The Psychedelics INTEGRATION HANDBOOK

RYAN WESTRUM PHD

Are you interested in knowing more?

Tune in to The Psychedelic Psychologist
found on your favorite streaming services.

Copyright © 2024 by Ryan Westrum
All rights reserved

This book, or parts thereof, may not be reproduced in any form without permission from the publisher; exceptions are made for brief excerpts used in published reviews.

Published by: Ryan P. Westrum

ISBN: 979-8-89316-966-9 (paperback)
ISBN: 979-8-89316-965-2 (ebook)

Printed in the United States of America

This book is intended as general information only and should not be used as recommendation or advocacy for use of psychedelics or any drug for any purpose. This book should not be used to diagnose or treat any health condition and is not intended to replace advice by a competent medical or psychological health practitioner. The ideas, processes, and suggestions in this book are intended to supplement, not replace, consultation with trained psychiatric, psychological or other professionals. Consider consulting your physician if you experience any condition that causes concern or suffering to you or others. The author and publisher disclaim any liability arising directly or indirectly from use of this book. This publication is sold with the understanding that the author and publisher are not engaged in rendering legal, medical, psychological, or other professional advice.

Cover and book design by Ryan Westrum
Art and illustrations by Ryan Westrum

PRAISE FOR *THE PSYCHEDELICS INTEGRATION HANDBOOK*

The Psychedelics Integration Handbook is coming to the market at an ideal time. The four decades of austere discrimination of psychedelic substances is now followed by a global renaissance of these remarkable medicines. Considering the avalanche of the new psychedelic experimentation and self-experimentation, it is essential to have a well-informed and reliable guidebook for the new psychonauts.

Ryan Westrum's new book meets this need. It offers an unprecedented rich pool of information about psychedelic and entheogenic substances. It explains what facilitators and sitters need for inner journeys and it answers their questions. The author covers in detail the preparation of the psychedelic session, conducting the journey itself, its challenges and interventions, its completion, and particularly the successful integration.

The book includes maps of the psyche, schools of depth psychology and systems that could be useful for running psychedelic sessions. It contains a great variety of ideas, examples of techniques, and exercises that readers can choose from. The author is a transpersonal psychologist and familiar with the academic literature around psychedelics, but the book is written in clear language and is not meant for an academic audience. Yet, the information in this manual is very detailed and comprehensible so that it can be useful both by people who are embarking on their first journeys as well as by those who are already on their way.

—Stanislav Grof, M.D, Author of *LSD Psychotherapy*
and *The Way of the Psychonaut*

This is, without a doubt, the most comprehensive and detailed book on psychedelic integration available. In addition, it is far more. Rather than being no more than an excellent manual of methods (which it is), it goes into great depth about every method, presents alternatives to almost every activity, includes a history of how and from whom the method developed, and then facilitates readers in making their own choices how to proceed through self-directed questions and practices.

While focusing primarily on psychedelic integration, the author, by presenting a diversity of approaches and describing other kinds of major traumas and interventions, offers paths to integrate other major life events as well.

Intensely practical, successfully designed to be useful, and just chock full of wonderful information related to mind-states that one encounters while taking psychedelic journeys, this book will be the necessary reference and guide for years to come.

—James Fadiman, Ph.D., Author of *The Psychedelic Explorer's Guide*

To All the Ancestors

And All the Descendants

TABLE OF CONTENTS

Prologue...ix
Fifth Anniversary Prologue..xi

Chapter 1: ENTRYWAY..1
    Integration Exercise 1: Basic Meditation.........................34

Chapter 2: More on Psychedelics...39
    Integration Exercise 2: Creating Sacred Space...............82

Chapter 3: Mindset and Setting...85
    Integration Exercise 3: Barefoot Walking Meditation...136

Chapter 4: Why Integrate?...139
    Integration Exercise 4: Mandala Spirit Collage.............154

Chapter 5: Introducing Maps of Consciousness................157
    Integration Exercise 5: Mind Mapping Your Psychedelic Journey.........202

Chapter 6: Channels of Integration...................................205
    Integration Exercise 6: Body Awareness.......................228

Chapter 7: Integration as Process......................................231
    Integration Exercise 7: Exploring with Divination Tools...258

Chapter 8: Integration and the Outer World....................261
    Integration Exercise 8: Sacred Circle: Group Sharing, Empathic Listening....283

Chapter 9: The Shadow Side..286
    Integration Exercise 9: Exploring Your Fears Surrounding Psychedelic Experiences: Digesting Your Strengths...........309

Chapter 10: Addiction...312
    Integration Exercise 10: Creating an Integration Altar....335

Chapter 11: Integration Stages: Possibilities and Pitfalls....338
    Integration Exercise 11: Food..367

Chapter 12: Letting Go, Death, and the Ultimate Mystery....371
    Integration Exercise 12: Exploring Your Relationship with Death..........391

Appendix A	395
Appendix B	401
Bibliography	403
About the Author	409
Index	411
Endnotes	415

PROLOGUE

It is important to honor those who have walked before us.

In writing about psychedelics, I am standing on the shoulders of the elders who came before me. I am stronger for their courage and I am wiser for their words. Their longing for an open-minded and a brighter hope elevates us. I am grateful for their vision and for their exploration within this universe.

Many others have shared their personal experiences in psychedelic realms. Their stories are filled with magic and mystical narration, drawn from courageous exploration and vivid descriptions of intimate lessons learned.

Their personal psychedelic journals burst with descriptions of what is possible through opening the doors of perception. I am abundantly entertained and profoundly grateful for their pioneering maps. Many times their stories have given us the courage to know we are not crazy and to believe in the paths opened up by working with psychedelics.

Others have written from an academic or scientific perspective to lay foundation for the legitimacy of working with psychedelics for psychological healing, personal growth, and increase in knowledge. I mention many of these people throughout this book. I have received personal mentoring from many of them and our gratitude for their contributions infuses this book.

While I draw on our elders, I hope this book is different than what has come before. This book is yours to use, yours to create and yours to make.

Psychedelic integration is a personal journey and a voyage of exploration that is unique to you as the individual seeker. Yes, you may have some of the classic experiences and find yourself in the white light or talking with the serpents. You may follow in some of the classic footprints or you may have experiences never before described.

In this prologue, I clear space as in a ritual for you to have your own experience and create what you create for your life. I hope you join us in thanking everyone who has come before and then accept your freedom to make your psychedelic journey your own. Remember this is your time to walk on this Earth, your preparation to leave this realm having made the most of your life. I hope *The Psychedelic Integration Handbook* supports you in making your journey clearer and more grounded in healing and wholeness.

—*Ryan*

FIFTH ANNIVERSARY PROLOGUE

It has been five years since the release of *The Psychedelics Integration Handbook*, and the world is consistently evolving within the realm's psychedelics across all paradigms, from legalization status of different psychedelic compounds to revolutionary developments in the clinical and academic settings. And please let's not forget the ever-trusted and sacred recreational, ceremonial, and spiritually important work many people are doing in "the underground."

This is a book of renewal. It is not simply about integrating psychedelics, but about the restoration of the heart, which occurs when we confront our life and death with compassion and awareness. When we bring a mindful practice of integrating psychedelics, it is an opportunity to resolve our denial of death as well as our denial of life in healing, reflection, revitalization, and above all, being gentle with oneself.

The book has touched many lives and contributed to a new practice of practically landing psychedelic work into the presence of our everyday life.

The book was designed to not follow a linear line. Indeed, readers are encouraged to experiment and create their own experience. I say "make it your own." Please continue to do just that!

May you have a WONDERFILLED journey.

Be Safe, Be Gentle.

—*Ryan*

CHAPTER 1

ENTRYWAY

Welcome to the world of integration. I am glad you're here. I am excited to share with you my passion for working with psychedelics.

In this Entryway, I want to give you a sense of what you will find in this handbook. To state the obvious, talking publicly about working with psychedelics is touchy. The potential benefits of exploring psychedelics are once again gaining attention in the mainstream media. But using psychedelics remains illegal in most places. You can get arrested and go to jail. Even worse, you could hurt yourself or end up hurting other people, including those you love.

To be clear, I am not advocating the use of psychedelics. That is your decision. But I know there are millions (yes, millions) of people around the world who have used psychedelics and untold numbers now considering exploring psychedelics for personal growth, healing, spiritual experience, and recreation. I believe these numbers will grow as more and more people find powerful, transformational, and exhilarating experiences with psychedelics.

Aside from "underground" experiences, there are legal research studies and clinics arising again after years of prohibition. Through the diligent and careful work of psychologists, psychiatrists, and researchers who know the healing potential of some psychedelics, legal use of these "medicines" is becoming available for treating post-traumatic stress disorder, anxiety, depression and addictions. To a large extent, these studies have picked up where other researchers were forced to leave off when the prohibition against psychedelics took hold in the 1970s.

Some of you reading this book may already be part of this "psychedelic renaissance." Others may be considering a journey or know someone who is using psychedelics. You may even be reading this book because you are worried about someone using psychedelics. While I do not want to encourage worry, anyone involved with psychedelics would be naïve not to proceed with caution. Concern and caution are appreciated and welcome in this book.

Working with psychedelics carries not only tremendous promise, but also perils and pitfalls. I borrow this phrase from a good friend, who has offered workshops for years to encourage discussion about the possible problems as well as benefits of working with psychedelics. Not only are there actual perils and pitfalls along with promise, but the entire subject of psychedelics carries enormous baggage. There are misconceptions, prejudices, and hysterics, mixed in with legitimate concerns about risks. I will unpack all this throughout the book.

From talking with many people in the psychedelics renaissance, I know there is a need for more attention to integration. Many explorers seem to be looking for guidance in connecting psychedelic experiences to their daily lives. Facilitators are looking for ways to help their communities grow from psychedelic experiences after a journey. Training programs are springing up for therapists, spiritual leaders, and research assistants who are working legally with psychedelics therapies. These programs discuss the importance of integration and offer important teaching. But even with the renaissance, there has been little practical guidance open to everyone interested in the work—and not much guidance focusing on you and what you want to make of your exploration.

As you will learn in this book, I will provide different parts of the spectrum with respect to psychedelics: a feeling of paradox, sometimes therapeutic and sometimes deeply recreational. But I will share the belief that you cannot experience the full potential of using psychedelics without some focused effort. I call this *integration*. I also believe that integration is difficult without guidance and ideas about how our minds, bodies, and emotions process experiences. To maximize the potential of your experiences, it helps to know where you are before, during, and after psychedelic experiences and to recognize where you might go wrong along the way.

I hope to be helpful to everyone and not lecture to anyone. I do not believe there is any one right way, and I know people come to psychedelics from all kinds of backgrounds and through many different paths. As for me, I have been exploring psychedelics since my early teens and followed my experiences into studying transpersonal psychology and becoming a psychologist and guide. Along the way, I realized the importance of integration in making full use of non-ordinary-state journeys.

There are many other books out there describing the psychedelic journey from academic, historical or personal perspectives. There are also many books relevant to understanding consciousness and integration work. I have read many of them and will point you toward some along the way. There are many others you will find on your own. I do not footnote books or articles in the text unless I use specific quotes and want you to be able to find them by page number. But at the end of the book is a bibliography with the details about all the books I reference in the text.

In the very instant I write this, I feel it is already obsolete. Since the rise of the Internet, numerous websites and blogs now offer advice and share experiential stories involving psychedelics. You will find many of these on your own, if you have not already. If you want some suggestions, you may want to check out these websites:

https://maps.org/
https://thethirdwave.co/
https://psychedelictimes.com/
https://tripsafe.org/
https://www.erowid.org/
https://www.healingsoulsllc.com/

Since I know there is so much out there on psychedelics, I wanted to write a fun and practical handbook for active engagement with non-ordinary states in your ordinary life. There is a lot of information here, and some of it will be more useful to you personally than other parts. I have tried to write in a way that lets you dip in here and there and then come back if you need to come back. More importantly, I will do my best to include you, because this is all about your experience and your journey. Integration is about making *your life* what you want it to be and what it is meant to be.

In the rest of this "Entryway," I will let you know some of the basics about my approach. All of these ideas will be unpacked throughout the book. For now, I want you to get a sense of how it all holds together.

Our Human Heritage in Psychedelics

From the vantage point of many people today, psychedelics are "drugs" that became popular in the 1960s with the hippies. This is true, but the real story reaches back into ancient times. Anthropologists believe our ancestors have been using plants, barks, and animal secretions for purposes of healing, visioning and celebration since the dawn of humanity. Sometimes individual "shamans" would use a psychedelic to enter a trance to develop their healing and visionary skills, to help someone in distress, or to answer questions for their tribes. Sometimes psychedelics were used in groups for sacred rituals, hedonistic festivities, or rites of passage.

Usually journeys with these "medicines" were accompanied by drumming, singing, and dancing. Sometimes fasting, sexuality, or trials of endurance (pain) were included. Deep breathing was often part of the picture. Even today, working in non-ordinary states almost always includes other elements in addition to the psychedelic substance, such as music, movement, guidance with voice, or focused breathing.

Why did our ancestors seek non-ordinary states?

Anthropologists (myself included) believe that non-ordinary states were accessed for these reasons:

- To connect with wise and powerful realms for purposes of healing and guidance
- To cure illnesses in individuals or groups
- To restore their communities to alignment with deities and with nature
- To understand and find solutions to challenges
- To celebrate and enjoy life.

These goals all involve integration. This is because these goals are met not just with a single experience, but when the experience becomes part of an intentional exploration for the chosen purpose. I believe it may have been easier to understand the importance of integration in past times. The key is to realize that ancient peoples understood there are spiritual realms with greater wisdom than humans. The wisdom from these spiritual realms needed to be *integrated* into life in the ordinary realm.

Usually these spiritual realms were understood as connected with nature. Receiving healing and guidance was for the purpose of returning the individual or the group to alignment with the wisdom of a sacred force. This was often felt as alignment with the non-human forces around which native people lived. In other words, energies or insights from another realm were *integrated* into the human energies of the individual, group or culture. This was felt as a restoration of balance—often as restoring balance in the relationship with natural forces on Earth.

> The western industrial civilization is the only group in the entire human history that doesn't hold non-ordinary states in great esteem, and doesn't have any use for them, actually has pathologized them; every other culture has spent a lot of time and energy trying to develop ways of inducing non-ordinary states.
>
> —Stanislav Grof

It is interesting to realize that many etymologists believe the word *religion* comes from the Latin *re-ligare*, meaning to reconnect or *re-bind*. I have no doubt that ancient religions involved practices and beliefs that were thought to integrate (or re-integrate) people and communities back into the sacred flow of life.

Fast forward to the present. I believe the current use of psychedelics by hundreds of thousands of people is a brave "standing with" our ancestors during a dangerous growing spurt in human history. The upshot of the dangerous growing spurt is that we have fallen out of balance with nature and have lost any sense of the sacred. Many of us are "remembering" that psychedelics were a sacred tool used by our ancestors when the human tribe was in trouble.

Sometimes in a psychedelic session, you can feel this. If you are in a ceremonial setting with lineage back into shamanic cultures (as many people experience Ayahuasca, for instance), you might feel how the ancient ways of this same tradition have come forward right into your very moment. Even if you are using psychedelics in a contemporary fashion (in a therapy office or in your friend's family room), you might feel ancestors or their spirits wishing you well and sending you the energies from how they celebrated and practiced their spirituality during their own times. You might feel them saying, *Yes, you are doing well, and this is how it is.*

Since I have mentioned religion, I want to recognize that organized religion (particularly Christianity) has been an enormous influence in the lives of many people in Western culture. I have found nothing in psychedelics (or non-ordinary state) work that is not consistent with the grace, power and comfort we find within many religions' traditions. Christianity has many beautiful, uplifting and guiding qualities—a sense of the unconditional love associated with Jesus and the Catholic tradition, which was an important part of my early life and spiritual journey. And then I found a Buddhist *sangha* and sewed a robe during my teens. My mother, to her great credit, accepted my path though her tradition was Catholic. She understood my need to sew a robe rather than go through Catholic confirmation.

As much as I respect anyone's religious tradition, I want to recognize that many of us have great disappointment and even wounding surrounding organized religion. I have found that working with psychedelics offers the possibility of releasing the negative overlays some of us have received from contemporary organized religions. Too often, people have incorporated into themselves confusing and even shameful influences from individuals or groups who claim religious authority. Psychedelic experiences often help us move past such limitations. If you know religious figures as demanding, shaming, judgmental forces, you may come to know another face of God (or Goddess) during your psychedelics work.

When I acknowledge that psychedelics have the potential to re-bind you to a spiritual realm, I am talking about an all-loving, all-knowing realm where everything is understood and forgiven, where the template for connection and wholeness exists. I am talking about an actual consciousness that is living and where you find your true home. There is no division between factions or tribes and no use of religious proclamations to divide and conquer.

That said, I do know some archetypal forces that may kick your butt during psychedelics work if you are not honest with yourself about your own life and history. The discovery with psychedelics, in the end, is the discovery of reality.

In modern times, how do we define psychedelics?

Humphrey Osmond (1917-2004) was a psychiatrist born in Great Britain who lived most of his life in Canada and the United States. In 1956, he decided to put together the Greek words "psyche" (meaning "mind") and "deloun" ("to make visible"). And then we had the word *psychedelic*. In other words, etymologically speaking, a psychedelic is something that makes visible what is in your mind. More recently, psychedelics researcher Rick Strassman, M.D., put it this way:

> Psychedelics show you what's in and on your mind, those subconscious thoughts and feelings that are hidden, covered up, forgotten, out of sight, maybe even completely unexpected, but nevertheless imminently present. [1]

Notice what psychedelic does **not** mean. A psychedelic is not something that only produces strange chemical effects or simple inebriation. Unfortunately, this is what many people believe as scientific truth—that psychedelics merely *alter* your mind and body in the same way that taking alcohol or many other drugs would alter you.

This perspective is often held as scientific because, even though physics has revealed for over a century that consciousness has the ability to participate with matter, the mainstream culture has still not found a way to integrate this knowledge into common understanding. It is hard for many people to realize that consciousness is more primary than matter and has the ability to connect with other layers of consciousness. For many people, "scientific truth" remains that your consciousness is nothing more than the accidental firing of neurons in your brain. From this perspective, there is nothing to "reveal" through psychedelics, so what is happening must just be a form of drunkenness. Usually, exploring psychedelics will convince you otherwise.

It is important to distinguish between psychedelics and "other drugs" because we work with psychedelics not just to get high (okay, psychedelics can be pretty cool) but because they bring us deeply within ourselves—and out into what is beyond ourselves in layers of consciousness and spiritual realms. Psychedelics open us to *what is* rather than just producing chemical reactions in our minds and bodies.

I believe psychedelics make visible what is in our minds to provide us the opportunity for integration of what becomes visible. We integrate what becomes visible into our existing selves so that we move toward our most healthy selves and our most authentic futures. The same goes for bringing what we learn back out into our communities and cultures in order to help restore health and balance to our external world.

Adding to Strassman's definition, I find that psychedelic journeys make visible not just what is in our minds, but what is in our bodies and our spirits. Sadly, most of us today do not have ready access to our bodies or our spirits. We experience the "body-mind" split. Our bodies seem separate to us. We may develop our bodies and "perform" them for the world. Or we may experience our bodies as a source of shame or illness. But it is not easy in our culture to experience our bodies truly as ourselves. Psychedelics push us toward making our bodies and minds one thing, but to get there, we often have to go through a lot of blocks and stored energies, many of which hurt to experience.

In our times, many of us do not even understand what spirituality is—we confuse it with religious dogma or belief in rules or mythological narratives. With psychedelics, we gain access to what is *really* out there in spiritual realms (or rather, *in here*, because the spiritual realms are accessible through us). But this is sometimes a complicated and difficult opening—particularly because many of us need to work through the shock of really accepting that there is something beyond our little selves.

Introducing "Transpersonal"

In addition to making visible what is on our minds, psychedelic journeys open us to energies coming from a universal sacred source. These energies are commonly experienced as offering (or sometimes requiring) an embodied experience of "what is in the universe" as well as what is "in your body" and "on your mind."

The word "transpersonal" was coined in the 1960s by Stanislav Grof, whom I consider the foremost theorist and writer in the field of psychedelics and non-ordinary states of consciousness. The prefix *trans* suggests that the deepest levels of our psyche connect us with what is "beyond" or "trans" our individual mind. Grof defined transpersonal states of awareness as follows:

> The common denominator of this otherwise rich and ramified group of phenomena is the feeling of the individual that his consciousness expanded beyond the usual ego boundaries and the limitations of time and space.[2]

It is interesting to consider the definition of the word *ramified* used by Grof. "Ramified" means to form branches or offshoots, to spread out. Transpersonal experiences tend to reach out beyond us in many possible directions, endlessly making connections, unfolding along lines of meaning and discovery. In a sense, this is the meaning-correspondence of the endlessly unfolding images that sometimes appear in psychedelic journeys, particularly in the early stages.

Psychiatrist Tim Read, author of *Walking Shadows: Archetype and Psyche in Crisis and Growth*, makes a crucial point about working with transpersonal energies. Grof, as I note in more detail in Chapter 4, describes different realms of the psyche that may be explored in non-ordinary state experiences. These include the following:

- Sensory
- Biographical
- Perinatal (from inside the womb or during birth)
- Transpersonal.

Read observes that sometimes we receive images or experiences that emerge from a transpersonal source and carry pure transpersonal energies. However, very often the transpersonal energies (or images or experiences) come to us mixed with our personal issues, complexes, traumas, and desires. In other words, while I believe (and know) very deeply that transpersonal energies and experiences are real, I note from the outset that the particular manifestation of these energies often draws from our personal psyches and issues.

As I explain in more detail later, Grof describes systems of condensed experience (COEXs) as constellations of experiences sharing an emotional charge. There may be a COEX that groups around a particular charge and has elements that are transpersonal, personal (biographical), perinatal, and sensory.

Read creates the word **cispersonal** (with *cis* meaning "near side") to suggest an area of the psyche where our personal issues, complexes, traumas, and desires are intermingled with transpersonal energies that seem to light them up. In other words, we might consider our psychedelic experiences as coming from a universal source, but working on us through a mixture of transpersonal and "this life" themes and issues. Sometimes it is helpful to talk about an experience (or image) as cispersonal because it suggests the blend between transpersonal and personal.

From a Grofian perspective, differentiating between transpersonal and cispersonal might miss the point that perinatal experiences are the bridge between personal and transpersonal. From the perspective of what is actually happening *during* non-ordinary state experiences, I completely agree with Grof that birth experiences often open the door to the transpersonal from the personal. However, from an integration perspective, I find it useful when working with images from non-ordinary states to consider whether any image that has transpersonal energies also has personal elements that may not have been obvious. This is where I think it helps to know the concept of cispersonal.

For example, imagine someone who has a strong experience of an evil archetypal mother strangling them during a non-ordinary state experience when they are also reliving the pressure of trying to be born. This is a classic illustration of a perinatal experience opening a door to the archetypal or transpersonal. Where the cispersonal idea might help us during integration work would be in suggesting to the experiencer that it might be helpful to consider whether the transpersonal image also has energies from the biographical realm.

In other words, as an integration guide, I might be neglectful if I did not explore the personal elements in the transpersonal image. Explaining Read's cispersonal idea might allow us to convey to the experiencer how it might help to look for both transpersonal and personal energies in the image. Describing a cispersonal realm might make this explanation easier.

I believe the transpersonal experiences coming to us through non-ordinary states light up those areas of our personalities, biographical and karmic history that are "up" for integration. Often this integration releases a charge that may have been sapping our energy and can now help propel us to our next level of development.

Stanislav Grof and other teachers in the Holotropic Breathwork movement describe an "inner healing intelligence" or "inner healer" that brings the most important "next" experiences. Psychedelics, broadly speaking, offer us the next experiences in our life journeys. Integration practices are essential to carry forward these stepping-stones in our lives, as well as providing for the resolution of old issues that have been lit up by non-ordinary-state work.

What are common psychedelics used today?

Today, the most commonly used psychedelics are the following:

- LSD-25 (Lysergic acid diethylamide)
- Psilocybin ("magic mushrooms")
- Ayahuasca, with active ingredient DMT (N,N-dimethyltryptamine)
- Mescaline and cactus derivatives containing mescaline, such as Peyote and San Pedro
- DMT
- Bufo alvarius, colloquially "toad medicine," with active ingredient 5-MeO-DMT but containing other natural substances contributing to a psychedelic experience
- Jaguar, synthesized 5-MeO-DMT
- MDMA ("Ecstasy" or "Molly"), actually an "empathogen-enactogen" rather than a psychedelic
- Other "Empathogen-enactogens" similar to MDMA, such as MDA, MDEA, and Methylone
- Ibogaine, from an African bark
- Ketamine ("K," "Ket," "Special K") and Salvia Divinorum are often considered psychedelics, but seem to work differently than the above "medicines."

In recent times, other words have been used for psychedelics. I find that many of these other words carry a charge and a certain slant or advocacy about the nature of psychedelics. "Feeling" into some of these words helps round out an understanding of different perspectives on the work. Some of these other words are:

- *entheogens* (derived from Greek meaning "that which causes God to be known or experienced within an individual")
- *hallucinogens* (causing hallucinations or other distortions in perception)
- *psychotomimetics* (mimicking psychotic states)
- *"medicines" or "plant medicines"* (informal and respectful terms, with "plant medicines" usually applied to natural psychoactive substances)
- *allies* (informal term suggesting that psychedelics offer help in personal growth and healing; the substances become allies with our own innate healing and spiritual potentials).

Using a label other than "psychedelic" for MDMA and similar compounds has its own particular history and discourse. At a scientific conference in 1983, the term **empathogen** was suggested by psychologist Ralph Metzner, who co-authored the classic 1964 book *The Psychedelic Experience* with Timothy Leary and Richard Alpert/Ram Dass.

Empathogen means "generating a state of empathy." This word reflects the experience of emotional openness, safety, connection, relatedness, and love that tends to accompany use of MDMA-related medicines. MDMA is one of the psychotropic medicines now part of the legal psychedelic renaissance in research and therapy. The current focus involves patients with "treatment-resistant" psychological conditions, such as difficult post-traumatic stress disorder. The emotional openness brought by empathogens assists with connection to the therapist and integrating traumatic experiences.

During the 1983-84 period, pharmacologist David Nichols independently used the term empathogen, but later preferred **entactogen**, meaning "touching within." Nichols was concerned the "path" root in empathogen would associate the MDMA-related substances with "suffering," as represented in words such as pathos and path-ology. Both "empathogen" and "entactogen" currently describe MDMA-related medicines, sometimes used in the combination "empathogen-entactogen."

I use the word "psychedelics" primarily in the book, but sometimes intersperse "medicines" or other terms. I am not in favor of argument over the words—unless you want to discuss and integrate why you feel strongly in favor or against some words. But I certainly respect people's preference. In part, I like using "psychedelics" because I feel the word is most inclusive of the modern history of psychedelics in the West, including shadow elements that I hope to integrate into our work with psychedelics.

An equally appropriate term for psychedelics, used by various researchers and facilitators, including Bufo alvarius carrier Octavio Rettig Hinojosa, M.D., is ***psycho-integrative***. To state the obvious, this term puts integration front and center in describing the impact of these substances. "Psycho-integrative" helps us distinguish other substances that produce "non-ordinary" or "altered" states of consciousness but do not offer the same level of integrative possibilities.

Some substances can be described as ***psycho-dissociative*** in that there is a distancing from what is most deeply present. Sometimes dissociation is a stress-relieving and enjoyable experience—sometimes even life-saving if we absolutely need to shut something down. But psycho-integrative medicines should not be lumped together with dissociating substances (e.g., alcohol, cocaine, methamphetamine). As I will discuss later, ketamine is considered a "dissociative" in some respects, but can hold healing potential when properly used and integrated.

Although not used to describe substances, the term ***holotropic*** must be brought into the mix. Stanislav Grof coined the word holotropic to suggest movement toward wholeness (from the Greek words "holos" for wholeness and "trepein" for moving towards). Grof describes "holotropic states" as a subcategory of all non-ordinary states. In holotropic states of consciousness, the inner healer is activated to help us move toward health and wholeness. This distinguishes holotropic states from the type of non-ordinary states (such as alcohol intoxication) that do not hold this potential.

Holotropic is another way of describing the psycho-integrative possibility of psychedelics. As I share in more detail later, after psychedelics were prohibited in the United States, Stanislav Grof and his late wife Christina Grof developed Holotropic Breathwork, a method of deep breathing combined with evocative music and supportive facilitation, to encourage the emergence of healing non-ordinary states.

In talking about the integrative potential of psychedelics, I do not want to leave the impression that I am excluding psychedelic journeys undertaken for exhilaration and enjoyment. Many people explore psychedelics to find a sense of connection, ecstasy, celebration, or just to feel good. I believe these are legitimate motives. I also believe experiences of this type may be brought mindfully into your life narrative through integration, if that is a choice you make.

What factors contribute to psychedelic experiences?

Ingesting a particular psychedelic substance does not create a uniform experience for everyone or for anyone at any given time. While there are commonalities and potentials relating to individual substances, other factors contribute toward your particular experience at any one time and place.

Six primary factors hold the potential to shape a particular psychedelic journey:

1. Substance and dose: the particular psychedelic and the amount you ingest.
2. Mindset (often referenced as "set"): what is on your mind before and during an experience, including what is present but not completely conscious.
3. Setting: the location, surroundings, and people who are part of the experience you create.
4. Intention: the conscious (or perhaps unconscious) goal you are bringing to an experience.
5. Your inner healer: what experience(s) your mind/body/spirit consider you ready to have in the ongoing unfolding of your self-discovery and healing.
6. Universal (archetypal, astrological) energies impacting you at the time of your journey.

I will unpack the importance of these six factors throughout the book. To help you understand our list, though, I will explain a few things now.

Mindset, intention and inner healer may look similar, but I hold them separately. This is because of the possible difference between what is on your mind, what you are intending (consciously, semi-consciously, or unconsciously), and what an "inner healing intelligence" may bring forward.

For instance, you might bring an intention "to heal" yourself into a non-ordinary state journey. But even with this intention, you might have a "mindset" of anxiety or fear surrounding the upcoming experience or when considering what you might uncover. In addition, your inner healer may simply feel that you are ready to understand secrets of the universe more than heal anything about your current situation.

Mindset is also interrelated with setting, because you may have an intention for a peaceful journey of discovery, but the setting in which you embark on the journey might not be safely held by people who have the maturity to guide others through deep work. You may pick up on this energy subliminally, and an unconscious or semi-conscious lack of safety may play out, at least in part, in your journey.

It may help to say more about the "inner healer" or "inner healing intelligence" as distinct from mindset or intention. Tav Sparks, who has trained facilitators of Holotropic Breathwork for several decades, explains:

> A psychoactive substance, or a breathing practice, activates the inner self's inherent healing power. This power then mobilizes the unconscious contents of the psyche. When activated by whatever strategy is employed, these previously immobile or static contents can be converted into what I might call a "stream of energy." At this point, this stream of energetic intra-psychic material emerges into consciousness, or the awareness of the experiencer.[3]

Sparks calls this activating potential "the power within." Healing or transformation does not occur, however, without the willingness of the experiencer to be moved and engaged by this energy. Sparks writes:

> The ability of the experiencer to become conscious of, or aware of, this unconscious material, plus the complementary ability to embrace, surrender to, or accept whatever emerges, constitutes the healing or transformational dynamic for the individual.
>
> Healing seems to occur through an inherent "cooperation" between the inner healing source and consciousness itself. *In fact, it appears that consciousness and the Inner Healer are one and the same dynamic.* They are two poises, two interrelated complementary characteristics, of the same process—like water and wetness, or fire and heat.[4]

Some non-ordinary state facilitators suggest *not* bringing any particular intention into non-ordinary state exploration. This is the approach recommended in the Holotropic Breathwork tradition pioneered by Stanislav and Christina Grof. I would frame this recommendation not so much as having *no* intention as holding an intention to be "open to what comes." You can see how this approach is consistent with an understanding that "an inner healing intelligence" will guide you to the experiences that you are ready to experience.

This intention of being "open to what comes" may be useful in making us aware that we do generally have an intention when we embark on a journey, even if that intention is simply to receive what our "inner healer" or "the universe" offers us on this day. Understanding even this "non-intention' as an intention may help keep us present when we journey. Focusing our will or awareness in "being open to what comes" may help us meet and engage with the energies that present themselves to us.

Of course, there is nothing wrong with having specific intentions. For example, someone might engage with holotropic work with a "hope for healing of my migraine headaches" or "learning to be more open to others" or "to accept my aging body." One facilitator I know suggests that we bring our "attention" to our "intention" during the non-ordinary state and be open to what unfolds. Maybe we *do* know consciously where we need to work.

To some extent, not bringing into focus an intention may overlook an intention that exists but just has not been made conscious. For this reason, I suggest focusing on the possibility of an intention in the weeks and, more importantly, days and hours before a journey.

A good approach might involve recognizing your intentions and yet remaining open to whatever comes in the journey. This attitude is consistent with a healthy approach to life and recognizes that even if we listen to advice "not to have any particular intention," we probably do have hopes, dreams, wants and needs that are with us.

Number six in our list—"universal energies impacting you at the time of your journey"—may seem somewhat mysterious or nebulous to some of you. Here we are back to accepting the reality of transpersonal realms beyond our brains and the material world around us.

Many of us working with psychedelics have a general sense of "the universe" as one of the sources of our experiences. As I will discuss throughout the book, the archetypes known in astrology (particularly those associated with the planets) often bring strong influence into our psychedelic journeys. It is also common to experience a particular personified intelligence as a source of non-ordinary state insight and experience. Those who participate in Ayahuasca, San Pedro, or Peyote circles often feel, hear, or see "Grandmother" (Ayahuasca), "Grandfather" (San Pedro), or the Creator (Peyote) as the spiritual (archetypal) power bringing experience.

For some of you, if you are questioning the "new age" or "woo-woo" nature of psychedelics work in general, hearing about the influence of personified intelligences, archetypes or astrology may be initially hard to swallow. It is perfectly fine to hold some skepticism about the reality of these influences or the possibility that universal energies shape psychedelic experiences. There is no way to prove them to you except through your own experience and observation, which working with psychedelics is likely to bring to you.

For now, I offer the story told by Stanislav Grof and cultural historian Richard Tarnas, who were both scholars in residence at the Esalen Institute in Big Sur, California, in the late 1970s and early 1980s. Grof and Tarnas were curious about whether there was any way to predict what experiences people might have in non-ordinary states of consciousness. They tried asking experiencers to complete various personality assessments, but none of the tests showed any relationship to the experiences people were having.

Eventually Grof and Tarnas considered examining people's astrological natal charts (where the planets were at the time and place of their birth) and the planetary transits impacting the experiencers on the particular day of the journey. They found powerful correspondences, which became an important element in their future work. Grof shares that he was particularly shocked given his scientific medical training and his prior dismissal of astrology.

Mindful of the potential impact of archetypal correspondences, some people seek out astrological information when planning non-ordinary state work. The book *Pathways to Wholeness: Archetypal Astrology and the Transpersonal Journey* by Renn Butler talks about the practice of considering archetypal astrology, an astrological approach developed by Tarnas, when trying to plan or understand non-ordinary state journeys.

If you do enough non-ordinary state work, you may come to understand the ways that all of these factors *integrate* together into a process that is your life unfolding. For instance, astrological influences on a particular day may have conspired to impact not just your internal state, but also the moods of others around you and the physical realities of your setting.

You might think your mindset and intention are completely internal to you, but once you start feeling the way your personal consciousness reaches into your personal unconscious, and beyond your personal unconscious into the collective unconscious (the realm of the archetypes), you may understand your inner healer as an expression of guidance that involves all of the factors I mention.

Internal versus External

It is important to me in this book to talk with everyone who is interested in psychedelics, no matter how you are constructing your exploration. But I would like to acknowledge the significant difference between experiences directed internally and those with an external focus. To some extent, this is a simple difference between whether you have your eyes opened or closed. And yet, it is much more. The most fundamental difference involves whether your attention is directed towards what is arising within you or what you're seeing or hearing outside yourself.

I have heard Stanislav Grof describe his realization after conducting many LSD therapy sessions that participants usually had more productive experiences if their attention was directed inward rather than in dialogue with the therapist. This involves the very fact that psychedelics reveal what lies deeply within the psyche and universal consciousness lying on the other side of the individual mind.

I agree that an internal focus is often an important part of therapeutic sessions. However, I believe healing and profound exploration also occur with externally directed experiences. As shared by a psilocybin guide I know, his touchstone in guidance is not so much internal versus external, but rather whether the experiencer is allowing what is emerging from inside to come forward or is defending against what is emerging.

In his sessions, after preparation, mindful ingestion of mushrooms, and body relaxation, most often the client will lie down with a blindfold. Some clients will easily turn inside and follow their internal process for their whole experience. Other clients will reach a point where they sit up and begin external conversation and engagement with what is outside themselves. My friend follows their process and is curious about whether their external focus is helping them bring forward and understand their experience, or whether they have reached a fear point or block that has halted a forward flow.

Sometimes external engagement allows the experience to come forward or the fear or blocks to release. On some occasions, the external focus itself may be defensive against the experience being offered by the medicine. But just as often, an external experience is exactly what the person needs—or even more importantly, what the person wants.

As my guide friend shares, once he rules out that an external focus is defensive, he simply helps the client find their most healing experience, even if the experience stays external for the rest of the session. What is most important to my guide friend is his commitment to helping clients make their experience their own.

When it comes to integration of the experience after a session, whether the integration is immediately following or taking place over the next weeks or months, all of the experiences—whether internal or external—are important elements for integration.

What do I mean by integration?

Well, you probably need to read the book to get it completely! But for now, I will describe integration as:

- Connecting the dots between experiences that may feel isolated or disjointed.
- Feeling your thoughts and thinking your feelings.
- Joining your thoughts and feelings and putting them into a single awareness.
- Reaching into your body to find feelings, memories, even thoughts.
- Experiencing your mind, spirit and body as one flow.
- Bringing consciousness to all that is happening to you.
- Bringing all your experiences into harmony.
- Moving into your life in a way that is authentic to all parts of you, even those that are not yet conscious.
- Remembering to experience yourself as always in a flow that includes transpersonal energies reaching into you from beyond your individual mind, body and spirit.
- Noticing the way synchronicities (meaningful coincidences) seem to encourage your unfolding process and bringing these experiences and their source into your reality.

What are we integrating?

Generally speaking, we are integrating what comes to us during and after our psychedelic experiences. Well, then, what sorts of things come to us during and after psychedelic experiences? Most psychedelic explorers would agree with many (and maybe all) of the following statements.

Experiencing psychedelics…

1. Offers profound insight into the nature of existence, including the reality of the universe as living consciousness.

2. Inspires (and possibly overwhelms) with the beauty, intelligence and power of creator consciousness.
3. Suggests your life purpose and meaning, which may move you toward making life changes.
4. Requires you to accept the reality of the eventual death of your physical body, and yet allows you to know you have an eternal place within universal consciousness.
5. Shows how your psychological and social issues, blocks or wounds have physical manifestation in your body.
6. Holds the potential to break through such blocks.
7. Invites (and sometimes requires) you to fully experience unprocessed trauma or difficult truths about yourself, others, or life in general.
8. Lets you see your assumptions, habits of mind, projections, and defenses and offers you the choice of letting them go.
9. Teaches you that letting go of assumptions, habits of mind, projections, and defenses leads toward freedom and a sense of wholeness.
10. Pushes you toward service and away from seeking power and control.
11. Orients you towards living in sync with nature and away from consumption, e.g., encourages you to look at eating habits, carbon footprint, where you live.
12. May leave you feeling isolated in the short term, and yet at the same time comforted by what you are coming to know.
13. Interacts with you on a karmic level, meaning you may be asked to experience and release traumatic experiences that feel as though they happened to you in a prior lifetime.
14. Whether or not you believe literally in reincarnation, you may begin to feel (and see or experience) the ways that all experiences throughout our human ancestry remain within a universal consciousness and may seek to manifest in your awareness and possibly resolve, reconnect, or express.
15. Could present you starkly with the impact of choices you have made in this or other incarnations and the possible impact of choices before you.
16. Offers the possibility for happiness, ecstasy, or fun.
17. Will likely bring you into community with people who feel like your tribe.
18. Could leave you confused or afraid on occasion.
19. Might cause you to receive the prejudices and projections of other people.
20. Could push you into beliefs you never thought you would have.

These are generalities. Then there are the specifics for any individual person. **What you integrate** are all the things (these and others) that come up for you as you do the work.

It is important to remember that psychedelics catalyze a process. I will talk several times in the book about the metaphor (and reality) that light is both a particle and a wave. You have a particular session at a particular time, like a particle. But really the session is part of a wave that is your life as you transform and move through time.

Right after the session, not everything that will become part of the wave is apparent. Many integration techniques are designed to help you feel into the particle and understand how to follow it out as a wave. As you continue the healing or discovery process that psychedelics has started, you will be integrating the experiences that came up in the session and then everything in your life that folds into the process.

Sometimes, the most important integration work involves specific experiences during a journey that are personally or existentially challenging. This can require a recalibration of your whole life story. For instance, one of my friends remembered during an Ayahuasca journey that he had been molested as a child. This realization was real on an experiential level and also made sense to him on an intellectual and emotional level in terms of explaining unclear memories and feelings.

Having the realization was a great relief. But integrating the experience, including all the buried emotions, became a process requiring a great deal of sensitivity, compassion for self, outside assistance, and energy. My friend needed, and sought, expert therapeutic help in processing the experience. So much about his entire life narrative had to shift. He needed strength, as some people around him did not believe his experience.

Having assistance from someone who understood psychedelics was very crucial, because encountering a therapist who dismissed the experience or the memory could have caused great suffering and additional trauma. This is not to say that all "memories" during psychedelics are literally true, but my friend needed to heal through holding onto the reality of what happened.

Your own experiences will be your own experiences. But the general categories listed above suggest some of the insights and experiences you may be integrating into your life. As you move through your integration journey, you might come back to these possible areas of integration from time to time and consider where you are being led. Ultimately, remember that the integration journey is fluid and constantly morphing and shifting.

Integration Compared to Aftercare

After non-ordinary state journeys, most facilitators offer suggestions for taking care of yourself right then, the next day, in the following week, and in the coming months. In Chapter 11, Integration Stages, I talk about some of the particulars that might be most helpful at various times following a session.

For now, I note that some of the "integration" recommendations I commonly hear are more about caring for yourself after a journey than about *integrating* your experience. To make the distinction, I use the term "aftercare." While I find the distinction useful, aftercare and integration are very much interrelated.

I bring up this distinction because integration is not just about being gentle with yourself or avoiding some experiences after a session, though these things are very important. Integration is about bringing conscious attention to the process catalyzed by your experience and bringing the experience into your life. Aftercare helps you do this, but integration eventually requires more active effort.

You will see the interplay between aftercare and integration in many of the exercises I share in this book. This is because taking care of yourself after an extraordinary journey is important simply because it is essential for you to learn to care for yourself. But aftercare is also important for your body-mind-spirit to be in the best place to hold onto and integrate the experience.

Here are some thoughts about Aftercare:

- Non-ordinary state experiences do not end all at once with a clear dividing line. Rather, we come back into our more customary state of mind gradually and with some lingering *afterglow*, or residual effects.
- How long this intermediate state lasts depends on all kinds of things, including the medicine you have explored, your experience that day, you, and all the other factors in the experience. Being gentle with yourself and others during this period of returning is essential aftercare.
- A major component of aftercare involves making sure you are safe as you move back into day-to-day living. Aftercare involves knowing you are vulnerable and may need help in various ways until you are fully back. If you work with a guide, facilitator, or co-explorers, they play an essential role in safety.
- Depending to some extent on the medicine and your particular experience, your body (and your mind and spirit along with your body) may have been through a metaphorical marathon. You need time, space, and aftercare in order to recover and recalibrate. I want to encourage you to hold this period of aftercare as its own unique experience. This is important because you may not want to really start focusing on deep questioning of the meaning of your experience and the transformation that seems to have begun until you have taken care of yourself in the aftercare sense.
- In the extended aftercare period (the hours and days after a journey), it is important to continue the gentleness you held right after the session. But then you gradually move from aftercare into integration, which can involve more challenge to yourself and more focused effort.

- I sometimes think of aftercare as a time of falling back into ourselves, gently feeling the space of ourselves without pushing. Later, integration involves taking some risks and reaching outwards or inwards with some energy and intention to push forward in process.
- Aftercare involves being highly sensitive to your own unique needs. Some people need to talk with someone, some people need to be held, some people need to have no conversation at all—it all depends on you.
- As you will find, the aftercare period blends into a lifestyle of integration. You will find throughout this book a seesaw blending of gentle caring for yourself as you integrate and challenging yourself to really bring your non-ordinary experience into your life in transformational ways. I encourage you to pay attention in the aftercare components to your emotional needs, your physical body, and any mental narratives that are developing or releasing.

What do you need for Integration: S-A-F-E-T-Y

Safety might be the most important thing in responsible use of psychedelics. For that reason, I created an acronym about integration drawing on the letters in "safety." Here are important elements I hope you find through integration:

S – Security
A – Accessibility
F – Fluidity
E – Empowerment
T – Transformational
Y – Yours

The English philosopher Sir Francis Bacon famously wrote, "Knowledge is power." I believe knowledge can also be safety.

From whatever vantage point you bring to this book, I believe safety increases with education, understanding, and learning from the experience of others. I will return to the specific elements of the S-A-F-E-T-Y acronym in Chapter 3, "Mindset and Setting."

Who is this book for?

This book is for you if

- You're curious about psychedelics.
- You've had some psychedelic experiences and you're trying to learn more about what happened.
- You're looking for God and suspect psychedelics might help.
- You are drawn to psychedelics as a path of self-exploration (or adventure) and want reassurance you're staying safe and sane.
- You want to use psychedelics for psychological (or what I will call psycho-spiritual) transformation and need some structure to get more out of your experiences.
- You want to feel like your use of psychedelics is going somewhere.
- You want to harness the power of psychedelics for creativity.
- You want to change the world and have the intuition that psychedelics have a place in that shift.

This book is also for you if

- You've had a "bad trip" and need clarification or healing.
- You have been diagnosed with a clinical mental illness (depression, anxiety, bipolar disorder, post-traumatic stress disorder, etc.) and wonder if psychedelics might help you heal, understand, and move forward.
- You are caught in one or more addictions and have heard psychedelics might help free you.

Even if you're not into "drugs" for adventure, self-exploration or psychological healing, this book may be for you if

- You are on a spiritual path and want some help with going more deeply, avoiding pitfalls, and integrating what is happening.
- You want to learn more about psychedelics as a cutting-edge healing modality.
- Someone important to you has become involved in psychedelics, and you want to understand, respect, and maybe even help.
- You want to clear up any misconceptions about psychedelics.
- You are interested in learning about "integration" of any life experiences.

What this book is not:

- Advocacy for using illegal substances.

- A substitute for therapy or advice from clinical professionals about how to handle any particular physical, emotional, or spiritual issue.
- Intended to force anyone in any particular direction.
- A quick fix (none of this is easy).

How can this book be used?

- As a reference for explorers, guides, professionals, or family/friends/ acquaintances of explorers.
- As a roadmap for an intentional and conscious use of psychedelics (or any tool for psychospiritual growth).
- As an overview of ideas and recommendations for integrating experiences in non-ordinary states of consciousness, with pointers for where to look for more information on particulars.

As I move toward the conclusion of the Entryway, I want to touch upon a few more topics...

Remembering Mental Health

In speaking about safety, I want to mention the two extremes of a polarity I would like to transcend in this book. The two extremes are represented by:

- People who insist (or pretend) there is no danger of psychedelics contributing to (or catalyzing) mental health problems.
- People who believe psychedelics are dangerous drugs that always lead to mental health problems.

From the perspective of people who *know* the extraordinary value of psychedelics, the portrayal of psychedelics as necessarily contributing to mental health problems feels not only unfair, but also ignorant and biased. Many of the people with this perspective, however, use psychedelics in safe settings, with appropriate support, and do not have much experience with serious negative effects of any lengthy duration.

Unfortunately, negative effects are possible. There are real examples of psychedelics seeming to instigate psychiatric decomposition. Some people become unable to care for themselves, raise concern about harm to self or others, or may show difficulty distinguishing between external reality and internal images and processes.

For example, I was recently contacted to help integrate the LSD experience of a young man who was convinced his skin was blue after a psychedelic experience. He had stopped taking showers and was not eating. My encounter with this young man and his family was not propaganda by an anti-psychedelics media, but a frightening and extremely painful predicament of real people. I believe these situations are very rare, but I do not believe it is prudent to pretend they are not possible.

The trouble with an either-or perspective is that we do not integrate the truths of a complicated set of realities about powerful substances and experiences. Throughout this book, I will try to *integrate* both perspectives into a balanced understanding of the perils as well as promises of working with psychedelics.

In Chapter 9, "The Shadow Side," I unpack many of the ways mainstream culture has mischaracterized psychedelics. This has often been through projecting fears and other charged emotional baggage that has more to do with those projecting than any reality about psychedelics. I suggest this involves avoidance of examining painful absences, deficiencies and harms in our own culture, including failures in our religions.

While I believe much of the negative spin about psychedelics is unjustified, I also believe strong elements of shadow exist within some parts of psychedelics culture. Particularly as psychedelics receive more and more attention in mainstream culture, I encourage us all to work with—and integrate—these various cultural and psychic components. This is the way the art and practice of working with psychedelics can continue to mature and stabilize.

For now, here are a few things that I personally believe are part of the reality about psychedelics:

- Some people have a genetic or social predilection towards difficult mental health conditions that may be more likely to come into full-blown presentation through use of psychedelics. This includes the conditions described in mainstream psychology as schizophrenia or bipolar disorder.
- Other people may be in a psychological (or psychosocial or psychospiritual) process that pulls them toward the use of psychedelics when their situation may not present the optimum time or circumstance to bring into their world experiences as powerful and potentially destabilizing as psychedelics.
- Sometimes a difficult psychedelic experience introduces a situation that can be understood and helped through a mainstream mental health perspective and treatment model. For instance, some psychedelic experiences bring trauma, grief or despair to the surface, and working with these experiences might be helped through mainstream therapy models. Some people might experience so much suffering and destabilization that medication may be prudent for a limited period of time.

Stanislav Grof and his late wife, Christina Grof, developed the concepts of **spiritual emergence** and **spiritual emergency.** The interplay between the words "emer-gence" and "emergency" captures the "emergency" that is sometimes experienced by people and their families through spiritual "emergence." I say more about these concepts later in the book, but want to introduce the idea that what seems like a mental health emergency from using psychedelics may in fact represent a healing process.

There is no doubt that spiritual awakenings sometimes occur in ways that look to mainstream medical professionals like serious psychiatric conditions. The perspective offered by the Grofs is that holding these "emergences" with compassion and skill, rather than as pathology, allows most people to pass through the difficult stages into increased health and wholeness—that in fact, movement toward wholeness is the impulse that has arisen through the emergence/emergency.

The Grofs' work on spiritual emergence/emergency does not focus on psychedelics as a catalyst, but rather on the spontaneous presentations that may seem to fit diagnostic criteria for "mental illnesses." Nevertheless, the spiritual emergence/ emergency model applies to difficulties arising through psychedelics. With appropriate support, I believe many people can get through the "emergence/emergency," but there is always the risk that a mental health "break" may occur that cannot be put back into the box.

More importantly, it is very difficult for many people to really find (or be able to afford) the support that would be necessary to get through a spiritual emergence/ emergency triggered by psychedelics that had serious lasting effects. For these reasons, I recommend great care in deciding whether to explore psychedelics, *and perhaps even more importantly,* in deciding whether to offer to support someone else's psychedelic experiences.

How do you know if you or someone else would be at serious risk for using psychedelics?

I discuss the spiritual emergence-emergency perspective and mental health issues in more depth in Chapter 7, "Integration as Process." For now, I would note that any genetic (family) history of mental health situations characterized as schizophrenia or bipolar disorder would cause some caution in exploring psychedelics or in escalating participation in psychedelics. Many facilitators will not work with people who are taking medications for depression or anxiety, so anyone taking those medications should explore carefully any use of psychedelics with or without a guide.

In general, I strongly recommend that anyone considering psychedelics begin by talking with an experienced guide. Discuss fully with that guide all issues relating to safety and possible mental health issues that could arise. I do not want to seem alarmist, but I want you to be safe. It would be easy to suggest that you "discuss this matter with your doctor"—as many commercials suggest about medications or health issues—but I realize that many medical providers know nothing about psychedelics and would be in potential legal trouble by supporting you in that journey. So you're going to have to do your best to discuss the issues with someone who is qualified and willing to have a confidential discussion.

One more word on this issue—and this is the hardest thing for me to say in this section. But the reality is that some people who are drawn to psychedelics are trying to avoid rather than face their issues. To state the obvious, it is dangerous to allow psychedelics to become part of someone's serious ongoing or emerging mental health challenge. On the other hand, many of us drawn to self-exploration are working out issues of depression anxiety, trauma, dissociation, or other experiences that could be labeled as mental health issues.

In the Holotropic Breathwork community, the line is often drawn between people who are able to work with unusual experiences as something happening to them on a psychological level and people who get caught in a storyline about the reality of the experience. For instance, if aliens come to you in a psychedelic experience, it is possible to hold the experience as real, but also to hold that reality loosely enough to continue with your ordinary life—and to work on the psychological implications of the experience. In this way, you recognize the "reality" held by most people around you, but make use of the experience for your own growth. It is another thing to tell everyone you know that you are in contact with aliens and still another to create a narrative about your special mission with aliens or the need to warn the world that they are coming or battle the government over a cover-up. None of this is to say that the experience is not real, but the focus and tone of what you do with it is different.

Some people have challenges in separating out the projections that come from their internal life from what is actually happening in the outside world. There can be some paranoia and delusions. Sometimes there can be a belief that exploring psychedelics will "prove" to the outside world that your internal state is not "crazy," but the world is crazy. Sometimes it may seem as though "spirits" or "God" are calling you to psychedelics because you have a mission to accomplish.

Many of us have these feelings and ideas to one degree or another. There is nothing wrong with feeling a sense of purpose and commitment to living out your life or helping the world. But please be honest with yourself about the complicated issue of separating internal projections from outside realities. You don't need to talk to people who will just tell you that you are crazy and deluded. Please talk with someone who is sympathetic to the positive benefits of psychedelic exploration, but who can advise you in a sober fashion about your risks. If psychedelics are not a good choice for you now, there are other avenues you can explore for your non-ordinary state adventures and life opening.

In closing this section, I return to the example mentioned above where I was asked to support the young man who seemed to decompose after an LSD experience. My initial contact was from the parents of the young man, then with the nurse who was responsible for his care in a hospital setting. The young man's parents were so alarmed by his presentation they placed him temporarily in a psychiatric facility.

Through being respectful of the perspective of the parents and nurse, I was able to introduce the possibility that integration of the experience might lead to greater health and wholeness for the young man. Without challenging their perspective, I introduced the possibility that the experience was not simply a pathological mistake, but an opportunity for psychological growth.

Fortunately, the parents and the individual nurse opened to the possibility of working *with* rather than against the experiences. At the same time, I supported their strong need to know the young man was safe. In addition to working with the experiences, the young man was able to receive the benefit of the stabilizing influence provided through the mainstream mental health system—which held him safely as he began to work with me on integration of his experience.

The young man returned to a safe and relatively stable baseline and moved back home with his parents. He has not (yet?) broken through into a more whole and independent lifestyle, but he became able to work on the immediate life issues that were part of his draw to psychedelics. These issues were serious and contributed the pressure that was part of his temporary decomposition. He remains in touch with me when he chooses to engage in integration work.

Don't do psychedelics because it's "the Next Big Thing people are doing"

In the last few years, psychedelics have received attention in the national media through books and commentaries by people respected in the mainstream media community. For instance, in 2018, renowned author Michael Pollan published *How to Change your Mind: What the New Science of Psychedelics Teaches Us About Consciousness, Dying, Addiction, Depression, and Transcendence*. I admire the book and share the excitement of many in the psychedelics community that Pollan brought his reputation and communications skills to the subject. This helped move psychedelics from "fringe" and "outdated" to "new" and "cutting edge" for many people who keep up with the conversations in the national media.

Pollan seems a perfect ambassador into mainstream culture for taking the positive possibilities of psychedelics seriously. But for people who know the history of psychedelics research in the 1950s and 1960s, there may be a hiccup in considering whether the "new science" is all that new. Describing the results of contemporary psychedelics research as "new" might be more about attracting attention than historical reality, though certainly, research teams once again receiving permission from the federal government to conduct lawful research is new—and phenomenally important.

Where I am going with this commentary is to say that some people may pick up an interest in psychedelics as "the next new thing" that people are doing—such as, just for instance, doing yoga was many years ago, and then mindfulness meditation, and then being vegan, or whatever else comes along. These are all terrific things to bring into your life, so no judgment. But I do feel called to say that doing serious work in psychedelics is very different than doing yoga during your lunch hour or after work, or quieting the chatter in your mind once a day, or changing your diet.

Psychedelics done seriously is *serious* business. I believe you should go down this road only if you are serious about opening yourself to very powerful energies of transformation. You should go down the road if you are interested in working on yourself in consultation with the spiritual realms of the universe, not if you are interested in "keeping up with the trends." You owe it to yourself to know the difference.

Psychedelics are not Pharmaceuticals

As psychedelics come into mainstream culture, there is the risk that psychedelic "medicines" are viewed as most people view pharmaceuticals— something synthesized by experts in order to take a problem away from them without any real effort on their part.

We have been conditioned by modern medicine to view our bodies as machines that may need a pharmaceutical intervention to set things straight. This applies to our minds and emotional lives when mental health is the issue. In many situations, medicines work in exactly this way. For instance, if you have an infection, antibiotics almost always defuse the problem. Various medicines can reduce high blood pressure, help with diabetes, remove dangerous cholesterol, or provide other chemicals to restore health or minimize suffering. In the mental health realm, the last fifty years have seen the growth of many pharmaceuticals to help with depression, anxiety, psychosis, and many other conditions. All of these medicines work without any participation of consciousness.

I call this the pharmaceutical effect. In these situations, you may have to pay attention not to ingest other substances that interact badly with the pharmaceutical, but you do not have to "work on yourself" as part of the solution. The pharmaceutical does something to you to take away the problem—just as replacing a part in a machine would restore functionality to the machine.

Psychedelics do not work in this way. You may have an "opening" to understanding the source of your suffering, and assistance in being able to process the suffering, but you have to do the processing. Your mind and body need to shift through your willingness—and almost always your *effort*—to shift and change. This is why Michael Pollan called his book *How to Change Your Mind*.

I understand that some clinics in the United States have been offering infusions of ketamine as treatment for depression through a practice of bringing the "patient" into the office, having a nurse practitioner administer an IV, and sending the patient on his or her way. Although a diagnosis allowing treatment will have been made by a medical provider, there is no ongoing processing or integration of the experience. I find this practice similar to electroshock therapy as used in the past. The idea is that the "medicine" resolves the problem on its own. There is no need for engagement or working through the life situation.

While I imagine some people have been helped, I have heard sad anecdotal reports of the problem with using ketamine as a "pharmaceutical" in this way. One young woman reported to us that the treatment did not alleviate her problem, though it gave her relief from her depression for limited periods of time. Perhaps this intervention bought her time and kept her from harming herself until something shifted on its own. But there may have been more productive and empowering ways to help her.

Another young woman said that after she stopped ketamine treatment, she realized she had lost a year of her life during the time she was receiving ketamine. No benefit and little sense of being alive. After she stopped ketamine infusions, she sought psychological help for processing what she felt was a traumatic experience during this year of treatment.

I am aware that studies have been and will be conducted into how to use ketamine for valuable assistance with mental health conditions. I do not want to argue based only on anecdotal reports, but I use this example to suggest the mistake in treating psychedelics as pharmaceuticals. Psychedelics are aids to healing by acting as allies for psychological processing. They are not pharmaceutical cures for passive subjects.

This issue shines a light on the broader question of whether mainstream culture encourages us to participate in our actual lives or act as consumers of products. I could talk for hours about broad cultural issues but will leave you with the idea that psychedelics are a tool for you to integrate what you learn about yourself and the universe, to process through challenging information, or absorb astoundingly beautiful realities. They are not a pharmaceutical to take away problems without your involvement.

Can Psychedelics be part of my "Sobriety"?

Maybe!

I understand there are growing numbers of people who have made the brave and difficult decision to let go of a lifestyle with heavy use of alcohol or drugs like cocaine—but who replace these drugs with psychedelics. Sometimes this involves small regular doses ("microdosing"), and sometimes the small doses keep getting larger, and sometimes the practice is more about frequent ceremonies with medicines like Ayahuasca or regular large dose trips.

I have an entire chapter on Addiction, Chapter 10. If you are curious about this issue, I recommend you read that chapter carefully, because this is a complicated topic. For now, I want to say three things:

- Absolutely I believe responsible use of psychedelics can play a life-changing role in releasing harmful addictions. Some psychedelics are more beneficial than others for this purpose. As I later describe, ibogaine (though dangerous) seems to offer an important physical and emotional break from the hold of addictions.
- On the other hand, when considering whether psychedelics can be part of your sobriety, please remember that addiction is addiction is addiction is addiction is addiction. Did I say addiction is addiction? Or that addiction is addiction is addiction? Honesty with yourself is the key—are you releasing something or just moving from one focus to another?
- If you really want to release yourself from addiction and still feel good about yourself and life (which is what I believe you want), then I recommend an integration focus that takes you deeply into yourself and all your wounds and needs and hopes and dreams. Psychedelics can absolutely play a role. I hope this book helps.

What about Cannabis?

Some people consider cannabis a psychedelic. Others, like me, do not. To be technical about it, some psychedelics are formally classified in the medical system as hallucinogens, some are empathogens, and some are dissociatives. Cannabis has its own different classification.

More importantly for me, cannabis in my experience does not open the mind to the same level of serious self-exploration psychedelics make possible. Some people definitely disagree with me on this point, and I do not want to argue. I definitely agree that cannabis is sometimes very useful as an adjunct to particular psychedelics in profound journeys. I've been there—let me repeat, I have been there. And to use it as a surrogate for psychedelics, I would rather just use it for what cannabis is and use psychedelics for what they are.

All this said, if cannabis is part of your repertoire, then by all means, use this book for help in integrating your experiences into your life adventure.

Can't I use Psychedelics Legally Now?

There is increasing publicity about psychedelics, including the research and ther-apy programs that have been authorized by the Food and Drug Administration in the United States and the equivalent governmental agencies in some other countries. Many articles in the mainstream media report on psychedelics now in positive terms, possibly leaving the impression that legal barriers have been lifted. BUT: just because you are now reading in Western publications about experiences with psychedelics, do not assume that such experiences are lawfully available to you.

I know many people who have been disappointed when they realize that they do not fit within the narrow criteria for participating in therapy programs or research projects. There are also many people who are surprised to learn they do not fit the criteria to train as psychedelic aides or research assistants.

While changes are happening at a fast pace, the research programs are carefully monitored and primarily staffed by people with appropriate licenses based on advanced degrees and clinical experience (e.g., medical degrees, clinical therapy licenses, and in some situations, ordination as a minister—and I don't think one of those online minister's licenses is going to work). I understand that there will be roles for assistants and sitters that might not require licenses. However, as of this writing, most "ordinary" people will not have the opportunity to train as the primary lawful facilitators for psychedelics work. This is a disappointment for many people because they were thinking they could get into the world of psychedelics for healing by working for one of the new programs.

You may have an opportunity to volunteer as a participant in certain research projects, but most of the projects have been approved for working with specific populations under careful criteria. For example, typical projects involve people with treatment resistant post-traumatic stress disorder, addictions, or anxiety while living with terminal illness. If you or your loved one fit into such categories, by all means look for existing programs, and you may find a perfect and life-changing experience.

One of the ironies in the psychedelics renaissance is that many guides and facilitators who have worked underground for years in assisting people during psychedelics experiences do not currently qualify to train or work as aides in the lawful research programs or clinics. As unfortunate as this may be for some people, it has been deemed important to require mainstream licenses and training to staff these projects—they would not be receiving government approval without these criteria.

On the other side of this issue, many people who *do* qualify to train and work as psychedelics facilitators have little or no experience in working with people in non-ordinary states. Fortunately, the programs have been providing—in increasing ways —opportunities (and requirements) to gain such experience, often through "sitting" during breathwork sessions.

I say this at the outset because I do not want to create the impression through this book that psychedelics can be easily used lawfully in the United States or many other countries. I am writing this book for everyone who uses or is thinking about using psychedelics, but please remember to have caution and forethought about the legality of your situation. Just because you now hear a lot about psychedelics does not mean you can use psychedelics legally in all settings. I am not endorsing or recommending illegal activity.

As I note in later chapters, lawful experiences with many "medicines" are available in many other countries. Also, while I do not advocate illegal activity, I know that underground experiences continue and seem to be growing. Finally, if you do find a guide to help you with an experience outside the recognized legal programs, please respect the guide's confidentiality and understand the trust they are placing in you to honor commitments of privacy and confidentiality.

Subjective and Objective

Now I want to encourage you to find a way to hold onto yourself as you use this book. I want you to hold onto your subjectivity.

The current worldview maintains there is an objective reality that is based on how science understands the material world. Even mainstream psychology pretends there are certain objective realities that categorize your mind and your experience. The *Diagnostic and Statistical Manual of Mental Disorders* used in psychology creates categories of psychological situations as though these are specific, separate realities that describe with certainty the variations of abnormalities that bring people into psychological suffering. These categories are useful in many ways, but the idea of an objective reality is something that needs to be recognized for what it is—kind of subjective. Adventuring with psychedelics plays with the fiction of objective reality and plays with your attachment to it.

An **objective** perspective is one that (in theory) is not influenced by emotions, opinions, or personal feelings—a perspective based in the assumption of material fact, in things quantifiable and measurable. A **subjective** perspective is based on personal feeling, emotion, aesthetics, and experiences. As you read this book, you may start to feel that I am giving you objective facts, describing realities about psychedelics, psychology, and integration. In a way I am creating a narrative that may look like objective reality, but it is very important that you see through and beyond whatever I say. See it as a portrait I am painting to give you something to see past.

Seeing integration with both an objective view and subjective view will give you more flexibility. Use the space in between objective and subjective. A lot of this book, particularly in the beginning, may feel very linear. There are definite statements about things, including maps in Chapter 3. But integration is definitely a non-linear process. In fact, integration involves learning to be non-linear. There I go saying "in fact."

The maps and objective descriptions in this book are not here to tell you where to go. The maps do not describe the places you will definitely encounter between Los Angeles and New York. The maps are rather to help you hold onto yourself when you find that you might not be sure where you are.

Chances are that adventuring with psychedelics will take you into realms where you have no idea where you are. Maps, linearity, and the objective are *only* something of value if they help you hold onto yourself while you let go. When you come back, the maps may help you frame your experiences, your learning, your life story, and your worldview.

I would like to offer an *AND* rather than an *OR* viewpoint when you work with objectivity and subjectivity in your integration. Play with a healthy balance between what your personal intuition is longing for while you lean onto some security about what others can tell you about psychedelics and non-ordinary state journeys.

It is also vital to lean on the ancestors, teachers, and elders to follow their paths of guidance. I try to share their experience in this book. The ancestors, teachers, and elders are both objective and subjective by nature and will come to you with fluidity as real people and spirits. As you form relationships with them, you will be in the space between objectivity and subjectivity. Feel into that space.

Who am I?

Probably fitting for a book about psychedelics, I am still exploring *who I am* in all the iterations of the concept of "who am I."

As I mentioned above, I come from a background of adventuring with psychedelics from teenage years through adulthood, finding my way to psychology and spiritual systems after many hours of psychedelic experience. One of the ways I describe myself involves a balance between Sigmund Freud's *Interpretation of Dreams,* Tom Wolfe's *Electric Kool-Aid Acid Test,* and Stanislav Grof's *LSD Psychotherapy.* After a career in culinary work in my twenties, I trained as an Adlerian therapist and then completed my doctoral degree in transpersonal psychology at Sofia University. I live in Minneapolis, Minnesota (where I was born and raised), with my wife, Myriah, two daughters, Greta and Asteya, and two sons, Levi and Bodhi. One truly psychedelic experience.

About the Integration Exercises

After every chapter I will invite you to engage in a particular exercise.

These are mandatory—NOT!

I encourage you to play with the exercises as you may be called to play with the exercises. If some appeal to you and some do not, that's fine. That said, please know that I have given some thought to offering exercises in a progression that might help you gather into yourself an approach to working with psychedelics.

Now Your Turn

Now I would encourage you to take some time to reflect on what brings you here. This is your first invitation to get this book dirty.

My intention in this book is not only to talk at you (well, at least not all the time). I also want you to engage with yourself and the information I share. After all, that is what integration is all about. Within most chapters there are places where I suggest questions for you to answer or things for you to consider. Usually this is midway in a chapter and then at the end.

Here is the question for the end of the first chapter:

What has been going on in your life that has led you to purchase this handbook?

Integration Exercise 1: Basic Meditation

What You Need

- Comfortable, loosely fitting clothing
- Pillows or cushions or a chair
- A timer or meditation bell
- Your journal.

General Background

Meditation, mindfulness, pondering, or concentration; there are many forms of this art both spiritual and scientifically cognitive. The practice of different forms of meditation can be learned in spiritual communities, modern training programs, or through searching for instructions on the Internet. For generations, people have spent hours, weeks, years or lifetimes practicing their chosen form of meditation. Each form of meditation has a particular focus. For those of you who have not found your own form of meditation, I offer an exercise based on following your breath.

The basic idea of meditation in this exercise is simple. Every time your mind begins to shift its focus away from your breath and you get lost in thought, you simply bring your attention back to your breath. And then you repeat this again and again until your meditation timer sounds. The idea is that every time you bring your attention back to your breath, you work out your "attention reflex." Then, over time, your focus, concentration, and attention span improve. This has benefits for meditation and all aspects of your life—and for our purposes, develops an attention "muscle" that helps you navigate through non-ordinary states.

Why This Exercise is Important for Psychedelics

Meditation, particularly meditation focusing on the breath, helps you develop an ability to place your attention on a focal point of awareness. You will find this is very different from allowing your thoughts, sensations, or emotions to create your experience.

By following your breath as it relates to your body, you build a relationship between something that feels like you at a deeply soul level—your awareness—and the "you" that is more subject to all that is going on inside you (sensations, emotions, instincts, desires, hurts) and all that is bombarding you from the outside, seeming to cause all those things to happen inside you.

Developing this **awareness** is the most important first step in almost all mystical traditions. Sometimes this is called a **witness consciousness** or **observer consciousness**. The practice of developing this awareness is sometimes called developing the **observer self**.

When a friend of mine was training with Helen Palmer in The Enneagram (see Chapter 5, "Introducing Maps of Consciousness"), Helen would lead the dozens of people in the training group in meditations designed to help develop this awareness. Helen would encourage each person to "feel" this awareness and to practice placing it in different places. She would ask:

- Can you place your awareness in your left foot?
- Can you place your awareness in your heart?
- Can you place your awareness at the top of your head?
- Can you place your awareness in the center of your torso?
- Can you place your awareness in the wall behind me?
- Can you place your awareness in one of the trees outside the window?

While you may not want to do this as you first develop your practice, eventually you will be able to "feel" what is in the places where you put your awareness. Some people do their own "chakra clearing" by placing their awareness in each of the energy centers of their bodies, feeling what is there, and working through what is to be worked through.

While there are many names for this sense of awareness or observer self, it is also that part of you (at least in the beginning of your practice) that is able to distance yourself from your emotions and habitual reactions in order to "see" what you are about to do and maybe decide to do something different. This is the point of the Enneagram—to help people find their particular habitual reactions and notice them before they are running you unconsciously. This is also the point of many of the techniques taught in therapy, including the popular Cognitive Behavior Therapy (CBT).

You can see that if there is a part of you that can distance yourself from the turmoil that arises in your thoughts or emotions, then that part of you can *work with* those thoughts and emotions as something to be worked with, not something that is controlling you without **your** participation.

Why is developing this awareness so very important for working with psychedelics (or in breathwork or any non-ordinary state work)?

If journeying with psychedelics is like venturing out into the ocean (a heavy surf sometimes?), you can think of your practiced awareness as a surfboard or even a life preserver. Being "in" your awareness helps you be able to experience what is being brought to you with enough self-possession to hold onto and learn from the experience. Placing yourself "in" this awareness can also help you make decisions about how to navigate through your experience. Literally, sometimes it may allow you to "go" into one thing or "not go" into another. This is because there is a "you" that is separate from what is coming at you, even if that also feels like you.

As Helen Palmer sometimes explained, a developed sense of awareness is also what allows "psychics" to venture into other realms and know the difference between the information they are finding and what is only internal to themselves. So this sense of awareness can move not just around your body or in the material world, but around many realms.

One caveat: do not get carried away with yourself. You are not trying to be a psychic or take a journey into other realms. You are just practicing meditation.

For this reason, it is a good idea to **stay close to your breath. Do not *try* to develop awareness or unusual abilities. Try to keep coming back to your breath no matter what happens.** The awareness will then develop. The same is true during psychedelic journeys. When you need to anchor yourself, your breath is there to bring you back to yourself.

Remember that your first breath is what anchored you in your body and in this material world. On the other side of your journey in this lifetime, your last breath is what releases you back into the other side (or oneness with all that is).

Recap: when you journey in non-ordinary states, the breath (and your focal point of attention) can become your navigational point in your explorations. One psychedelics guide I know puts it this way: take your intention for exploration and bring your attention to it. "That's how you navigate in these realms."

Your breath is also a point of refuge and safety where you can return and adjust what you are experiencing. Being one with your focal point of attention, as you will discover, allows you to make choices during your journeys. Your breath, inhabited through your attention, allows you to stay with and begin integrating experiences that might otherwise be overwhelming.

How To Do It

Preparation in advance

1. Create a safe and sacred space that you have devoted to meditating.
2. After Integration Exercise 2, you may have an altar that speaks to you, with both spiritual and physical interests of yours being represented, near where you meditate.
3. Have your chair and pillow (or cushion) set up in a comfortable position.
4. Have your timer set up, probably on your phone.

Instructions for the exercise (Time: 2 minutes to 30 minutes)

- Dim the lights a bit, or shut them off completely to help you focus better. Some enjoy the natural daylight. Get comfortable, open the timer on your phone, or ring the bell three times; this opens your meditation.
- Start your timer.
- Sit up straight. Having a strong posture is an important part of meditation, but be comfortable as you explore your experience. The more you get to know your body in meditation, the more your body will find its own best posture for the flow within you.
- Bring your attention/focus to your breath. Focus is what meditation is all about, and this is what makes meditation both difficult and worthwhile. In this step, close your mouth and focus entirely on your breath as it enters and leaves your nose. You can focus on any element of your breath that you want—from how the air feels as it enters and exits your nose, to how the air feels as you inflate and deflate your lungs, to the sensation under your nose as you breathe in and out, to the sound you make as you breathe. Don't force your breathing here—just breathe naturally and observe your breath without thinking too much about it.
- Don't think. This is the hard part. Don't analyze your breath; just bring your attention and focus to your breath, without thinking about it or analyzing it.
- Bring your attention back to your breath when it wanders. And it will. When your mind wanders, and it will, gently bring your attention back to your breath once you realize that your mind has wandered. You may not clue in at first that your mind has started thinking again, but when you do, gently bring your attention back. Don't be hard on yourself during this stage. Just gently bring your attention back.
- Again, bring your mind back when it wanders. When your mind begins to think, gently bring your attention back to only your breath. When your mind begins to think about your past psychedelic session or your excitement to "trip" again, simply breathe. When your mind becomes restless, bring in your attention again. Keep doing this until your meditation timer sounds.

How long should you meditate? You can start with two minutes, then work up to five, ten, a half-hour. Some people meditate all day at retreats.

Generally, I find that it is helpful to have a pre-set commitment to meditate for a particular period of time. This not only keeps you in your chair or on your cushion, but it develops discipline that is important for your commitment to integration. Having the commitment and carrying it through seems to "awaken" something in the spiritual realm for you.

There are many possible points of concentration for meditation, but the breath is more than just a focal point. Learning to merge your attention with your breath gets you in touch with an entry point into your spiritual process. Psychedelics can blow open the doors and windows of your spiritual process. Building the muscle of containing yourself through your breath enables you to integrate. The breath may be the single most important entry point into integration.

CHAPTER 2

MORE ON PSYCHEDELICS

Psychedelics Come to Western Culture

In recent times, psychedelics returned to Western culture following the accidental discovery of LSD by Swiss chemist Albert Hofmann (1906-2008). Having synthesized an early version of LSD in 1938, Hofmann's intuition led him back to the substance in 1943, when Switzerland was an island of neutrality with World War II raging all around.

Albert Hofmann

Hofmann tells his own story in *LSD, My Problem Child: Reflections on Sacred Drugs, Mysticism and Science*. His famous "bicycle ride" on April 19, 1943, while on the first intentional acid trip, is immortalized in the history of psychedelics. Some people celebrate April 19 every year as a psychedelics history holiday. I share more about Hofmann's astounding discovery (and the bicycle ride) when I talk about LSD later in this chapter.

In 1953, Aldous Huxley (1894-1963), famous author of the dystopian novel *Brave New World*, read a research paper about psychedelics by Humphrey Osmond (inventor of the word *psychedelic*). Huxley invited Osmond to his home in Los Angeles, where he convinced Osmond to guide him in an experience of mescaline. This led to Huxley's 1954 book *The Doors of Perception*, a classic in the literature of psychedelics. In 1965, Jim Morrison suggested the name The Doors for the iconic rock band. This honored both Huxley's book and the famous quote by English poet William Blake (1757-1827):

> If the doors of perception were cleansed, everything would appear to man as it is, infinite.

The history of "magic mushrooms" in the West began differently, but around the same time. In 1956, R. Gordon Wasson (1898-1986), a banker, author, and amateur anthropologist, traveled to Mexico with his wife, Valentina Pavlovna Wasson (Guercken), who was originally from Russia. Their goal was to investigate the ceremonial use of mushrooms by indigenous peoples. Native healer Maria Sabina allowed the Wassons to participate in a Mazatec mushroom ritual, making them some of the first Westerners to experience the psychedelic possibilities of psilocybin, the active ingredient in "magic mushrooms."

Maria Sab.ina

In 1957, Gordon Wasson wrote his legendary article about the experience for *Life* magazine, titled "Seeking the Magic Mushroom." An interview with Valentina appeared around the same time in the magazine *This Week*, using the title "Sacred Mushrooms," the description preferred by the Wassons. (An interesting side story: the Wasson expedition was sponsored by the Geschickter Fund for Medical Research, later revealed as a front for the CIA. I would not be surprised if additional information comes forward in the next several years indicating the involvement of the CIA and other covert government agencies in experimentation and political manipulation involving LSD and other psychedelics.)

Maria Sabina lived to regret her invitation to the Wassons. Despite her request to remain anonymous, her story became well known, leading Westerners to descend on her village for many years. Sabina herself found God through Catholicism, considering herself a healer of the sick in her community, not a guide for Western enlightenment.

"From the moment the foreigners arrived, the 'holy children' lost their purity," Sabina said about sacred mushrooms. "They lost their force; the foreigners spoiled them." Sabina thought the "young people" were the ones who were the most disrespectful. "They take the children at any time and in any place," she said. "They don't do it during the night or under the direction of the Wise Ones, and they don't use them to cure any sickness either." [5] Sabina's community unraveled, and even the police harassed her. This is but one example of the complexity of the entry of psychedelics to Western culture.

Early Use of Psychedelics in Psychotherapy

Meanwhile, back in Europe, psychedelics had come to the attention of Ronald Sandison and other psychiatrists in the United Kingdom. In 1952, Sandison visited Switzerland and met Hofmann, whose lab provided him with samples of LSD for research with psychiatric patients. Through their research, Sandison and his colleagues became convinced LSD sessions assisted people suffering from severe treatment-resistant neurosis or depression. They wrote about their work, which received international attention.

In 1956, Stanislav Grof (b. 1931) was a medical student at Charles University in Prague, Czechoslovakia. When one of his professors asked for volunteers to experience LSD-25 as part of a research project, Grof raised his hand. His experience with LSD, in combination with the stimulus of an oscillating white strobe light, evoked, to use Grof's words, "a powerful mystical experience that radically changed my personal and professional life."

Stan Grof

For over a decade, Grof conducted and supervised hundreds of psychedelic sessions in Czechoslovakia and later Maryland, USA. His meticulous research shaped the scientific understanding of the psychological benefits of psychedelics when used in appropriate settings. His research is summarized in *LSD: Doorway to the Numinous: The Groundbreaking Psychedelic Research into Realms of the Human Unconscious*. For a time, Grof and many others believed the discovery of psychedelics in psychiatry would be looked upon as the equivalent of the discovery of the microscope in modern physical medicine.

As you work with this book, you will note the seminal role Grof has played in the development of transpersonal psychology and in working with non-ordinary states of consciousness for healing and self-discovery. His maps of consciousness and understanding of the human psyche provide important guidance for those of us hoping to integrate psychedelic experiences.

> If I am the father of LSD, Stan Grof is the godfather.
> —Albert Hofmann

"Timothy Leary's dead—No, no, no, no."

For better or worse, the name Timothy Leary (1920-1996) is synonymous for many people with LSD. Any mention of Leary brings to mind the phrase "turn on, tune in, drop out." This was the famous (infamous?) advice Leary gave at the "Be-In" gathering of 30,000 hippies in Golden Gate Park, San Francisco, in 1967.

Tim Leary

One of the best pieces of evidence for the hysteria about psychedelics generated by the United States government in the 1960s and 1970s is the description of Leary by President Richard Nixon as "the most dangerous man in America." Seriously?

Leary is immortalized in many ways in our culture, including in the classic song "Legend of a Mind" by the Moody Blues. You get the flavor from some of the lyrics:

Timothy Leary's dead
No, no, no, no, He's outside looking in
….
He'll fly his astral plane
Takes you trips around the bay
Brings you back the same day
….
He'll take you up, he'll bring you down
He'll plant your feet back firmly on the ground
He flies so high, he swoops so low
He knows exactly which way he's gonna go

Sadly, Leary was unjustifiably persecuted by the conservative elements in academics and government. In Chapter 9, I talk through the enormous cultural shadow projected into psychedelics and carried by people like Leary. Though eventually spending time in prison and as an internationally wanted man, Leary was once a respected Harvard professor of psychology, where he worked with Richard Alpert, later known as spiritual teacher Ram Dass (b.1931).

Ram Dass

In 1959, Leary and Alpert began The Harvard Psilocybin project with the goal of documenting the effects of psilocybin on human consciousness. The most famous of these experiments, conducted in 1962, is known as "The Good Friday Experiment." Graduate students in divinity (religion) were divided into two groups: one ingesting psilocybin and one receiving a placebo. The students ingesting psilocybin all reported profound religious experiences, in contrast to those in the control group.

Leary and Alpert were criticized for this experiment and eventually fired by Harvard for giving psilocybin to undergraduate students off campus. They became social activists, Leary of the more unapologetically provocative kind, while Ram Dass transitioned into non-drug-related spiritual teachings, including authoring the spiritual classic *Be Here Now*. No matter where you come down on the explosion of LSD in the 1960s, it is important to remember that Leary and his associates were real people serving the culture by carrying a wave that had come to the world. As a person, Leary had a tough ride and is remembered touchingly by his youngest son as a kind and present father. Zach Leary wrote about his father's last moments, when Tim repeatedly clenched and unclenched his fist, asking "Why?" and then "Why not?", with his final word being, "Beautiful."

Interestingly, Leary is one of the few people whose cremated ashes were buried in space after his passing in 1996 from prostate cancer. A rocket containing some of Leary's ashes, along with those of several other people, including Gene Roddenberry, creator of the *Star Trek* mythology, was launched into space in 1997, where it remained in orbit for several years before burning up on reentry. Seems very appropriate.

After Leary and his crowd, no one is more responsible for spreading the psychedelic movement than Ken Kesey (1935-2001) and his band of Merry Pranksters. The author of *One Flew Over the Cuckoo's Nest*, Kesey used funds from his successful novel to spread the word about LSD (the "Electric Kool-Aid"). He arranged "happenings" in California and documented a famous bus trip across the United States. Kesey also mentored the rock band The Grateful Dead, formed the same year as The Doors (1965).

In their separate ways, both bands embodied the energy of the psychedelic movement. Jim Morrison's performances in The Doors often veered into poetry recital accompanied by music, with his message sounding like the perennial wisdom of mystical traditions. One of their most famous songs, "Break on Through (to the Other Side)," captures the psychedelic drive to find what lies beyond the surface levels of life.

Jim Morrison

If you want to get into the spirit of the times, listen to some of the songs that capture the sense of inner exploration hitting the culture through psychedelics. You can find them on YouTube and get a sense of the colors, sounds, and exuberance that came with the psychedelics movement. Some of my favorites are:

- "Magic Carpet Ride" by Steppenwolf:
  "Close your eyes girl, Look inside girl,
  Let the sound take you away."

- "Lucy in the Sky with Diamonds" by the Beatles:
  "Follow her down to a bridge by a fountain,
  Where rocking horse people eat marshmallow pies.
  Everyone smiles as you drift past the flowers,
  That grow so incredible high.
  Newspaper taxis appear on the shore,

Waiting to take you away.
Climb in the back with your head in the clouds,
And you're gone."
(Notice that the initials of the main words in the song, Lucy-Sky-Diamonds, spell LSD.)

- "Purple Haze" by Jimi Hendrix:

"Purple Haze was in my brain,
Lately things don't seem the same,
Actin' funny, but I don't know why.
'Scuse me while I kiss the sky."

- "I Feel Free" by Cream:
"Feel when I dance with you,
I move like the sea,
You, you're all I want to know,
I feel free, I feel free."

- "Eight Miles High" by The Byrds:
"Nowhere is
There warmth to be found,
Among those afraid
Of losing their ground."

- "White Rabbit" by Jefferson Airplane, with Grace Slick's amazing voice and lyrics suggesting the ominous undertone of some LSD experiences:
"One pill makes you larger
and one pill makes you small
and the ones that Mother gives you
don't do anything at all."

- Just about anything from the 1969 festival Woodstock.

Some of the most notable books on the history and most influential personalities of psychedelics coming into Western culture are:

- *The Electric Kool-Aid Acid Test* by Tom Wolfe

- *The Most Dangerous Man in America* by Bill Minutaglio and Steven Davis
- *Tripping the Bardo with Tim Leary* by Joanna Harcourt-Smith
- *Acid Test* by Tom Shroder

The Illegal Turn

During the late 1960s, the governments of the United States, the United Kingdom, and many other countries banned most psychedelics and, sadly, shut down all research into their healing potential. As other mind-opening substances have become recreationally popular (for instance, MDMA in the 1980s and 5-MeO-DMT in the 2000s), prohibition of those substances has followed suit.

Many writers document the history and sociology behind "the illegal turn." Here are a few reasons I believe this happened:

- Using psychedelics can be dangerous, particularly outside a safe setting and without experienced and trustworthy guides.
- Media coverage in the mid-1960s sensationalized stories about people "thinking they could fly" and "jumping off roofs" while under the influence of LSD, probably an urban legend (or propaganda) as I have not found reliable evidence this ever occurred.
- In 1969, when beloved television personality Art Linkletter's daughter died tragically after falling from her sixth story West Hollywood apartment, her family blamed LSD, and Linkletter's campaign against psychedelics cemented the image of dying because "you think you can fly."
- The psychologically and spiritually transformational impact of psychedelics on many people contributed to a counter-culture movement threatening the values of many people, including the parents of younger people using psychedelics, as well as many people in social, organized religious, and political power.
- Powerful people controlling governmental and other institutions perceived the counter-culture movement, linked with psychedelics, as threatening the viability of the war conducted by the United States in Viet Nam, which many believed "could not be lost" given the "fight against Communism" and the desire for the United States to remain the dominant world power.

In 1971, President Nixon launched a "War on Drugs" that has continued in many ways into the present. By including psychedelics along with drugs that are actually addictive and harmful, Nixon (and the popular media of the time) swept under the carpet all the research proving the potentially healing properties of psychedelics. Lawful research was put on hold for several decades. And yet, use of psychedelics continued, mostly underground.

Now Your Turn

Where do you personally connect with the history of psychedelics in the West?
_____
_____
_____
_____
_____

Whom do you relate to?
_____
_____
_____
_____
_____

What is your personal vision for the place of psychedelics in global society?
_____
_____
_____
_____
_____

Psychedelics in the 1980s and Beyond

Entering the "scene" of a new generation in the 1980s was MDMA ("Ecstasy" or "E" or "Molly" or "Adam"). Urban legend says the original street name was *Empathy*, but the market seemed to find *Ecstasy* more profitable than *Empathy*, something to think about. Perhaps this was an echo of the popular preference of "magic" to "sacred" mushrooms in the 1950s.

Often described as an empathogen (that is, producing empathy), MDMA offers an experience of "heart-opening" or compassion for self and others. The world feels like a good place, and love is everywhere. This worked for many as a party drug in the late 1980s and 1990s dance club scene. But MDMA had a prior incarnation as an aide in serious psychotherapy, a reincarnated use now in the last stages of research heading toward limited approval by the United States Food and Drug Administration.

Like LSD, MDMA (*3,4-methylenedioxy-methamphetamine*) was discovered accidentally in a pharmaceutical laboratory many years before it became popular. In 1912, a chemist named Anton Kollisch, working for Merck, synthesized MDMA while seeking a compound to stem the flow of abnormal bleeding. Merck patented the substance and later studied some of its effects on the nervous system, but without much public attention.

It was not until the 1970s that Alexander "Sasha" Shulgin, a biochemist, "rediscovered" MDMA through his own synthesis. Like Albert Hofmann with LSD, when Shulgin tried MDMA, he realized the potential power it had for psychological work. He then introduced the "empathogen" to psychotherapists for use with their clients.

Alexander Shulgin

During the era of President Ronald Reagan, another push against drugs pulled MDMA into emergency classification as an illegal substance. During the summer of 1985, amidst Nancy Reagan's "Just say No" campaign, MDMA was placed on Schedule I as a drug with no accepted medical use. This was based on a study linking the substance to brain damage in rats. We might notice the cyclical nature of expansion of mind-expanding substances into our culture, followed by a closing-down reaction by conservative factions.

And yet, interest in mind expansion continued. An important figure in the psychedelic movement of the 1980s and 1990s was Terence McKenna (1946-2000). Like many of his generation, McKenna read Huxley's *The Doors of Perception* as he was coming of age. Following Leary's advice to turn on, tune in, and drop out, McKenna spent time in Nepal investigating hallucinogens, followed by a trip to the Amazon with his brother Dennis (b. 1950). The McKenna brothers were seeking Ayahuasca, but coincidentally also found psilocybin.

Terence McKenna

Known to some as the Timothy Leary of the '90s, Terence McKenna spoke widely about the healing benefits of psychedelic plants, in particular psilocybin and Ayahuasca. McKenna bridged into the underground rave scene of the '90s and beyond, where MDMA took hold in the psychedelic movement. Sadly, Terence passed away in 2000, but Dennis remains influential today in discussions and education about psychedelics.

Given the significance of MDMA in the experience of the '80s and '90s generations, I want to bring in the flavor of the dance and rave scene with mention of Electronic Dance Music (EDM). Interestingly, some of this music finds its way into breathwork sessions as a means to help launch non-ordinary states without mind-altering substances. You might consider feeling into this sound experience by searching the Internet for EDM music or rave music. In this music, you might feel the thumpa-thumpa of the beating heart, opening to what is, opening to flow. If you can, feel the love behind the pulse of life.

Psychedelics Today

It has been estimated that over 30 million Americans now living have used psychedelics at least once in their lives. These are not all aging baby-boomers remembering their acid trips in the 1960s. Roughly the same percentages of younger people explore psychedelics today as in the era of the Merry Pranksters and The Beatles' Yellow Submarine.[6]

Most use of psychedelics in the United States and European countries remains illegal. But, as I have noted, the rules for allowing research studies have loosened up over the last few decades. This has come about through the diligent and wise work of many people.

In *DMT, The Spirit Molecule: A Doctor's Revolutionary Research into the Biology of Near-Death and Mystical Experiences*, Rick Strassman, M.D., describes the labyrinthine process he went through to obtain permission from the university where he worked (the University of New Mexico) and the United States Food and Drug Administration (FDA) to study the effects of DMT on humans. He finally passed all the hurdles and conducted groundbreaking research over the years 1990-1995 (discussed later in the book).

Several prominent organizations have been instrumental in ushering in the psychedelic renaissance. In 1986, the **Multidisciplinary Association for Psychedelic Studies (MAPS)** was founded as a non-profit research and educational organization. Spearheaded by Rick Doblin, the mission of MAPS has been to develop medical, legal, and cultural contexts for people to benefit from the careful uses of psychedelics and marijuana. MAPS envisions a time when psychedelics may be lawfully prescribed by knowledgeable medical providers and psychedelic experiences supported by trained professionals. Research sponsored by MAPS has begun to provide a contemporary "evidence base" for the safe and beneficial use of psychedelics.

Rick Doblin

In 1993, the **Heffter Research Institute** was incorporated in New Mexico as a non-profit scientific organization. Named in honor of Dr. Arthur Heffter, who identified mescaline as the active ingredient in the peyote cactus, the Heffter Research Institute designs, reviews and funds studies involving psychedelics, primarily psilocybin. Some of the projects sponsored by the institute have been conducted at prominent research institutions in the United States and Europe. Seminal studies have investigated the benefits of psilocybin for the treatment of cancer-related distress and addiction; others have examined the relationship between psychedelic experience and spirituality.

Other organizations important in the study of psychedelics include:

- **Erowid,** a non-profit educational organization founded in 1995, providing information about psychoactive plants and chemicals, as well as other modalities that can alter one's state of consciousness, such as dreaming, meditation, yoga, and breathing exercises.
- **ICEERS,** the "International Center for Ethnobotanical Education Research and Service," an international non-profit organization based in Barcelona, Spain, undertaking to renovate society's relationship with psychoactive plants.
- **The Beckley Foundation,** a policy foundation in the United Kingdom devoted to reforming drug policy around the world based upon education and research.

In the 2000s through the present, one of the important leaders in psychedelics research has been Charles Grob, professor of psychiatry and biobehavioral sciences at Harbor-UCLA Medical Center. Grob was one of the first contemporary researchers to receive FDA approval to study the effects of MDMA and Ayahuasca.

Charles Grob

Some of the most important universities conducting psychedelics research include:

- Johns Hopkins
- New York University (NYU)
- University of New Mexico (UNM)
- Harbor-UCLA
- Imperial College in London, UK
- University of Zurich, Switzerland.

Having told you about some of the contemporary lawful research projects involving psychedelics, I will throw the whole thing open for the rest of the book. In other words, I want to talk to everyone, whether you are involved in the projects authorized by the government or not. I am also mindful that most of you "are not."

While I do not advocate illegal activity, I know there are thousands if not millions of people around the world showing greater interest than ever in psychedelic experiences. I am guided by the following observation of MAPS founder Rick Doblin:

> The cultural integration of psychedelics won't happen overnight, and the question of young people is perhaps the most difficult involved. The first step is for people who have knowledge of these substances to share it, "coming out" about their own experiences. Drug education should be honest and present a balanced picture of risks and benefits.

A growing number of publications, including numerous websites, describe experiences with various psychedelic medicines. I encourage you to explore according to your time and interest. For now, I want to share some information about the ways many people are exploring psychedelics today.

Ayahuasca

Ayahuasca has become a worldwide phenomenon in the last few decades. Thousands of people have traveled to South America to experience Ayahuasca rituals, giving rise to what is known as Ayahuasca tourism. Within the United States and other countries, underground Ayahuasca groups meet regularly, particularly in California and the East Coast.

Ayahuasca is brewed as a tea from the combination of the chacruna plant (providing DMT, the psychoactive compound) and the bark/root of the caapi vine, providing an MAO (monoamine-oxidase) inhibitor. The MAO inhibitor allows us to digest the DMT, which would otherwise be neutralized in our stomachs.

Amazonian shamans discovered the power of combining these two plants centuries ago. Given the multitude of plants in the Amazonian basin, the odds of accidentally combining chacruna and caapi in a brewed tea are staggering. The shamans will tell you the plants made themselves known to the people as an offering into their healing world.

The Internet abounds with tales of Ayahuasca exploration in the South American Amazonian region (Peru, Ecuador, Brazil and Colombia). The classic experience takes place in a ritual setting with a group of experiencers, a leader, helpers, and usually musicians or singers. Whether or not the leaders actually carry forward an authentic lineage in which they trained, the surroundings of the experience typically suggest heritage from an indigenous spiritual tradition.

Some people are concerned that participation by Westerners in Ayahuasca ceremonies represents a form of *cultural appropriation*. The concept of cultural appropriation is probably better understood as cultural *mis*appropriation. The idea is that elements of an indigenous culture are adopted by a dominant (often imperialist) culture in a way that works as a "taking" not much different from the taking of land and the robbing of self-determination.

The issue of cultural appropriation can be very charged and painful. Years ago, a Native American friend of mine pushed back in a group setting when some people of European descent began to use indigenous ceremonial customs. Through angry tears, she said, "Western soul retrieval is your problem, not mine. Find your own traditions." This is definitely not the attitude held by all indigenous people and healers, but it is a concern we all need to hold closely in awareness.

Increasingly, Westerners are training with indigenous leaders and then offering Ayahuasca ceremony. Ongoing communities are arising in many locations. I know very grounded and authentic Westerners who trained with South and North American elders and now offer Ayahuasca ceremony in suburban towns. From speaking with many people who have experienced Ayahuasca ceremony in South America, and those who have worked with Western "shamanic practitioners" in the United States, I am firmly convinced of one thing: the safety and sacred nature of the ceremony depends on the individuals involved much more than whether ancestry and lineage is claimed or advertised.

On the issue of cultural appropriation, one of the Western Ayahuasca guides I know speaks openly about these issues. He feels that much of the debate takes place on a level involving human power issues. His Native elder instructors taught him that once you are in touch with the spirits of nature and the plants, if you stay grounded with the actual physicality of where you are, the angst on these issues begins to loosen. I also know several people who have experienced being "told" by the spirit of Ayahuasca that she wants to come to Western countries to help us with our current spiritual and ecological crises. All this said, the issue of cultural misappropriation is serious and must be handled with deep respect.

Ayahuasca Ceremony

In keeping with indigenous tradition, Ayahuasca ceremonies are usually held overnight and include drumming, flute, rattle, voice, and energetic assistance by the shaman/facilitator and trained assistants. The psychedelic experience tends to begin a half hour after drinking the tea and reaches an apex within a couple of hours. Often a second cup is taken after the effect of the first cup begins to wane. Sound (singing, drumming, etc.) and the intention of experienced facilitators helps "hold" and protect the journeyers, as well as assist in working through energetic manifestations that arise.

The psychedelic effects of Ayahuasca include visual and auditory stimulation, the mixing of sensory modalities, and psychological introspection that may lead to great elation, fear, or illumination. Effects are commonly fairly strong, highly visual, and very energetic.

Purging (vomiting, known as *la purga* or "the purge") is common, and diarrhea is not unusual. Both experiences tend to feel as though the body is being cleansed of toxicity that is simultaneously physical, emotional, spiritual and even karmic. (By *karmic* I mean issues and physical/energetic residue brought into this life from experiences in prior incarnations). Conscious attention to what is being brought forward and purged—on psychological, biographical, and karmic levels—helps clear the toxicity while typically providing great insight into oneself and others.

Many people avoid Ayahuasca because they do not want the physical upheaval of vomiting or diarrhea. These experiences are not always part of the journey, but Ayahuasca does work through the body and focuses on physical release as a means of assisting emotional and spiritual processing.

Many people experience Ayahuasca as offering entrance into a realm of nature that feels wise and healing, though the experience may feel like "tough love." Ayahuasca is often known as Grandmother, but she is a grandmother who may deliver hard truths about you, even ultimatums about what you must do if you want the life you claim you want. Even with the possibility of "hard journeys," many people have experiences of astounding beauty, love, and connection, as well as insights that change their lives overnight.

Because Ayahuasca is typically experienced in groups, it is common to feel as though a shared field is created, with the experience of one person impacted by the experiences of others. This seems to happen not only because of the sounds and activities in the room, but on an energetic level. The facilitators, typically sharing in the tea themselves, enter into and work in the field, providing assistance on both physical and energetic levels.

Perhaps more so than with other psychedelics, transformation and healing may occur even without conscious recollection or processing of the experience. This is because Ayahuasca works deeply on physical and energetic levels. Nevertheless, I believe integration after the experience is critical. For some people, Grandmother Ayahuasca brings trauma to the surface, which may require ongoing processing on both physical and emotional levels.

On occasion, difficult aspects of the experience themselves need to be processed and integrated. Repeated Ayahuasca journeys without integration may lead to the sense of "I keep doing the same thing; why I am doing this?" That experience itself is a doorway for integration.

Peyote and San Pedro (Mescaline)

Mescaline, an amphetamine, is the principal active psychedelic compound in Peyote and San Pedro. Mescaline was the first psychedelic to come into mainstream Western culture, before LSD and psilocybin. In *The Doors of Perception,* Aldous Huxley made famous his experiences with mescaline, such as through the following classic description:

> As the Mind At Large seeps past the no longer watertight valve, all kinds of biologically useless things start to happen. In some cases there may be extra-sensory perceptions. Other persons discover a world of visionary beauty. To others again is revealed the glory, the infinite value and meaningfulness of naked existence, of the given, unconceptualized event. In the final stages of egolessness there is an "obscure knowledge" that All is in all—that All is actually each. This is as near, I take it, as a finite mind can ever come to "perceiving everything that is happening everywhere in the universe."[7]

San Pedro is the name given to a large South American cactus mainly found in the Andes. Mescaline is most highly concentrated in the skin, which can be peeled, dried and made into a powder for consumption. The cactus can also be sliced into sections and boiled in water, making a liquid to drink. The effects of San Pedro vary for many individuals, with an onset of one to two hours and lasting anywhere from eight to fifteen hours. San Pedro is often known as *huachuma* or *chuma* (meaning dizzy). Similar to Ayahuasca, San Pedro has been used for centuries by South American shamans, typically in ritual settings. Chuma is sometimes called Grandfather, a corollary to Ayahuasca's Grandmother.

I have a European friend who carries San Pedro medicine with her partner after training for several months in South America. She describes their ritual as follows:

> So with Grandfather, it is a different setting than with Grandmother. Usually, I do it in a ceremony around a fire, so in an ancient design... the altar, fire, people in the circle... all is aligned in sacred geometry, and the movement in the circle contributes to creating the safe setting for everyone (people and spirits).
>
> We move like Earth... clockwise. It is much more disciplined [than Ayahuasca rituals I have experienced]; there are some moments when it's okay

to go out from the circle to the bathroom, but otherwise, everyone's attention is called in the circle. With drum and rattle, people who know the songs can offer prayers. When presented, the drum also goes around in the circle.

There are crucial moments in the ceremony... when the *curandero* is praying with a tobacco or the medicine is presented several times during the night. During these moments, people are invited to maintain special attention (no lying down or sleeping).

The effects of the medicine are felt first in the body... usually you are more awake and open, and the sensations are sometimes like there are horses running through your veins... it opens the heart chakra... relaxes our defenses, and I can connect with everyone and everything... I feel the Oneness.

The inner dialogue is somewhat like with the Grandmother... but for me, it is more straightforward and with a masculine energy... like "no bullshit, man up and live" kind of thing....

Purging is quite common... you get a bag and face the fire... that connection with the Grandfather Fire through the night is helping you process everything that comes... everything you want to release, you offer to the fire... pain, love, fears, joy... and the purging part is usually a short relief... for me it often grows into opening to the collective and creating a path for healing.

Emotions flow and people release a lot during the singing... all these prayers are invoking certain spirits through certain vibrations... so this creates a healing journey. The spirits of the land, the intentions in the prayers, processes of people in the circle, it all feels like an orchestra.

Visions are also common... distorted reality, similar to mushrooms' effect. In fact, in our (European) lands, I also add them, the children of light [mushrooms], to the paste, to connect with our ancient traditions and sacred plants that are almost forgotten in Europe....

The effects of the medicine last much longer than the ceremony itself... so in the morning I continue to sing... in a more informal circle... and usually the "chumada sagrada" ("sacred drunkness") offers opportunity to see things differently... contemplate and integrate.

I am all okay to drive after some hours, but the underlying feeling of connection and openness for some people stays for weeks....

Peyote is to North America what San Pedro is to South America. When connected with ritual in Native American churches, peyote is lawfully used in the United States, Canada and Mexico. As with San Pedro and Ayahuasca, peyote rituals date back thousands of years. Records from the first colonial conquerors of Mexico and the southwestern United States demonized peyote. Along with other aspects of native culture, using peyote was forbidden in colonized areas for over two centuries.

During the 1800s, as the various Indian tribes were forced into reservation life in North America, peyote found a new life in changed cultural context. *Peyote Way* rituals arose as one of the means to preserve and celebrate indigenous heritage and spirituality.

Peyote Ritual

Leaders of peyote ceremonies became known as peyote roadmen. They traveled around North America to places where natives lived (typically reservations) and brought the sacrament. Similar to the evolution of many indigenous rituals after colonization, elements of Christianity and even American patriotism found their way into peyote ceremonies. Along with carrying the peyote medicine itself, the roadmen taught values and pride in tradition.

In *Peyote: The Divine Cactus*, Edward F. Anderson describes the typical peyote ritual as "an all-night meeting in which participants sit inside a tipi or other structure facing a fire and a crescent-shaped altar." [8] Ceremonies usually have four parts: praying, singing, eating peyote, and silently contemplating. Most participants spend much of the night quietly looking into the fire and listening to "Father Peyote" inside themselves. Nevertheless, peyote ceremonies are a collective ritual.

Anderson describes:

> The prayers, songs, and quiet contemplation, coupled with the effects of peyote, frequently lead to personal revelations. These are often in the form of visions and audible messages directly from Peyote or the Great Spirit. Peyote often "speaks" to the participants and promises them forgiveness of their sins; members are confident that Peyote will overcome both bodily and spiritual ills, for it is the "comfort, healer and guide of us poor Indians" [quoting *The Peyote Religion*, by J.S. Slotkin.][9]

One of my Canadian friends with European heritage, but strong ties to native communities, has been invited to many peyote ceremonies. She explains that some groups may be inclusive of non-natives, but many peyote communities are very sensitive about reserving the ceremonies for those with indigenous lineage, an issue that is spiritual, cultural and legal. Preservation of the right to use peyote lawfully is an essential consideration, which in the eyes of the law involves use only by Native American church members.

LSD

Lysergic acid diethylamide (LSD-25) and psilocybin are probably still the most commonly used psychedelics for personal exploration. Millions of people trip on these substances on their own, with friends, and in recreational settings (concerts, hikes, etc.). Therapeutic use in underground sessions with experienced guides has also continued for people able to find the right connections.

I return to the story of the discovery of LSD by Albert Hofmann in 1938. Working in a Sandoz laboratory in Basel, Switzerland, Hofmann was seeking compounds potentially useful as pharmaceuticals. Ergot, a natural substance related to LSD, had properties considered helpful in folk healing, often used by midwives for assisting uterine contractions and stopping bleeding after childbirth.

Hofmann put LSD-25 aside until 1943, when intuition brought him back to the compound. After handling the purified salt of LSD-25, he began to feel "unusual sensations." In a report sent to his colleague, he wrote:

> Last Friday, April 16, 1943, I was forced to interrupt my work in the laboratory in the middle of the afternoon and proceed home, being affected by a remarkable restlessness, combined with a slight dizziness. At home I lay down and sank into a not unpleasant intoxicated-like condition, characterized by an extremely stimulated imagination. In a dreamlike state, with eyes closed

(I found the daylight to be unpleasantly glaring), I perceived an uninterrupted stream of fantastic pictures, extraordinary shapes with intense, kaleidoscopic play of colors. After some two hours this condition faded away.[10]

Three days later, Hofmann drank .25 milligrams of LSD mixed with water, an extraordinarily large dose by later standards. He was trying to learn the properties of the substance by using himself as a test subject. Hofmann's suspicion that the compound had caused his earlier reaction was immediately confirmed. With the .25-milligram dose, he soon began to feel incapacitated.

In notes he made that day, Hofmann wrote, "I had to struggle to speak intelligibly. I asked my laboratory assistant, who was informed of the self-experiment, to escort me home." Because of wartime conditions, they traveled by bicycle, leading to the famous LSD "bicycle ride" that continues to be celebrated in some circles on April 19.

Bicycle Day 1943

Once home, Hofmann became terrified that he might be going insane or had ingested a substance that would lead to irreparable harm. When a concerned neighbor looked in, Hofmann thought she was a witch. Much later, he wrote:

> Every exertion of my will, every attempt to put an end to the disintegration of the outer world and the dissolution of my ego, seemed to be wasted effort. A demon had invaded me, had taken possession of my body, mind and soul. I jumped up and screamed, trying to free myself from him, but then sank down again and lay helplessly on the sofa. The substance, with which I had wanted to experiment, had vanquished me.[11]

As the difficult aspects of the experience subsided, Hofmann began to enjoy "the unprecedented colors and plays of shapes that persisted behind my closed eyes." He watched fantastic kaleidoscopic images that arose from within, shifting and exploding in "colored foundations, rearranging and hybridizing themselves in constant flux."

Hofmann was particularly intrigued by the transformation of sounds into visual perceptions (known as synesthesia). Eventually, he slept and woke up with a sensation of well-being and renewal. He wrote:

> Breakfast tasted delicious and gave me extraordinary pleasure. When I later walked out into the garden, in which the sun shone now after a spring rain, everything glistened and sparkled in a fresh light. The world was as if newly created. [12]

Thirty-six years later, when writing *LSD, My Problem Child*, Hofmann summarized his initial conclusions back in 1943:

- LSD was a psychoactive substance with extraordinary properties and potency; he knew of no other compound invoking such profound psychic effects in low dosage.
- He was able to remember the experience in every detail, "the conscious recording function was not interrupted, even in the climax of the LSD experience, despite the profound breakdown of the normal worldview."
- Everything in the LSD experience was perceived as completely real, "alarming, because the picture of the other, familiar everyday reality was still fully preserved in the memory for comparison."
- LSD left no hangover, but rather produced "the day after" what felt like remarkable clarity and health.
- He was immediately aware that LSD would have significant use in pharmacology, neurology and especially psychiatry.
- He had no idea the compound would come to be used as an inebriant in the worldwide drug scene that would develop a few decades later. [13]

Given the potential of LSD, Sandoz Laboratory offered samples of the compound for experimentation by other professionals. Stanislav Grof, as a young psychiatrist in Prague, Czechoslovakia, accepted the invitation from Sandoz to investigate the potential therapeutic uses of the compound. Grof worked with hundreds of patients ingesting LSD under controlled circumstances. He also experimented with the drug himself.

Grof considered LSD to offer direct encounter with the unconscious. From his own experiences, he described "an intoxicating fugue of emotions, visions, and illuminating insights into my life and existence in general that became available to me on this level of my psyche." [14]

Pointing towards his eventual role in founding transpersonal psychology, Grof realized that LSD offered an opening into realms beyond individual consciousness. He found access to information about the universe, the biological realities of other living creatures, spiritual beings, and what Swiss psychologist Carl Gustav Jung had called the collective unconscious and archetypal realms. As noted in more detail below, even after research with LSD was halted, Grof continued exploring and describing the healing potential of non-ordinary states of consciousness through working with Holotropic Breathwork.

Today, while illegal, LSD remains available to many people "from someone who has it." Typically, an edible blotting paper is infused with liquid LSD, which is then ingested through the tongue. Since the 1960s, there has been a tradition of colorful art on the blotting paper and nicknames such as orange sunshine, purple haze, Felix White, Leary Head, and other names associated with LSD lore.

> The true importance of LSD and related hallucinogens lies in their capacity to shift the wavelength setting of the receiving "self," and thereby to evoke alterations in reality consciousness. This ability to allow different, new pictures of reality to arise, this truly cosmogonic power, makes the cultish worship of hallucinogenic plants as sacred drugs understandable."
>
> —Albert Hofmann

Turning to the properties of LSD, the compound is a tryptamine, which stimulates serotonin production in the cortex and deep structures of the brain. In contrast to some other psychedelics, LSD experiences can have a long duration. Depending on dosage, the onset of the experience typically starts within thirty to sixty minutes and can last six to twelve hours.

LSD did not enter the world with a background from indigenous tradition including established ceremonies and spiritual worldview. Nevertheless, some facilitators or guides may offer group experiences of LSD grounded in a spiritual worldview borrowed from world traditions and/or described in transpersonal psychology.

As discussed later in the book, very small doses of LSD (micro-doses) are now being used by some people for assistance with depression, anxiety, creativity, stamina, and in seeking other general life benefits.

Psilocybin

Psilocybin is the psychoactive compound within hundreds of mushrooms found all around the world. Unlike Ayahuasca and the mescaline-based psychedelics found in the Americas, psilocybin has heritage in Europe and Asia. While lost for many centuries, ceremonial traditions involving psychedelics on these continents (very likely with mushrooms) are suggested by cave paintings and prehistoric artifacts.

Psilocybin Mushrooms

From digesting any of the "sacred mushrooms," our bodies produce the substance psilocin as we metabolize psilocybin. Psilocin interacts with serotonin receptors in the brain to allow experiences very similar to what I described with respect to LSD. The duration of psilocybin experience is generally shorter than with LSD, typically lasting from four to six hours.

Some people find significant or nuanced differences between experience with LSD and psilocybin, while others find the experiences hard to differentiate. Nausea can develop for some people with mushrooms (but this may depend on the particular mushroom), while others find mushrooms "natural" and LSD to have a less desirable synthetic quality. Mushrooms definitely have low toxicity and harm potential; you could never eat the amount of psilocybin mushrooms it would take to cause you serious physical harm.

The *Psilocybe cubensis* mushroom is currently one of the most popular and commonly available natural psychedelics. This species is known under several other names and is often referenced as the "Mexican mushroom." Because this mushroom is relatively easy to grow, it is one of the most widely used hallucinogens all over the world. Effective dosage depends on species and variety.

As noted above, "magic mushrooms" came into mainstream world culture through the visit of Gordon and Valentina Wasson to Mexico in 1956. From that time forward, LSD and psilocybin have been the sources of psychedelic experience for millions of people in a wide range of circumstances. As with LSD, psilocybin is not generally used within traditional settings carried forward by long lineage, though some guides worldwide are bringing "the children of light" back into ceremonial use.

Many people grow their own "magic mushrooms" and may offer experiences to friends or people looking for guides. Psilocin in pharmaceutical form has been used recently in research studies. This may allow more careful attention to dosage, though experienced guides have familiarity with their mushrooms and expertise in recommending an appropriate dose for particular people.

Because psilocybin is a very commonly used psychedelic in underground therapy sessions, I asked an underground therapist friend to share his version of the work. The story is a three-day event with one client and one therapist in the room, told from the vantage point of the therapist.

> I start with a one-hour pre-session *intentional* meeting to confirm the details of the experience with the client, address dosage, establish contracts, and discuss both the practical details and talk about any percolating emotions; really prime the person for their psilocybin experience.
>
> Then on the next day (psychedelic session), the client and I meet early in the morning around eight a.m. and start the experience. Because it is not a "traditional" therapeutic session, I invite the client to bring in tokens of appreciation for an altar, and this is when the psychedelic session begins. The participant offers up gratitude and intention for the work and instantly ingests the mushrooms, all the while I am invoking trance with a rhythmic drumming. After the person eats the mushrooms, I immediately do ten to fifteen minutes of gentle stretching to open up the body. It is a very important aspect of psychedelic work to have your body open and loose as the psilocybin "comes on."
>
> After the stretching, I invite the client to lie down on the cushion (mat) with a blindfold on, and I guide them into their journey with a ritual of poetry, guided imagery, body scan, and honoring that they have taken this day for themselves. The music then starts and goes for roughly three hours or so. People have a large range of different experiences. For some people there is an embodied or somatic experience of moving through energies. Other people have strong emotional cathartic releases. For still others, there is mostly cognitive exploration or problem solving. This is where work on a specific intention seems to be the focus.
>
> At the end of the music, the session goes from directive and structured to formless and fluid. Usually, the person will sit up and want to attend to their physical needs. They start to intuitively engage with me or otherwise just

come back into a closer sense of ordinary awareness: asking for help to resolve something, bask in the afterglow, visit the bathroom, or desire a conversation.

Because integration is a strong focus of my work, I start to bring attention to this process. I believe in a series of incremental shifts like slowly coming out of water. I put away the mat, blankets, pillows, and eyeshades. Now there is a gentle movement from internal to external. I invite the client to sit on the couch, and I sit near them in my rocking chair.

I follow an organic process depending upon where the client is in their journey. There is usually some continued exploration, maybe putting words to experience, and often some reassurance from me to them. I try not to shut down the experience but to help the client to come back into this reality. There is usually a gentle time of one foot in and one foot out that I try to respect.

At this point, I always invite the client on a walk outside. This is a two-fold process. I like to help the client return to external reality and also have the chance to make sure they are safe to be involved in the world. Prior to the session, I would have already discussed how the client would get home, usually with a partner or support person coming to get them.

After forty-eight hours, I invite the client back for hour-long integration sessions where I talk about what the experience was like and what is on the horizon for their psychedelic integration. Throughout the entire experience from start to finish, I am with the participant or available by phone.

MDMA

As noted above, MDMA was first synthesized in 1912, rediscovered by Alexander "Sasha" Shulgin in the 1970s, and popularized as a party drug in the 1980s, particularly associated with rave and electronic dance music (EDM) culture. In contrast to psychedelics, which open the door to the unconscious and collective or spiritual realms, MDMA more typically alters mood and awareness, comparable to stimulants and hallucinogens. 3,4-Methyl-enedioxy-methamphetamine generates feelings of amplified energy, pleasure, emotional warmth, and distorted sensory and time perception. Ralph Metzner described MDMA as an *empathogen* due to the state of empathy that comes with the experience.

In a party setting, MDMA helps us fall in love with the world, all experience, and everyone around us. In a therapeutic setting, or in personal work of self-healing, MDMA allows us to face traumatic issues and experiences with compassion for ourselves and for those who have caused us harm. Rather than continue to block the full impact of difficult experiences, we may see (and feel) them in a context of acceptance and forgiveness, making it possible to more completely process the experiences and move toward solutions and new life directions. Even when not focusing on past traumas, the empathogenic qualities of MDMA allow us to feel that anything is possible with love and to imagine ways to reconstruct our lives and relationships based in love.

With an onset of anywhere from twenty to ninety minutes, the typical duration of an MDMA experience is three to five hours without a "booster" dose. This relatively short duration makes MDMA useful in clinical therapeutic settings. Through Sasha Shulgin, some West Coast therapists in the 1970s began to use MDMA to assist patients in becoming more willing to communicate, establish connection with their therapist, and participate in the therapy process. MDMA was sometimes called "Adam" because therapy clients seemed to return to a more innocent state.

MDMA Session

While not carrying a spiritual or indigenous lineage, MDMA is the "ally" used by many underground facilitators in private and group settings for psychospiritual work and empowerment. While MDMA is the most well-known empathogen, there are many analogous substances providing a similar heart-opening, such as MDA, MDEA, and methylone.

Some of the potential downsides to MDMA include after-effects involving clenching of muscles, particularly in the jaw, teeth clenching, or a rebound depressive effect in some people. There are ways to help prevent or lessen these problems (for instance, using supplements such as magnesium). In the context of purchasing MDMA outside legal settings, there may be concerns about purity, as it continues to be a substance produced en masse for distribution through sale on the underground drug market.

Through the hard work of MAPS and Annie and Michael Mithoefer (see therapy section in Chapter 3), MDMA has advanced toward FDA approval for treating people with treatment-resistant post-traumatic stress disorder (PTSD). This is known as MDMA-assisted psychotherapy, with specific treatment protocols involving therapeutic connection with licensed professionals (including integration of the experiences). During 2017, the FDA designated MDMA with "breakthrough therapy" status, meaning that if ongoing research trials continue to show the same promise as those already conducted, expedited approval for use of MDMA in therapy might be forthcoming as early as 2024.

DMT

DMT (N,N-dimethyltryptamine) is the active ingredient in Ayahuasca, but can be used alone as a launch into psychedelic experience. When digested without the MAO inhibitor present in Ayahuasca, DMT does not produce psychedelic effect. But when smoked or vaporized at sufficient dose, most people have an extraordinarily powerful experience.

N,N-Dimethyltryptamine was synthesized in 1931 by Richard Manske, but is remarkable for its natural presence in mammals and plants. As a synthetic psychedelic, DMT was known during the 1960s as the "businessman's trip" because the experience usually lasts only five to twenty minutes, short enough for a lunch break. While brief, DMT experiences can involve intense visuals with bright, vibrant light and complex kaleidoscopic patterns, along with a sense of being in an "alternate" realm.

As noted above, Rick Strassman, M.D., conducted federally approved research with DMT in New Mexico from 1990 to 1995. *In DMT, the Spirit Molecule*, he describes the extraordinary experiences of his research participants, which led him to conclude DMT opened a door for consciousness to perceive (or perhaps enter into) other dimensions that have objective existence separate from our plane of reality. Strassman came to believe DMT, which is produced in the human brain, might trigger an opening for the soul to "enter" and "exit" the body. [15]

Summarizing his research, Strassman wrote:

> Our volunteers unquestionably had some of the most intense, unusual, and unexpected experiences of their lives during the DMT research. The spirit molecule dragged, pushed, pulled, and thrust research subjects into themselves, out of their bodies, and through various planes of reality. I've read about all manner of sessions, many of which seem to help people better understand their relationship with themselves and the outside world. I've also read about the toll some experiences took on our recruits. [16]

Strassman did not continue the research after his scheduled rounds. He felt the research setting was not the right place for people to process intense DMT experiences in beneficial ways. In other words, there was no context for integration. Strassman was especially disappointed that none of the research participants began psychotherapy or a spiritual discipline to carry forward the insights brought by DMT. Strassman was forced to conclude, therefore, "DMT was not inherently therapeutic." He continued:

> Instead, I had to face the crucial importance of set and setting. What the volunteers brought to their sessions, and the fuller context of their lives, was as important, if not more so, than the drug itself in determining how they felt with their experiences. Without a suitable framework—spiritual, psychotherapeutic, or otherwise—in which to process their journeys with DMT, their sessions became just another series of intense psychedelic encounters. [17]

Strassman was also concerned that he had no framework himself to hold the frequent reports of "real" contact with beings and realms outside our own material universe. Experiences that feel spiritual or archetypal are one thing; but experiences of the journey of consciousness to alternative realities bring up a different level of challenge. As Strassman wrote, "the reports of contact with invisible worlds and their inhabitants, while utterly amazing, left me grasping at conceptual straws as to their reality and meaning." [18]

While Strassman's concerns were directed toward the research setting, his words resonate with my reasons for writing this book—and for encouraging integration. For most people, it is necessary to have a framework for understanding and integrating psychedelic experiences for those experiences to have maximum impact in changing lives and relieving suffering. Just as importantly, it is necessary to have ideas and support for sticking with the experiences as part of an integration process and not holding (and then forgetting) them as a single strange event.

5-MeO-DMT

5-MeO-DMT is a different substance than DMT, but also with very strong psychedelic impact. Synthesized, this psychedelic is known as **Jaguar**, a name first used by a group working with Ralph Metzner before the substance became illegal. Metzner explains, "The *Jaguar* process" was used as a "code name because the rapid onset of the medicine powder when smoked or inhaled was reminiscent of ancient Mayan mythic images of the open mouth of a jaguar, with the face of a human shaman looking out from within its jaws." [19]

Jaguar

A powerful natural form of 5-MeO-DMT is found in the venom of the *Bufo Alvarius* toad, which lives in the Sonoran desert along the border between Mexico and the United States. Some experiencers find **Bufo** or **toad medicine** to carry a more otherworldly effect than Jaguar, perhaps due to other substances in the toad venom. Mesoamerican shamans may have used dried toad venom to engender psychedelic experiences, but there is no living tradition associated with *Bufo Alvarius* with lineage back into ancient times. This is in contrast to San Pedro and Ayahuasca.

Bufo Alvarius

Octavio Rettig Hinojosa, M.D., is convinced toad medicine was used in Incan and Mayan rituals engendering mystical states. He writes:

> Upon analyzing the figures found in the Frieze of the Four Kings in the Mayan ruins in Balamku, Campeche, I clearly see four Otacs [the Seri Comcaac language word for toad]. There are also four human figures in a meditational-submissive position with the same elements that appear consistently as effigies of *Bufo alvarius*, their glands like visionary rings and spirals, symbols of transformation and the Olioliuqui vine. These beings emerge from the jaws of the toad dressed allegorically as though participating in an entheogenic

festivity. I can only imagine what actually happened, due to the subsequent destruction of practically all written records of the time.[20]

Octavio Rettig Hinojosa

Rettig is a Mexican physician who leads healing ceremonies with "toad medicine" throughout Mexico, the United States, Australia and Europe. He came to this medicine after his own hard journey with other substances, including addictive experiences with alcohol and street drugs. Introduced to toad medicine by a friend, Rettig recalls:

> I puffed on it three times and began to feel the psychedelic effects. I continued to pull and inhale with all my strength when suddenly colors, electricity, magic, and beauty began to get more and more intense. I did it with the intention of having a good time and getting really "messed up," as young people commonly say. [Having experienced other psychedelics,] I assumed it would once again be celestial music, colors, and magical feelings. But what actually happened was the most shocking experience of my life.
>
> Within my atheism and arrogance, I found the greatest learning that anyone can have in the world: a truly mystical experience and an actual encounter with the creator. It was a reunion with my true spiritual nature and my true self, with the infinite knowledge of cosmic intention and what I typically call God.[21]

In his first experience, Rettig heard a loud, clear voice he felt was God. He began shuddering, trembling and crying. While feeling his own fear and emptiness, he heard God say: "I am the

Alpha and Omega, the beginning and end, life and death, everything and nothing, I am you, I am he, I am they, I am everyone, I am no one."[22] Rettig felt he was "in front of the mirror and seeing all my beliefs and values shattered." The experience was a "holistic reset that allows for a deep release of destructive emotional and mental patterns, as well as an influx of life force that is both inspirational and healing."[23] Rettig writes:

> Your visions won't be as colorful as those triggered by other tryptamines, as the colors and fractals are so fast. What's most significant is the feeling you experience, a melding with the universe, a feeling of oneness. You experience a dissolution of your "self"…
>
> With the majority of psycho-integrators, the person becomes very susceptible to emotion. There may be childhood traumas, frustrated desires, repressed memories, or dreams impossible to achieve in a state of "normalcy."[24]

Both toad medicine and synthetic 5-MeO-DMT (aka Jaguar) are discussed in Ralph Metzner's brief book *The Toad and The Jaguar*, which is based on his extensive research and lawful use of Jaguar in group settings prior to its banning in January of 2011. The book contains Metzner's insights from working with the medicine, as well as descriptions of the experience shared by several people. For instance, from one experiencer:

> As my breath went out, I went in. And still I fell. The last vestige of resistance, a mere quiver of anxiety, subsided. I was fearlessly falling into an incredibly spacious, powerfully radiant, ancient but ever-present center, at once still and moving, a Core from which all things were arising, would arise, had arisen. I had let go and I had arrived. I was Home. That which I called "I" hung suspended in a vast, spacious and imperturbable Universe. I felt freed from my usual burden of aches, tensions and fears, unconstructed, deeply and profoundly relaxed, at home in life, in a state of no struggle, deliciously, effortlessly healed.[25]

I have friends who carry Jaguar medicine and describe consistent experiences by those in their medicine circles similar to those related by Rettig and Metzner. In an experience usually lasting twenty to forty minutes, a person's entire understanding of life and the reality of God can change. My friends offer these experiences in weekend workshops with six to eight people, allowing plenty of time for community processing and the start of integration.

The Experience

People emerging from an experience of 5-MeO-DMT often feel they have been in a place from which knowing itself emerges, a place of total freedom from personality and personality structures. During re-entry, there can be confusion as to "why have I come back to someplace so confining?" Realizing it is ourselves that provide the confinement can be liberating but also upsetting. Integration can involve learning to move from that place of knowing and just allow the structures to evolve with compassion and love.

Martin Ball is author of *Entheogenic Liberation: Unraveling the Enigma of Nonduality with 5-MEO-DMT Energetic Therapy*. He considers 5-MeO-DMT the most potent and profound psychedelic existing on the planet. Ball makes clear the path of 5-MeO-DMT is not an easy road. He conveys the seriousness of having a "face-to-face encounter with God":

> Any first-time use should always be done in the presence of an experienced guide or facilitator. Some people have very dramatic reactions to 5-MeO-DMT ranging from desperately trying to run away and escape the experience to wildly and uncontrollably thrashing about. Assistance might be necessary to keep someone from hurting him or herself. Some people become hyper-violent and even attack others who are in the space with a "flight or fight" reaction. While these reactions are relatively rare, they do happen, and keep in mind that until you personally experience 5-MeO-DMT, you will have no idea how you might react, or what the experience might inspire you to do.[26]

Because there is no living tradition of working with 5-MeO-DMT, guides offering the experience develop their own styles. Rettig tends to work in groups of friends and acquaintances, who provide support to each other and can process their experiences together after the session. My friends who support Jaguar experiences in weekend workshops recently organized a gathering of other Jaguar carriers. Their goal was to share intentions and practices for developing their own traditions for offering this "new" and extraordinarily powerful psychedelic.

Other compounds

The psychedelics mentioned above are most likely the medicines you will encounter during our times. However, here are a few more substances to know about:

Ketamine ("K," "Ket," "Special K") is a dissociative drug long used in pediatric and veterinary medicine, with history as a street drug that can be addictive and potentially dangerous. In *The Ketamine Papers: Science, Therapy and Transformation*, Phil Wolfson, M.D., and Glenn Hartelius, Ph.D., gather writings pointing toward the potential (and growing) lawful use of ketamine in treating depression, PTSD and other psychological conditions. As I noted in Chapter 1, I have heard anecdotal stories of people trying ketamine in clinical settings but not experiencing much support or context for integration.

On the other hand, when held in a spiritual context, some people report transformational experiences. As a dissociative, ketamine separates consciousness from identification with successive layers of the physical, emotional, and energetic bodies. At the physical level, ketamine allows one to move away from pain or suffering that exists in the body, which is why the substance has been used in medical settings with children and animals when it is necessary to cause temporary extreme pain such as when setting a broken bone.

If experiencers have the ability to move further into the experience, they may separate from layers of emotional suffering and longstanding psychological issues —seeing these experiences as manifestations that might be released rather than unchangeable realities. Beyond this, layers of tethering to cultural and social realities may be understood, as well as the very anchoring of consciousness in our plane of reality. If supported by the appropriate psychological and cosmological understandings, these experiences can set the stage for release from conditions of suffering and beneficial transformation.

Slvia divinorum has been used by Mazatec shamans since ancient times. In recent years, it has come into some psychedelic circles, often as an adjunct to working with other psychedelics. Considered dangerous by some people, salvia divinorum is experienced by others as a swift but temporary portal to what feels like the other side. Ross Heaven, a psychologist and healer who experienced many psychedelic medicines before his passing in early 2018, believed in the value of salvia. In *Shamanic Quest for the Spirit of Salvia: The Divinatory, Visionary, and Healing Powers of the Sage of the Seers*, Heaven described salvia as having the ability to connect people with their higher purpose.

Ibogaine is a powerful substance made from the African rain forest shrub Tabernanthe iboga. The Bwiti people of Western Africa have long used the plant to combat fatigue, hunger and thirst, and, in higher doses, in spiritual initiation ceremonies. Ibogaine has been described as the best cure for addiction to heroin, alcohol or other physically and psychologically addictive substances. (See *Ibogaine Explained: Everything You Need to Know About the World's Most Powerful Psychedelic* by Peter Frank & Eric Taub and/or *Rehab Doesn't Work: Ibogaine Does*, by Willers T. Darenvogt). [27]

Ibogaine Tree

Using ibogaine tends to overwhelm the person physically for a few days, but then offers a period of several weeks without strong cravings for the addictive substance. This allows the committed individual to begin changing the structure of their lives, helping to avoid return to addiction. People taking ibogaine should only use this compound under close supervision due to medical concerns; possible issues are asphyxiation or heart problems.

The only person I know who experienced ibogaine was given the substance (little shredded pieces of fibrous root bark) from a healer in Gabon, a country on the west coast of Africa. Not so mindful about mindset and setting, but an adventurous soul, my friend ate some of the iboga before a solo bicycle trip on the northwest coast of Oahu. He intended to ride along Keana point, a rugged but beautiful area, but soon found himself on his own wobbly bicycle ride. Eventually he dropped the bike and stumbled onto the sand, where he took refuge under a bush.

My friend thought he was dying. As he felt closer and closer to death, thorns from the bush were pushing into his back, an archetypal if terrifying encounter. The experience lasted eight hours. After he realized he might not die, he had powerful insights into his place in our physical world, which he realized had entry points into other worlds. He does not regret the experience, but he wished he had brought water.

Ever the inner adventurer, my friend tried another sample with his girlfriend when he was back home in rural New England. My friend and his friend lay in a field. This time, he soon realized he should have eaten, believing this was likely his problem before. Again he felt he was dying, but doors opened to different dimensions. That was fascinating, but every time he opened his eyes, he was terrified because tree branches shading the moon morphed into dangerous creatures.

My friend's girlfriend sat up to go the bathroom but was gone for what seemed like hours. Eventually my friend was able to stand up and look for her. She was swaying on her feet in another field. He asked her what she was doing. She said, "I don't know. I was trying to get to the emergency room." He knew enough to say, "What, are you crazy?" and get her back down on the ground. She later said she had visions and insights that changed her life for the better. They were both nauseated for days afterward.

My friend had been told by his Gabonese friend that one in one hundred people who experience ibogaine die of a heart attack. He was not afraid of the odds, but I am. My friend is clear on one thing: the next time he does ibogaine will be with a healer in Gabon.

In my next chapter, I talk about the importance of Mindset and Setting. My friend, a sophisticated and brilliant journalist and human rights advocate, was aware of what he was doing even if his settings could have been safer. I tell his tale with some humor because this is how he holds it. But he advises great caution to others interested in ibogaine.

Breathwork (and Breathing in Psychedelics Sessions)

I know that our ancestors have been using natural "medicines" to enter non-ordinary states of consciousness for thousands of years. I also know indigenous people everywhere have always used deep or rhythmic breathing to journey into other realms for healing and transformation.

As I suggested in Exercise 1 above, the breath goes hand in hand with deep experiential work of almost any kind. Most of us working with psychedelics recognize the important role that breathing plays in many psychedelic experiences.

I return to the story of the development of Holotropic Breathwork, the method in which I trained as a facilitator. After almost all psychedelics became illegal in the 1970s, Stanislav Grof and his late wife, Christina, developed a method for experiencing non-ordinary states without drugs. The method combines deep breathing and evocative music with the support of trained facilitators and a "breathing partner" called a sitter. This is but one of many similar methods that draw on the innate relationship between the breath—particularly deep breathing—and the opening of channels in the body and energetic system for processing and transformation.

Having trained in Holotropic Breathwork facilitation, I have deep respect for this particular method, but I recognize it draws on simple techniques and practices long known to many peoples. My training included what is called "energetic release work" or "body-work" as a means to assist people, upon their request, with the release of what feels like "stuck" energy in the body.

Breathwork

Energetic release work uses matched pressure to parts of the body and gentle encouragement of vocalization, weeping, movement, or whatever else arises within the person and seems to allow opening and movement of energies. Often facilitators encourage experiencers to "breathe into" a place in the body where something feels "stuck" in order to bring forward a release.

How does this relate to working with psychedelics?

To begin with, I note that Stan Grof and I both report a similar experience in working with people having psychedelic experiences. Quite often people in psychedelic journeys will spontaneously begin breathing deeply or otherwise focusing on their breath as part of their navigation through the psychedelic experience. In fact, Grof has shared that knowing this tendency of people to begin deep breathing when working through psychedelic experiences contributed to his realization that deep breathing could invite non-ordinary states without psychedelic medicines.

I believe there are as many ways to use the breath during psychedelic experiences as there are people and experiences. Sometimes the breath can be used as a catalyst to begin or renew an experience, and sometimes the breath is used to ground oneself towards the end of an experience or to slow down experience when it becomes overwhelming at any point in a session.

Often our breath will spontaneously shift in order to match or help an experience —or as a result of the experience. Often the breath becomes shallow or even seems to stop. Just before a major shift, you may feel as though your breath has stopped completely; this may even feel as if you are going to die. Knowing this can help you relax if and when this happens. On the other hand, sometimes the breath spontaneously accelerates and even pumps air into the body. All of this is normal to experiencing non-ordinary states.

Becoming familiar with your breath as a manifestation (or tool) of your awareness can help you navigate through psychedelic experiences. If you practice moving into bodily or psychic space with your breath as a point of awareness, you will develop your ability to focus on internal experience and to maneuver through internal realms.

Sometimes returning to deep breathing during an intense experience helps someone "come back" from an experience that has gotten overly intense or may feel out of hand. The breath can be a "grounding cord" or a "tether" to human experience and the body that may keep you safe when you feel your consciousness has journeyed or expanded into unfamiliar terrain.

As I shared above, Ralph Metzner was one of the early pioneers in the serious study of psychedelics in the 1960s and through the decades ever since. Without fanfare, Metzner continued studying psychedelics in lawful settings even after the prohibition of many psychedelic substances, as described in his many books. Metzner makes an important point for consideration when comparing customary breathwork techniques with psychedelics work:

> I do not believe it is appropriate and perhaps counter-productive to combine forceful breathing or bodywork methods with entheogenic substances such as 5-MeO-DMT (or Ayahuasca, psilocybin or LSD, for that matter). These intensive breathing and body-methods use dynamic energy to break through conditioned inertia-resistances imprinted into the cellular and organic tissues of the body. The subtle high-frequency energy perceptions possible with entheogenic amplified meditation may be overwhelmed and overshadowed by the lower-frequency but high-intensity body sensations and tension-release movements.[28]

Ralph Metzner

I completely agree with Metzner that many psychedelic experiences involve a very subtle level of experiencing that is different from the intense "energy release" processing that often happens with breathwork. "Forceful breathing or bodywork methods" may in fact disrupt the delicate nature of the psyche's exploration during psychedelic sessions.

However, I would not discourage experiencers, or their guides, from remembering that "returning to the breath" can be a way to navigate through psychedelic experiences, particularly if they become challenging. More importantly, as Grof and I have observed, sometimes the breath comes into play naturally as an innate response of the body-mind-spirit in processing through psychedelic experiences. Sometimes the breath gets you to the next place in the journey, including closure and beginning of integration.

I also note that some psychedelics—for instance, Ayahuasca—invite a release at a body level (including purging) that does seem related to the types of releases that happen in breathwork journeys. Sometimes I have seen people "stuck" during Ayahuasca journeys until a guide encourages them to sit up and breathe into what is happening, which often then leads to purging, release, shifting, and perhaps even the emergence of the "core" of the experiences being offered during that journey. And yet, sometimes the more effective shifts happen in those settings with the voice, rattle, and energetic work of the shamanic practitioner without touching or changing the breath of the experiencer.

Another perspective on breathing and psychedelic experience comes from Martin Ball, whose work has focused on 5-MeO-DMT. Ball is adamant that anything other than slow and quiet breathing indicates resistant ego-control rather than release into the healing non-dual experience offered by 5-MeO-DMT. While I would not take such an adamant position, I suspect there might be some truth in his observation. Sometimes, focus on breathing might be defensive and used to avoid experience.

On the other hand, Octavio Rettig, who carries *Bufo Alvarius* medicine (another form of 5-MeO-DMT), writes about *the importance of breathing* during 5-MeO-DMT experiences. He believes this helps people stay present to the experience, because "it requires a lot of control and concentration not to fall into either panic or ecstasy, in order to feel what the medicine does for the body, brain, and soul."[29]

As I suggested above and in Exercise 1, I believe you can use your breath as a focal point of awareness in order to reach places in your body or in the realms of consciousness. This can help you access what is present and perhaps release what needs to be released by entering into what is there. But I recognize this is an active process to some extent. Your will is doing something to engage with what is present.

I understand Ball to suggest the most important experience happens when all effort to *do anything* is released during psychedelics work. Ball likens releasing your breath in 5-MeO-DMT experiences to releasing conscious focus on breathing when you go to sleep. "When you sleep, you set aside all your thoughts, all your plans, all your agendas… and you give yourself over to the energy of sleep, trusting that you'll make it through just fine without any effort or control on your part." [30]

Ball believes psychedelic experience should be similar:

> The more you get out of the way, and the less control you try to exert over it, the more easily your ego will get out of the way and the more you'll gain from the experience by allowing the energy that arises to flow and transform naturally. [31]

I suspect Ball's adamancy may have something to do with the strength of 5-MeO-DMT to work most effectively with complete surrender. It may be that relaxing the breath is uniquely suited to this particular medicine. However, his point is worth considering with respect to *any* use of breath in non-ordinary state experiences.

Returning to the value of the breath in many psychedelics experiences—and particularly as you turn to integration—I have found that following your breath is one of the most valuable ways to **stay with** whatever experience you are having. For many of us, the issue with non-ordinary state work is often finding a way not to dissociate from the experience, to **be** with it as it begins to integrate into our lives. There is nothing like the breath for unifying your body-mind-spirit into one flow, which is one of the main tools and goals of integration. If you have a particularly important experience in a non-ordinary state and want to *hold onto it*, then you might *breathe into it* as an embodied request to remember.

In closing this section, I return to Ralph Metzner for another point he has made:

> [A]lternating the different methods of accessing deep unconscious body memories on different occasions, comparing findings and consolidating healing changes, can of course be very valuable. I know, for example, that some holotropic breathwork practitioners who are also familiar with entheogenic media such as Ayahuasca, have practiced the two different methods on different days. [32]

I also want to stress the recommendation made by Diane Haug, who is one of the leading teachers in the Holotropic Breathwork movement and in the training programs relating to lawful psychedelics use. Haug emphasizes there is no better tool for learning how to navigate through the complex world of psychedelics—whether as an experiencer, sitter, or guide—than gaining experience of Holotropic Breathwork in the careful model used by many facilitators worldwide.

Diane Haug

In this recommendation, Haug makes three points:

- The careful attendance to "mindset and setting" shown in Holotropic Breathwork communities models the safety that can be so crucial in any type of psychedelics work.
- Breathwork, with its ability for the breather to modulate the intensity of non-ordinary state experiences by slowing down the breath, provides a way to experience non-ordinary states with training wheels, so to speak.
- For people who have had challenging experiences in psychedelics, breathwork experiences can often help with completion, resolution or healing (that is, integration).

Like my friend Diane, I strongly recommend experience in safely held breathwork sessions for anyone with serious interest in psychedelics.

Now Your Turn

Throughout this chapter I have paid homage to some of our psychedelics elders. I will not be able to mention all of them, but I hope you will gain a sense of the respect I owe to all those who have come before us in working with psychedelic medicines. As I keep saying, this work is part of our human heritage—and it is sacred work.

Indigenous cultures understood the sacred importance of respecting elders and ancestors. Sadly, this has been lost to many of us today. The more you work with psychedelics, the more you will understand the beauty and necessity of remembering elders and ancestors. The elders you meet in our times and the ancestors you meet in your journeys will share their wisdom with you—and they will help you if you let them.

For this "your turn," I invite you to feel into a poem I have written. Then I invite you to respond to the poem and to your feeling about psychedelic lineage with whatever comes to you.

Lived In a Time…

They lived in a time when every member of the tribe held knowledge of the body—the magic of healing and the holiness of sex and the miracle of birth and the necessity of death.

They couldn't thrive otherwise.

They lived in a time creating—driving onward this need to expand, live and understand.

They lived in a time when reverence and a sense of the sacred spoke to them in hallowed whispers throughout the mundane tasks of daily life. They couldn't find meaning in the universe otherwise.

They lived in a time blazing forth the trails through passion and love. Creating a new destiny for us to awaken to.

And today many of us ache for these old ways, yearn for the wisdom that seems so inaccessible to us in our denatured, hyper-speed modern life.

Awake to the memory of our elders.

—Ryan Westrum

What comes may be your own poem, your own narrative, a picture, some random doodling, a photograph or magazine cutout, or something you print from the Internet and paste below. Try not to think about it—try to feel it and let yourself be guided by your heart and intuition.

Integration Exercise 2: Creating Sacred Space

What You Need

- Comfortable, loose-fitting clothing
- Pillows, cushions, or a chair
- A timer or meditation bell
- Music
- Meaningful objects to you (e.g., pictures, statues, notes, and cloth)
- Items that represent four elements (e.g., Earth, Air, Wind, and Fire)
- Your journal.

General Background

Creating a sacred space is an important part of integrating your psychedelic experiences. It's also a very important part of integrating your life. A sacred space can be as simple as a bathtub with candles and incense or as intricate as a room with a personal altar. It can be permanent or small enough to be carried with you. It can be inside a room or outside in nature. Retreat centers are sacred spaces today for many of us, as are many places in nature. I cannot tell you what to put in your sacred space; however, I would like to offer suggestions to develop a sanctuary for integrating your psychedelic experiences.

Sacred space is a place to renew and create. It is a safe environment to meditate, reflect and integrate your life. Sacred space is a place to focus on your "inner self." A meaningful space is created to embody what is important to you. The environment is an extension of your divine being. As it relates to working with psychedelic integration, sacred space is a valuable part of cultivating and growing your connection with all you are and all that is within the world.

Sacred space is a subjective experience; it is an organically grown opportunity to become whole. Sacred Space can be:

- A room
- A bookshelf
- A backyard garden
- A labyrinth at a religious site
- A shoebox filled with personal, sacred items you travel with
- A park
- A symbolic landmark.

Why this Exercise is Important for Psychedelics

Creating sacred space is important so that you have a physical place where you can feel safe enough to explore your integration—and connected enough to spirit to feel you are inspired and held by the universe or your spiritual guides or helpers. Creating a sacred space is also important in terms of the actual work with psychedelics. In Integrative Exercise 1, I talked about the importance of meditation in helping you gather yourself into an awareness that is useful to psychospiritual work and for navigating in psychedelic space.

Working with sacred space in the external world can help you develop an orientation to what is other than you in psychedelic journeys. When you start relating to sacred space you have created in the external world (for instance, as an altar, or in a room, or around some trees), you start to develop an offering of yourself and a relationship to space that is not you but that is related to you. You learn how *to be* in this space and draw from it and be comfortable with it. As the space becomes more and more yours, and yet anchored in a sacred realm, you can allow yourself to expand, contract, feel, and think in the space. Your relationship to the space you have created will grow stronger the more attention you bring to yourself and the space. This will help you have more confidence and fluidity in the spaces that exist within your psychedelic journeys.

Like sacred spaces you create in the external world, some part of you participates in creating the spaces you will feel and see in your journeys, but they will be more than you. If you get comfortable with them and with relating to them, you will gain comfort in your journeys, and then after your journeys, you will be able to feel the sacredness of the journey space in and through the sacredness of the external sacred space you have created.

And as I always say, there is no right way, there is only your way—and there is really only the way you make it today, because tomorrow you can do something new.

How To Do It

Preparation in advance

1. Spend time thinking of what makes a sacred space for you.
2. Get creative thinking about where you want to create your sacred space.
3. Start to collect items that have significance to you (e.g., pictures, statues, candle, blankets…).
4. Choose your space: I recommend starting with just one or two places. For example, one inside your home and one that is connected to nature.

Instructions for the exercise (Time: Two minutes to thirty minutes)

- After you have decided on your sacred space, start to focus sacred attention on your space.
- Using all your senses, start to add organically what will make you feel comfortable. Your comfort is of significant importance.
- Unclutter the space you have chosen. Clean the space.
- Start to add items to your space or altar.
- Have a special ceremony to inaugurate the sacred space.

Allow your sacred space to evolve over time. As you develop this space, it is important to remember that there is no wrong way to do this. Your well-being is vital as you integrate your psychedelic experiences. The process of creating a sacred space is a valuable exchange of energy that will help illuminate your focus on integrating your life.

CHAPTER 3

MINDSET AND SETTING

Choices, Choices, Decisions

In the last chapter, I described different psychedelics being used around the world at this time. While there are overall similarities, there are differences, including the typical settings in which certain psychedelics tend to be used. For instance, Ayahuasca is usually experienced within group ritual settings, with a leader carrying forward traditions and shamanic techniques. LSD and psilocybin are more customary for individual experiences, with a few friends, or with a guide.

In this chapter, I want to step back and take a broad look at the impact and importance of the multi-layered variables that will contribute to your experience no matter what psychedelic you have chosen to explore. I talk about "choices, choices, decisions" because ultimately your choices play a large role in your experience. I encourage you to really own your choices and to make conscious decisions about how to use psychedelics.

That said, I do not want to sound as though I am saying you will have complete control over your experience if you just pay attention to your choices. In fact, exploring psychedelics relinquishes control from your conscious mind; surrendering is a major part of the experience. Depending on dosage, substance, and circumstances, you will still have some control, but you are deciding to release yourself into what your unconscious and the realms "beyond" may have to offer you.

While you probably need to be at peace with what comes, there is no doubt that your choices influence your experience. To be blunt, if you dive into a psychedelic experience without mindful preparation about the setting and your mental framework, you might invite the kind of chaos that will not be particularly helpful for serious personal exploration—and will make your experiences more difficult to integrate into your life journey.

Before turning to the details of this chapter, I will offer an analogy of getting ready for a vacation. You would want to be mindful about where you are going, make some choices about whether you want to set up reservations beforehand, and know what places you want to visit based on what is most interesting to you and what you want to learn. But you also want flexibility for spontaneity and joy and the unexpected. Within the mix, you also want to stay aware of the things that may be outside of your planning, such as whether it rains during your beach vacation, or whether the museums are suddenly closed for circumstances you did not expect, or whether you pick up a bug that requires you to stay close to your bathroom.

To bring the analogy back into psychedelic exploration, depending on who you are and what you want, you may *decide* to set up a particular circumstance, and bring a particular intention, but you may be wise to recognize the probabilities and the possibilities of what you will actually experience—which brings us back to the interplay between the probabilities of experience with certain psychedelics and the probabilities that arise from the combination of environment and intention.

Mindset: Choice of Internal Experience

The phrase **"set and setting"** is typically used to describe two main things that influence non-ordinary state experiences:

- The frame of mind you bring to an experience (the set), and
- The environment you choose for a non-ordinary state journey (the setting).

Rather than use the word "set," I am using "mindset" because I think "mindset" is much easier to understand than "set." (To be honest, every time I hear "set" I have to translate in my head into "mindset.") **Mindset** is the internal piece of the picture, what you bring from inside yourself. This necessarily includes what is in your head, your heart, and your body. Dictionary.com defines "mindset" as including:

- Attitude
- Disposition
- Mood
- Intention
- Inclination.

Mindset

Awareness can be brought to all of these aspects of mindset.

Attitude can be broken down into some interesting components. This includes "a settled way of thinking or feeling about something" or a "view, viewpoint, orientation, approach or reaction." What opinions are you bringing to the situation? Sometimes analogy is made to a physical or embodied attitude, such as "position, posture, pose, stance or bearing." You might consider not only your conscious attitude in your mind, but also the attitude that is brought by your body (position, posture, pose, stance or bearing) as you enter into a session. These are clues to what might influence your experience.

Disposition involves "a person's inherent qualities of mind and character." This involves knowing yourself and considering what you know about yourself and might be bringing to a session. For example, someone might take a deep breath before a session and realize, "Here I go again, expecting too much of myself and the world… let me please accept what comes."

Mood is defined as "a temporary state of mind or feeling." Are you bringing in something from your week, from your relationship, from your job, from what someone told you and you have not yet processed? Is there something in the setting that is influencing your mood? How are you really feeling today and right now?

In considering these aspects of *mindset*, it is important to bear in mind that some of your attitudes, disposition, and mood may be conscious, and some may not.

This brings us to the importance of preparation—including the possibility of working with a therapist or guide. I will talk more about this later in the chapter. For now, just consider the value of unpacking before any psychedelic session what you are bringing to the session from your settled views, your temporary moods, your conscious attitudes, your unconscious disposition—and all of the nuances that can be unpacked from the definitions suggested above.

This unpacking can happen in a pre-session meeting with a guide the day before the session or in a relatively quick check-in just before you begin. On your own, you can simply check in with yourself with some compassion and gentleness. In the Holotropic Breathwork tradition, facilitators typically check in briefly with experiencers right before a session begins. Usually this is just to ask, "How are you doing?" and to wish a good journey, often with a hug. Bringing even brief consciousness to "how you're doing" can help clear you for the journey.

Getting back to other elements of mindset, I return to *intention* ("a thing intended; an aim or plan") and *inclination* ("a person's natural tendency or urge to act or feel in a particular way; a slope or slant.")

Intention is the word most commonly used to describe the *conscious* part of what you bring to a non-ordinary state experience. As I mentioned in the Entryway, there are different opinions about whether one should bring a conscious intention for a particular experience into a session or whether one should show up with openness to whatever comes. I will touch on the different possibilities for intention throughout the book, but for now, I emphasize that whether you have an intention, and what intention you may have, could shape the *probabilities* of your experience, but will not guarantee what you experience.

Getting to *inclination*, I like this word for the metaphor it suggests about the angle through which you dive into your non-ordinary state experience. If you are going to dive into a body of water, here are some possibilities of what you could do:

- Cannonball in with the notion of making a big splash.
- Stand carefully for minutes to be sure you hit the water exactly when you are ready.
- Jump as far as you can, flailing your arms and legs around.
- Try to accomplish a beautiful controlled dive into the most perfect place in the water.
- Or any number of other possibilities.

Which possibility you choose probably involves the body of water you are entering into. With a lake, you might not know the depth of the water and could hit your head on rocks. So you might want to jump feet first or make a shallow dive. If you're on the top of a high dive and are an experienced diver, you can probably make an excellent controlled dive, but if you have never jumped before, you might have a more cautious and less ambitious approach. All of these things play into the *inclination* you choose when you make your dive.

Coming back to psychedelics, consider your inclination in terms of your goals and desires, but also with respect to your level of experience, the substance, who is supporting you, and the setting in which you're taking your journey.

Pre-Session Mindset (Preparation)

Before talking about pre-session recommendations, I want to mention one of the common ways facilitators break down the stages of non-ordinary state work: *Preparation, Session, and Integration*. This is a useful way to focus attention on the importance of preparing for a journey and the need for integration following a psychedelic experience. It helps to make preparation, session, integration a linear progression so that we remember to pay attention to both the before and after, as well as the journey itself, which often takes most of the focus.

But... from my perspective, this approach can leave integration as something of an afterthought, more or less a reminder: "Take care of yourself afterwards, and don't forget to integrate." This basic reminder is important, but I believe you can do more. I believe it is possible to approach all stages with an integration intention, including what happens pre-session. This will make more sense as I talk you through it. Just keep remembering that exploring psychedelics invites you into a *process* into which everything is folded on an ongoing basis.

I labeled this subsection *Pre-Session Mindset (Preparation)* because the mindset you develop *leading up to* a psychedelic session is an essential part of preparation for your session, but it is much more than this. Your mindset before your journey sets the stage not only for your session, but also for your ongoing integration after your session. **You prepare not just to have an experience, but to have an experience that you can integrate.**

Preparation is not just about making sure the room is set up in a way you want, and your facilitator gives you a hug if you want a hug, but bringing focused attention to your upcoming journey over a period of time prior to the session. Treat the upcoming journey as though it is an important and sacred ritual. Integrate all that comes up for you consciously before the journey—and reach into what is there but may not yet be conscious. Start integrating what is coming up for you even before your session.

James Fadiman is one of the early pioneers and leading academic experts in psychedelics. A dear friend of mine was fortunate to take several classes with Fadiman at the Institute of Transpersonal Psychology; one involved exploring Sufism, the mystical side of Islam. Sitting on the floor in a circle, participants shared parts of sacred teaching stories and texts that had meaning for them—and everyone took the time and space to feel into the parts of the stories that touched them. This is practice reaching into yourself to find what is there.

James Fadiman

Fadiman is the author of *The Psychedelic Explorer's Guide: Safe, Therapeutic and Sacred Journeys*, one of the leading contemporary texts on psychedelics. Fadiman recommends some areas for exploration prior to a session:

- Clarifying "your personal preconceptions about psychedelic experiences" and substances.
- Reflecting on "your understanding of mystical experience, cosmic consciousness, or whatever else you may have heard described that may arise."
- Sharing your "expectations, concerns, and hopes."
- Discussing the range of possible experiences you may have. [33]

In discussion groups for people who are considering experiencing psychedelics, I have a set of questions to focus exploration of pre-session mindset. Using the word P-R-E-P as an acronym, he invites consideration of Purpose, Reflection, Expectations, and Potential.

I encourage people to go from a macro level (universal) down to a micro level (personal) when contemplating working with psychedelics. As always, I remind you not to judge what comes up for you in the manner of good or bad, but rather to observe and bring awareness. Feel free to type or write out your answers to these questions and to save what you write for comparison to where you might evolve down the road of your psychedelics journey.

P – Purpose

How do you see this work being developed throughout the world, where you live, from your own lenses? What is the commitment or draw to this work? Are you aware of any specific questions you are looking for? In other words, what is your intention for this work?

R – Reflection

How do you see the history of psychedelics? What are the stories you have heard? What have your experiences been?

E – Expectations

What are your beliefs for the future of this work, both globally and directly within yourself? Do you have any narrative that is in your head about this work?

P – Potential

What is the potential you see for this work? What will this work become? The difference between expectations and potential might seem minor; however, I encourage you to dream big and think outside the box. Maybe you are interested in helping psychedelics therapy became more and more legal and mainstream; or maybe your interest is spiritual or based in community. Whatever it may be, feel into it and make it your own.

Prior to a session, it is important to think, feel, and talk through these issues (and anything else that may come up). This is particularly important if you are taking your first journey but remains important no matter how many times you have explored psychedelics. Sometimes it is the second, third, fourth or fiftieth journey when it really hits you what the possibilities are—and you begin to feel seriously into your pre-session reflections.

As for preparation to integrate as you are about to enter a non-ordinary state, Stan and Christina Grof recommend that you:

- Keep your attention on your inner process.
- Surrender fully to your experience.
- Express without judgment the emotions and physical energies that come up for you.
- Suspend your rational analysis and trust your inner healing intelligence more than your intellect. [34]

These guidelines not only help you maximize the potential of your non-ordinary journey, but prepare your body, mind, and soul to integrate the experience by carrying it forward into your life.

Mindset Interacts with Setting

Many of the psychedelics experts advise very specific circumstances for the setting of a journey. I will share some of my own thoughts on this later in this chapter. Experience has shown without any doubt that the circumstances surrounding your dive into a non-ordinary state (both internal and external) shape your experience. However, rather than lecture you on those circumstances, I want to empower you to make conscious decisions and to process through all that is arising for you no matter what circumstances you develop and choose.

How you prepare for a journey depends on all the variables—including the setting you choose. One person may never have used psychedelics and may plan for months toward a trip to South America for an Ayahuasca retreat. This person may read extensively online about

Ayahuasca and prepare for the trip to South America, but may not realize how to feel into herself about her expectations, hopes, fears, and all the possibilities. Another person may enjoy the spontaneity of an unplanned psychedelic journey at a festival, house party, or evening alone or with a friend. The invitation may present itself suddenly, and the invitation may be accepted.

> It is natural to hope that one's first full sexual experience will be loving and pleasurable. However, for many people that initiation can be awkward and uncomfortable—even traumatic. Unfortunately, self-administered psychedelics also can have severely disturbing, long-lasting effects. A well-structured session makes it far more likely that early psychedelic experience will be meaningful, healthy, and life enhancing.
>
> —James Fadiman

Even without months of preparation, it is possible to take a few moments to set a sacred internal tone of gratitude and respect for what is coming, even if the atmosphere is full of fun and partying. The mindset you bring to your particular journey depends on your choices about the journey, but also depends very much on your internal attitude.

Later in the chapter, I will discuss the choice you have whether to work with a guide, facilitator, or therapist. For now, just note that your ability to explore and integrate where you are pre-session can be influenced significantly by your choice of your companion (or lack of companion) in the work. No one else can do the pre-session reflection for you, but you can ask for and find support to help you. I want you to take ownership of this choice and even begin to integrate your "choice process" as you choose who may impact your pre-session mindset. In other words, ask yourself, why am I deciding to involve or not involve others? If others are involved, why this particular person or group?

Some facilitated journeys are designed to assist you in exploring questions or intentions that emerge from deep within yourself. I have participated in weekend workshops where the facilitator leads the group through exploration of a particular spiritual system used by some of our ancestors for guidance (for instance, the Celtic Tree of Life, the Kabbalah, the Egyptian mystery schools). Each individual's psychedelic journey is held within the group sharing and the guidance from this system. A weekend retreat setting with a group that spends time getting to know each other helps focus the pre-session mindset for everyone.

When experiences are framed in a small-group retreat setting, an appropriate psychedelic may be one that allows some measure of conscious reflection by the explorer during the experience. MDMA typically allows a fair amount of conscious reflection and sometimes interaction with a guide during the experience. For such experiences, an example of advice for pre-session mindset could be: "Allow your intention to emerge with regard to what you wish to learn about yourself or to be shown during the retreat. The most important preparation is becoming clear about your intentions or questions." The intentions or questions then become an entry point into the experience given the nature of the group journey.

In contrast, if the upcoming experience involves 5-MeO-DMT, the most sensible pre-session mindset might involve preparing to surrender into the experience. Rituals helping to prepare the body and mind for release into the potentially *very* strong experience will likely prove more fruitful than any focus on specific conscious intention involving worldly issues.

There are countless possibilities for setting. I encourage you to remember to blend your mindset with the appropriate setting and consider what setting will work best for the mindset you think you are creating.

Mindset on a Countdown

Speaking very generally, it might help to consider mindset preparation in the **weeks before** a session, the **days before**, and the **moments before**. I make this suggestion because you may find different things arising and shifting in each of these time frames, though you will likely have some consistency in themes and issues depending on you and your purpose for the journey.

To draw an analogy, I have some experience with skydiving. I know that my awareness starts to move towards an upcoming dive as soon as I contemplate the possibility of another jump. Exploring what is emerging is helpful in the weeks before an actual jump, but the intensity increases in the days just before I head to the drop zone. The intensity might peak as I step onto the airplane and incrementally shifts each and every moment the altitude increases.

In the weeks, days, and moments leading up the jump, the issues for exploration in my body, mind, and spirit may be similar all along, or may shift as the time for the jump approaches. I readily acknowledge that the tendency to dissociate from the fact that I will be jumping into free fall at 125 miles an hour increases as I near the jump zone and the time to step out of the airplane. In those moments, the main mindset focus might involve just managing to stay present to what is about to happen so that I maximize my presence during the jump. The focus may shift to a form of self-care rather than detailed and nuanced exploration.

The Dive

I feel there is a strong analogy here to psychedelics work. Speaking very candidly from my experience, the tendency to dissociate from what is about to happen may well increase as the time for a psychedelic journey approaches. So I am suggesting the possibility of building a presence to yourself and to what you are undertaking throughout the trajectory of the journey, beginning weeks before, moving into days before, and up to the moments before diving into a non-ordinary state. You might even develop little (or big) rituals designed to maintain your presence and whatever attitude you want to bring to the experience.

In the **weeks before** a session, you may be attending to the questions noted by Fadiman and myself—or similar questions developed by your guide or yourself. Even in the preparation stage, I feel it is fair to call this undertaking by the name of integration. This is because all along you are integrating all that is arising within yourself and all that is coming from outside yourself. If you find you are stepping outside yourself as the experience nears, then you can simply try to integrate yourself back into yourself. Remembering your preparation can help. Rather than defend against or dissociate from what is arising, you are bringing everything into your conscious awareness and presence, allowing yourself to experience and process what is emerging. You are facing what is coming through with an embodied and conscious awareness.

All this said, I also understand that none of us is able to fully process what is moving within us at any given moment. For this reason, I do not want to suggest that there is success or failure at any moment in staying present to what is emerging. Rather, I simply want to bring attention to this process as important throughout the preparation-mindset experience.

Turning to **the days before a session**, you might notice that your approach to the session in some ways begins to consolidate. You might feel that the same issues and sensations and feelings are flowing around you, but the process starts to coalesce into a more focused movement towards the experience. It might feel as though the experience begins to tunnel in towards the moment when you will surrender yourself into an intense and transformative journey.

In the days before an experience, you may start to feel that a process has started to emerge that is already like a non-ordinary state. Sometimes it feels as though you have opened into something that is much bigger and broader than your own individual mind or body. Synchronicities (coincidences) might occur. You might feel as though a higher power or specific spirits have started to join with you in preparation for your experience. I want to encourage you to respectfully and mindfully open into whatever is happening for you. You might frame this as emerging intention, but only if that makes sense to you.

In the days before a psychedelic journey, particular questions or issues for exploration may start to come to your attention. You may notice that narratives (pre-conceived expectations) may begin to take shape. It is also common to find yourself free-associating about your intentions for the journey. Treat yourself gently and with compassion for whatever emerges.

It is important to emphasize freedom for shifting intentions and expectations—though I encourage you to notice and keep track of the variety of what is coming up. Starting your notebook for the upcoming session may be a good idea. This is an excellent time to journal about what is happening—including writing down potential intentions or questions for the journey that may begin to appear on their own. Remember to put anything into the notebook that comes to you. This can range from free-flowing words, to dreams you are having, to printing pictures from the Internet or taking cutouts from magazines that capture your attention.

I recommend using complementary practices for focusing intention and allowing spontaneous emergence. You may want to play with a mind map (see Integration Exercise 5) to find some of your more linear intentions; or you may want to let yourself doodle, draw, or daydream to notice what is coming up without conscious thought. By giving space for both of these possibilities, and everything in between, you will be metaphorically and literally accountable for fueling yourself up and setting yourself down in a ready space for a psychedelic dive.

In closing this section, I want to emphasize the idea of …S…P…A…C…E….

Finding enough time for easing into a psychedelic journey is probably the most difficult thing for many of us with our busy lifestyles. Please do not add to your burden by judging yourself for any difficulties in making space for both finding intention and allowing spontaneous emergence in the weeks and days before a session. But if you can find time to let yourself *be* and *feel into* and *think into* the upcoming experience, that giving of space may itself by your best preparation.

Surrender

Just Before the Session

No matter how you have attended to your mindset in the weeks and days before a session, you will eventually find yourself about to digest some form of medicine and engage with what comes. You might find yourself flooded with many different kinds of emotions just before the journey. These may range from exhilaration to panic—with maybe some middle-of-the-road jitters or anxiety.

I encourage you to consider the source of whatever may come up for you. Sometimes just a brief check-in with yourself will help you realize you're worried about something that is no longer applicable or that you are simply responding to the knowledge you are doing something big. Whatever it is, breathing into it and through it can be helpful. It can also be very helpful to check in with your support, whether that is your guide or facilitator, the person sitting next to you in a group, or your higher power. Reassurance from whatever source is usually the best medicine.

Just before a session, there is no need to "figure out" or find a clarifying answer for whatever may be emerging. But it may be important to be honest with yourself, and whoever is helping you, about exactly what you are feeling. Most often, this helps you let go of whatever is there and be ready for whatever emerges.

As for the few moments right before a session, a close friend of mine jokes that just before the start of any non-ordinary state journey, he asks himself, "Why the f— am I doing this?" He asks this question because he has some pre-session jitters and also because he knows the session will likely involve some challenging emotional and physical work. These feelings are normal. In fact, I might be worried if you did not have some version of these feelings before taking the dive.

As practice for gearing up for a journey, I now invite you to feel into yourself right now.

Now your turn

In the weeks before my next session, I envision....

_____
_____
_____
_____
_____

In the days before my next session, I envision:

_____
_____
_____
_____
_____

In the moments before my next session, I envision:

_____
_____
_____
_____
_____

Pre-Journey Suggestions

As you work towards a journey, the following activities might be helpful:

Baths or Showers

Water is a great way to prepare for an experience as well as truly integrate an exploration with psychedelics. Many different spiritual communities use bathing and cleansing as preparation for ritual work.

Fasting

As the day gets closer, you may want to limit your intake of certain foods. Many facilitators request that you refrain from meat, caffeine, alcohol, or even solid food in the days or at least day before a journey. (On the other hand, sometimes not having enough food in your system can make a journey difficult.) By mindfully exploring your eating habits as they relate to your individual desires, you will also connect more deeply with your intuition. A week away from an experience is a great time to start to crystalize your understanding of your eating.

Yoga

Gentle yoga (not necessarily the fast core-building yoga common today) may offer you the opportunity to feel into your relationship with your body. Depending on the form of yoga, it can be a wonderful way to ease into a grounded state, and aid in harmonizing your body.

Meditation

Contemplation and attention towards the internal is a great way to recover peace of mind and a deeper sense of your body.

General Physical Activity

Exercise or physical hobbies can help to ground you and remind you of your loves and enjoyments in life. Walking, biking, hiking, swimming, and running are all wonderful explorations of your physical self.

Journal Writing

Stepping into a linear, left-brain frame of mind is a way to articulate your needs and desires before a session, and a fantastic way to put some foundation to an experience you had after a session. I encourage you not to get too "tied-up" on the linguistics of words and the meanings. More importantly, explore the art of writing as a fulcrum to your preparation or integration.

Surrendering Mindset

Having emphasized the importance of mindset, I am well aware of the *paradoxical* nature of entering into any non-ordinary state journey. You might prepare for weeks with a specific intention and focus yourself in the days before the journey with all kinds of preparatory techniques—and even feel yourself surrendering calmly into a healing space. And yet, the medicine in any particular situation may have its own plans for your experience. I like the word paradoxical in relation to mindset because I find attending to mindset to be crucial and important; and yet I find it undeniable that none of us has control over a psychedelic journey.

When I say that we do not have control over the experience, I need to say a few words about the difference between conscious control and unconscious influences. At one end of a spectrum, we may have a clear intention, for instance, to look into why we have difficulties again and again in our personal relationships. We may have a fantasy that the session will bring some form of intellectual clarity around the issue, perhaps including biographical memories that are relevant, and emotional or embodied energetic releases that may help us move toward what we want. This may very well happen just as imagined.

On the other hand, outside of our conscious awareness, our body-mind-spirit may have a deeper understanding of our life path than we hold in conscious awareness. Similarly, we may have some form of karma or karmic commitment that needs to play out in our life for reasons not having much to do with our understanding of our relationship issues. These things within us could be considered a form of unconscious *invitation* coming from our body-mind-spirit for what our session will involve.

I am suggesting that your mindset could be considered very broadly as including things that are outside your conscious awareness. This mindset considered broadly will very likely contribute to your psychedelic experience. It may even be inevitable that your broadly-considered mindset builds the experience that you will have. However, you always have a role to play with your consciousness, your awareness, your intentionality, moment by moment, throughout all your experiences.

Your mindset can be analogized to a set of train tracks that lead out of a central terminal. Your mindset may control the switches that allow or disallow your experience to proceed down any particular tracks. In this way, mindset can be held as a general form of "intention" for any particular non-ordinary state journey. Since some of your mindset is likely unconscious, you might have a conscious intention but an unconscious mindset that supersedes your conscious intention with respect to controlling those train track switches.

This is why I encourage you to think about integration at every stage of working with psychedelics, from preparation to session to afterwards. If you give conscious attention to integrating into yourself all that is going on for you prior to a session, then you may increase your openness to all that you are bringing to the experience and *understand* moment by moment the implications of everything emerging during your non-ordinary state adventure.

It is also important to allow your mindset and intention to shift as the experience unfolds. Empowerment includes the ability to shift with what is happening and continue to own your experience. For instance, a friend undertook a journey not long ago where he thought he was microdosing psilocybin based on his prior experience with that substance. He had a museum activity planned with friends. However, for whatever reason—environmentally, astrologically, interpersonally, or personally—he found himself in a challenging situation that completely changed his approach to the journey.

My friend found he would not be able to flow with external circumstances but needed to surrender himself completely into what was arising from inside himself. Given his prior experience with psychedelics, and with the assistance of those around him, he was able to *react* to what was happening in order to manifest the most productive and safe experience for himself. His mindset shifted from an intention for an externally-based experience to needing to go deeply inside with whatever emerged while asking for support from friends.

Having spent some time with *mindset*, I now turn to the second part of the dyad typically known as "set and setting." Before unpacking the idea of setting, I want to share a story that illustrates the unity of mindset (set) and setting with respect to emerging psychedelic experience.

Jeff and Alyssa's Story

Alyssa and Jeff are a newly married couple in their thirties. Jeff has much more experience with psilocybin than Alyssa and wanted to offer her an adventure in this realm. Though they had talked beforehand about taking a journey that afternoon, Alyssa happened to have just returned from running errands at a big box store with an intention to clean the house that weekend.

She had just unpacked several varieties of cleaning supplies, which were sitting on the kitchen counter in their open ground floor townhouse.

With no focus on the cleaning supplies and without sharing Alyssa's intention to clean house that afternoon, Jeff reminded Alyssa they had talked about a Saturday afternoon mushroom journey. Alyssa got back on board with the plan with no apparent concern. After the psychedelic experience began, Alyssa became consumed with the need to clean the house. She took Jeff by the hand and brought him around the house, noticing in minute detail every little bit of dirt or lack of cleanliness. Alyssa began saying, "This place is so dirty; it's like a meth house; how can we live like this?"

Objectively, the house was actually very clean. Jeff found the house completely cool as it was and talked Alyssa through her experience of the lack of cleanliness. He asked her, "What would you like to do about it?" Alyssa wanted to use the cleaning supplies, which were prominently right in front of them, to clean the house. They spent much of their psychedelic experience cleaning.

There was nothing wrong with this experience for Jeff, but he was aware of how much the experience flowed from not only Alyssa's mindset coming home that afternoon, but from the cleaning supplies that sat prominently on the counter around them. In retrospect, Jeff thought there was probably no way the experience could not have unfolded as it did with the cleaning supplies dominating the room and Alyssa having just come home with an intention to clean. He wondered whether Alyssa had some feelings about "drugs"—which they had never discussed— that might have influenced her sense their house was like a "meth" house.

Jeff enjoyed the experience for what it was and was grateful for the opportunity to support Alyssa in engaging with what emerged for her. There was something good about their intense focus on their house. Alyssa shares that she was disappointed with the experience and felt a fair amount of fear and discomfort through an intense focus on dirt and the need to clean. She is reluctant to have additional experiences with psychedelics.

I want to emphasize there is nothing "wrong" with Alyssa's experience. She did not seek an immediate opportunity to explore the experience further. If she had wanted to explore what happened, healthy integration of her journey could well have answered some unresolved feelings. Even more importantly, her experience could have been an entry point—a golden opportunity— to explore her psyche around many possible issues. On the other hand, I completely respect that she was simply not interested in going any further with the experience.

This story suggests an extreme example of the influence of setting. To state the obvious, you can use psychedelics just about anywhere you want. I want to avoid judging anyone for their choices around using psychedelics. On the other hand, I want to be clear about the possibilities that exist through not paying careful attention to the settings in which you enter into a non-ordinary state journey. As the example of Jeff and Alyssa suggests, every nuance of setting combines with mindset to shape the experience you will have with psychedelics. The variables cannot be quantified but should without a doubt be taken into consideration.

Setting: Choice of External Experience

Your choice of setting may seem much more in your control than your mindset—and yet many people lack information about the possibilities for setting. I recognize that using psychedelics in your home country may be illegal, so I do not want to imply that you have a wide range of easy choices or even should choose to do something illegal. But I would like to take you through my understanding of some of the possibilities.

In a broad-brush stroke, I can say that in choosing setting, you should consider the psychedelic, the dose, and your intention for the experience. Staying safe within your setting depends on these factors. For instance, you might choose to take a relatively low dose at a festival where you want to enjoy yourself with friends you know well. On the other hand, if you wanted to work through some deep-rooted trauma with a mind-opening psychedelic and a trained facilitator-therapist, you might go with a relatively high dose.

As I shared in earlier chapters, some psychedelics (for instance, Ayahuasca) tend to be used in a ceremonial setting, carrying forward rituals and structure from particular cultures or lineages. Others are more typically used individually or with a one-on-one guide. There is no way for us to unpack all the possibilities for setting, so I will touch upon some of the general choices that exist for how to experience psychedelic journeys.

Guided v. Self-Guided

Most experts in psychedelic experience would strongly recommend working with a guide rather than alone. In *The Psychedelic Explorer's Guide,* James Fadiman puts it this way:

> Many of those who have never had a guided session appreciate how psychedelic experiences have impacted and improved their lives. However, the presence of a knowledgeable guide greatly facilitates the probability of reaching expanded levels of consciousness and recalling and integrating the experiences. The fact that a guide makes a significant difference in the quality of the experience underscores the difference between psychedelics and almost all other medications. That difference is not only that the plant or "drug" opens one to a wider range of experiences, but also that the direction, content, and overall quality of the experiences can be focused and enhanced with guidance.[35]

A knowledgeable guide is not so much there to help you through a potentially difficult "drug" experience, but to assist your entry into the powerful depths of yourself and what lies beyond your individual ego.

"For most people," Fadiman writes, "the predominant feeling during a session is not of discovering something new, alien or foreign, but of recalling and reuniting with an unassailable clarity what had been latent in one's own mind." [36] Psychedelics often open those "doors of perception" into what Fadiman describes as "an eternal flow of energies and understandings." [37]

Experiencing this flow can be exhilarating and life changing in an instant, but the power of what comes upon you can be like standing alone before a blocked dam when the floodgate is opened. As Fadiman observes: "During the experience of awakening to oneself, it is invaluable to be with someone who supports you. Your guide knows the terrain, can sense where you are, and will be able to give you advice or caution you as appropriate."

I find this sound advice—and I am also mindful that many people do not have ready access to an experienced guide where they live. If you are going to another country where "medicine" is legal, you want to be sure that the programs you are considering have a good reputation. You may want to ask your contact for the names of some people who have experienced the program and try to talk with these people yourself. I say more on vetting when I talk about group experiences overseas. Of course, if you are experiencing psychedelics within one of the legal programs, then you will just want to be sure that the particular people helping you have experience and are a good fit for you personally.

If you are looking for an underground guide, I cannot give you any referrals! But I recommend attending conferences or discussion groups involving the subject of psychedelics or other transpersonal topics, including workshops involving other means for entering non-ordinary states of consciousness, such as breathwork. Be yourself and talk to people. Ask intelligent questions. Do some reading beforehand (including this book!).

In such settings, be open for coincidences to happen that put you in touch with people who might point you in the right direction. Most legitimate underground guides will be extremely cautious about what they are doing and will not talk about the possibility of guidance unless and until they trust you. This will involve some assessment on their part as to whether you are in a place in your life and journey where you could responsibly benefit from the experience. So expect general conversation before there is even any acknowledgment that you are talking to a possible guide. Humility and curiosity more than posturing or showing knowledge are often good ideas when getting to know anyone—in any context.

Some guides will only talk openly with people who are only a few (one or two) degrees of separation from someone they know very well and trust completely. The guide will rely on their very trusted friend only to refer someone *they* know well and trust completely. In other words, you may need to get to know some people very well so that they trust you completely; then they may put you in touch with a guide or with someone who knows the guide.

When you meet a guide, not only will the responsible guide evaluate you, but you will also evaluate the guide. To be perfectly honest, many people holding themselves out as guides in today's "psychedelics renaissance" bring their own issues, beliefs, inexperience, or agendas into their work. This is not to judge anyone, but to recommend that you bring a great deal of consciousness to your decision about a guide. If you have a history of having certain blind spots with respect to bringing new people into your life, pay great attention to those blind spots.

Martin Ball

Martin Ball, author of *Entheogenic Liberation: Unraveling the Enigma of Nonduality with 5-MeO-DMT Energetic Therapy*, stresses the importance of working with a clear facilitator, particularly if you are using one of the more powerful psychedelics, such as 5-MeO-DMT. He writes:

> Always keep in mind that who you take any medicine with, and the context and setting they provide, can have both a strong impact on the quality of your experience, and your ability to integrate and ground the experience, post-session.... Taking medicines with inexperienced people can be an invitation for disaster. Taking medicines with manipulative and narcissistic individuals is an invitation for personal struggle and difficulty. [38]

Although focusing on 5-MeO-DMT, Ball envisions the positive qualities of a facilitator that I find apply to any facilitator of non-ordinary state work:

- Energetically grounded and present.
- Not reactive and not prone to confusing their thoughts with reality.
- Having very little "story" involved with their practice (in other words, no self-mythologizing or embellishment about significance beyond the simplicity of what is being offered).
- Body language communicating a calm presence and clarity, rather than nervous energy.
- Good listener.
- Patience.
- Compassion and empathy, "but not necessarily the overly-sincere and often uncomfortable form of gushing compassion and 'honoring of others' that all too often shows up in overly-spiritual folk."
- "They may also be stern, and not tolerant of bullshit, illusion, and other forms of storytelling, and they won't be afraid to say so."
- Not presenting as victims or heroes.
- Confident without spiritual or religious justification.
- "Able to answer your questions and listen to your concerns and issues."
- "Honest and realistic in their statements and actions."
- Without artificial or forced humility.
- "They will know what they can and can't do, and will be confident in knowing the distinction."
- "Furthermore, they should have good relationships, be reasonably happy (but not too happy—over-enthusiasm and artificial goodwill are signs of overcompensation), and have a reasonably stable lifestyle."[39]

When reading Ball's list, I am humbly reminded that none of us is perfect. In other words, he describes a tall order for a person to fill—and yet I completely endorse his criteria. As you learn about potential guides for psychedelic experience, please hold these professionals with compassion in their imperfections while also making sure you find an experienced and healthy facilitator.

Another healthy characteristic mentioned by Ball involves having a sense of humor and the ability to recognize the balance between seriousness and non-seriousness in life. One of the reasons I have learned to trust an Ayahuasca facilitator so strongly involves the facilitator's ability to laugh at himself and with the hilarious paradoxes and circumstances built into the universe. He never laughs at the expense of others, but his presence encourages people to consider that laughter, like love, rests at the center of the cosmos. A strong and clear sense of humor does not suggest a lack of compassion for suffering, but an awareness of the level of love and joy implicit within universal consciousness.

If you are working with an individual guide, that person may or may not be available for ongoing integration work after the session. This is another point to consider when looking for a guide. In my view, in a perfect world, the person guiding you through an experience would be available (for appropriate compensation, of course) for regular integration sessions following the experience. On the other hand, you might work with a facilitator for the experience only—preferably with a discussion meeting beforehand and some integration afterwards—and then work with someone else in ongoing integration.

Having talked at length about guidance in psychedelics work, I return to the legitimate choice of working without a guide. In reality, the vast majority of people who have experienced psychedelics—and many of them reporting that the experience was among the most profound of their lives—have not worked with a guide. As long as you are mindful about what you are doing, to embark on an adventure on your own is your choice. And yet, once again, I agree with Fadiman and Ball that journeys with a guide are more likely to open you fully to the experience.

At the end of this chapter, I stress the importance of S-A-F-E-T-Y on all levels. While I want you to stay safe, I want to respect your wisdom and choices about your own psychedelic path. In fact, I have written this book in part to provide you with some of the guidance you might find when working with others, so that your journeys—whether alone or with guidance—can be rich with integration, awakening and healing.

Like many serious psychedelics explorers, you may find that over time you engage in both solo and guided exploration as well as one-on-one and group experiences. I hope this book helps you create a thread *of yourself* that runs through all your experiences.

Sexual Boundaries

All ethical practitioners stress the importance of **clear sexual boundaries** between healing professionals and experiencers. Sadly, there are hundreds of stories of seekers (usually but not exclusively women) who have found themselves taken advantage of sexually by guides in non-ordinary state work. This includes not only psychedelics work but also other modalities of spiritual seeking.

Most of us seeking healing or spiritual awakening bring to our search a sense of longing, vulnerability, and willingness to surrender. Desire for connection with an idealized spiritual "other" can be astoundingly strong. These urges can be easily projected onto guides in psychedelics work, similar to "transference" in any therapeutic work, but with heightened hazard given the vulnerability inherent in non-ordinary state work.

Although this is less commonly discussed, some people (both women and men) experience an awakening of healthy sexuality on their psychospiritual journeys, including when working with psychedelics. Even with the sexual revolution of the 1960s and beyond, many people have learned to repress their sexuality (or some aspects of their sexuality). Sometimes the release of repression may happen through shifting energies in non-ordinary state work in ways that feel as though following sexuality is the path to finding God.

As illuminated beautifully in her book, *Transcendent Sex: When Lovemaking Opens the Veil*, Jenny Wade brings attention to the many people who find spiritual awakening through sexuality.[40] Often these people gravitate toward non-ordinary state work to continue their spiritual journeys. It is important for these people not to feel shamed for their awakenings, but also to meet clear boundaries in the professionals with whom they work. It goes without saying that you should avoid guides who give you a vibe of sexual interest. You should have a discussion with any guide about the level of touching you may feel is appropriate—and you may want some touch to support you. Partially in recognition of the importance of clear sexual boundaries—including considering appearances as well as realities—most of the lawful research and therapy programs have a dyad of supporters, one woman and one man, working simultaneously with experiencers.

Suppose you feel the urge to develop a friendship or relationship with a guide? Some practitioners maintain a rule of never pursuing romantic relationships (or even deep personal friendships) with people they facilitate in non-ordinary state work. Others practice a rule of "six months" or "a year" with the idea that if a relationship is meant to happen, it can happen after a cooling off period. Within group experiences, facilitators will often obtain agreement from group members to avoid touching between participants that may carry or be perceived as carrying a sexual edge.

5-MeO-DMT guides I know (a man and a woman who work as a team) tell the story of a workshop where they offered an initial group experience and had forgotten to talk about sexual boundaries. Two men, in the height of the experience, looked at each other and immediately joined together passionately. The male guide broke them apart as gently as he could, but some trauma was introduced into the group. The men were angry at having been broken apart. Some others felt violated by the bringing of sexual energy into the circle. Much processing needed to happen about this occurrence.

If the setting had included an initial agreement not to engage in touching that could be perceived as sexual, the incident may not have happened. Even if the men had still come together, at least the prior clear statement about sexual boundaries by the guides would have been part of a group agreement and the "breaking apart" would have had a different feel. Again, if a relationship is meant to happen, it will commence after the heightened nature of the non-ordinary state work has a chance to integrate.

All this said, I have noticed that over-emphasis of sexual boundary awareness may transfer onto innocent seekers the issues around sexuality held by some facilitators and the culture at large. In other words, sometimes there is an "edge" to the description and imposition of sexual boundaries that contains some of the "stuff" of the facilitator or carry-over from cultural shame.

During sessions of Holotropic Breathwork I have seen some facilitators rush to push pillows between facilitators and experiencers, or to counsel apprentices who themselves are very clear with their sexuality, in ways that seem to create an issue (and potential shame) around intimacy and touch. Similarly, I have seen some facilitators project their sexual issues on those who exhibit healthy sexual charisma in ways that can be damaging for all concerned. In some worst-case (but actual) examples, sexual charisma is demonized and ostracized and innocent individuals harmed.

To state the obvious, whether you are in a facilitator role or just assisting your peers in non-ordinary state work, take responsibility for knowing when your sexuality (or your repression of sexuality) is leaking out from your experience onto that of others. Of course, this is easier said than done as the problems arise from unconscious acting-out, but I hope this section might encourage you to seek consciousness around this extremely important issue.

Individual vs. Group

One of your main choices of setting involves whether you will experience psychedelics in a group or individually. Given the prevalence of Ayahuasca ceremonies in current times, many people are introduced to psychedelics in a group ritual setting. Sometimes this involves planning an adventure to a faraway land.

There is something to be said for taking an *external* journey in order to take an *internal* journey. Our long-ago ancestors may have traveled long distances by foot to join with others from different tribes to celebrate rituals involving non-ordinary states. Probably this was how religions developed. There are anthropological theories that sites began to exist where people would join to experience the kinds of rituals I would recognize as involving non-ordinary states. Eventually some people would become shamans or leaders and would stay at these sites. Teachings and world-views would develop that set the groundwork for what later became religions.

Since Ayahuasca ceremonies in other countries may be the most available group experiences, I will say a few words about them. These can be amazing experiences, as evidenced by the thousands of North Americans and Europeans who have traveled to the Amazonian basin countries in the last few decades.

As with any group experience you seek, I recommend thorough vetting of any individual or organization you trust to host a psychedelic experience, particularly in an unfamiliar country or culture. A quick Internet search might take you to reports of difficult, traumatic, even dangerous experiences; some people have felt exploited or abused. On the other hand, thousands of people have found life-changing transformation through an experience with "Grandmother" in her natural habitat.

For this book, I am more interested in the group experiences now offered in Western countries. Because almost all psychedelics are not legal in Western countries, these group experiences necessarily take place discreetly and typically only with people the facilitator has decided to trust based on referral from a trusted person, meeting in another context, and/or individual interview.

As I recommended when looking for a guide for an individual experience, I suggest that you attend personal growth workshops of a serious and deep nature and pay attention to the people around you and the conversations that open up to you. Some guides offer individual experiences first and then follow with an invitation to group experiences if the person seems ready for the experience. Other guides for group experiences are more open to new people as long as the approach is handled discreetly.

Also, while this is no guarantee, I have found that if you begin the serious work on yourself that is required for serious use of psychedelics, when you are ready for a group experience, the universe may present circumstances to you that you know to follow. I would suggest these general categories of group experience now available in North America and Europe:

- Single or periodic experiences (often with long interims) offered by traveling indigenous healers from countries with psychedelic medicine heritage, usually coordinated through a local host, often with the traveling healer referenced as a shaman.
- More regular experiences offered by people who have trained with such indigenous facilitators in the particular lineage, often in a regular setting in a particular locale, making possible the growth of a healing community of people who regularly or periodically participate.
- Periodic group sessions offered by an experienced facilitator (or better yet, team of facilitators) in the underground psychedelics tradition without any direct affiliation with shamanic lineage; often these facilitators are grounded in their own deep psychological work within a transpersonal psychology context; these facilitators have often worked extensively with mentor facilitators.
- Groups offered by self-trained people called to psychedelic facilitation work and knowledgeable from their own personal experiences and studies.
- Peer groups arising among people who explore psychedelics and enjoy group experience.

Certainly these are not exclusive categories but suggest the possible orientation of particular groups. It is interesting to consider that we may be witnessing the development of a new profession and new type of spiritual community.

Turning to the nature of group experiences, some groups last only as long as the medicine journeys, but may follow a format involving the three stages of *preparation, session, and integration*. For group work, I am most comfortable with overnight or weekend formats. Depending on the particular group, ritual elements may or may not be involved, but almost always there will be a stage where community forms through introduction by the facilitator, followed by individual introductions and sharing of intentions. The medicine may be ingested by everyone at once or in stages, depending largely on the medicine and particular style of the leader. The facilitator (or facilitators) may ingest the medicine themselves, a somewhat controversial issue (see discussion in next subsection below). After the session, there is generally rest (and often sleep). Then the group will typically reform for sharing and closure.

What might be different for you in a group (as opposed to individual) experience? Well, of course that depends on the facilitator, on the group, on the medicine, on the dose, on the developing culture of the group, and on the intention everyone holds. But I note the following:

- In a group, you may feel part of a ritual that holds significant power in addition to the power of the particular medicine.
- Even if the group is not long-term, intimate community tends to form in groups focusing on deep exploratory work; this group intimacy itself may be healing and transformational.
- You might find what feels like your "tribe" of like-minded people who come to play an important role in your life.
- In groups, many facilitators offer teachings about how to work with the medicine—or how to integrate the medicine—that may make an enormous difference in your experience; experiencing the teaching in a group rather than individual conversation may feel more profound.
- Some group leaders (particularly in longer experiences) offer teachings about particular spiritual or mythological systems that inform the time together and may guide the medicine sessions (for instance, Celtic, Egyptian, Native American, Shamanic).
- Depending on the medicine, some group leaders offer guided imagery journeys during the psychedelic experience, or as the group emerges from the experience, which may help frame recollection and integration.
- Experiencing medicine in a group almost certainly involves development of a group energetic field that may provide healing potential that would not exist if you had an individual experience.
- During the introduction and integration phases, you will almost certainly learn from the shared experience of other psychedelic journeyers, developing not only a breadth of knowledge but a deepened compassion for others.

- It can be a lot of fun to experience psychedelics in a group—not a party exactly, but a profound sharing experience potentially involving the highs and challenges of human life.
- Some of us experience spirit coming more powerfully to gathered groups of people than when alone.

Returning to integration, the best group experiences provide guidance regarding the importance of integration. Opportunities are often provided to begin integration and/or continue your ongoing integration habits. In addition to community sharing, the group may undertake integration experiences such as drawing, dancing, other movement activities, walks in nature, shared eating experiences, etc. Some of the best integration experiences happen overnight in a shared room with a co-experiencer (or a few co-experiencers in a dorm setting) as you get to know each other and share your life journeys.

That said, it is common now among psychedelic group leaders to talk about the importance of providing more opportunities for integration. In part, this is because facilitators are beginning to notice that some of their regular participants move forward in their growth by leaps and bounds while others seem to have trouble shifting their life (and non-ordinary state) experience. The solution seems to involve more emphasis on integration.

Integration after Group Experiences

If you experience psychedelics in a group setting, probably your integration will begin in the group. However, you will have the choice whether to continue integrating in community or mostly within yourself. As a matter of integration before, during and after a session, I encourage you to consider your relationship to integration: are you drawn more to communication (groups) or to contemplation (alone)?

Being alone or in community is a complex question regarding psychedelic work. I have talked a great deal regarding the multitude of variables that are to be contemplated when getting ready to do a psychedelic session. Integrating psychedelic experience can raise the same spider web of questions:

- Do you thrive by processing externally or within yourself?
- What are your values, experiences and expectations in the gradations between contemplation and community?
- How do you understand the territory of integrating alone and/or in a community?

Here are some points to consider:

Integrating Alone:

- Deep and quiet contemplation
- Understanding what is yours
- Safety to explore your boundaries and new insights
- Continuing to develop and practice your dialogue of expression without an audience.

If you integrate alone, you may want to consider, at some point, sharing with others. This may be a trusted partner or friend, a therapist, or a sympathetic group. Then the question comes up: When should you check in with someone else? Do you want to give it more time?

Integrating in Community:

- Expression
- Exploring vulnerability
- Validating similarities
- Advancing your empathic listening
- Sharing your authentic voice
- Sharing with support.

I encourage you to feel into yourself (alone or with others!) on all of these issues.

Role of the Facilitator

Each facilitator brings his or her own style and intention to working with individuals or groups. Without suggesting hard and fast distinctions, I think it is helpful to note some different ways of working. I begin with some words used to describe different types of psychedelic guidance.

In the Ayahuasca tradition, a distinction can be made between an **ayahuascero** and a **curandero**. An *ayahuascero* knows how to brew the Ayahuasca tea, set up the space for the ceremony, and lead the ritual. But a *curandero* actually enters into the energetic space of the participant and actively works to heal blocks, problems or illnesses existing or developing. As explained by Zach at the caminodoamor.org website:

> An *ayahuascero* is generally not a healer, or they are a healer still in training. (Note: when I use the words "healer" or "healing," I am talking about healing

on all levels—physical, mental, and energetic/spiritual, as Ayahuasca is a truly holistic medicine.) *Ayahuasceros* are relying on the medicine to provide the insights and healing. *Ayahuasceros* are not actively working with the guests' energies or the medicine to maximize healing and insights. They may notice that there is something "off" in the guest's body or energetic body, but usually an *ayahuascero* does not have the training to do anything about it. In fact, a good *ayahuascero* that sees something is amiss in a guest will refer that guest to a *curandero* for actual healing.[41]

While Zach draws a clear distinction, the experience most of us have with Ayahuasca facilitators in Western countries is likely somewhere between these two poles. Remember my comment that we may be witnessing the development in the West of a new profession of psychedelic facilitator. Particularly in Ayahuasca ceremonies, I would expect a responsible facilitator to follow along with the experience of those in the group on all the levels Zach mentions—physical, mental, and energetic/spiritual —and to help within that facilitator's skill set. Sometimes this may be just providing a safe physical setting, sometimes it may involve verbal or physical support, and sometimes it may involve "working on" the experiencer's energetic space.

The Tradition

In an Ayahuasca ceremony, the facilitator may or may not have taken the tea along with participants. Likely the facilitator is not working alone but with other facilitators holding the group. Even if not "working on" individuals, the facilitators will likely be using drums, rattle, flute, or other forms of music to help move the experience through the group.

Facilitators may notice that one or more participants are moving through challenging energies that may be individual or may in some sense belong to the group. With rattling, smudging, use of feathers, voice, or touch, the facilitator may assist the individual with the experience. Possibly the facilitator is "seeing" something within the energetic body of the participant as well as the outward presentation of the participant on physical and mental/emotional levels. As noted, the facilitator may perform some version of the traditional work of a *curandero* in entering the energetic space for healing.

Some psychedelics facilitators work in a way that is similar to the facilitator training in Holotropic Breathwork, a method known as "doing/not-doing." In the Holotropic Breathwork tradition, facilitators do not intervene based on their own ideas or templates about what is happening to the participant. This is a strict protocol based on respect for the wisdom of the individual and a mandate not to overlay the facilitator's projections onto the participant.

While not interfering with the participant, the Holotropic Breathwork facilitator is trained to follow a participant's invitation to assist with focused energy work, containment in a boundary of the mat, supportive presence, and/or whispered communication, usually of encouragement. This loose form of intervention happens when the participant might be entering a place where they are putting themselves in a challenging situation or have asked for assistance. Both those possibilities tend to occur when the participant is approaching or moving through an embodied or emotional transformational point.

From his reference point of working with 5-MeO-DMT, Martin Ball draws a distinction analogous to *ayahuascero* and *curandero*. Ball describes a 5-MeO-DMT **practitioner** as someone who has done a profound level of personal work with the particular medicine. "Such an individual would be able to take the medicine with the client," he writes, "and be able to work with the client through all the ebbs, flows, and releases of energy to help the client remain calm, present, and authentically grounded." [42]

Ball considers anyone with less than these abilities to be a medicine **provider**. This is "someone who makes the medicine experience available to others and 'holds space' for the experience to unfold. By contrast, practitioners don't 'hold space'—they work the energy and ground it into the reality of the nondual." [43]

From these examples, and from our experience, I can outline four general categories of facilitation:

- **Keeping the individual or group safe physically,** and being responsive to their requests relating to water, bathroom, blanket, etc., without any intentional approach to holding the energy of the experience.
- **"Holding space"**—which I will define as a compassionate (with boundaries) energetic attention to what is emerging in the room, including the mood, tone, and feeling sense, as well as keeping people safe physically and being responsive to their mental and emotional presentations and needs.

- **"Doing/Not-doing"**—as noted above, this is a phrase borrowed from Holotropic Breathwork, and written about by Holotropic Breathwork teacher Tav Sparks, involving a stance of non-interpretation and non-intervention, but willingness to assist the transformational movements emerging solely from the participant's energy, with the facilitator using some touch, bodywork, voice, containment, or possible use of drums or rattles; the facilitator intends to follow emerging energy and assist its movement as it arises, not to actively move or work with the energy themselves.
- **Interventional healing work**, where the healer (often in a non-ordinary state themselves) intentionally feels into and moves or grounds the experiencer's energies; this is necessarily based on an extraordinary level of expertise, probably a gift, and a depth of training, which **absolutely requires** a very rare ability to discern between the facilitator's own projections and needs and actual energetic/spiritual/karmic presentations of the participant.

Does the Facilitator Take Medicine?

When reading the above, you may have noticed the question of whether or not the facilitator enters a non-ordinary state of consciousness through the ingestion of particular medicine during the experience. As I mentioned previously, this is a controversial question. From one point of view, to keep a psychedelic experiencer safe, the guide should remain sober and focused on the experiencer. The reasoning is that there is so much to manage in a psychedelic experience, and so many potential pitfalls, it is not responsible for the facilitator not to have all their normal faculties.

In this line of thinking, if the experiencer enters into situations of fear, grief, or confusion, the full sober attention of the guide is necessary for safety as well as respect of the experience. With some forms of medicine, the experiencer may attempt to leave the safe space of a careful setting and venture out into the world. If the guide is having his or her own journey, he or she may not be prepared to keep the experiencer within the safe setting without jarring the experience.

From another point of view, the facilitator "joins" with the experiencer or group through entering the same psychedelic space. To appreciate this point of view, you need to remember that psychedelics are not drugs simply offering a wild experience. Rather, they open the doors for consciousness to participate in usually hidden realities of the individual mind and beyond the individual mind. This can include immersion into complicated and potentially confusing realms of the universe with which individual consciousness participates and potentially merges. These realms are not just products of an individual mind but are actual realms with a real existence, even if that existence is not tangible in the same ways as the material world.

With this in mind, would you want a guide to a foreign territory who was not actually in the foreign territory with you? Do you enter a potentially challenging wilderness with your guide staying home on the telephone?

But the matter is not that simple. For a guide to be useful and protective in the wilderness with you, the guide absolutely needs to know the terrain and needs to be able to focus on you and your experience without their own distractions. If the guide has the propensity to get lost on their own, and to pull you with them, then you are better off if they stayed home. But if they are sufficiently trained, gifted and experienced, they may be able to help you through doors and remove blocks that transform your life or heal deeply entrenched wounds.

Admittedly, if the guide is to perform *healing* work *on you,* this is the realm of magic and is not to be taken lightly. In the tradition of shamanism, the shaman (healer) knows how to work in non-ordinary realms and enters those realms for your benefit. This is not something new in humanity, but an ancient tradition lost in mainstream culture, but preserved in some psychedelic medicine lineages.

In my experience there are more people around who mistakenly *think* they can perform this level of work than there are people who can safely perform the work. Be careful. But if a person has this gift, then their work may well be done most profoundly when they are "with you" in the space of the medicine.

Even when the facilitators are not performing healing work, some traditions involve the facilitators sharing the medicine with experiencers. This is often the case with Ayahuasca. If the ceremonial space is set up carefully and with agreement that no one leaves during the experience, and the facilitators are experienced with "holding space" or "doing/not-doing" while sharing the medicine, a great deal of safety and community can be experienced.

Facilitation as Shamanic Work

If you are interested in psychedelics, you will come across people who are described as shamans and ceremonies or experiences that are called shamanism. I want to unpack these references just a bit from our perspective. I also want to note that I feel psychedelics facilitation is "shamanism" at some levels.

The root word for "shaman" comes from the Asian language Tungusic, which is spoken in Northern Asia in the areas that are now Russian Siberia, northeast China (old Manchuria), and parts of Inner Mongolia. Shamans in these parts of the world —like healers in many other indigenous cultures—entered into non-ordinary states in order to heal illness or solve problems in their communities. They worked with the powerful energies I call archetypal in order to find the root causes of disease and move or process energies to facilitate cures.

After the 1951 book by historian of religion Mircea Eliade, *Shamanism: Archaic Techniques of Ecstasy*, and the 1981 book by anthropologist Michael Harner, *The Way of the Shaman*, the words "shaman," "shamanism," "and shamanic" have been generally used to describe indigenous practices of healing and journeying from cultures across the world. Fair enough; I needed some words in English to offer these descriptions. "Medicine man" was an earlier term but might have carried some condescending or colonial baggage.

Comparisons between the actual practices in northeast Asia and other parts of the world will be the work of anthropologists for years to come. But as Eliade and Harner described, I believe there are many similarities across cultures because this work is our human heritage and because the realms in which "shamans" work are actually *real* realms that are accessible by all of us. The images, worldviews, entry points and ways of working vary according to land and culture, but the essence of the work involves entering non-ordinary states to interact with strong energies for a healing purpose.

The word "shaman" is sometimes applied to facilitators of psychedelic experiences, particularly those offering group work with medicines having lineage back into indigenous communities. As I have noted elsewhere, sometimes these facilitators have years of arduous training in a very real lineage that requires the utmost respect. The word "shaman" would be appropriately used with them—or even better would be the words used in their indigenous languages to describe their role and their work. *Curandero* is the Spanish word most often used relating to South American shamans.

Without disrespecting the shamanic work taking place by many healers around the world, I want to recommend mindfulness as you encounter people holding themselves out as shamans or their work as shamanism. These labels do not necessarily guarantee the authenticity or safety of the work being offered. Indeed, a long-term journeyer and guide in psychedelics work has shared with me that she has trouble trusting any Westerners who describe themselves as shamans.

As with anyone you may encounter in the psychedelics community, I recommend that you trust yourself in feeling into the actual work being offered. Try to get to know the differences between "performance" by potential facilitators and their actual ability to offer you safety and assistance in your healing and exploration. Notice the difference between image and authenticity.

Unpacking your "feeling into" these differences can become important integration work. This can help you feel through with your own integrity the complicated issues involving the return of non-ordinary state work to our contemporary culture. For instance, consider the question whether this work will become commercialized and trivialized with the surface-level marketing we are used to with advertising and performance. This can happen even in underground communities. Or will we find ways to work through these issues and find the stillness and sacred elements of this work that are our human heritage?

Having said that, I want to emphasize that I believe facilitating experiences with psychedelics is in fact shamanic work. I do not mean that all facilitators are trying to enter non-ordinary states for shamanic purposes but that, with psychedelics, doors may be opened into personal, collective, and universal energies that are complex and powerful. These are realms that are not governed by the thinking minds we associate with modern science (even modern psychology), but involve deep and ancient levels of instinct and energetic integrity, safety, resilience, and power.

In fact, some contemporary practitioners of psychedelics work (particularly with groups) are concerned that opening the door to psychedelics work within a medical or modern therapeutic model might be hazardous given that, at the most fundamental level, this is shamanic work, and the skills that may be most appropriate for facilitation are not well understood within these models.

Integrating Your Facilitator Experience

Returning to the question of integration, I hope you are beginning to understand how the facilitator you have chosen becomes part of what you integrate. *What* you integrate and *how* you integrate are necessarily intertwined with the role played by the psychedelic facilitator with whom you work.

For example, if you are drawn to working with a "healer," that's great, but I encourage you to examine and integrate as much as possible relating to this draw for you. Do you need to turn your development over to someone else? Is your model of healing linked to Western medicine, where some substance or person acts to heal you, rather than you participating in your own healing? Is it too painful to face your demons on your own? Or have you realized you need help and you are brave enough to seek it?

On the other end of the spectrum, if you recoil with fear at the possibility your guide might work on you—particularly from a non-ordinary state themselves—I encourage you to feel and think into this fear. I'm not saying it is not a prudent concern, but is there anything behind your aversion that might be helpful to understand and unpack? Do you have trust issues? Does your history include caretakers who became absent through addictions or substance use? Or do you just need to know that a grown-up is in the room to help you when you ask?

When you are integrating an experience that has happened, do not forget to hold your guides in awareness, gratitude and compassion. What they provided for you (or were not able to provide for you) is a crucial part of what you will integrate. All of the tools, perspectives and exercises in this book can be used to examine the important experience of guides.

Therapeutic Sessions

I almost included a fifth category of **therapist** in our general list of types of facilitators. But I decided this type of facilitation emerges from a somewhat different tradition and perspective that I wanted to address separately.

As noted above, after decades of prohibition, the U.S. Food and Drug Administration has begun to allow use of some substances with psychedelic properties in therapeutic treatment. Therapist and research partners Michael and Annie Mithoefer (also husband and wife) have been instrumental in the new wave of legal psychedelic therapy. Michael's background as a psychiatrist and Annie's as a psychiatric nurse bring a wealth of important experience to this growing field. Their work includes assisting military veterans in coping with the impact of combat-related post-traumatic stress disorder, a condition that takes the lives of thousands of veterans every year through suicide.

Michael & Annie Mithoefer

On August 18, 2017, MAPS announced that the FDA had granted "Breakthrough Therapy Designation" to MDMA for the treatment of post-traumatic stress disorder (PTSD). This approval follows years of careful FDA-approved research into the therapeutic effects of MDMA for treatment-resistant PTSD. The dire needs of military veterans, and the lack of responsiveness of many to traditional treatments, encouraged the medical and bureaucratic establishment, traditionally hostile to psychedelics, to authorize such studies.

As noted in a previous chapter, psychedelics expert Ralph Metzner offered the designation *empathogen* for MDMA, distinguishing this "medicine" from other substances with a more classic range of psychedelic properties. Nevertheless, I consider the openings for profound healing and transformation provided by MDMA within the range of medicine work.

Psychedelic Therapy

For several years, the FDA has approved studies sponsored by MAPS and other organizations into the therapeutic effects of MDMA, psilocybin, and, more recently, LSD, for a range of psychological issues. These have included the anxiety experienced by people facing terminal illness, obsessive-compulsive disorder, alcoholism, depression, trauma, grief, and anxiety. Studies sponsored by MAPS in Mexico and New Zealand have begun formal investigation into the effectiveness of ibogaine in treating addiction, particularly to opiates. The Center for Psychedelic Therapies and Research at the California Institute of Integral Studies (CIIS) in San Francisco now offers a certificate program training sitters or guides for psychedelic experiencers. Admission to this pioneering program is limited to licensed mental health clinicians, specific medical professionals, and ordained/commissioned clergy and chaplains.

From these studies and programs emerges a setting for psychedelic/empathogen experience facilitated by a therapeutically-oriented guide. While some of the professionals providing training for future psychedelic therapists/guides and researchers come from the underground tradition, the emerging setting is shaped by the therapy tradition. Guides draw from mainstream therapeutic techniques as well as techniques from the non-ordinary state "sitting" tradition. Actual experience in "sitting" comes from sessions of Holotropic Breathwork or other lawful modalities for inviting expanded states of awareness.

While a therapy practice using psychedelics is emerging within the mainstream medical community (and hooray for that!), underground therapeutic settings continue for psychedelics work. Courageous people who have trained as therapists (some of them risking their licenses) guide clients in psychedelic experiences as part of their ongoing work in therapy. The medicines used are often psilocybin, LSD, or MDMA or similar compounds. Such arrangements permit the client and therapist to fold the psychedelic experience into ongoing psychotherapy, in a situation where trust has been developed and the therapist and client have joined into ongoing work.

Focusing on Holotropic Breathwork and psychedelics, I wrote my master's thesis on the value of blending psychotherapy with non-ordinary state work. After experiencing several Holotropic Breathwork workshops, I realized the formats allowed only limited focus on integration. Typically, experiencers were provided space to share the most important aspects of their experiences in a closing circle or debriefing. But there was no ongoing possibility for using the experience as an entry point into processing the person's psychological history or current challenges and goals.

If non-ordinary state experiences became part of ongoing therapy, I believed the experiences could be integrated into the person's life and would be less likely to stand alone as one-time strange happenings. Too often, I thought, an experience with psychedelics was left as an island in a separate ocean of life—with some part of the experiencer's soul left alone on that island.

Through my master's thesis, I realized there were skills and techniques that might be employed by a therapist in assisting experiencers in using their non-ordinary state journeys as ongoing catalysts for healing, growth, and change. The techniques of various traditional forms of therapies could be very useful in unpacking and integrating the psychedelic experiences. But there was also the need for the therapist to understand the possible terrains and pitfalls of working with non-ordinary states, particularly psychedelics, without judgment or projection.

I would never suggest that anyone should experience psychedelics without a true calling to that work. Nevertheless, I note that it may be difficult for therapists without experience in psychedelics to walk the walk with clients who want to bring their psychedelic experiences into the therapy. One way to consider this issue is this: if the therapist only holds a perspective from consensus reality in present materialist culture, then the probability exists that the client's experiences in psychedelics might be pulled into that perspective.

One of the gifts of working with psychedelics is the opening these medicines provide into perspectives vastly larger than those held in current consensus reality in Western culture. It may be difficult for a therapist without a sense of this realm to appreciate the "reality" of your experiences. I am reminded of the saying shared with me by a friend when I was heading for India several years ago: "If you have been to India, no explanation is necessary. If you have not been to India, no explanation is sufficient."

In closing this section on "therapy" as a setting for psychedelics, I will draw on Stanislav Grof's distinctions of the types of therapy that can be employed *during* a psychedelic experience. These are:

- **Psycholytic** therapy, a term coined by British researcher and psychedelic pioneer Ronald A. Sandison, meaning the therapist helps the experiencer release or dissolve tension

existing in the mind through talk therapy similar to psychoanalysis, but assisted by the client's use of a medium dose of psychedelics.
- **Psychedelic** therapy, where large doses of a psychedelic are administered to make possible the experience of "ego-death" or other transcendent experience, with the goal of allowing a deep transformational shift in consciousness that may break a dysfunctional pattern or pathology, such as alcoholism or obsessive-compulsive disorder, and establish a connection to a higher power that may provide ongoing assistance.
- **Aggregated** psychedelic therapy "en masse," where clients take a medium or high dose in a group setting, with a set of facilitators, in order to experience community bonding and to learn from the potentially diverse set of experiences in the group.

By no means have I exhausted the possibilities for offering a "therapeutic" setting for psychedelic work. Rather, I hope to suggest the possibilities for blending the modalities and ranges of traditional therapy with the possibilities of psychedelic work.

Creativity Sessions

From the inception of contemporary psychedelics usage nearly seventy years ago, in places such as California, New England, and old England, to the hotbeds of creativity in contemporary Silicon Valley and the entertainment industry, intentional sessions with psychedelics have focused on increasing creativity for particular projects or general discoveries.

Just after Timothy Leary and Richard Alpert (Ram Dass) were ousted from Harvard, heiress Peggy Hitchcock offered Leary, Alpert, and their Harvard colleague Ralph Metzner a temporary home in her family mansion at Millbrook in upstate New York. Some of the stories of visitors and communal living at Millbrook in those times have become practically mythical. But it bears noting there was intentionality to using psychedelics (primarily LSD) to learn about human potential, creativity, and uncharted intellectual terrain.

Millbrook Mansion

Until the United States government halted lawful research into the potentials of LSD and other psychedelics in 1966, James Fadiman and Willis Harmon headed careful and responsible studies involving the benefits of psychedelics for catalyzing creativity. The "set and setting" for these sessions was carefully crafted to maximize the possibility of creative breakthroughs that could be remembered and recorded. The goal was not only to provide settings for these breakthroughs, but also to document the power of psychedelics for assisting innovation in science, technology, academics, and business.

Though necessarily underground from 1966 through recent times, it is likely that history will eventually acknowledge the role played by psychedelics in the innovations of computer and Internet pioneers, such as Steve Jobs. In other words, history may show the important role psychedelics played in the unfolding of the world in which we live today.

Dosages

Mindset and setting are important in shaping your experience. But nothing is more important than considering the particular psychedelic you are ingesting and the dosage of that psychedelic compound. I gave you an overview of our understanding of different psychedelics in Chapter 2. Here I come back to dosage.

Getting the right dose of medicine involves objective knowledge about the impact of the medicine on the human system, but the nuances of dosage are to a large extent subjective. There are a multitude of different factors when I talk about dosage:

- Personal experience with sensitivity to any substances (e.g., food, alcohol, etc.)
- Prior experience (confidence) with the particular psychedelic medicine
- Body type
- Medicine purity
- Whether you have eaten that day
- Personal trepidation.

The only real way to figure out a good dose for you is through trial and error. Of course, if you are participating in a research study, there are exacting rules for the dosage of a substance and the timing of ingestion. However, most of us working with psychedelics for personal growth have to figure out dosage on our own or through the guidance of a facilitator. Without a doubt, I recommend working with a facilitator or expert on beginning dosage, as well as choice of psychedelic.

Purity of the compound is an extremely important reason to be very prudent about selecting a facilitator or, if you are working on your own or with non-professionals, the source of your particular medicine. It goes without saying that you need to be very careful about the safety of any particular drug provided to you, particularly those that are provided in the underground.

I think some of the horror stories about harmful additives to psychedelic allies have been exaggerated over the years as scare tactics or for political reasons. Nevertheless, in contemporary times, the world is a dangerous place, and there are many misguided or wounded people out there with sad motives to harm other people. Either know your source sufficiently to trust the purity of what is provided to you, or test the substances you use on your own. Fortunately, there is now a great deal of guidance available on the Internet for understanding how to test psychedelic substances, including kits you may purchase to test the substances you are considering using.

Also, it is important to remember that different medicines work differently, both in general and with respect to individuals. If you have experience with a certain medicine, you cannot assume that it will transfer over with other psychedelics. Remember, when working with your dosage, it is vital to know what you are dealing with, who you are working with, and what you are working towards. If you are worried about getting lost in the void of psychedelics through too high a dose—or you have been lost and now feel stuck—I would like to recommend *underdosing* rather than *overdosing*. The idea is to find your "goldilocks" experience. That is the place of "not too hot" and "not too cold," but as Goldilocks found, "just right."

One of the most responsible guides I know—who specializes in guiding experiences with 5-MeO-DMT—begins a weekend group session with an evening of experimentation with small samples of "Jaguar" for each individual. This allows everyone, on their own and with the advice of the facilitator and his co-facilitator, to incrementally explore the nuances of the dosage in order to find the level with which they are most comfortable.

As with every aspect of psychedelic exploration, I recommend that you pay attention to the depths of the *why* question of your motivation in gravitating toward any particular dosage. I guarantee that your attitude toward dose will be part of your overall personality and life trajectory—so that when you integrate your psychedelic experience, considering your choice of dose is an important aspect for integration in the very biggest picture.

Staying Conscious, Remembering, and Whiteouts

One of the most important dosage considerations involves whether you remain able to stay **conscious and present** to what is happening in your experience. A corollary consideration is whether you will be able to **remember** what happened—or at least some important highlights—even if you are able to be present to what is happening as it unfolds.

Sometimes with psychedelics one may have an experience known as a **whiteout**. Different people might use the term in different ways, and there are different experiences that might be grouped under the phrase *whiteout*. Most generally I consider a whiteout an experience that is not remembered, but involves a sense that you were taken somewhere else, into some other realm. You may know your consciousness went somewhere outside your ordinary experience, but you are not able to bring back any specific elements, either emotional or content based. Or, a whiteout may simply be an experience you can't remember. I suppose this is similar to a blackout talked about with alcohol or other substances, though I do not want to give the experience that negative connotation.

In the Holotropic Breathwork community, there is talk of an experience of **yogic sleep.** The idea is that you went to a deep place of profound rest when you "breathed" during a Breathwork workshop, suggesting an advanced spiritual experience. Sometimes I suspect facilitators talk about yogic sleep to people who simply fell asleep during their experience, as a way to help them not feel bad about their slumber (or feel they still got their money's worth!). Nevertheless, I do not discount that sometimes you may enter into a profound resting state (some version of sleep), and this might be exactly what you needed—or inevitable given your circumstances.

Experiencing a whiteout can be disappointing, even to the extent that you are not sure whether you want to ever experience psychedelics again. It is easy to personalize an experience of whiteout along the lines of "I can't do this" or "This does not work for me." It can be very demoralizing not to remember anything that happened and have nothing to share, particularly when others in a group are talking about an amazing experience and what they saw or learned. Very often, this sense of "nothing happened" fits into an ongoing narrative that a person has about their life and the lack of a sense of agency in their life.

And you know what I'm going to say next—if you have disappointment or other feelings around this experience, that is an excellent entry point into integration. To state the obvious, your lines of thought or emotion around a whiteout become fruits for integration—and might themselves be considered a gift of the experience and catalyst for transformation, whether now or down the road. I guarantee that many things about you and your current life will come to the surface.

Psycho-integrative vs. Dissociative Dose

To use more technical terms than "whiteout," I might talk about a *psycho-integrative dose* versus a *dissociative dose*. A psycho-integrative dose might have the following characteristics:

- Enough medicine to profoundly open the doors of perception.
- Not so much to overwhelm you so that you are not able to consciously experience the experience.

- While most psychedelics take hold of you in a practically demanding way, a psycho-integrative dose allows you to hold onto yourself enough so that there is someone having the experience (that said, one of the most profound experiences in psychedelics involves releasing the sense of yourself, but a psycho-integrative dose would allow you to hold onto yourself enough to witness the release of yourself).
- Some psychedelics necessarily involve a period of feeling nauseous or having other side effects (often including purging)—and while this may be an important component of the experience, a psycho-integrative dose would be low enough not to leave you with an entire experience of illness or misery.
- As suggested by the phrase, a psycho-integrative dose would allow you to bring enough of the experience back to work consciously with integration.

In contrast, a **dissociative dose** suggests that you have moved away from conscious experience of yourself. I do not want to leave you with the impression that I think this is necessarily a negative experience. For example, ketamine (which is not, strictly speaking, a psychedelic) is known for its dissociative qualities. Sometimes, taking yourself away from your typical frame of reference or state of mind is exactly what you need in order for your doors of perception to crack open. I often hear this from people suffering from depression or anxiety—just a break from the difficult blanketing mood can be very healing. However, the phrase **falling into a K-hole** emerged to describe the "lost" quality that may accompany an experience of dissociation through ketamine.

Ultimately, the continuum between psycho-integrative and dissociative doses is something for you to work with on your own terms. And I want to return to our ongoing stance of non-judgment. I do not discount the human need—particularly in a stressful culture like our own, and particularly in the tumultuous time in which we are living—to release ourselves so that we lose our stress-based identities.

If psychedelics give you an escape that you need, then I do not want to suggest this escape cannot have healing qualities or become part of an integration journey. Certainly, responsible escape through psychedelics could be argued to be much healthier than through alcohol or other drugs. And yet, I am advocating some conscious attention to the "whys" of your dosage and considering whether you are seeking escape or self-actualization.

Psychedelics Working Outside your Awareness

Some psychedelic medicines do part of their work outside your conscious awareness. For example, Ayahuasca can work to purify blocks in your unconscious mind-body-emotional system deep inside your body and energetic system. You might have awareness of those blocks as they come to the surface for release, or you may not. You might know you are purging—or Grandmother Ayahuasca is helping you release—something that is toxic and blocking you, but you might not know what is being released. Even without complete consciousness of the *what*, you might experience healing or transformation.

I offer the analogy of having dreams. Science tells us that each of us dreams consistently every night and through a large portion of our sleep cycles. However, we almost never remember all of our dreams and commonly remember only particular dreams or fragments of dreams. Nevertheless, I believe many dreams are working on us through releasing clogs or blocks in our systems to allow more flow in our lives and a sense of freedom. Dreams may also guide us to our best futures without our conscious awareness.

With integration after a session—just as with dreams—some of what you were not conscious of may come back to you. Many of us have the experience of not consciously remembering a dream and yet having a piece of a dream come back to us as an event happens in life. This happens with psychedelic experiences as well—you may think you do not remember much of what happened, but elements of the experience may suddenly or gradually return to you at the appropriate time.

Sometimes a synchronicity occurs in life that seems to bring everything together at just the right moment. The memory of some part of a psychedelic journey emerges just when you need it. I have found that using some of the integration practices—and practicing an integration lifestyle—increases the potential for bringing even "lost" experiences during psychedelics to light and back into our life flow.

Microdosing

Having just spoken about the impact of psychedelics outside conscious awareness, I come to an important practice that has received increasing attention the last several years. "Microdosing" involves ingesting a small amount of a psychedelic substance—typically LSD or psilocybin—to assist day-to-day functioning.

Microdosing

In *The Psychedelic Explorer's Guide,* James Fadiman asks the question, "Can sub-perceptual doses of psychedelics improve normal functioning?" Fadiman shares stories from several people who have worked with LSD or psilocybin through small doses on a regular basis. While controlled research studies into the benefits of microdosing are only just beginning, the anecdotal reports from many people suggest positive effects. Drawing from the reports shared by Fadiman, these positive effects may include:

- Feeling more consistently in a positive and healthy flow of life
- Living with a sense of gratitude for what you have
- Emotional balance and resilience
- Increased focus and creative output
- Decreased anger or anxiety
- Expanded spiritual awareness
- Better understanding of the bigger picture of how everything fits together
- Increased connection with one's body, emotions, and the surrounding world.

Some people have switched from pharmaceutical anti-depressant or anti-anxiety drugs to microdosing psychedelics. As Fadiman notes, the preliminary evidence does not indicate harmful effects of microdosing but rather "better than normal" life functioning and enjoyment. However, you know I am going to tell you that I am not recommending microdosing and that you should check with appropriate professionals before trying this on your own. In particular, I would be cautious against stopping any prescribed medications in favor of microdosing without professional guidance. That seems a prescription for disaster, even life-threatening disaster.

"Good Time" External Experiences

Much of this book is directed toward maximizing your internal experience with psychedelics. As I near the end of our chapter on Mindset and Setting, I want to talk about the value of psychedelic experiences with a strong focus on the external, where you are not holding an intention to do internal psychospiritual work. I am talking about activities where you are out to have a good time. A few common settings for such experiences include:

- Festivals
- Nature
- Parties
- Concerts.

In all likelihood, if you are drawn to these experiences, you understand the euphoria or heightened awareness that might come with combining psychedelics with time in nature or when watching a performance or while interacting with a lively community experiencing music or dance. For example, attending a rock concert may get you into the flow of life, heightened to amazing levels by psychedelics.

The Festival

I have a friend who lives to attend Cirque De Soleil productions. He says the experience is extraordinary in his ordinary state of awareness, but deeply euphoric for him with an appropriate psychedelic dose. He finds himself merged with the music, beautiful human bodies, lights, and artistic showmanship in a way that rejuvenates him for his busy life.

Experiencing nature through psychedelics can feel like an archetypal immersion in the reality that spirit manifests into form. You might realize you are actually alive on a living planet. Connections with life forms or minerals or the land itself may occur at what feels like microscopic levels. In other words, there are very good reasons that so many people gravitate towards nature or the wilderness for psychedelic experiences.

On the other hand, at times many people forget that nature is real and can be dangerous. We may not have much experience with actual wilderness and may project our ideas about the benign and healing aspects of "Mother" onto "Mother Nature." While tripping in a park or a rural setting close to home might raise minimal concern, trekking out into the wilderness with psychedelics requires experience both with wilderness and with the medicine you bring. Real nature is not Disneyland nature and often holds real challenges and even life-threatening dangers.

As for the combination of psychedelics and "partying," I do not want to come across as a downer; I respect everyone's right to choose how to experience their life. In a later chapter, I will discuss in more detail the shadow side of psychedelics as that applies to integration. For now, I just note that a partying atmosphere might be the most challenging for maintaining safety and *respecting* the medicine.

Finally, I will just note that an external experience of psychedelics during any of these activities still calls into question mindset and setting. If you want to experience psychedelics with friends as a recreational event, you still might consider how to frame your experience in ways that minimize the potential for negative experiences and maximize the possibility for personal growth and insight as well as escape and enjoyment.

Psychedelics and festivals of a certain kind (did anyone say *Burning Man*?) have gone hand in hand for decades. I am happy to note that many organizations now offer safe havens or guidance for those who might find themselves struggling with a psychedelic experience at a festival. I say more about some of these organizations a few pages from now. If you do have a challenging experience in an external situation (such as a festival), you might later bring the *entirety* of that experience into an integration process. For some people, an experience of this kind becomes the introduction into integration involving psychedelics.

The Psychedelic Integration Handbag

How many times have you been out in the woods or on a car trip and that one friend always comes through with the goods, be it a simple piece of gauze for a cut or a complex tool that you need to keep the trip going?

Here I would like to share with you the importance of building *The Psychedelic Integration Handbag*. The details will be up to you, and of course it really depends on where you are, what you are doing and who you are with, but the most important thing is finding healing, safety and understanding of your experience.

When you get ready for a psychedelics journey, imagine yourself packing a metaphorical—and then literal—handbag. The following are examples of different things you might want to have as a part of *The Psychedelic Integration Handbag*:

- *Non-Alcoholic Hydration* – Water, tea, coffee, fruit juice or your favorite drink.
- *Layers of Clothing* – The more layers the better, especially if your experience is outside.
- *Favorite Blankets or Pillows* – Comfort will help you when you need an integrative grounding.
- *Tissue and Plastic Bags* – Both can be valuable and always practical.
- *Chocolate or Sweets* – The sugar is a great benefit at the end of a long experience when food might not have been consumed before.

- *Other Snacks* – Fruit, raw veggies and other snacks that you have a tendency to be drawn to.
- *Your Journal or a Notebook and Writing Utensil* – It's a great way to start to come out of your experience without the need to verbally talk with anyone.
- *Music* – Everyone has some sort of device that has music. Often a therapeutic session is focused around music, and a festival has music. Still, it is nice to have "go to" artists and songs that bring you comfort.
- *Pictures of Loved Ones* – This one could be seen as potentially activating; however, this is up to you if you want these photos with you.
- *First Aid Basics* – Ointment, gauze and Band-Aids can always be helpful.
- *The Psychedelic Integration Handbook* – Just like a map on a camping trip, never leave home without it.

The above are just a few examples that can start your Psychedelic Integration Handbag.

If you are interested in a safe internal journey that maximizes the potential for personal growth, here are some tips for setting:

- Warm colors in the room
- Soothing sheet, blanket or fabrics
- Cozy bed, mattress or couch ("the mat")
- Comfortable clothing
- Appropriate scents (sometimes depending on the particular psychedelic)
- Ritual objects or talisman you are drawn to bring
- Mindfulness about safety: no sharp corners or objects that might hurt you.

What happens if you (or a friend) did not plan for safety— or you did plan and something got difficult?

This takes us to the concept of harm reduction, which is an important part of integration. While harm reduction has relevance to psychedelic work, the concept is usually applied to drugs that do have more harmful consequences (such as strong addictive qualities and negative social impact). I want you to be familiar with harm reduction as an idea and as a practice, but please do not let the negativity that may be associated with "harm reduction" carry over into your psychedelic work. In other words, I hope you do not expect the negative but are mindful about the possibilities.

Harm reduction is an arrangement of practical strategies and ideas to reduce the negative consequences associated with drug use. Harm reduction is also a movement for social justice built on a principle in, and respect for, the rights of people who use drugs. The central belief is that it is possible to modify the more high-risk behaviors in our culture with means other than prohibition.

Harm reduction incorporates a perspective of meeting users "where they are," which happens to reflect a deep spiritual and therapeutic practice as well. If you are helping someone with a difficult experience, or counseling someone with psychedelic usage issues that seem to be getting problematic, the harm reduction model requests that you be with them in their experience rather than lecture or judge them.

The following are key points surrounding the general harm reduction model:

- Recognizes that drug use is part of our world and works to minimize its harmful effects rather than simply discount or criticize the user or situation.
- Appreciates drug use as a complex, multi-faceted phenomenon that encompasses a variety of physical, mental, emotional and spiritual behaviors; this can include the predisposition toward addiction of any individual using drugs.
- Looks to the quality of individual and community life and well-being as the criteria for successful interventions and policies.
- Involves the non-judgmental, non-violent arrangement of services and resources.
- Safeguards that people have an authentic voice when asking for what they need.
- Encourages understanding and empowerment through the sharing of stories, experiences, and support of one another.
- Acknowledges that the realities of financial positions, social experiences, past trauma, discrimination, and other cultural factors affect people's ability to have or gain support.
- Emphasizes the need of respecting a process and staying with the person.
- Does not minimize or overlook the real and tragic harm and danger associated with some forms of drug use.

Every situation is different. The harm reduction strategies that I just recommended may not be suitable for everyone or every experience. Explore what works for you, and more importantly, follow your intuition regarding what you and your explorers need at any given time.

How does harm reduction apply in psychedelic work? In any given year millions of people are consuming psychedelics outside the framework of a structured, guided session. The potential for any variety of things to "go wrong" can happen; this could be using a new compound or an unexpected reaction to a familiar medicine. It is especially important to recognize that taking any form of psychedelics can lead to overpowering and unimaginable experiences that no one could be ready for. If you have a hard time, or find yourself helping others, exploring these experiences with the harm-reduction guidelines will help. Remember, the primary guideline is to offer a reassuring, supportive and compassionate environment.

An important organization promoting harm reduction in the realm of psychedelics is the Zendo Project. The organization was founded in 2012 as a collaborative venture with MAPS. Their first focus was providing support at the Burning Man Festival for people having challenging experiences, along with developing education through training and workshops.

Zendo Project

Over the years, the Zendo Project has continued to sponsor presences at festivals and events to give hands-on support to people as situations arise. One of the practical results is the possibility of avoiding or limiting unhelpful interactions with law enforcement. The Zendo Project now operates in Europe as well as North America. At zendoproject.org, the organization envisions "a world where communities are engaged in providing safety and support for people having psychedelic and psychological challenges; and harm reduction principles are used foremost to reduce the risks associated with substance use."

The following are four principles of psychedelic harm reduction followed by the Zendo Project:

- **Safe Place**: If someone is having a challenging experience, try to move them into a comfortable, warm, and calm environment.
- **Talk through, not down**: Without distracting from the experience, help the person connect with what they are feeling.
- **Sitting, not guiding**: Be a calm meditative presence of acceptance, compassion, and caring. Promote feelings of trust and security. Let the person's unfolding experience be the guide.

- **Difficult is not bad:** Challenging experiences can wind up being our most valuable, and may lead to learning and growth.

Mental health and medical professionals are often the people staffing a presence of the Zendo Project at festivals. They work alongside lay people, who may have more experience with psychedelics and "bad trips." One of the results has been an organically designed think tank, where people learning and working with these experiences can share and compare methods from their own cultures, communities and respective backgrounds. It also is ultimately important to work alongside trained mental health and medical professionals when working with both emotional and physical manifestations of experiences.

When providing support and education surrounding psychedelic harm reduction, offering a welcoming community is extremely important. This is in contrast to what might happen with legal or "mainstream medical" intervention. The central approach is that you are providing care for a friend or family member, acting as a welcoming tribe through compassion and safety. In itself, this is a contribution to our culture and emerges from the central moral and ethical teachings of psychedelics.

The Zendo Project is not the only organization supporting people who need help when using psychedelics. The following are some other organizations that you might encounter at your next festival or gathering:

- **CALM (Center for Alternative Living Medicine)** has been, since 1972, a group of volunteers of the Rainbow Gathering.
- **White Bird** is a non-profit human service agency based in Eugene, Oregon, established over 40 years ago. This community of volunteers delivers education and services on site at festivals, as well as offering services to the estimated 12,000 homeless people of Eugene at their three clinics.
- **Green Dot Rangers and Sanctuary at Burning Man** is a group of trained support staff working with Burning Man's Emergency Service Department (ESD); they provide the Black Rock City with fire, medical, mental health, and communication services for the Burning Man event. Black Rock Rangers specifically address safety issues and mediation for the collective community.
- **DanceSafe** is an organization founded in 1998 with the purpose of promoting health and safety within the electronic music and nightlife society. DanceSafe is another non-profit, harm reduction group with community outreach through-out the United States and Canada. DanceSafe also supplies pill-testing and additive/ingredient screening for MDMA users.

- **Full Circle Tea House** is a California-based group established in 2011 to offer a safe place for festival enthusiasts to rejuvenate, rest, restore, and integrate transformative experiences. This environment is also conceived as an alcohol-free social space.

By spending time with the harm reduction concept and organizations offering harm reduction services, I hope I have encouraged you to be mindful of your ability to ask for help when you need it. Also, without lecturing you on where to engage in psychedelic journeys, I hope I have given you a sense that there are safer places to take journeys than others, even if you choose an external experience without intentional guidance.

Now your turn

What makes you feel safe?

_____
_____
_____
_____
_____

Are there certain environments or individuals that help you feel safe?

_____
_____
_____
_____
_____

What about the opposite—are you aware of some circumstances that make it difficult for you to relax and feel at ease?

_____
_____
_____
_____
_____

Different psychedelic traditions take place at different times of day—do you happen to feel safer journeying during the day or overnight? What length of time feels most safe for you to journey?

_____

Integration Exercise 3: Barefoot Walking Meditation

What You Need

- A pair of sandals or shoes if your feet hurt (only after you go barefoot)
- Comfortable layers of clothing
- Your journal.

General Background

The soles of our feet are a great way to feel on a deeper level. When you connect to the Earth, you are free to experience a closer connection to a more dynamic sensation in your body. Your first few barefoot walks outdoors should be short in duration. The general background of this exercise is to expand your sensations and reconnect to your body. By taking short barefoot walks two or three times directly after your psychedelic experience, you will have the potential to integrate and align yourself with nature and your higher physical body.

- Walking barefoot is a way to bring attention and focus to yourself and Mother Earth.
- By engaging in this exercise, you will harness more balance and stability.

Why this Exercise is Important for Psychedelics

Almost everyone who dives deeply into psychedelics—or any non-ordinary state work—ends up finding a deep and meaningful reconnection with nature. A former teacher of mine, Jay Dufrechou, wrote a book called *Moving through Grief: Reconnecting with Nature* that shares his own story, and the similar stories of people from around the world who realize the deep loss hiding inside them from the loss of intimate connection with nature for most of us living in global culture. Engaging with psychedelics holds the potential to bring you back into connection with how we humans evolved on this beautiful blue-green planet. Placing your bare feet on the ground can be one of the most profound ways for you to remember and integrate this experience through your body.

By putting your bare feet on the Earth, there is a grounding sensation that happens in your body-mind-spirit without you having to *do* anything to make it happen. This is a sensory experience—because truth be told, the feet are very sensual and remain the place where you most often connect with the planet. When you take your shoes off or put your shoes on, you may want to remember what it would be like not to always have a barrier between you and the

Earth—and to feel what it is like to have this sensual part of your body in direct skin-to-Earth contact with the planet.

How To Do It

Preparation in advance

1. Create a sacred space. These walks are best accomplished when you begin with the intention of learning something about you and the space you are in. Carry a sacred object; prepare a small space no larger than 10 x 10 feet.
2. Develop a safe space. Create an emotional and comfortable physical environment. It is encouraged to clear any debris away from your space.
3. The main rule is to use common sense; don't go into woods during hunting season, and stay away from ledges on mountaintops.
4. Wear layers.

Instructions for the exercise (Time: Five minutes to thirty minutes)

- To begin, stand with your feet shoulder-width apart.
- Feel the sensation under you, your bare feet touching the Earth and ground.
- Take a moment and engage your core and take one inhale (in) breath and one exhale (out) breath.
- Take a step forward with your left foot and leave the right foot fully placed on the Earth where it is.
- Position your upper body slightly forward with more of your weight still positioned on your back right foot.
- Position your arms comfortably at your sides or in your version of a prayer.
- Take a few more breaths. Begin walking in silence, moving with your own rhythm, what feels natural to you. Continue to move in an intentional manner.
- As you continue to walk, focus on your breathing, working to match the pattern of your walk.
- Begin to focus your attention on your surroundings: the sights, sounds, scents and other elements.
- Be attentive to how your body is feeling.
- Walk five to ten feet forward and simply turn around. Or walk in a circle if you are drawn to that instead.

As with any integrative exercise, there is no "wrong" way or "right" way to practice this skill. Walking barefoot and in silence opens the doors to experiences that are separate from the familiar "everyday" walking. Creating a rhythm with your breath and barefoot walking meditation will help you integrate your psychedelic experience, helping you to connect more deeply with your body and the Earth under you.

CHAPTER 4

WHY INTEGRATE?

This chapter is a little bit different.

I talked about integration in an overview kind of way in our Entryway into the book. In this chapter, I want to give you a sense of the variety of meanings and applications of integration in real life situations. I will unpack all of this throughout the rest of the book. For now, I give you some "quotes" of what I hear from people that have given me the sure knowledge that there is a lack of understanding about integration and a real desire to bring integration into contemporary use of psychedelics.

The "quotes" that head each section in this chapter are fictional, but based on things I actually hear from people. I then unpack the issues I see behind the dilemmas presented—just enough for you to understand why integration is important. Each section includes some suggestions I might give to people who bring a yearning for integration through the "quote" presented. The remainder of the book unpacks the elements of integration in detail.

You may resonate with some of these issues, or maybe not at all. I hope this chapter will give you a sense of the broad range of situations that call out for integrating psychedelics experience as well as the different needs for integration that different people present. You may also begin to see that integration in each situation holds the commonality of helping people move toward healing and wholeness—which in our culture and times often involves an enormous shift in outlook and life paradigm.

Although I give suggestions for working with each integration "problem" presented, I want to emphasize once again that there is no one answer for any situation. <u>Integration in any context is about *you* finding what you need to hold onto your non-ordinary state experiences and allow your experiences to move through you and take you toward the life you want.</u>

"It was amazing, but what was the point?"

Many people report that an experience while using psychedelics was one of the most important experiences of their lives, if not *the* most important experience. And yet, they may describe what happened as an isolated adventure, even as an adventure that disappeared like a single raindrop back into the ocean. Sometimes I hear this from people who had LSD or psilocybin experiences decades ago—but sometimes I hear this from people who recently had an experience and then have uncertainty about what happened and begin to question the significance.

When people tell me something like this, they may be coming from many different directions—and sometimes several directions at once, not all of them fully conscious. Some of the emotions that seem to be involved are:

- Elation
- Embarrassment
- Guilt
- Excitement
- Sadness
- Anger
- Frustration.

You may be asking, what's up with these emotions?

Well, what is up with these emotions would be an entry point to integration and will depend on the person. But just for instance, someone might feel lingering elation or excitement but not know what to do with those emotions. Because they don't know what to *do* with the elation and excitement, they may end up with, "What was the point?"

Embarrassment and guilt sometimes seem to involve an internal and not fully conscious "push-back" from some part of them that feels they were not entitled to the experience or cannot find a way to hold onto it while they are also rejoining mainstream culture. For example, someone felt the urge to tell her conservative mother about the experience and then when she started to "go there," she could find no words for the experience, so she began to sense a voice insider her saying, "I should never have done this." That may have been her voice, or it may have been her mother's, and this would certainly be an amazing entry point into integration.

Sometimes people seem to have a deep sadness or even a hidden anger that may hide behind the comment, "What was the point?" The sadness is usually closer to the surface. Anger, when it exists, may come across as sarcasm or even challenge to anyone who thinks psychedelic experiences (or even life) holds any meaning. Again, this might arise from not understanding what could have been *done* with the experience.

Rick Strassman, after conducting powerful research using DMT, was left with the concern—so great that it contributed to his discontinuing psychedelic research —"that isolated experiences, occurring without any sort of spiritual or therapeutic context, were not especially effective in producing long-term serious change in our volunteers."[44]

A variation on "It was amazing, but what was the point?" is sometimes, "Well, it was fun, but I think it was just my head doing things." Sometimes this latter comment feels a bit defensive, as though the person is protecting their inner self from possible disappointment by saying there was no *reality* behind the experience—and you can take that a little bit further into *there's no meaning to life* or *there is no God*. Unpacking the psychedelic experience and the life and cultural history behind these feelings can lead to profound work.

Another variety I hear is: "Wow, I remember feeling like I understood everything and had love for everything and everybody, but that all just faded away." The people who make this last comment may be those whose sadness might be coming very close to the surface.

What might these people do? Again, I unpack what could be helpful throughout the book, but to give some broad-brush strokes:

- Feel into the body and access emotions.
- Explore into the uncertainty and where it comes from.
- If there is difficulty in getting back to the experience, remember next time to record enough about the experience (art, writing, etc.) to have an entry point for returning to the experience for integration.
- Feel back into the excitement, elation, love, or understanding and expand out from that experience, following where it goes.
- Simplification can be helpful: find one word about the experience and build from that word.

"It's slipping through my hands quicker than I thought."

When I work with people on integration not long after they have an experience, this is the kind of thing that some people share. Through exploring what is going on, I might point out that when you come back from a vacation, you don't expect to still be on the beach, but you can look for ways to work your vacation into your life. Daniel Pinchbeck, who writes about shamanic and visionary experiences, notes that Ken Wilber, a well-known psychologist and philosopher, "draws a distinction between the experience of temporary 'states' and the development of permanent 'traits.'"[45] Pinchbeck goes on to say:

While psychedelics can allow us to access different levels of awareness, their use does not necessarily compel a transformation that would turn the developmental possibilities glimpsed in those states—such as greater levels of empathy, a wider intellectual scope, a more refined aesthetic and sensuous engagement with the physical world, and so on—into positive character traits.[46]

Saying this more simply: a psychedelic experience may take you to a place possible for the future you—one full of understanding, beautiful engagement with the world, and love—but *having* that experience once does not mean it will stay with you. For these "states" to turn into "positive character traits," you need to do some work to transform the experience of a "state" into a lasting part of who you are. This is *integration*.

Because I have experienced such positive transformation from psychedelic experiences, I have a deep belief that they can be positively integrated to support long-term serious change. Yet, much of what I have read about psychedelics, even though stressing the importance of integration, falls short of giving detailed recommendations for *how* to integrate appropriately. I believe the way to *hold onto* these experiences—for them to *have* a point—is through conscious attention to specific activities and awareness around integration.

Again, all this unfolds throughout the book, but for people making this statement, I might suggest:

- Creating some way to externalize the experience enough to be able to have it reflect back to them (for instance, artwork or writing).
- Guided meditation to get back to the experience.
- I have used music that reminds me of non-ordinary state experiences every morning to bring back the embodied sensation of the experience in order for it to "stoke the day."
- I also suggest that people find a totem to symbolize what they loved about the experience—a souvenir, so to speak—perhaps a crystal or rock, so that they can carry a symbol of the experience around with them and touch it or pull it out when they want.

"I don't really understand what happened."

From talking to people who guide psychedelic experiencers, I can share a number of variations on this comment. Right after a session, when asked about their experience, experiencers may say:

- "Whoa! Give me a second. That was weird."

- "Where do I even start?"
- "I get it, but I can't explain it."
- "I feel great…I don't need to talk about it." Or sometimes people are just speechless.

Throughout this book, I will talk about the importance of gentleness and timing of integration. So I would not suggest people should be guided into "talking" or "doing anything" before they are ready, but I would offer that without some eventual cataloging of the experience, be it nonverbal or verbal, they might always be left with "an experience I did not understand." For people in this situation, I would recommend that they find some way, *any way*, to create something tangible to have a way back to the experience. Then follow this lead and just openly see where it goes.

Sometimes, people may have the sense that they do understand what happened after the session, only later to become confused. All of the suggestions noted above continue to apply, but for this issue, I would talk about:

- Did you have an intention or clear purpose before the session that might work as a guidepost after the session?
- Though I believe the person's **own experience** is always the best place to start, this is a situation where reading about maps of consciousness and the possibilities of journeys as written by theorists and other experiencers could be helpful.
- Alternating the type of integration exercises, for instance, shifting from verbal to non-verbal or from writing to movement, etc.

"That had nothing to do with what I was intending."

I have a recollection of a time when I set the intention for a psilocybin experience to explore how I could better understand and manage my professional practice. I was particularly interested in learning how I could balance family and work life. However, in the session, on the surface, there was nothing that looked like direct answers for these questions.

What did my session look like? I ended up crying for most of the session in complete empathy with how much my clients needed me. At first, I was confused at what the medicine was telling me. I was not so much disappointed not to have concrete answers, but I was not sure how to draw a connection between my intention and what happened, if there even was any connection.

This experience helped me understand the importance of integration to try to go back and connect those dots. In this instance, I completed a free association art project, took a walk in nature, had a great conversation with my wife, and started an inner dialogue about how the emotional experience might help clear out something between myself and getting information in a linear way about my intention.

"I'm in an Ayahuasca circle and I meet every month. I love the community, but I don't feel like my life is any different."

I hear a variation on this theme from some medicine circle leaders: "I have some beautiful people who keep coming back, but some of them seem to have the same experience every time and then they keep talking about the same things as problems in their lives, as though nothing is happening in the sessions. I feel like I should do something else to help them."

In Chapter 11, I talk about a situation some facilitators call "looping." Without seeming to judge anyone's experience, if you feel like you keep having the same thing happen in psychedelic journeys, but want something more, then consider creating a conscious integration practice. Consider really working with this book or with others for an intention to integrate. Keep going through the spots where it feels like nothing is happening. And then keep going some more.

This is also a time when you might consider other ways into your experience besides your psychedelic medicine and "setting" of choice. If you have only been going to circles, maybe try an individual session with a guide who will be with *you* only for pre-session preparation, post-session unpacking, and even ongoing integration discussions without journeying.

I also talk later about the value of breathwork (or other modalities focusing on the body) in helping you reach blocked parts of yourself that may need some work other than through psychedelics. Starting with (or going back to) a traditional therapist who is at least sympathetic to psychedelics is an idea. Easy for me to say, but if you really do want to move into transformation, you may need to explore places that hold pain, trauma or grief, and you may need to recognize some things about yourself or others in your life that may be hard to face. The good news: when you are ready, psychedelics can help you look at these places and heal what is there or what has been missing.

"Ever since my husband did mushrooms, he's been so angry."

To begin with, this might be a relationship issue. Within that issue may be a "judging" issue—that is, a judgment that there is something wrong with anger or any negative emotions. On the other hand, I "hear" this spouse as vocalizing genuine concern about what might be *increasing* suffering of her/his husband. Certainly the spouse is worried. There might be a very real problem (or even a potential physical danger) that lurks behind these kinds of experiences that come out of psychedelics.

There is no way I can explore all the possible scenarios and issues that may lie behind this kind of "entryway" into integration work. Later I talk about the sensitive issues that arise when one person in an intimate partnership begins exploring psychedelics. For now, let me suggest that psychedelics invite not just work on yourself, but also work on your relationships, which almost always involves dealing with the family of origin (and ancestral) issues of everyone involved.

Sometimes an experience with psychedelics stirs up something inside us that cannot work itself out on its own. In Chapter 8 I talk about integration and the outer world. Sometimes to continue your inner exploration, you need to engage with important people and circumstances in your outer world.

I work with people in customary marriage and family therapy as well as integration of non-ordinary state experiences. In both these contexts, I use the expression, "Once the toothpaste leaves the container, you can't get it back in." What is now out in the open needs to be processed and integrated.

The invitation here is not just to work with the psychedelic experiences themselves, but to consider the "medicine" to have opened a door into deep psychological, relationship, family systems and ancestral work. Trained therapists of various specialties and group work (for instance, family systems groups) can transform lives.

It is also important to recognize that things often get more difficult before they get easier. I know a guide who shares the story of a psychedelic experiencer (I will call him Tyler) who thought he had resolved an issue of pornography addiction. Tyler wanted a psilocybin session to celebrate a new phase of his life. Only a few weeks after the session, he returned to his guide and said, "Dude, I'm deeper in than ever. I'm using porn all week, increasing my risky behaviors, and fighting all the time with my wife. I think the mushrooms brought it all back."

Some people might reach the conclusion Tyler should have left well enough alone and not tried his psychedelic celebration. Maybe. But I believe there was something left still unresolved in Tyler that was brought back by his psilocybin experience. Integrating the experience, perhaps through continued psychotherapy and other non-verbal techniques, would offer the possibility of working with the energy still calling to him. On the other hand, if Tyler decides he needs to keep the lid on whatever is fueling his addiction and not squeeze out any more toothpaste, I am not going to judge him. I would support him.

"I had a bad trip."

My approach to psychedelics understands we may be venturing into rough surf or standing on top of a mountain in a gale force wind. The potential for an amazing experience calls us forward. But we bow to forces much stronger than ourselves and engage with caution, prudence and humility.

Information from a Global Drug Survey suggests that between 15% and 40% of people who have used LSD or sacred mushrooms report at least one "bad" experience. This usually means an experience involving anxiety, fear, or other challenging emotions. From decades working with 5-MeO-DMT and DMT, Ralph Metzner estimates that "dissociative, psychotic or fear-panic reactions have occurred in about 10% of cases."[47] With these short-acting psychedelics, these reactions lasted only a few minutes.

Metzner's ten percent estimate comes from working with "seasoned adults, mostly with considerable experience with psychedelics, participating in small group settings with conscious intention and careful preparation."[48] He believes bad trips are more likely when psychedelics are used in "haphazard settings such as rave events or parties, with little or no preparation."[49] As I discussed in Chapter 3, attention to Mindset and Setting should help you have productive experiences.

And yet, difficult experiences sometimes open the door to the deepest transformation. Roland Griffiths of Johns Hopkins University surveyed almost two thousand adults about their single worst "bad trip" on psilocybin. The average dose leading to the difficult experience was around four grams. Sixty-two percent of the participants said the bad trip was one of the most difficult psychological experiences of their lives. Eleven percent said it was *the* most difficult experience. And yet thirty-four percent reported the bad trip was in the top five of their most personally meaningful experiences, with thirty-one percent saying it was among the top five of the most spiritually significant experiences of their lives. Seventy-six percent said the bad trip, in the end, increased their sense of well-being and overall life satisfaction. Forty-six percent were willing to experience the bad trip all over again for this reason.[50]

Of course, this is easy to say from a distance and not when you are in a hellish experience. I also know a good number of people who still have a form of post-traumatic stress from bad trips. Some do not want to re-traumatize themselves by exploring the experience, though some do have breakthroughs when they attempt to integrate what happened.

In navigating hard experiences, I believe it helps to have developed an observer consciousness through meditation, breathwork, or focused attention on working on yourself. This gives you practice witnessing your experiences with the capacity for some separation between a safe part of yourself and hard experiences. If you know "this is just an experience I am having," then even "bad" experiences can help you move through energies that present themselves for experience—and quite possibly release things inside yourself that are ready to be released.

During a psychedelic experience, sometimes it is possible to notice "fear" or "dread" or even "terror" as what seems like a presence, an opening, or an area of "inner space" in a physical-psychological sense. You may be able to make a choice not to be pulled into that area, to willfully move toward something else, or simply to allow yourself to hover close enough to the energy to modulate how it teaches or feels, but without becoming overwhelmed or lost. This might feel more like a directional movement or physical orientation of your will or awareness than a thought in the head.

Staying centered in your witness consciousness might help. It might be like becoming familiar with a dangerous animal from a safe distance, encountering the animal energetically for learning without coming too close. Again, this is easy for us to say, but not always possible. This technique may not have any application with fast-acting psychedelics such as DMT, though a general invocation to stand with the sacred in all forms before the session may not hurt.

In *The Toad and the Jaguar*, Metzner shares a poem he wrote about an experience with 5-MeO-DMT, also recorded in his *Spirit Soundings*. One stanza speaks perfectly to this experience:

> You are seeking the pearls
> Of golden energy-essence,
> Guarded by the dragon...
> That dragon's name is
> *Pain-fear-threat-scream.*
> Speak softly to that dragon,
> Or sing to him soothingly, like Orpheus.
> Then, you may take the precious pearls
> From his frightful, flaming jaws. [51]

Of course, sometimes all you can do with a bad experience is to see it through. Having someone there to hold your hand, hug you, or sit near you can make all the difference. But it is important for these people to follow your lead and not intrude in ways to make the experience worse. Some people are only too happy to offer too much comfort, which brings in their own needs to be needed or to comfort. That kind of overlay can do more harm than good.

After a bad trip, you have the choice whether (and how) to work with it. I draw an analogy to working with dreams. Even nightmares bring information. Dream worker Jeremy Taylor shares the following:

> All dreams speak a universal language and come in the service of health and wholeness. There is no such thing as a "bad dream"—only dreams that sometimes take a dramatically negative form in order to grab our attention. [52]

But this is where integration is crucial. If you are left only with the visceral memory of fear, it is hard to find the learning. Slowly, with integration, you might move closer toward the "dangerous animal" with safe steps that bring the wisdom into your body, mind and spirit. Again, it helps to choose some small pieces of the experience as ways to enter back into what was there. A guide or therapist can help.

Even years later, reaching back towards a "bad trip" for integration can be a truly healing experience. A difficult journey may be an invitation to explore the deepest part of ourselves, where the gems for transformation lay hidden. Returning to the dream analogy, one of my friend's nightmares from childhood continues decades later to provide entry points into the depths of his instincts and vital life forces.

There is also the reality that difficult journeys sometimes involve negativity coming from other people and the setting around us. Please do not take this comment as permission to blame other people for your experiences—that could be a terrible form of projection. However, in your integration, particularly with a trained integration therapist, you might explore the setting in which you had a difficult journey. Integrating this reality can help you learn about your relationships and where you invest your energy, as well as about what is inside you. It is possible that someone else's energy impacted you—even possible that somehow you carried or processed it for them.

Metzner writes about difficulties that may come from negative spiritual energies that somehow gravitate to us. This is the realm of shamans from indigenous cultures and beyond our personal experience, but may be worthy of consideration even in contemporary cultures.[53] Hundreds of people are now participating in Ayahuasca ceremonies either in their home country or in another country through "Ayahuasca tourism." Many leaders of Ayahuasca rituals are deeply spiritual people capable of keeping participants as safe as possible. But some have their own issues of power or various forms of negativity. Anthropological readings can inform you about centuries-old traditions of using negative energies in such settings. While I hesitate to seem like I know this terrain, I do hold it as very real—and potentially related to bad trips.

Integrating what happened in "bad experiences" involving other people is much like working through any type of trauma, but even more complicated because of the psychedelic. It can be very important to provide space for integration of these experiences.

"Now that I know what this is, if I do it again, I want to be sure I'm doing it right."

I would not want to say there is any one "right" way to do anything in life. On the other hand, there are ways to do things that have more safety, more authenticity, or more service of your health and wholeness than some other possibilities. When I hear people say something like "I want to be sure I'm doing it right," I hear an urge to make the most out of their psychedelic experiences. I hear someone who has realized the potential of the work, even if they do not yet understand exactly what that potential may be for them personally or for the world. I may also hear someone who puts a lot of pressure on themselves. All these things can be unpacked through integration—including integration of "where you are" and "what you want" before you decide to embark on a psychedelic session.

I have heard people want reassurance about *how* they are using psychedelics. Some of the reassurance is kind of nuts and bolts—ideas for what is out there and what is possible and what to avoid. If this is you, I hope this book can answer some of your questions, point you in helpful directions, and most of all, give you confidence to believe in yourself.

"I'm on a Spiritual Path."

Many people come to psychedelics hoping for a mystical experience, a sense of God/Goddess, oneness, unity, the Universe, connection with past lives, experience of the place between lives, or many other aspects of spiritual realities. On the one hand, I want to say, "Well, you came to the right place." On the other hand, I return to the question of bringing a specific intention, desire, or need to a session versus being open to whatever comes—or whatever your inner healer may bring to you. Mystical experiences, even with psychedelics, tend to be a matter of grace and not within our grasp. More importantly, sudden blasts of God experience may provide ecstasy and change lives, but very often *then the real work begins.*

What is this real work? That might be the work of feeling into all your wounds, defenses, projections, needs, past wrongs, grudges, relationship issues, unconscious legacies of family lineage, aspirations, hopes, and dreams. You might also be called to become responsible in a new way for what is going on in your community, your country, the world—not to mention what has been happening to nature over the past several decades.

God forbid, but you may have to change your mind about a lot of things. You may be called upon to alter your behavior, to work with your ways of thinking and feeling, even to give up things (or people) you love for your (or their) greater good and wholeness. All kinds of things may happen.

Without doing the hard work that "God experiences" may offer, we run the risk of what is called Spiritual Bypassing. Integral psychotherapist Robert Augustus Masters explains:

> Spiritual bypassing, a term first coined by psychologist John Welwood in 1984, is the use of spiritual practices and beliefs to avoid dealing with our painful feelings, unresolved wounds, and developmental needs. It is much

more common than we might think and, in fact, so pervasive as to go largely unnoticed, except in its more obvious extremes.[54]

Masters believes spiritual bypassing is common because our culture prefers "pain-numbing" solutions to facing and working through our pain. He writes:

> Because this preference has so deeply and thoroughly infiltrated our culture that it has become all but normalized, spiritual bypassing fits almost seamlessly into our collective habit of turning away from what is painful, as a kind of higher analgesic with seemingly minimal side effects. It is a spiritualized strategy for not only avoiding pain but also for legitimizing such avoidance, in ways ranging from the blatantly obvious to the extremely subtle.[55]

Masters describes spiritual bypassing as a "very persistent shadow of spirituality." I talk throughout this book about the hazard of using psychedelics to avoid rather than face problems and needs. I talk about shadow issues in Chapter 9 and Addiction issues in Chapter 10. While we are one with everyone coming to psychedelics hoping to experience God, I do hope you will use those experiences as energy for transformation, as well as solace, more than ways to avoid facing what may be missing or hurting or pressing for development.

Very often an experience of God provides the energy and commitment needed to make real changes in your own life and in the world around you. After the God experiences, the work may begin when you try to bring what you have experienced into your daily life, particularly if you want to be open (at least to some degree) to others about what you have experienced.

Importantly, there is also a big difference between spiritual experience in non-ordinary states and finding a way to live moment-to-moment with a sense of the sacred. The God experiences help to understand what a sense of the sacred even feels like—for there are few examples in our culture, this being one of the places organized religions typically fail most of us. It is usually a slow and steady process to be able to live within the sacred.

Integration is about all these things.

"I'm in therapy, but I don't talk about this kind of thing."

As I have already shared, I wrote my master's thesis on the value of talk therapy for integrating experiences from non-ordinary states of consciousness. Using psychedelics gets really interesting when you are able to explore particular insights, feelings, memories, fantasies, fears, images and hopes that come up in non-ordinary states. As I suggested above, the major openings with psychedelics often just *start* the work.

Talk therapy can be extremely valuable, but you need a therapist whose view of the mind (and the universe) is open to working with your experiences. Unfortunately, many therapists do not have this kind of openness to psychedelics. Fortunately, there are more and more therapists—or guides, counselors, etc.—who do hold the framework that can help you unpack your experiences and follow your path.

For working on your own, the exercises in this book are designed to help with post- and pre-session exploration. In the next chapter, I will share some of the most useful "maps of consciousness" to frame understanding of the depths of the unconscious. While the work is *always* something you must do personally, it can really help to have a trained integration therapist walk the path with you. Your work with the right therapist is integration work.

"My friend is a military veteran with PTSD. Now he is also an alcoholic. I heard psilocybin or ketamine could help. Is this true?"

Under the right circumstances, with appropriate guidance, psychedelics can help with recovery from addiction and treatment-resistant psychological challenges. Here I enter the realm of the lawful research studies and the promise of legal psychedelics therapy beginning in some clinics right now and, if things keep going well, in many clinics in the next several years.

I sincerely hope the veteran mentioned in this quote will be able to get help through psychedelics therapy—if that is his or her choice—now or very soon. The terrible plight of such service people may have helped the United States government finally lift the ban on research and treatment involving psychedelics. For years, the United States Department of Veterans Affairs has reported that an average of twenty veterans commit suicide every day.[56] Beginning in 2012, suicide outranked war, cancer, heart disease, homicide, transportation accidents, and other causes as the leading cause of military deaths.[57]

In answer to this person, I might suggest their friend explore the possibility of treatment with MDMA, as that may be the easier course both for legal and treatment reasons. Some of the initial FDA-approved research has involved using MDMA in connection with supportive therapy for treatment-resistant post-traumatic stress disorder. The projects undertaking treatment of PTSD with MDMA take advantage of the heart-opening properties of this empathogen.

As I note elsewhere, MDMA seems to allow many people to face experiences with love and compassion and to begin to process the emotions that may be locked in the body, often including grief. To state the obvious, many service people have experienced horrendous situations overseas and/or lost faith in systems they previously thought they understood and supported. The toll taken on marriages, families and friendships by military service is well known and tragic.

As mentioned previously, ketamine is a substance that has never been completely prohibited. Some professionals with the ability to prescribe ketamine offer treatments for psychological conditions (such as depression) with ketamine. Research suggests ketamine can be very effective in the short-term relief of severe and treatment-resistant depression, with quick onset and lasting at least a few days. [58] From anecdotal reports, I am not as sure about long-lasting effects, but I am sure that ongoing integrative therapy is almost certainly necessary for any lasting recovery. For our military veteran friend, I would probably suggest looking first toward MDMA treatment, then toward psilocybin or other medicines under strict professional support.

"I just use shrooms (or acid) (or "Molly") for fun."

Cool, as long as you're keeping safe. And, just for fun, you might try some of the exercises in this book. And, remember, we're still in a culture where this is not legal, so be mindful.

"My girlfriend discovered psychedelics and is tripping every weekend. I feel like I'm losing her."

I hear you!

I have come across people who have used psychedelics hundreds of times and continue using at a brisk pace. I am not in the business of judging anyone's private choices, but I understand the concern that family and friends may have about someone's frequent use of psychedelics.

If you are the partner concerned about your girlfriend's frequent use, you might be "right" in some sense. However, you might also consider trying to "hold space" for better understanding that this is *her* journey. And, you might leave a copy of *The Psychedelics Integration Handbook* in an obvious place in your house. And finally, it is possible that some relationship work with a couples and family therapist might help you uncover what is underlying *both* of your situations.

Back to the concern about "tripping every weekend." Psychedelics do not seem to be physically addicting like alcohol, amphetamines, opiates, or some other drugs. But using psychedelics can be emotionally addicting. I mentioned spiritual bypassing a few pages back. Repeated use of psychedelics without integration could actually help you avoid the psychological or spiritual work you might be thinking has drawn you to psychedelics. Such repeated use could help you avoid issues in your life or relationships and might be easier than changing things in your actual life that need to change.

"Once I started integrating psychedelic experiences, it all started to get real."

Another way of describing integration, more metaphorical, comes from another thought I tumble around and offer this: anyone can go into an Ayahuasca ceremony, drink the tea, and spend the night throwing up and having visions of jaguars; or do the "heroic" dose of five grams of psilocybin and meet some aliens; or even go to a festival and trip out on Ecstasy or LSD and dance the day away.

But, to me, this may be like having sex—cool, but there may be more to the story. Integration in our minds is similar to becoming a mother or father after enjoying the sexual experience. That's when you really start taking responsibility for the consequences of your actions, and raising the "infant" that comes out of your experience.

One more metaphor I have: if psychedelic experience is looked at like an algebraic equation, then integration is the "x" in the equation. You need to *solve* for it. You need to figure out what is that "x" in the context of everything else in the equation of your life, your past, your present, and your future.

All this said (about integration), I want to make clear that I am talking about integrating your experiences into *your* life, not into others' lives or into someone else's idea about what your life should be.

Now your turn

What questions do you have about using psychedelics?
_____
_____
_____
_____
_____

What questions do you have about integration?
_____
_____
_____
_____
_____

Integration Exercise 4: Mandala Spirit Collage

What You Need

- Collection of images (e.g., stacks of *National Geographic* magazines)
- Glue sticks
- Large white paper (20 x 20 or larger)
- Scissors
- Pencil
- Sharpie markers
- Large circle dinner plate
- Your journal.

General Background

This experience is to connect with the archetype Carl Jung has called the "Collective Unconscious." It brings forth the ability to tie your experience into tangible images. You can create a Mandala Spirit collage whenever you are moved to the process—for instance, at this point in your work with this book, just to see how you are connecting with what you are reading and learning.

Creating a collage is particularly powerful for beginning to integrate non-ordinary state journeys. Throughout our psychedelic sessions there are a great deal of emotions and non-tangible visuals, as well as a kaleidoscope of images at a rapid pace. The mandala spirit collage is designed to integrate the journey into images that illuminate and create the story of your experience.

- If you're by yourself, set up your space prior to your journey.
- If you're working with a sitter/guide, ask them to set up the materials for you away from your session environment.
- This exercise is to be done immediately after or within three hours after the psychedelic session. The closer to the completion of your psychedelic session, the more vivid and capable you will be to translate your experience.

Why this Exercise is Important for Psychedelics Integration

I will start to focus more and more on the actual process of integration. This involves drawing from inside all the parts of yourself that have been touched by your experience and finding a way to manifest them in the external world. Because the unconscious speaks to us primarily through images, looking through magazines rich with images from all parts of the world allows your unconscious to call out, "That resonates!" You may not have been able to come up with the image until you see it, but when you see it, you know.

If you are using magazines with many images from nature, from geography, from different cultures, you give your unconscious a chance to resonate with memories from our human past—and maybe from past lives you may have lived. You allow yourself to connect with specific images from nature that will help you to feel more part of nature—which is one of the trajectories that seem to come from non-ordinary state experiences. Most importantly, you will **create** something from your journey that you can tangibly hold onto and **know that your journey happened.**

How To Do It

Preparation in advance

1. Prior to the session, have your table prepared with collage material.
2. Taking the large dinner plate, outline a circle with the pencil.
3. Place all the magazines and pictures in order on the table with the glue stick next to the paper.

Instructions for the exercise (Time: Individually determined)

- When you are ready and feeling comfortable with your surroundings, find your way to the collage table.
- Take a moment to reflect on your experience. Focus on a non-judgmental mindset regarding the project.
- Look through your magazine and just let your eyes, heart, and soul feel into what you are seeing. You may *know* immediately upon seeing an image that you need to use it. Or you may pass some by and then come back to them later.
- Start to gather images that you are drawn to.
- Organize images in a way that is organic to you.
- Start to place images in the mandala circle. Don't limit yourself to the initial place of the image. Play with the placement of your images.
- When you have found comfort in the final placement of your images, start to glue the images down.

The completion of this exercise is when you feel it is done. Many times I have started a mandala only to walk away from it for hours or even days. The most important part of the exercise is tapping into your experience and intuitive process.

Creating a spirit mandala is one way of beginning to notice the different parts or channels within you that may be calling for expression in an external sense. As you work with each of the images you are called to include in your collage, I invite you to notice where this image touches inside yourself.

CHAPTER 5

INTRODUCING MAPS OF CONSCIOUSNESS

Why use Maps of Consciousness?

Psychedelics can take us into places where there is no orientation. Maps help us know where we are and where we might be going. When we come back, we may have a framework (some words or concepts) to help us hold onto where we have been and talk about our journey with other people.

When maps are shared by groups of people, talking about experiences in terms of the maps can help develop community. New maps may even develop once the basic contours of the old maps are understood by a group of people. New places may be found within the maps. With maps, cultures can transform.

And yet, when I use maps, I need to be careful I do not force experience into maps. Then I may miss the novelty of the experience and may lose its point.

Here are several maps I find useful. Some may be familiar to you. Some maps are associated with the people who created them. Others are more generally cultural or scientific. The maps are not necessarily about psychedelic journeys, but they are about the psyche, which is opened through journey. These maps of the psyche may help you make sense of your psychedelic journey as one stop along the way of an ongoing journey of consciousness.

Most importantly, as you integrate your journeys into your life—and begin to follow an unfolding process—the maps may help you orient yourself, understand conflicts, blocks and obstacles, and keep moving toward wholeness.

Sigmund Freud (1856-1939)

The man with the cigar. The father of psychoanalysis, Freud is known for "discovering" the unconscious. If you look back through history, you will find that many other people have known things similar to what Freud described, but he brought these ideas into the modern Western world. He did this just as science was replacing religion as the main description of reality for many people. So his theories were right on time and stuck.

Sigmund Freud

Freud's description of the unconscious, boiled down to basics, says that what we think and know consciously is just the tip of an enormous iceberg. Much of the time, we are thinking, feeling, and acting based on motivation that is outside our conscious awareness.

A good modern atheist, Freud believed our consciousness (and our unconsciousness) comes only from the experiences we have had since birth. Freud saw the trajectory of our life as beginning with a blank slate (the famous "tabula rasa"). In other words, he did not believe in a soul that brings into life information or problems that are continuing to be worked on. This is a significant difference between the map Freud offers and some other maps important in psychedelic work.

Importantly, Freud did not believe we are able to remember our actual birth. But he thought infancy and early childhood were extremely important in shaping who we become. For Freud, many experiences that have a large psychological "charge" are repressed along the way as we grow up. These experiences sink down into the unconscious, but may cause psychological problems or influence our behaviors, emotions and thoughts.

This is important for working with psychedelics because repressed experiences often resurface during work in non-ordinary states. For example, if you had an experience as a child that was terrifying, but that you could not fully process at the time, that experience might come back to you in psychedelic work as a chance to move through whatever happened.

Another important part of Freud's map involves stages of development. Freud thought psychological problems could be traced back to stages we did not fully complete when growing up. The basic stages are oral, anal, phallic, latency, and genital. The well-known Oedipal Conflict proposes that males reach a stage when they desire their mothers and want to kill their fathers. The corollary, the Electra Complex (a term actually invented by Carl Gustav Jung), proposes that daughters desire their fathers and become jealous of their mothers.

Freud believed we all have very strong impulses towards sex, aggression, and even death, but have difficulty facing and feeling these instincts. He wrote about a life instinct (Eros) expressed through sexuality and a death instinct (Thanatos) expressed through aggression and urges toward destruction. When the energy of these instincts (the life energy is called *libido*) cannot flow freely, strong unconscious forces may turn inwards against ourselves (for instance, depression) or may twist into strange thoughts or behaviors directed outwardly.

While these energies are instinctual (part of our bodies and evolutionary heritage), Freud believed we internalize limitations and rules from our culture. In other words, civilization has developed ways to stop the reckless acting out of sexual and aggressive instincts. These internalized rules put the brakes on our instinctual urges.

You can see the conflicts that develop inside us. One part wants to move toward something with huge energy; another part holds us back. All of this takes place mostly outside our conscious awareness. Freud also described a third part of the psyche, which mediates the conflict between these other parts.

Freud's basic "model of the psyche" involved these three elements:

- the *Id* (our instincts, including aggression and raw sexuality)
- the *Super-ego* (the restraining internal police officer who enforces the rules of society we have been taught)
- and the *Ego* (the part that seems like "me" and navigates between the Id and Superego).

A basic idea of psychoanalysis is that repressed instincts, desires and conflicts linger in the unconscious, later causing neurosis or psychosis. Add the unresolved energies of the stages of development and you get the stormy seas of the unconscious. Freud's psychoanalysis had a goal of getting people back to these experiences so they could consciously work with them. For many people, it seems absurd to think that children have the feelings Freud described or that we necessarily move through the strange stages in his theory. It may also seem crazy to think we are all walking sex fiends and murderers. Freud would say that our tendency to question these ideas involves our denial and repression of instinctual but forbidden feelings.

Once you venture into this "taboo" terrain, you might see that repressed instincts are a hidden but very rich part of the psyche. It is interesting to note that Jim Morrison, one of the cultural icons raising consciousness about psychedelics, wrote a song called "The End." While under the influence of LSD, Morrison envisioned a narrative feeling through the dynamics of the Oedipal conflict in graphic terms. I suspect he had experienced the power of reaching into forbidden terrains of the psyche while experiencing LSD. The reason for knowing these dynamics is that if they come to you, you may be able to accept them and allow them just to be, rather than fight against them.

Many feelings come during psychedelic experiences that appear only vaguely or through images. If you understand that sexual and violent instincts may be repressed in the psyche, you may be able to reach behind strange images and find instinctual energies that can actually help free you.

> Out of your vulnerabilities will come your strengths.
>
> —Sigmund Freud

It also seems to be true that early experiences involving sexuality or violence are often repressed, but may resurface during non-ordinary states. This can involve violations of you that occurred and are not remembered consciously—or even feelings you had that were repressed as "wrong." Such experiences do not resurface to hurt you, but in order to help you heal.

Knowing some of the possibilities of how the psyche works, even if it all seems strange, can help you make sense of what might appear for you. While you might not want to go immediately into "story" or diagnosing yourself, you might be able to make sense of certain things in order to process them.

In the Freudian map, it is the **energy** of these hidden instincts that is important to allow into your life. Part of Freud's genius was that he realized that bringing these stages and conflicts into conscious awareness could help resolve psychological issues and free psychic energy, or "libido." The reason for freeing libido was to live a more satisfying life, which Freud thought involved "love and work… work and love, that's all there is."

One of the main techniques used by Freud in psychoanalysis was dream interpretation. He understood the importance of dream symbols in helping us uncover what was unknown in the unconscious. Oftentimes, characters in our non-ordinary state experiences (just like in our dreams) may be carrying the energies of parts of our psyche, sometimes playing out conflicts. While Freud worked with words, I recommend in our exercises many techniques for letting the energies carried by symbols to come out of the unconscious (through art or movement, for example) and act as a bridge to awareness.

How does Freud help understand experiences in psychedelics?

It may help to understand that some of the experiences we have in psychedelics:

- Are bringing back into view unresolved conflicts or stages from other times in our life, including early childhood.
- Appear to us through symbols (maybe even disguises) rather than as literal memories.
- Involve different parts of us arguing or battling it out with each other (and sometimes only one of the combatants appears in a session).

In the 1950s and 1960s, many psychiatrists were so excited about the possibilities of LSD-25 because the drug lifted repressions against remembering and feeling the sorts of memories (and feelings) that Freud found so important. These memories and feelings are important because they may still be running around in the unconscious and sapping psychic energy from us—energy that could be used for living a more fulfilling life.

Carl Gustav Jung (1875-1961)

Considered the grandfather of transpersonal psychology, Jung was a Swiss psychiatrist, originally a protégé of Freud. Unlike his erstwhile mentor, Jung believed there was more to the human unconscious than our animal instincts and what we repress.

Of huge significance for working in non-ordinary states of consciousness, Jung described the *collective unconscious*, an area of the psyche common to all humans. The collective unconscious "contains the whole spiritual heritage of mankind's evolution, born anew in the brain structure of every individual."[59] Jung understood the collective unconscious as holding all of the "mythological motifs or primordial images, for which reason the myths of all nations are its real exponents."[60] In other words, if we bring our awareness deep inside our individual psyche, we enter a place common to all humanity, where we can encounter spiritual realities that are expressed in myths and religions from all over the world.

Carl Gustav Jung

Living within the collective unconscious are the symbols, complexes, and archetypes from all human cultures back through our history and pre-history. I will define each of these words in Jungian terms:

- A **symbol** is something that comes from the unconscious (often the collective unconscious) with a charge that we cannot completely explain in a linear or analytical way. A symbol carries a sense of mystery and can never be completely nailed down with the rational mind. Symbols must be experienced, feeling their power and the emotions and associations they bring up. They must be lived, held closely, and experienced over time.
- A **complex** is an association of emotions, memories, ideas, and desires that are not conscious but influence our behaviors, reactions, and emotional charges around what happens in our lives. If we are "acting out" of a complex, we may not make sense to other people, but we usually feel righteous, at least at the moment. If we are "in" a complex, we may be in a "blind spot." A stereotypical example is an "inferiority complex," where someone might unconsciously feel less worthy than others and act in ways to compensate or prove his worth.
- **Archetypes** are patterns of experience that guide the trajectories of our lives, sometimes taking form as powerful people, gods or demons, or forces of nature, or stages of life, or ways of behaving. Archetypes take shape for us individually but draw their energy from the collective unconscious, resonating far beyond our own lives, often reverberating within myths and spiritual themes. It is important to understand archetypes as patterns acting through our lives and perceptions, not static people or events.

To my knowledge, Jung did not himself work with psychedelics. But he ventured deeply into his own unconscious in ways that feel very similar to non-ordinary state journeys. In a sense, we could say that Jung found ways to open the doors of perception into the unconscious without medicine allies. One of his biographers, Sonu Shamdasani, wrote that Jung intentionally immersed himself in fantasy states, bordering on what could be described as psychosis, to allow his unconscious to come forward. Shamdasani compared Jung's method with "taking mescaline."

Many of Jung's images and writings from such journeys appear in a beautiful journal published in 2009 known as *The Red Book*. Taking a look at this book will give you examples of creative ways to work with the images and narratives that come out of non-ordinary states. Interestingly, Jung drew a figure that acted as a guide for him, whom he named Philemon. Responding to a letter from someone asking about this figure, Jung said Philemon was "only myself," but then wrote: "Philemon (= kiss), the loving one, the simple old loving couple, close to the Earth and aware of the Gods, the complete opposite to the Superman Faust, the product of the devil." Finding a guide living within your psyche can be a powerful help for people in non-ordinary state work.

Jung developed a process called **active imagination.** This is a meditative technique that is very useful for integration work. You allow images, narratives, or figures to come into awareness as though they are emerging from the deepest parts of yourself. Trying to let your conscious mind rest, you watch what develops as though you are seeing something unfold separately from you. You put your attention into what seems to hold deep resonance or meaning, even if you do not understand rationally what this may be.

Jung considered active imagination to work as a bridge between the unconscious and conscious parts of your mind. You might start with an image from a dream, a memory, or a significant occurrence in a psychedelic journey. You can start with anything, including a feeling or a hunch or something that feels just beyond awareness. Jung seemed to sense a way of "falling back" and allowing these experiences to emerge. But he thought it was important to treat them as real.

Active imagination is a useful way to bridge from mysterious or unformed parts of your psychedelics journey into journaling, drawing, painting, or moving. Then you may find yourself with internal companions, like Philemon, who seem to emerge as ongoing guides to your process. What you produce may also be important if you are working with an integration guide or therapist, who can help you process even further from what you have brought forward.

Jung also drew attention to experiences of **synchronicity**. These are meaningful coincidences that feel as though fate is involved, with a "numinous" charge. (You hear the word "numinous" in ordinary state work; this means, "having a strong spiritual quality," "a presence of divinity," "a nod from the divine.") Synchronicities seem to pull us forward into the way our life is supposed to unfold, validating our path.

A famous story from Jung about synchronicity involves a patient in analysis with him. The patient was locked in a rational view of the world, not believing in spirituality or the more magical side of life. She was telling Jung about a dream involving a scarab, a species of beetle carrying spiritual significance in ancient Egypt and other cultures.

While Jung's patient was in the midst of her rational interpretation of the dream, a bug began knocking on the window next to Jung. He opened the window and found an insect very close in appearance to the scarab, as close as you could come in Switzerland. This was a rare occurrence. Jung grabbed the insect and showed it to his patient, saying, "Here is your scarab." Realizing there was no way to rationally explain how this could have happened in a material-only world, her "defense" of rationality melted.

Jung described a model of the psyche vaster than what Freud imagined. I believe this is because he included the reality of guidance from spiritual sources. In Jungian psychology, we have:

- The *persona*, that part of us I show to the world—a mask, to some extent.
- The *ego*, similar to what Freud understood, the part of us navigating our life.
- The *personal unconscious*, similar to Freud's unconscious, containing those parts of ourselves that are forgotten or repressed.
- The *shadow*, holding those forgotten or repressed elements as well as instincts that I may not fully live due to social constraints or our own personalities (e.g., sex, aggression).
- The *collective unconscious*, which we can reach "beyond" our personal unconscious, where the archetypes live, containing the collective shadow.
- The *anima* or *animus*, feminine or masculine figures that help us reach loving and transformational energies (watch for them in dreams and active imagination).
- The *Self*, an archetype, but related to us individually—a God image that awakens and pulls us toward our highest self and most fulfilling life.

For Jung, the process of psychological growth involved separating out from the unconscious masses and finding your own true path. He called this process **individuation**. In a lecture, he described individuation as "the psychological process that makes of a human being an *individual*—a indivisible unit or whole man."

In one of his writings, he asked the question: "What is it, in the end, that induces a man to go his own way and to rise out of unconscious identity with the mass as out of a swathing mist?"

His answer: "It is what is commonly called vocation: an irrational factor that destines a man to emancipate himself from the herd and from its well-worn paths .... Anyone with a vocation hears the voice of the inner man: he is called." [61]

In many ways, Jung's process of individuation is very similar to what I am calling integration. Jung saw the process as gradually incorporating into your conscious sense of yourself what was pressing into awareness from your personal unconscious, from the collective unconscious, and from archetypal realms. Individuation essentially integrates your shadow and complexes into consciousness, making you a more mature and responsible individual.

Bringing into yourself elements of the collective unconscious and the timeless transpersonal realms aligns you with our ancient heritage and the possibilities for our collective future. Since psychedelics tend to show you these same elements, the integration of what comes from psychedelics is essentially an individuation process.

How does Jung help us with psychedelics?

In any experience of non-ordinary consciousness, we have access to a realm that is beyond our personal selves, where archetypal energies live. Sometimes they show themselves to us or reach out to us. The images and experiences that come to us in psychedelics may take the form of any of the archetypes that have arisen in any of the cultures of the world from the beginning of time. Jung teaches us that these images and experiences may hold energies of our personal complexes—things for us to work out and through—or may take the form of mysterious and mystical figures that pull us toward our highest and most whole selves.

Jung suggested, and I have found to be true, that when you make the effort to bring consciousness to what appears to you in non-ordinary states, when you try to understand your issues and let go of them, when you truly accept the mystery from the "other side," synchronicities tend to emerge to help pull you forward. New people may come your way to help you. Books may fall off the shelf to give you information you need. A song with perfect lyrics may come on the radio just as you acknowledge to yourself the work you have to do. In other words, when working with non-ordinary states of consciousness, be ready for surprising coincidences, and be ready to integrate their meaning, helping them stay with you and take you into the next step of your life journey.

Stanislav Grof (b. 1931)

In earlier chapters, I introduced Stan Grof as one of the founders of transpersonal psychology and a leading early psychedelics researcher. From working with thousands of people in psychedelic or breathwork sessions, Grof developed a **cartography of the psyche** to describe the types of experiences people tend to have in non-ordinary states. His four categories can also be envisioned as the "source" of experiences:

- *Sensory experience*, in the past described by Grof as a "sensory barrier."
- *Biographical experience*, or the "recollective-biographical," including conscious memories that may not have been completely processed.
- *Perinatal experience,* involving the imprint and recollection of experiences in the mother's womb and through the stages of the birth process.
- *Transpersonal experience*, including what Jung described as the collective unconscious and all sources beyond the individual self, including archetypes, myths, gods and goddesses, nature, past life experiences, etc.

Later in his work, Grof focused less on sensory experience than on the biographical, perinatal and transpersonal. These layers typically provide sources of meaning with clearer psychological implications. I believe recognizing the sensory layer of experience in non-ordinary states is helpful because sensory experiences are often the beginning point of entry into psychedelic realms. In addition, processing what may be stored in the body or in energetic levels often begins through the sensory levels.

Sensory experiences themselves can be amazing entry points for integration, and they may also function as places that transition into other experiences with conscious attention. This brings me back to the idea that sensory experiences are sometimes a barrier to moving more deeply into the unconscious. In my experience, sometimes it can be useful in psychedelics work to "look beyond" what initially feels only like sensory experience.

Grof's description of the **Basic Perinatal Matrices** (BPMs) represents a unique contribution to psychology. He describes four stages of birth:

- *BPM I*, the oceanic experience of being in the mother's womb, ideally a peaceful sense of being "whole" and provided for without effort, but sometimes an experience of a "toxic womb" through impact of physical or emotional intrusion into the experience (e.g., drug use, smoking, difficult emotional states of the mother or those around her).
- *BPM II*, a difficult and seemingly endless "no exit" experience when contractions have begun but the mother's cervix has not yet opened, involving the sense of pressure that cannot be solved or avoided, sometimes corresponding to depression.
- *BPM III*, when the cervix has opened and the baby struggles to be born, seemingly a life-or-death battle, involving high arousal, corresponding to sexual and aggressive feelings.
- *BPM IV*, the release of being born into a new life, a liberating and often euphoric experience.

Grof observed that perinatal experiences often open into transpersonal experiences, acting as a bridge into realms beyond the personal. Given this possibility, when perinatal experiences emerge during non-ordinary states of consciousness, processing through these experiences can lead to deep insights and healing. Returning to the remembered felt-sense of these states during integration work can open doors for continued insights, spiritual awakening, and psychological healing.

> The human psyche shows that each individual is an extension of all existence.
> —Stanislav Grof

Over more than half a century, Grof worked extensively with people experiencing non-ordinary states of consciousness. Because experiencing a non-ordinary state involves **the entire body**, Grof's base of experience went further than Freud's or Jung's. These great predecessors worked deeply with the unconscious, but not much with the embodied processes that emerge when the unconscious is activated through non-ordinary states.

The map of the psyche described by Grof thus understands that a healing process may emerge in many different ways. For instance, in addition to memories or insights, strong emotions may surface (often grief or rage), or body movements or positions may enact themselves without conscious will of the experiencer. Often these look like what I see in yoga or other embodied spiritual practices, suggesting that the healing process finds the precise movements or postures for processing what is emerging, spontaneously repeating the discoveries of ancient masters. In Chapter 6, I will discuss channels of integration, encouraging you to bring together many different ways of experiencing and processing into your integration journey.

In the history of transpersonal psychology, different terms have been used for what I am calling non-ordinary states of consciousness. First these were called altered states of consciousness, but then we realized that many of these states are actually quite normal to the human condition. *Altered* suggested that there was something changed for the worse, which is not always true. Still, there are some states of consciousness that result from problems with brain functioning, or "drunkenness," that are not particularly healthy states.

As I introduced in the first chapter, Grof coined the word **holotropic** from the Greek words *holos* (meaning whole) and *trepein* (meaning movement towards). When applied to states of consciousness, holotropic indicates a non-ordinary state that offers assistances in moving towards wholeness. "Holotropic states of consciousness" is actually better than non-ordinary states because it does not carry the baggage of "not being ordinary." Nevertheless, I use both non-ordinary and holotropic in the book.

Grof used the term **inner healing mechanism** to describe a part of us that seems to bring forward experiences in non-ordinary states that help us move toward wholeness. Others have used a shorthand term, **inner healer**, which many people find easier. For some people, it seems useful to personify that part of us offering healing. My experience has been that different people imagine the inner healer in different ways. For instance, you might be most comfortable thinking about a psychological process, or you may feel that God or spirit is sending experiences to you in order to help you.

Depending on the psychedelic you are experiencing, the culture of that medicine may involve an understanding of the healing source, for instance, as Grandmother Ayahuasca or Grandfather San Pedro. Many medicine workers understand the healing source as the plant itself. This is based on their experience of a deep intelligence within specific plant species. Many books about specific psychedelics can help you learn more about the intelligence of particular plant medicines.

Similar to the complexes described by Jung, Grof talks about **COEXs**, or systems of condensed experiences. This is his way of bringing attention to the fact that people tend to have emotional wounds, psychological issues, or places of learning and challenge that seem to group themselves around particular themes. To understand COEXs, you need to remember that the body-mind-spirit unfolds within an embodied life process pulling from all levels of experience and manifesting through many different channels.

For instance, you may have a life theme of being unable to speak your truth and feeling frozen in the face of injustice or burden. If this is one of your COEXs, during a non-ordinary state, you may:

- Remember incidents in life when you were unfairly accused of something and were not able to respond.
- Feel yourself stuck in the womb with pressure all around you and unable to move (or without the memory, find yourself in a non-ordinary state putting pillows all around you and asking people to push against you).
- Experience yourself as Jesus on the cross being abandoned by God and killed by people you tried to help, perhaps even lingering without being able to die.
- Recall a past life when you were hanged based on false accusations and sense that you are not quite able to get to the point where your neck breaks.
- Find yourself feeling as though you are choking during your non-ordinary state and grabbing your neck as though you need to put pressure there.
- Start weeping endlessly about injustice all around you in the world, all the people who are not treated fairly and need help and cannot get it.
- Or any number of other possibilities.

As you can see, a COEX may emerge through various images, symbols, memories, stories, or expressions of emotion or movement, and may switch back and forth between expressions. Like complexes, if COEXs are not resolved, they tend to pull experiences toward you in life as well as in dreams and imagination. In other words, you may not only skew your interpretation of occurrences based on your COEXs, but you may also, through what I could call fate, pull actual experiences toward you, reenacting your COEXs until you find a way to release them. Integrating all the aspects of a COEX can free life energy for moving in new directions.

As I close our section on Grofian maps, I want to remember one more way to understand what appears from your psyche during non-ordinary states. This comes from British psychiatrist Tim Read, who studied Grofian psychology after working for years in the mainstream mental health system.

As I mentioned briefly in our Entryway, Read developed the idea of a **cispersonal** source of experiences during non-ordinary states of consciousness. As I have stated, "trans" is the Latin meaning "across" or "beyond," "on the far side of." The Latin word meaning "on the near side of" is *cis*. In the time of ancient Rome, *trans* Alps meant an area far away from Rome, whereas *cis* Alps was closer to home.

If there is a transpersonal source of energies that come to us in psychedelics, Read suggests some of what appears can be considered "on the near side" of our psyche. Our consciousness can participate in the transpersonal, but there is a closer realm, the cispersonal, which, as Read describes, opens "to material from the deeper layers of the unconscious, but this material is rooted predominantly in the personal or the psycho-social layer of the psyche." [62]

From working with people experiencing holotropic states, Grof observed that the bridge into a transpersonal source of experience is often perinatal memory or experience. When considering the source of experience, there is not necessarily a place in the psyche that has a blending. However, from an integration perspective, I find it useful to look for both transpersonal and biographical elements in any image.

When I do integration work, I believe it helps to explain the cispersonal realm as the place in our psyche where personal and transpersonal energies blend. Particular images may have roots in both our biographical lives and the transpersonal realms. Read believes there is hard work in really moving consciousness into the transpersonal realm, just as it was hard for Romans to cross the Alps into the "trans" land beyond. Psychedelics very often help you make this journey, yet it remains true that much of what appears to you is rooted in *you*, even if energized by transpersonal contact.

In my view, the concept of a cispersonal realm can be helpful when working with the Grofian maps. For instance, if the archetypal Gorgon Medusa came to you in a session with her snakes for hair hissing at you, the energy would likely feel transpersonal. But in working with the energy during integration, you might feel into your experience of threatening or poisonous female figures in your biographical life, as well as your internal conception of the archetypal feminine. In the end, there is a strong relationship between the transpersonal, cispersonal and biographical elements of manifestation, often understood through the commonalities of a COEX.

In working with such images, I find it helpful to understand them as having reality in another realm—the transpersonal realm—and yet your most fruitful work may remain within your biographical life. If you do not include focus on your personal life, you may end up with amazing transpersonal narratives but not really unlock stuck energy in your system. In the worst case, this could lead to what has been called spiritual bypass. Processing through your experiences and feelings **in this life** may then open you more to transpersonal energies—as a gateway. In other words, it is through deeply processing our personal lives in *this lifetime* that we experience most fully the spiritual realms.

How does Grof help us with psychedelics?

Grofian psychology in some ways builds upon the work of Freud, Jung and others, but Grof describes a comprehensive and unique frame of reference that grew out of his work with non-ordinary states, including psychedelics. His map of the psyche may be the most useful single resource for your psychedelics integration work. By expanding the view of the psyche into an **embodied process** involving transpersonal, biographical, and perinatal realms, all manifesting into the present, Grof presents a comprehensive understanding into which everything seems to be enfolded. Importantly, the body and its expressions are included as part of the psyche.

Rather than focus on simply relieving symptoms, Grof encourages us to follow our process into the deepest sources of imbalances and blocks that are ready for release. Non-ordinary states, particularly when integrated, help you do this work.

Grof does not pretend the psychospiritual work we do in our lifetime cures us or makes us perfect. Rather, he created the word *holotropic* to describe gradual movement toward our own unique wholeness, with no illusion that we ever completely arrive. Your wholeness is entirely individual to you and is best considered an evolutionary process. Discovering that evolution is an exciting, always-changing journey. Integration as a life practice is essential to this process.

New Science of Consciousness

Even if you are drawn to psychedelics, spirituality, and psychological exploration, since you were born in our times, there is probably some part of you stuck in the idea that the "material world" is *really* the only thing going on. You may think psychology is cool, particularly transpersonal psychology, but there may be some part of you thinking *science is real and this psychology stuff is not real.*

If you have studied psychology in mainstream settings, you may also have been taught that consciousness is just a by-product of the firing of neurons in the physical brain. With the "material world only" perspective all around us, it is hard not to worry we are kidding ourselves by believing in what we experience from the inside out. The complexity in understanding what comes to us from inside can contribute to a lack of trust. In other words, it can be so confusing to sort through all that emerges from our consciousness that we give up and think "none of this is real."

For these reasons I want to put the world revealed through psychedelics on the grid of mainstream science, particularly physics. Finding "proof" through science helps us leave behind our doubts about the reality of consciousness. Plus, the correspondences between some of the basic realities known to physics and what you find through psychedelics are just downright amazing.

I begin with Albert Einstein (1879-1955), probably the most famous physicist of modern times. Two of the most essential discoveries of modern physics—brought forth a century ago by Einstein—are that:

- Matter is a form of energy; and energy involves patterns and dynamic unfolding.
- Space and time are not separate, but are "fused into a four-dimensional continuum," to use the phrase of scientist and writer Fritjof Capra.

Albert Einstein

Also proven scientific fact is that human consciousness interacts with matter. I am not talking about the reality of extrasensory perception (that's a different and also true story), but the discovery nearly a hundred years ago by Werner Heisenberg. He showed that human observation of a particle/wave has an impact on the particle/ wave. In other words, hard laboratory physics has shown that our consciousness participates in the four-dimensional continuum.

Before relating these realities to psychedelics, I want to spend a little time with Einstein's famous commentary on God. In 1954, he wrote a letter to a Jewish philosopher (Einstein was born Jewish) in which he said: "The word God is for me nothing more than the expression and product of human weaknesses, the Bible a collection of honorable, but still primitive legends which are nevertheless pretty childish."[63] Predictably, these words have been taken as rejection of spirituality by the most famous scientist of the last few centuries.

But if you look further at what Einstein really believed, you see without doubt that he understood "the universe" in a very spiritual way, essentially as God. Einstein wrote about his "cosmic religion," which he described as a "rapturous amazement at the harmony of natural law, which reveals an intelligence of such superiority that, compared with it, all the systematic thinking and acting of human beings is an utterly insignificant reflection."[64]

Science writer Eugene Mallove wrote that "Einstein's God was the Universe itself, not an external 'grand puppeteer.'"[65] Another journalist, Avi Selk, wrote:

> For Einstein, the mystery in the architecture of the physical universe—an architecture he helped reveal with his breakthroughs in relativity and the nature of space and time—was more profound than any wonder he read about in the Talmud or the Bible.[66]

There is even more orientation I can find from psychics for what we may experience in psychedelics work. Another twentieth century physicist, David Bohm (1917-1992), brought forth within theoretical physics the idea of an implicate order. In order to explain the behavior of electrons in plasma, Bohm came to believe that any individual particle of matter could reveal information about an interconnected wholeness. At the most fundamental level, there is **holomovement** in which everything is in a state of process or becoming.

In an oft-quoted passage from his book, *Wholeness and the Implicate Order*, Bohm wrote:

> Throughout this book the central underlying theme has been the unbroken wholeness of the totality of existence as an undivided flowing movement without borders. It seems clear . . . that the implicate order is particularly suitable for the understanding of such unbroken wholeness in flowing movement, for in the implicate order the totality of existence is enfolded within each region of space (and time). So, whatever part, element, or aspect I may abstract in

thought, this still enfolds the whole and is therefore intrinsically related to the totality from which it has been abstracted.[67]

Over the last three or four decades, numerous books have been written that describe a relationship between spiritual experience and the realities of physics. Among the most well known of these books is Fritjof Capra's *The Tao of Physics*, followed several years later by his *The Turning Point*. In *The Turning Point*, Capra explains, "subatomic particles are not isolated grains of matter but are probability patterns, interconnections in an inseparable cosmic web that includes the human observer and her consciousness."[68] The dynamic character of the cosmic web is the very essence of its being.

As Capra puts it, the image of the universe as a machine has been replaced by a view of "one indivisible, dynamic whole whose parts are essentially interrelated and can only be understood as patterns of a cosmic process."[69] He continued:

> At the subatomic level the interrelations and interactions between the parts of the whole are more fundamental than the parts themselves. There is motion but there are, ultimately, no moving objects; there is activity but there are no actors; there are no dancers, there is only the dance.[70]

Interestingly, in the preface to the first edition of *The Tao of Physics*, Capra reveals that "power plants" or psychedelics helped him in understanding the relationship between physics and mysticism. He wrote that glimpsing this reality was "so overwhelming that I burst into tears, at the same time, not unlike [contemporary shaman's apprentice Carlos] Casteneda pouring out my impressions to a piece of paper."[71]

This is not just a strange isolated use of psychedelics by one scientist. Some of the most impactful scientific discoveries in the last few centuries have been assisted by psychedelics, such as the understanding of the DNA double helix by Francis Crick and the development of computer technologies by Steve Jobs and others.

For me, drawing a parallel between the *unified field* theory of physics and the ancient Hindu idea of the Akashic records is very helpful in linking psychedelic experience and science. In *The Akashic Experience: Science and the Cosmic Memory Field*, Ervin Laszlo describes the unified field recognized in contemporary physics as the all-encompassing reality of the universe. Laszlo explains:

> Science is currently undergoing a fundamental paradigm shift. The currently dominant paradigm of separate material things connected by mechanistic relations of cause and effect is failing; there are ever more things and processes

it cannot account for. Classical science's conception of the universe has turned out to be flawed. The primary "stuff" of the universe is energy and not matter, and space is neither empty nor passive—it's filled with virtual energies and information.

As scientists now realize, the unified vacuum—now widely known as the unified field—is the originating ground as well as the ultimate destination of all the things that arise and evolve in space and time.[72]

Now I turn to the ancient Hindu idea of the Akashic field, and you will see the correspondence:

- Akasha is a Sanskrit word meaning "sky," "space" or "ether."
- The Akashic records are a field from which all the cosmos is formed and holds all that ever was, is or will be.
- Hinduism uses two terms—Atman (individual soul) and Brahman (world soul)—to describe the way *everything that ever was, is or will be* is contained both inside us and outside us.
- The universe is infinite and our bodies are made of many levels of consciousness and never-ending cycles that are also infinite.

During psychedelic experiences, you may feel that something like this cosmic *field* becomes available to you. Indeed, you may come to feel that you are within the field and being swept along or overwhelmed by a flowing field of *everything that ever was, is or will be*. This can feel just as if you are floating along inside a tumultuous four-dimensional river.

You might also become aware that actions you have taken or could take (or actions taken by others in your life, particularly your ancestors) seem like boulders that were put into a field or flow. Some seem to create a dam and there are eddies; some may guide future developments; some have been worn down by later actions or releases. You might feel as though you could "go into" some of these places and learn about what has happened, particularly on the emotional levels or the levels of consequences (karma).

Another way of thinking about the Akashic field is that it contains the active and passive energetic records of all souls in the sense of past lives, present lives, and *possible* future lives. What is hard to fathom, even if you are in it, is that this is all happening at the same time, though it also happens sequentially in the sense of consequences.

Hindus believe every soul has its Akashic Records, like a succession of books with each book signifying one lifetime. The Gallery (or Library) of the Akashic Records holds the energetic resonance of all that has ever happened. But the Akashic Records are not a dry compilation of events—they are the record of human experience as lived. These records also contain our collective wisdom, which may correlate to what Carl Jung called the collective unconscious.

Drawing on your vision of the Akashic Records for explaining and integrating psychedelic experiences only seems natural to us. These records may be referenced as a card catalog of your life (and past lives) as well as a *true north* to your psychedelic work. Some ways to use the basics of the Akashic when working with psychedelics can be:

- Exploration of what feels like a prior lived experience—throughout your psychedelic journeys, have you connected to similarities in your prior "lived" experiences?
- Investigating the experience—have there been psychedelic experiences that have invited new questions and a further desire to research something new?
- Taking charge of the experience—learning, exploring and investigating the experiences is important as a foundation. Now what will you do to live with these psychedelic experiences as realities of your soul as an enduring consciousness?

By understanding and using the Akashic field as a guide, you may be able to integrate your psychedelic experiences on a multitude of levels, opening up a logical and more detailed mode to understand not only past behaviors but also future possibilities. Using the Akashic Records within the field of psychedelic experiences reminds us that we have everything within us that is represented by everything outside of us.

I find it helpful to ponder these kinds of questions on an ongoing basis. What kind of Akashic experiences have you had? Have you had any of the following Akashic experiences when working with psychedelics?

- What is the meaning of your life? Why were you born?
- Everything in life is purposeful: What is the purpose of this or that?
- What are your perceptions of the inner and outer realities of the world we live in?

If this all seems pretty trippy to you, work your way back from the trippiness into the new science—and try to hold it all as absolutely real. Read again through our descriptions at the beginning of this section, or read some of the books on the new science and spirituality. Understand that through exploring psychedelics, you are exploring reality.

Astrology

The ancient science of astrology provides an astoundingly important map relating to consciousness and psychedelics work. Because of the depth and complexity of astrology, I can only touch upon the subject in this book. I will give you a sense of how astrology fits into working with non-ordinary states of consciousness. Here is the basic idea: Each of us is born at a moment in time at a particular place on Earth. Even though we know the Earth and the other planets revolve around the sun, astrology looks out at the cosmos from our place on the Earth at the time of our birth. The idea is that archetypal energies represented by the planets and stars are imprinted on us at our time of birth.

At the moment you were born, all the "planets" and the star constellations were in a particular place in relation to you. (In astrology, the Sun and the Moon are considered planets.) Our time and place of birth creates the bull's-eye around which astrology considers the archetypal energies corresponding to the planets and signs. The snapshot of the archetypal energies imprinting on you at the moment of your birth is called your "natal chart." This is another map that can help you when working with psychedelic experiences.

Most people only know their Zodiac "Sun sign" (e.g., Aries, Taurus, Gemini, etc.), which involves the star constellation influencing the Sun at the time of your birth. But you also have influencing energies associated with the placement of the Moon, Mercury, Venus, Mars, Jupiter, Saturn, Uranus, Neptune and Pluto in your natal chart. There are also other planetoids that provide information, but we are already getting complicated enough.

Archetypal astrology, a discipline developed by cultural historian Richard Tarnas, focuses on the relationships between planets rather than on the Zodiac sign of your planets. Traditional astrology places just as much emphasis on the *signs* as on the planets. You can think of planets and Zodiac signs as all representing archetypes that have influence relevant to your life journey. This can apply to what is likely to happen for you when working with non-ordinary states.

Richard Tarnas

There is no way I can describe the rich and multivalent meanings of the astrological archetypes, but I want to suggest very briefly the nature of the archetypes. The below chart on planetary archetypes is drawn from the work of archetypal astrologer and Jungian scholar Keiron Le Grice; the chart on Zodiac archetypes is summarized from the work of evolutionary astrologer Steven Forrest. Their summaries draw from hundreds of years of astrological work by our ancestors.

Planetary Archetypes (Keiron Le Grice)

Sun	Selfhood, identity, the urge to self-expression
Moon	Feelings, emotional responses, the inner self, home, family, mother, child
Mercury	Thinking, perception, communication, analysis
Venus	Romantic love, beauty, pleasure, harmony
Mars	Self-assertion, action, fight, struggle, warrior, strength
Jupiter	Expansion, abundance, trust, desire to connect to larger wholes
Saturn	Contraction and restriction, structures and boundaries, limitations, time and mortality, death and endings
Uranus	Freedom and individualism, rebellion, liberation, sudden unexpected change
Neptune	Transcendence and spiritual experience, dissolution, myth and dreams
Pluto	Primal power of destruction and creation, unconscious compulsion, evolution, instinctual energy

Archetypes of the Signs (Steven Forrest)

Aries	Beginning fire: warrior, pioneer, daredevil, survivor
Taurus	Steady Earth: nature, physicality, inner stillness
Gemini	Dispersing air: perceiving, communicating, informing
Cancer	Beginning water: mother, nurturing, healing
Leo	Steady fire: performing, warmth, royalty, divine child
Virgo	Dispersing Earth: analyzing, sacrificing, perfecting
Libra	Beginning air: lover, artist, peacemaker
Scorpio	Steady water: intensity, essence, no pretense
Sagittarius	Dispersing fire: traveler, philosopher, student, flying fast
Capricorn	Beginning Earth: ambition, materialism, public presentation
Aquarius	Steady air: revolutionary, idealist, exile
Pisces	Dispersing water: mystic, dreamer, observing mind

When we first start learning about astrology, probably the three most powerful indicators on our personal astrological map are the Sun, the Moon, and the "Rising Sign." (The Rising Sign, also known as the Ascendant, is the sign "rising" on the horizon when and where you were born.) For instance, my Sun sign is Gemini, my Moon sign is Cancer, and my Rising Sign is Sagittarius.

Perhaps the strongest influences come from the relationships between the planets at your time of birth. For instance, if Saturn is in close relationship with your Sun, the experience of discipline, constriction, and developing wisdom over time may be an important theme (COEX? Complex?) in your experience of yourself and your life journey—and in your non-ordinary state experiences.

In *Archetypal Cosmos: Rediscovering the Gods in Myth, Science and Astrology*, Keiron Le Grice synthesizes much of the "new science" with the principles of archetypal astrology and the psychologies of Carl Jung and Stanislav Grof. Le Grice understands the collective unconscious as extending "from the farthest reaches of the psyche to the transcendent background of reality." [73] He continues:

> As the matrix of experience, the collective unconscious, at its deepest level, merges seamlessly into what might be called the *dynamic ground*—the creative source, the generating and sustaining matrix of being from which all life springs. It is here that I can, I believe, locate the transcendent archetypal principles, the patterning forces that are the very basis of the phenomenal world. [74]

As Le Grice explains, in our lives on Earth, each "slice of space-time" carries the unique archetypal qualities of the moment and place, reflecting one precise snapshot of the constant "dynamic ever-changing nature of the universe." [75] Referencing Grof, Le Grice notes that the birth process (the perinatal domain) "appears to be a mysterious point of intersection between the personal-biographical and the transpersonal, between the individual and the collective." [76] The moment of birth is when the creative-generation of the archetypal cosmos intersects with the material reality of biological life on the planet.

Le Grice brings things together:

> The birth experience seems to serve as a kind of archetypal imprint or stamp, as it were, in which biographical, perinatal, familial, cultural, ancestral, phylogenetic, and transpersonal "memories" appear to constellate around the archetypal pattern of the birth moment. Each individual life seems to give concrete form to the underlying archetypal dynamics of that moment as a particularized expression of the cosmos.

> In this sense, we cannot separate the purpose and meaning of our coming into existence from the life of the universe as a whole. While our birth is our own individual beginning, it is also in some sense a cosmic event. Our coming into existence is a creative action of the cosmos as a whole. At biological birth the whole seems to individualize itself in and through the human being.[77]

Your natal chart (reflecting your moment and place of birth) thus becomes a map for your life journey that links you to the transpersonal realms. Because psychedelics open the door into the depths of the psyche and the universe beyond, knowing your natal chart can help you understand what appears in your experiences and, more broadly, the important influences in your unique life journey.

Now, those of you who have no experience with astrology might be wondering: how do I find out about my own astrology? The good news is that you can generate charts for yourself through free programs on the Internet, or (much more advisable) you can consult an astrologer. The not-so-good news is that understanding your astrological influences is a complicated process. But there are many informative books out there, as well as astrology teachers and guides.

I know I am making things complicated, but I need to mention one more thing about your astrological map. As you would imagine, the planets and stars kept moving after you were born. As they move, they are always changing alignment ("transiting") in relationship to where the planets were when you were born. The relationship between the changing placement of planets and your natal chart gives important insight into the archetypal "winds" that will be blowing your way at any given time.

Importantly, noticing the impact of the "transiting" planets can provide information about psychedelic experiences as well as the "work" you are doing in your psychological and spiritual journeys. The planets I study the most for their "archetypal winds" are the outer planets: Saturn, Uranus, Neptune and Pluto. To recap: the archetype of the planet Saturn involves constriction and discipline; Uranus involves freedom and breakthroughs; Neptune involves mysticism and dissolving of boundaries; and Pluto involves struggle and digging down deep to bring up powerful (and often troublesome) energies.

Amazingly enough, these four outer planets correspond to Stan Grof's four Basic Perinatal Matrices (BPM I = Neptune; BPM II = Saturn; BPM III = Pluto; and BPM IV = Uranus). As I mentioned in Chapter 1, Grof and Tarnas discovered that astrology is the only system that seems to offer some prediction about the experiences people will have during non-ordinary states. Knowing what transits are active for you during a non-ordinary state experience can help you understand and integrate the experiences you have. I will say more about this in Chapter 7.

If you believe our souls reincarnate, you might be interested in the idea that we incarnate at a moment and place on the planet where some of the energies from our past lives (karma) imprint on us through the astrological archetypes as we are born into "this life." In other words, we might be "pulled into" incarnation at the precise moment in space-time that allows us (or requires us) to carry forward our karma. This means we "continuing working" where we left off in prior lives. The discipline of evolutionary astrology (represented by Steven Forrest) works with this principle. At the risk of really confusing you, the relationship between the planes of the Moon's orbit and those of the Sun's apparent path around the Earth at your time of birth seems important in this karmic imprint. The points used in astrology for looking at this impact are called the Nodes of the Moon.

Learning about your astrology can help you integrate psychedelic experiences and make your life journey all the more conscious and interesting.

The Enneagram

Many people want to let go of their "ego" through working with psychedelics. If you really want freedom from your ego constructs, you need to begin seeing your unconscious motivations. Behind your behaviors, thoughts, projections, and defenses are motivations that hold the key to unlocking the boxes where we are trapped. These motivations remain unconscious until you do some hard work of looking at parts of yourself you would rather not see.

One of the best tools for doing this work is a nine-pointed personality system called the Enneagram. Passed down mostly through oral tradition until the late 1980s, knowledge of the Enneagram in the West is often traced back to George Ivanovich Gurdjieff, a charismatic Greek/Armenian spiritual teacher and mystic.

Gurdjieff said his teachings came through his expeditions to foreign lands in search of ancient wisdom. His "Fourth Way" is based on three established methods of spiritual discipline he learned in his travels:

- Mental discipline from yogis,
- Emotional discipline from monks, and
- Control of the body (i.e. asceticism) from Muslim fakirs.

The Enneagram is based on nine different styles of personality motivation; three lead with the mental function (head), three with the emotional (heart), and three with the body (gut). As you will find, I encourage you through integration to pay attention to all these functions—the mind, heart and body are all ways into your process.

Gurdjieff taught in Russia before the Bolshevik Revolution, then in Paris and other places. Through his students, Gurdjieff's teachings found their way to many other countries. In South America, the Bolivian-born philosopher Oscar Ichazo taught "Fourth Way" principles, including the Enneagram, in his Arica School. A Chilean-born psychiatrist, Claudio Naranjo, brought Enneagram teachings to California, where he shared them with various spiritual groups, including around Berkeley.

I mention this history because I would like you to become familiar with our spiritual ancestors, but also because Naranjo took part in some of the early experimental trials of psychedelic compounds synthesized by Alexander "Sasha" Shulgin. Naranjo has been one of the most important teachers for inner explorers, with roots, as you can see, in both ancient mysticism and contemporary psychedelic exploration.

There is no possibility of doing justice to the Enneagram here, but I point you toward any of the books by Helen Palmer, Don Riso and Russ Hudson, Sandra Maitri, or Naranjo.[78] Palmer and Riso/Hudson are probably the easiest to read.

In brief, the nine personality types as named and described by Palmer and Riso are:

Enneagram Type	Helen Palmer	Don Riso
One	Perfectionist	Reformer
Two	Giver	Helper
Three	Performer	Motivator
Four	Tragic Romantic	Artist
Five	Observer	Thinker
Six	Devil's Advocate	Loyalist
Seven	Epicure	Generalist
Eight	Boss	Leader
Nine	Mediator	Peacemaker

The value of the Enneagram comes in the little (or big) "ahas" you get about your unconscious motivating forces. To give you a sense of how this works, I draw from a brilliant little book by Riso, *Enneagram Transformations: Releases and Affirmations for Healing Your Personality Type*.[79] In addition to being brilliant, the book is brutal if you are honest enough with yourself to recognize some of your least appealing motivations. For instance, consider these "transformations" offered by Riso as examples of the kind of self-realizations that you could have about unconscious motivations you might release:

As a One, I now release…	Driving myself and others to perfection.	My fear of losing control and becoming irrational.	Believing that I am in a position to judge others.
As a Two, I now release…	All attempts to justify my aggressive feelings.	All attachment to feeling victimized and abused.	All attempts to force others to love me.
As a Three, I now release…	Feeling jealous of others and their good fortune.	My fear of failing and being humiliated.	Using arrogance to compensate for my own insecurity.
As a Four, I now release…	Turning my anger and aggressions against myself.	All feelings of hopelessness and despair.	Feeling that people always let me down.
As a Five, I now release…	My fear of being violated and overwhelmed by others.	Desiring to antagonize others and ruin their peace of mind.	Being cynical and contemptuous of the normalcy of others.
As a Six, I now release	All feelings of dread about the future.	Overreacting and exaggerating my problems.	Taking out my fears and anxieties on others.
As a Seven, I now release…	Always feeling that I need more.	Running away from the consequences of my actions.	Insulting or abusing others to vent my frustrations.
As an Eight, I now release…	Believing that taking vengeance will free me from my own pain.	Believing that I do not need others.	Hardening my heart against suffering.
As a Nine, I now release…	Turning away from whatever is unpleasant or difficult.	Refusing to see my own aggressions.	Living through others and not developing myself.

And there is more… which you can find for yourself. I give these few examples because in my experience these are the sorts of insights about ourselves that often become available during psychedelics work—and which can be released in an energetic sense during the work. You probably need a lot of intention and stamina to feel your way into these sorts of motivations, but once you do, there is enormous freedom.

We might "know" about some of our tendencies (or have heard about them repeatedly from loved ones), but with psychedelics we might *feel* such things deeply within our bodies. Particularly in working with Ayahuasca or other medicines that assist purging, these sorts of "egoic" tendencies can often be purged from the body, where they may have taken hold as entrenched (and physically lodged) character structures.

I wish you Godspeed working with these depths.

World Mythologies

Some psychedelic guides offer experiences that include teaching about a particular spiritual tradition. Usually this occurs over a few days, such as a long weekend. During the non-ordinary state experience, the guide may suggest stages or images for the journey drawing from the particular mythology. The particular mythology becomes a map for the experience—and perhaps also for the broader journey of psychospiritual work.

In your psychedelics work, it can be fun to explore different mythologies and spiritual systems. There are many sources in books, movies, and of course the Internet. Because working with psychedelics can feel like a heroic undertaking, there are many myths about transformative and challenging journeys that can deepen your experience.

One of the most famous mythologists in the last several decades was Joseph Campbell, a university professor and author. As he explained in his book *Hero with a Thousand Faces*, almost all world cultures have a story about a challenging heroic journey. There are common elements to all the stories, which indicates the heroic journey is an archetype deep in our collective unconscious.

Star Wars creator George Lucas famously drew on Campbell's work when finalizing his vision of interplanetary adventure for his crew of characters. Generations of people worldwide have incorporated Luke Skywalker, Princess Leia and Han Solo into their psyches as heroes on a journey. You can also see the heroic journey in many other movies, such as *The Matrix*, *Jason and the Argonauts*, and *Lord of the Rings*. In *The Rebirth of the Hero: Mythology as a Guide to Spiritual Transformation*, Keiron Le Grice uses many popular films to illustrate stages, pitfalls, and promises of the heroic journey.[80]

Here are some of the common elements of the heroic journey:

- A call to adventure
- Refusing the call—the hero at first does not want to face what they must do
- Circumstances of fate pulling the hero into a journey
- Meeting strange characters, some trustworthy, some betraying, and often some animal familiars
- A time of confusion or illness (setbacks)
- The need to surrender (face failure) in order to "cross the final threshold"
- Finding the treasure and bringing it home, not just for you but for everyone.

You can see how psychedelic journeys draw on these archetypal elements. Sometimes when we approach a journey or when the medicine first starts to affect us, we resist the call—perhaps not wanting to face the arduous journey ahead. The resistance can involve holding back from really letting go into the journey.

Then we are pulled into the adventure despite ourselves (heck, we took the medicine, what can we do?). We are hoping for insight and discovery about the universe and ourselves. We probably meet all kinds of strange characters and worry what to make of them. Can we trust what they try to say to us? We may be confused, lose our way, feel sick, and reach way down into our most wounded places. And then, somehow, we break through and there is a precious jewel of awareness, which we bring back for integration into ourselves, our loved ones, our families, and our culture.

Several years ago, an old friend of mine attended a weekend workshop drawing on Norse mythology. The facilitator shared teachings about this spiritual system before the medicine journey. During the medicine experience, she offered guided imagery as a prompt and map for a journey of awareness and insight.

Norse mythology envisions a world tree (the Ash Tree for the Norse, known as Yggdrasill) on which the gods and goddesses (and certain humans) travel. The image of a tree with limbs branching above and roots branching down below seems to resonate deeply with many of us. This may touch upon our sense of having many ancestors behind us—whose genetic offering comes together into our life—and the knowledge that we leave our impact on many people, those who will follow us, whether biological descendants or people we have touched.

"The World Tree"

In the journey he took through the map of Norse mythology, the guide invited participants to move along Yggdrasill and encounter various beings who might offer wisdom or healing. All along the way, he found treasures of insight and also felt very deeply connected to the mythology of a people who lived on the land and the seas. Synchronistically, not long after this journey, he moved into a home with prominent ash trees. Several months later, through genetic research, he discovered nearly a third of his DNA comes from Scandinavia, something he had never known given what he knew about his ancestors.

You are encouraged to find your own mythologies that help you understand your psychedelic work and life path. I offer an exercise at the end of this chapter to invite you to find your own map for psychedelic work.

Mainstream Mental Health Perspective: Diagnostic and Statistical Manual of Mental Disorders, 5th Edition (DSM-5)

When considering the integration of psychedelics, it is also valuable to have a basic understanding of mainstream mental health language and perspective. While this is not the first map I would bring to working with psychedelics, it is a map that you should know exists—and not be afraid to consider.

Though I want to offer this information, I am by no means endorsing the reduction that some mainstream professionals make with psychedelics—that is, assuming that psychedelics produce hallucinations that may be harmful or at best meaningless; or that they have a strong tendency in everyone to lead to mental health problems. Nor am I suggesting that the ways of being and behaving that are described as "disorders" in the mainstream system mean that people with these ways of being and behaving are flawed, broken or inadequate in any way.

The clinical resource book that sorts out all mental health concerns from the mainstream perspective is the ***Diagnostic and Statistical Manual of Mental Disorders***, now known as the **DSM-5**. I consider the DSM through some of its history and purpose in order to help those of us who have negative reactions to the DSM begin to ease into the potential value it can sometimes hold.

It helps to know how this book came into being. Within our Western society the necessity for categorization of everything and anything has always taken precedence over more holistic ways of understanding. The classification of mental disorders has been around throughout the history of medicine, but until recently there was little agreement on which disorders should be included and the optimal method for their organization. Once the original DSM was introduced in the year 1952 (as a variant to the world health organization's ICD-6), the DSM through its various incarnations has become the "bible" resource for clinicians, insurance companies and other professionals.

The American Psychiatric Association (APA) published the DSM-5 in 2013. APA is a national medical group whose more than 37,000 physician members specialize in the diagnosis, treatment, prevention and research of mental illnesses, including substance use disorders. The DSM-5 sets out criteria for mental health professionals to diagnose particular conditions. It took thirteen years to organize, re-write, edit and publish this edition. The primary goals for the manual's new framework are to help clinicians make more accurate and consistent diagnoses, and to help researchers better study how "disorders" relate to one another, which can lead to better treatment for patients.

Here are the reasons I recommend you have some familiarity with the mainstream diagnostic system:

- Some of what presents in non-ordinary states (and in spiritual awakening in general) seems to match diagnostic criteria for what are considered serious mental disorders, including schizophrenia and bipolar disorder.
- If you really enter into a process of transformation with psychedelics as one of your tools, the road may be bumpy, and some people may begin to pathologize and diagnose you—so it helps to know what they may be thinking and saying.
- As I shared in the Entryway, for some people, psychedelics may hasten or start a process that could be most safely handled (at least temporarily) through the mainstream mental health system.
- Having a sense of the mainstream diagnostic system helps you see the basic conflict in paradigms between mainstream psychological understandings and those of transpersonal psychology.
- Probably most importantly, having a label (even from the mainstream perspective) for certain experiences or behaviors you may find in yourself and others in psychedelic communities can help you navigate through your journey.

On this last most important point, having a label for some experiences can help you see and feel into them more deeply—and get some observational distance from them. In other words, you might reduce the chance you are unconsciously caught in behaviors and experiences. I am not asking you to buy into the ideologies and perspectives of the psychiatric model, but just to have some familiarity with frames of reference that can sometimes be helpful. This knowledge can go a long way as you support others and yourself in the exploration of psychedelics.

Turning to the DSM, whole courses and programs are taught for people to learn the DSM system. Just very briefly, take a look at the chapter headings to get an overview:

- Neurodevelopmental Disorders

- Schizophrenia Spectrum and Other Psychotic Disorders
- Bipolar and Related Disorders
- Depressive Disorders
- Anxiety Disorders
- Obsessive-Compulsive and Related Disorders
- Trauma and Stressor Related Disorders
- Dissociative Disorders
- Somatic Symptom Disorders
- Feeding and Eating Disorders
- Elimination Disorders
- Sleep-Wake Disorders
- Sexual Dysfunctions
- Gender Dysphoria
- Disruptive, Impulse Control and Conduct Disorders
- Substance Use and Addictive Disorders
- Neurocognitive Disorders
- Personality Disorders
- Paraphilic Disorders
- Other Disorders

There are three important diagnoses I want to discuss at some length:

Hallucinogen Persisting Perception Disorder

This diagnosis harkens back to the 1960s and 1970s when the media stirred up public concern about flashbacks, usually focusing on LSD. The DSM criteria for the diagnosis of Hallucinogen Persisting Perception Disorder are:

- The reexperiencing, following cessation of use of a hallucinogen, of one or more of the perceptual symptoms that were experienced while intoxicated with the hallucinogen (e.g., geometric hallucinations, false perceptions of movement in the peripheral visual fields, flashes of color, intensified colors, trails of images of moving objects, positive afterimages, halos around objects, macropsia or things looking larger than they are, and micropsia or things looking smaller).
- The symptoms cause clinically significant distress or impairment in social, occupational, or other important areas of functioning.

- The symptoms are not due to a general medical condition and are not better accounted for by another mental disorder (e.g., delirium, dementia, and schizophrenia) or hypnopompic hallucinations.[81]

The DSM claims that approximately 4.2% of people who use hallucinogens have this experience, but I question whether this number of people actually have this sort of experience, and I question how many find it troubling. Some research suggests post-psychedelic perception problems are not at all common or may be caused by non-psychedelic substances when they occur. One study interviewed 500 Native American church members who had experienced Peyote on numerous occasions, but found no evidence of these symptoms occurring.[82] Other studies from decades ago suggest that the people having post-psychedelic perception issues may be continual users of cannabis and/or may have other preexisting conditions.[83]

While the DSM treats this experience as a physical condition, I would encourage anyone having persisting images to consider integrating what comes up in response to working with the images, perhaps with an integration guide. I would never discourage treatment in the medical system, only suggest the possibility of moving through the symptoms to see whether a helpful process occurs.

Schizophrenia

A diagnosis of schizophrenia represents a serious event in one's life. While not discounting the utility of the diagnosis for helping people (and having that help covered by insurance), I want to be careful with the idea that "schizophrenia" is one thing, that is, one clear-cut disorder, in the same way that having the flu from one particular virus is "the same" for everyone. Even in the case of a flu virus, different people would likely react differently to the virus. I would rather hold "schizophrenia" as a label that comes out of matching certain criteria in the DSM.

The DSM proposes diagnosing schizophrenia when two (or more) of the following symptoms have been present for at least a month (or not as long if medication or other treatment stops the symptoms):

- Delusions
- Hallucinations
- Disorganized speech (e.g., frequent derailment or incoherence)
- Grossly disorganized or catatonic behavior
- Other negative symptoms, such as flat affect or lack of motivation.

There must also be:

- *Social/occupational dysfunction*, meaning a change in work functioning, interpersonal relations, or self-care that is judged as a negative change.
- Persistence for six months or more, though the specified symptoms may lessen and the diagnosis remain, particularly if the person continues with "odd beliefs or unusual perceptual experiences."
- Ruling out other conditions; some of the conditions to rule out are physical and some psychological (and I might add, ruling out spiritual awakening would be an appropriate addition.)

You can probably see how medical providers, family, significant others, friends and acquaintances might confuse what you tell them after a non-ordinary state experience—and during spiritual awakening in general—with several of the diagnostic criteria for schizophrenia.

From a "material world only" perspective, your sharing about archetypal or transpersonal experiences may sound like the sharing of delusions or hallucinations. If your life is transforming as the result of what you are learning about yourself and the universe, you may well have a period of functioning differently as you gain your footing in a new reality. Particularly if other people are threatened by the changes happening within you (for instance, significant others), it becomes easy for them to consider that you have become schizophrenic.

As I noted in the Entryway, Stan and Christina Grof developed the concept of spiritual emergence/emergency to help people understand that when spiritual awakening occurs, there may be presentations that look to others as symptoms of mental illness. Along with other experts, they explore the problem of this possible confusion in the classic book, *Spiritual Emergency: When Personal Transformation Becomes a Crisis*.[84] In their essay on the evolutionary crisis of spiritual emergence, Stan and Christina wrote:

> Feelings of oneness with the entire universe. Visions and images of distant times and places. Sensations of vibrant currents of energy coursing through the body, accompanied by spasms and violent trembling. Visions of deities, demigods, and demons. Vivid flashes of brilliant light and rainbow colors. Fears of impending insanity, even death.
>
> Anyone experiencing such extreme mental and physical phenomena would instantly be labeled psychotic by most modern Westerners. Yet increasing numbers of people seem to be having unusual experiences similar to those described above, and instead of plunging irrevocably into insanity, they often emerge from these extraordinary states of mind with an increased sense of

well-being, and a higher level of functioning in daily life. In many cases, long-standing emotional, mental, and physical problems are healed in the process.[85]

Christina Grof

In 1980, Christina Grof (1941-2014) founded the **Spiritual Emergency Network (SEN)**, an organization dedicated to helping people in psychospiritual crisis avoid psychiatric stigma and find alternative treatment. Christina had experienced spiritual awakening through the activation of *kundalini* energy, a challenging process often confused with various other physical and psychological conditions. She tells her story in the prologue of her book, *The Stormy Search for the Self*.[86]

The story begins with the spontaneous emergence of *kundalini* energy during the birth of her first child. She felt "enormous electrical tremors" throughout her body and saw "brilliant mosaics of white light" exploding in her head. She was shaking, had visions, and began an involuntary breathing process. Christina had similar but even more challenging experiences during the birth of her second child two years later.

A few years later, in the context of a disintegrating first marriage, Christina attended a retreat led by South Indian guru Swami Muktananda, known as Baba. During a meditation, he looked at her and then touched her, giving a transmission known as *shaktipat*. She describes the experience:

> Suddenly I felt as though I had been plugged into a high-voltage socket as I started to shake uncontrollably. My breathing fell into an automatic, rapid rhythm that seemed beyond my control, and a multitude of visions flooded my consciousness. I wept as I felt myself being born; I experienced death; I plunged into pain and ecstasy, strength and gentleness, love and fear, depths and heights.

I was on an experiential roller coaster, and I knew I could no longer contain it.

The genie was out of the bottle.[87]

Along with this experience came life difficulties that might be diagnosed as "social/occupational dysfunction" within the modern DSM criteria. Searching for a way to understand what was happening, Christina met with Joseph Campbell, a longtime friend since her college years. Campbell suggested she visit Stan Grof, who was then in residency at Esalen. She met with Stan and read his writings on LSD experiences and the maps of consciousness that emerged from detailed records of the experiences of his patients.

In Christina's words, it was a "revelation to suddenly have guidelines that helped me understand what had been happening to me." Just as important was Stan's strategy of encouraging her to "stay with the process" even though some of her experiences were "dramatic, arduous, disorganizing, and frightening." Stan felt that "if these experiences are properly supported, confronted, and integrated, they can be transformative, therapeutic, healing—perhaps even evolutionary."

Christina's own experiences became a template for her work with Stan in developing the understanding that experiences looking like presentations of mental or physical illness can actually represent a transformational process of spiritual emergence. Even with this understanding, the experiences may also represent challenging "emergencies."

How to Distinguish Between Spiritual Emergence and Psychosis

Stan Grof sometimes asks the question in teaching circles, "What is the difference between a mystic and a psychotic?" The answer is: "A mystic knows who not to talk to."

Grof is suggesting that the difference between spiritual emergence (mysticism) and psychosis depends on whether you tell your experiences to someone in the mainstream medical system—or someone who will convince or require you to engage with mainstream psychiatry professionals who do not credit the possibility of spiritual emergence. This can be literally true. I am quite clear that some people believed I was having a psychotic break in my twenties when spiritual experiences entered my life. Fortunately, I found the medicines; mentors and academics to ground me rather than a psychiatric hospital to help me integrate and follow the experiences rather than repress and diagnose them.

But there is another element to Grof's teaching question. By knowing who not to talk with, the hypothetical mystic is able to distinguish between what is presented to her internally and what is held as "real" in the outside world. Being able to integrate and follow spiritual emergence while not insisting on any particular realities to a skeptical medical system indicates an ability to work with the experiences.

Without a doubt, there are many "crossovers" in the experiences described as mysticism and those recognized as psychosis. Psychiatrist Roberto Tomas Agosin made some very useful observations about the similarities and differences between mysticism and psychosis. Before his death in 1991, Agosin was the Associate Director of Residency Training at the Bronx Psychiatric Center. In his article called *Mysticism and Psychosis,* he described these similarities:

- *Intense subjectivity.* The person is totally focused inwardly. There is a compelling attraction to what is happening inside so that the outside world and daily ordinary aspects of life seem irrelevant.
- *Sense of noesis.* Something very important is happening to the person. In both types of experiences, the person's attention is riveted with a sense that an important message or knowledge is being discovered.
- *Ineffable quality.* Both psychosis and mystical experience are very intense situations which the person has trouble putting into words. Both types of experience transcend the rational and usual, ordinary way of experiencing life.
- *Loss of self-object boundaries.* One experiences a sense of oneness with others, nature, the universe as a whole. The clear boundaries of inside (self) and outside (other) are blurred.
- *Distortion of time sense.* In both situations, the linear sense of time (past—present—future) is lost, with the present appearing as the only reality.
- *Perceptual changes.* Heightened perceptions in all sensory modalities, synesthesia and hallucinatory phenomena (especially visual and auditory) are very common.
- *Intense affective experiences.* Great ecstasy and great moments of terror are often described. Negative affective experiences tend to be more common in psychosis, but they can be experienced in either.
- *Attempt at renewal and healing.* The mystical experience is the attempt of the psyche to transcend a limited identification of self. It is the psyche's effort to break the boundaries of the personality totally trapped in the ego. The mystic sees his/her connection with all of life, and through that new vision expands his/her identity and sense of self. Psychosis is also an attempt at renewal and healing. The person has reached an impasse in his/her psychological life, and the only way it can be resolved is through such a drastic transformation.[88]

A number of other psychological professionals over the years have considered psychosis as a presentation that may be worked through if held appropriately. In *The Far Side of Madness* and other books, Jungian psychiatrist John Weir Perry describes psychosis as the attempt of the psyche to borrow energy and images from the archetypal realms in order to heal a fractured sense of self. Perry believed the archetypal energies could be integrated through artistic expressions such as painting, dance, other movement, and conversation.

Ronald David Laing (usually known as R. D. Laing) was a psychiatrist originally from Scotland who became well known for resisting the medical model of mental illness. Laing wrote about psychosis as a transformational process that could be compared to a shamanic journey. Rejecting the idea that schizophrenia was a biological illness, he viewed the presentations of psychosis as symbolic expressions of distress that could be understood and processed toward resolution.

R. D. Laing

After his death in 1989, Laing has been described as a celebrity psychiatrist, admired by the Beatles, Jim Morrison and others in the transformational times of the 1960s. Some people considered Laing to be Britain's answer to America's Timothy Leary. Several years ago, it was revealed that Laing guided actor Sean Connery on an LSD journey when Connery was learning to cope with his James Bond fame. Connery's wife shared that Laing took a smaller dose of LSD during the session.

I share these transformational perspectives on psychosis, but I am mindful of the practical limits of assistance that is available in this flawed world. In other words, even if all presentations of "psychosis" could be safely held for the experiencer to break through into health, in real life, it is difficult to find (or be able to afford) the necessary level of assistance. Just as importantly, our experience suggests that many people with presentations of psychosis are not able to hold the "distanced" perspective necessary to work productively with the experiences.

I find it helpful to bear in mind some of the **differences** between psychosis and mysticism found by psychiatrist Agosin:

- *Attachment to the world.* The mystic detaches from the material world as the source of all reality. The psychotic also detaches from the world in that he/she focuses on inner experiences to the exclusion of socially established rules of behavior. But the psychotic is also highly vulnerable to profound and intense reactions to whatever is in front of him/her. His/her ego boundaries are easily broken down, and because of the incapacity to control emotions, it is easy for the psychotic to shift from one state to another very quickly, leaving a disruption of any sense of continuity in his/her sense of self and the world.

- *Self-image.* The mystic wants to be an infinitesimal point of consciousness, with the smallest possible ego, so that he/she can perceive life in the least distorted way. The personality is seen as a barrier, a filter that does not allow one's consciousness to perceive life in its truest form. Humility before the enormity of the universe is a common attitude in the mystic. In contrast, the psychotic often sees him/herself as omnipotent and omniscient. There is a great increase in self-centeredness, with a feeling of being all-important. He/she is the center of the world, and only he/she is sufficiently important to matter.
- *Ego-identity is shed by the mystic.* He/she works to transcend the smallness of ego and tries to find a more expansive sense of self. The psychotic has never acquired a strong ego identity and often clings to whatever fragments he or she can find of him/herself.
- *Serenity increases in the mystic through detachment to the temporal and transient.* The mystic identifies with the eternal, that which is most sacred and valuable. In that deep identification, the mystic finds peace and inner tranquility. The psychotic, however, finds little serenity in his/her life. The emotional and mental life of the psychotic is completely fragmented: fear and lack of control of one's mind are the predominant states.
- *Change is welcomed by the mystic, who is open to new possibilities.* The psychotic person tends to reject change, for anything new brings with it a whole set of circumstances to learn to deal with. This frightens the psychotic patient since he/she has little ego-identity or inner strength with which to meet the new situation.
- *Thought processes are not disrupted in the mystical experience.* In the psychotic experience, thinking usually becomes fragmented and disordered.
- *Aggressive or paranoid elements* are found exclusively in the psychotic experience, sometimes to the point of being impossible to control.
- *Hallucinatory experiences* tend to be visual in nature for the mystic. Often these are described as visions of light, superior beings and beautiful panoramic phenomena of a most positive nature. The psychotic tends more often to experience auditory hallucinations, which are usually negative and frightening because they are projected, unacceptable thoughts that person has and can no longer keep buried in the unconscious.
- *Limited in time* characterizes the mystical experience. It is usually short-lived, but it always leaves an intense impression upon the memory and has a profound impact on

the person who experiences it. It leaves one with a new sense of oneself and the world. Psychosis can become a chronic condition.

Agosin believed the consequences of the experiences of mysticism/psychosis are the most important indication of difference. He wrote:

- The mystical experience leaves the mystic more connected and involved in the world. He/she expands his/her capacity to love and to serve. The mystic becomes more appreciative of the beauty and the miracle of life. The mystical experience leaves the individual with a feeling of reverence for all life, embracing every aspect of life and death as sacred.
- Psychosis unfortunately most often leaves the person more self-centered. It narrows his/her possibilities of connection with the world because the psychotic needs to protect him/herself from the anxiety that such a connection produces. The psychotic reduces his/her capacity to love because he/she cannot forget him/herself. The psychotic spends so much energy on survival that there is little psychic energy left for more.[89]

While I believe these are useful distinctions to bear in mind, my experience suggests the distinction between mysticism and psychosis is definitely not either/or. As the work of Stanislav and Christina Grof makes clear, during the period of "stormy search for the self," many of the presentations described by Agosin as psychosis may come from someone who will eventually break through into a higher mode of functioning and being. As long as the experiencer is able to work psychologically, many of the symptoms described as psychotic may lessen as adjustment is made to a new way of being.

> The mystic, endowed with native talents… and following… the instruction of a master, enters the waters and finds he can swim; whereas the schizophrenic, unprepared, unguided, and ungifted, has fallen or has intentionally plunged and is drowning.
>
> —Joseph Campbell

Tim Read uses the term **archetypal penetrance** to describe the degree to which different people may be "influenced by an archetypal ocean with tides, currents, waves and undertows."[90] This varies from person to person and depending on different times of life. Astrology helps understand these personal tendencies and times of high archetypal penetrance.

I would say people who look like either mystics or psychotics are people who share a high degree of archetypal penetrance. Though I hesitate to make a sweeping statement or open a can of worms, I strongly suspect research would indicate that people who "succeed" on a transpersonal path often have genetic or family relatives who have struggled with "psychotic" tendencies. Levels of archetypal penetrance may thus have genetic or familial components.

Whether there is the positive outcome—allowing description of the experiencer as a "mystic" rather than a "psychotic"—almost certainly depends on the support the person receives. Equally important is whether the person finds a way to hold the experiences as positive and transformative, rather than fall into the medical model's desire to pathologize and prescribe medication. I think exploring maps such as those offered in this chapter can help. No matter what, integrating the experiences through your witness consciousness and working with all levels of your body-mind-spirit is the way forward. As the poet Robert Frost has said, "The only way out is through."

Bipolar Disorder

In the DSM-5, there are three varieties of bipolar disorder, but I do not need to focus on the distinctions between the varieties. What seems important is to note some of the "diagnostic criteria" that may overlap with presentations in people who are drawn to working with psychedelics. A diagnosis of bipolar disorder involves a "distinct period of abnormally and persistently elevated, expansive, or irritable mood, and increased goal-directed activity or energy lasting more than a week, present most of the day, nearly every day." The following behaviors/experiences may be present:

- Inflated self-esteem or grandiosity
- Decreased need for sleep
- Pressured speech
- Racing thoughts or flight of ideas
- Distractibility
- Increased activity
- Excess pleasurable or risky activity.

Of course, not all of these experiences follow from using psychedelics! But I would be less than honest if I did not own up to some similarities.

There is often a sense of euphoria from working with non-ordinary states that may lead to presentations that look like some of these criteria. For instance, having just been in a place (during psychedelic experience) where there is unconditional love and "everything is okay just as it is," you may find yourself, at least for a period of time, feeling pretty pumped-up. You might not feel any need for limits. You might start wondering, "Why am I worried about all this usual stuff?" This may go further into, "Who needs this job? Everything is going to work out."

Sometimes you may get to, "I'm sick of this relationship, she doesn't understand what's real, let's just be done."

With a sense of a better way of being, there may be rumination about how to get there as well as excited explanations to others about what you have experienced. Because various repressions or energetic blocks may have been lifted, you may find yourself wanting to explore your sexuality further or experience the highs of life through various activities you might ordinarily find risky. For these reasons, in the breathwork community, guidance is provided to experiencers after a session about being mindful in sharing about your experience and delaying any decisions about life changes until the non-ordinary state experience has settled into one's life.

"Inflated self-esteem or grandiosity" needs some special attention. After you have experienced yourself as God—even if you also know that everyone else is God—you can be forgiven if you are in a place where you feel divine. I can go back to the distinction made by Agosin between humble release of your sense of self into something larger as compared to a fragile holding onto yourself as chosen and special because of your fractured sense of self. But the situation is more complicated because when you have amazing non-ordinary experiences, you may enter periods of inflation when your ego is still fragile—even if you are moving toward the experience of the mystic.

Martin Ball writes effectively and pointedly about what he calls the problem of **self-aggrandizement**. "It isn't easy for the ego to process the reality that you are God," he writes. "Some people come out of the experience with a messiah complex, thinking that *they are THE ONE*." Ball would like to let you know otherwise:

> So, let's just get it out of the way: you are not the savior of humanity. You are not the chosen one. You are not the messiah. You are not Maitreya or the Mahdi or the Christ—at least not exclusively. *Everyone* is…. Yes, you are beautiful. You are powerful. You are infinite. You are everything.
>
> But get over yourself. You still need to wipe your ass and brush your teeth and pay your bills, just like everyone else. Accepting your divinity does not translate into miracle-working, psychic powers, or walking on water and transforming water into wine. That's just mythological thinking. Life, reality, and being already are all the miracles you will ever need.[91]

Ball also describes an "evangelical stage" that may come with intense experiences of psychedelics. This could look like "pressured speech" or "racing thoughts and flights of ideas" or "increased activity." Ball flat-out advises against trying to talk others into finding what you have found. "Let other people make up their own minds. Share the information, but check your enthusiasm. Be ebullient and forthcoming, but not excessive." [92]

Similarly, Ball cautions against allowing inflated energy to lead you quickly into thinking you will be a "medicine carrier." He also warns about projecting your God-sense onto others you meet in the psychedelics realm, such as your facilitator, in a way that glorifies them inappropriately. Moderation in all things is probably more "godlike" than excess or rushing.

On the other hand, some level of inflation during spiritual awakening may be necessary to help you "make it." Edward Edinger, a psychiatrist and Jungian analyst, wrote one of the essential early books about spiritual development from a transpersonal perspective, *Ego and Archetype: Individuation and the Religious Function of the Psyche*. The book begins with discussion of "the inflated ego" as the initial stage of psychospiritual growth. Edinger quotes a dictionary definition of inflation as, "Blown up, distended with air, unrealistically large and unrealistically important, beyond the limits of one's proper size; hence to be vain, pompous, proud and presumptuous." [93]

In Jungian terminology, Edinger describes inflation in spiritual development as the individual ego's identification with the archetypal Self, which is essentially a God image. This is also the state of the infant, an experience of God-like wholeness and perfection. As adults, when we move toward spirituality, Edinger believes we alternate between periods of inflation—identification with an internal sense of God—and periods of depression, when we feel separation from God and a sense of unworthiness. The stages of inflation often give us the energy we need to deal with the internal changes that are happening, but we need to be prepared to cope with cycles of loss.

Bipolar disorder was previously known as manic-depressive disorder. This is because some people cycle through phases of inflation and phases of deep depression. Edinger recognizes a form of this cycling as natural to spiritual development. But even if such cycles are normal, they can be brutal. If you have tasted the euphoria of the sacred, to fall back into a sense of alienation and lack of meaning can be devastatingly painful.

In the sixteenth century, St. John of the Cross, a Spanish Christian mystic, wrote the classic poem *Dark Night of the Soul*. The title may be more evocative about the experience of alienation than the actual poem (no offense, St. John!), but the concept of "dark night" resonates with many of us. It also helps to imagine that the Sun will rise again, and you may once again be infused with light.

How can it help to know about this possible cycling? Observe yourself. Have compassion for yourself. Get help when you need it. Integrate what is happening. Most importantly, recognize that stages of inflation provide us with enough energy and self-esteem to meet the challenges that come with changing our lives and attitudes.

In the euphoric phases, gather yourself toward your journey and draw from the wellspring of energy you have received. If you then descend into dark phases, work on the meaning spiritually and psychologically. This is the perfect opportunity to explore any issues in your family of origin or in your relationships—or in your view of our culture. These are probably the recollections of reality that are fueling your sense of separation and depression. In addition to finding compassion for yourself, you may develop compassion for others as deep as the oceans from your own depths of aloneness and despair.

And not least important to say—during psychedelic experience, you may visit places of darkness that seem so very hard to endure. If you can fathom them as stages in a process, as darkness from which later connection to light is made, you may find a deep sense of inner peace.

Cleansing the Doors of Perception

In closing my chapter on Maps of Consciousness, I want to leave you with a basic model of "open and close." This involves an opening to the energies of the universe (sometimes including a feeling of inflation) and then using those energies to cleanse your doors of perception. This is a model of "receive" and then "use to create." The creation involves living your life through interaction with others and the world.

In an interview, Jim Morrison of The Doors put it this way:

> When we perform, we're participating in the creation of the world, and we celebrate that creation with the audience. It becomes the sculpture of bodies in action. That's the political part, but our power is sexual. We make concerts sexual politics. The sex starts with me then moves out to include the charmed circle of musicians onstage. The music we make goes out to the audience and interacts with them. They go home and interact with their reality, then I get it all back by interacting with that reality. So the whole sex thing turns out to be one big ball of fire.
>
> I offer images, I conjure memories of... freedom. But I can only open doors; I can't drag people through.
>
> Our work, our performing, it's striving for metamorphosis. It's like the purification in the alchemical sense. First you have the period of disorder, chaos, returning to a primeval disaster region. Out of that you purify the elements and find a new seed of life, which transforms all life and all matter and the personality until finally, hopefully, you emerge and marry all those dualism and opposites. Then you're not talking about evil and good anymore but something unified and pure.[94]

Two basic movements are happening in non-ordinary state journeys, sometimes one or the other, sometimes both, usually spread out over time. The two movements are inseparably intertwined, like lovers, working themselves against each other. There is a way in which the movement between these ways reflects feminine and masculine energies and the act of making love. But you have to remember that masculine and feminine energies are alive and well within all of us, regardless of gender orientation or sexuality.

One movement opens to the energy from the universal source. That energy, if you open to it, penetrates the blocks in you that may be causing suffering for you or holding you back from moving toward your most whole self. You *receive* this energy. You allow it to penetrate you. You can feel this as a feminine experience if you like, but you don't need to get into gender wars on it. Just feel yourself opening and receiving. Transpersonal teacher Hillevi Ruumet describes feminine processing as "more organic, internal processes with a relational, feelings-based and nurturing focus."[95]

The second movement involves you doing the psychological (or psychospiritual) work to continue dissolving the blocks. This is active energy from you into yourself. Here is where knowing some maps and classifications can help you understand or conceptualize what is arising and find the best people and tools to work with (that is, integrate) what is coming forward.

You can consider this "working on yourself" a masculine experience if you like (avoiding falling into gender issues). By this I mean that you gather energy and penetrate what may be there within you that is ready to dissolve and release. Ruumet describes masculine energy as "a more active, externally focused, analytical, goal directed orientation."[96] By externally focused, I mean focused on something within you that you want to understand and process through. This is internal to you, but feels like something you are witnessing and can work with.

I hear Jim Morrison as describing a version of this process when he talks about the music of The Doors as participating in the creation of the world and as a sexual process. As you open yourself to your experiences, as you then move yourself back into them, you engage in a creative act—the act of creating yourself. In that dance, that lovemaking, you integrate.

Now Your Turn

My intent in this chapter has been to give you some maps that might help you engage with the path that exploring psychedelics opens for you. Now I want to invite you to remember some of your own individual frames of reference that have been helpful to you in your life, including those developed during any psychedelics experiences you have had.

Your frames of references may seem like they have nothing to do with the kind of map you can explain in words or with linear thought. For instance, I sometimes bring a small wooden statute of the Hindu god Ganesh to non-ordinary state sessions. Ganesh is known as the remover of all obstacles. For me, Ganesh acts as a map to help me find my way during experiences. The map is to follow the path that seems to remove obstacles.

Ganesh

What are some symbols that provide meaning or guidance to you? Can you understand them as maps of guidance?

___
___
___
___
___

Do you have sources of inspiration outside of yourself that you might want to bring into non-ordinary state work?

___
___
___
___
___

Integration Exercise 5: Mind Mapping Your Psychedelic Journey

What You Need

- Pen
- Markers
- Blank paper (legal size or bigger)
- Your journal.

General Background

Mind mapping is a highly effective way of getting information in and out of your brain. This is another psychedelic integration exercise that can be done before any psychedelic experience to work with your intentions or as integration to understanding your journey after it has happened. I will explain the exercise in terms of using it after a journey, but you can easily adapt it to working with where you are before an experience.

Often times a psychedelic experience can be "loaded" with information that can create more confusion if not appropriately integrated. Mind mapping is a creative and logical means of note taking and note making that literally "maps out" your ideas. All mind maps have some things in common. They have a natural organizational structure that radiates from the center and use lines, symbols, words, colors, and images according to simple, brain-friendly concepts. Mind mapping converts a long list of monotonous information into a colorful, memorable and highly organized diagram that works in line with your brain's natural way of doing things.

One simple way to understand a mind map is by comparing it to a picture of a tree. The tree trunk is the base of the tree where all the main body is. The trunk represents the main idea; the main branches leading from the center represent the key thoughts in your thinking process; the twigs or smaller branches represent your secondary thoughts, and so on. Special images or shapes can represent breakthroughs of interest or particularly related ideas.

You can think of it this way:

- The main idea, psychedelic experience or focus is crystallized in a central image.
- The main themes radiate from the central image as "branches."
- The branches comprise a key image, symbol or key word drawn or printed on its related line (don't let yourself feel limited to words).
- Topics of lesser importance are represented as "twigs" of the relevant branch; they are potentially open for more integration.
- The branches form a connected nodal structure.

Why this Exercise is Important for Psychedelics Integration

Mind mapping pulls information from a part of you that is not necessarily linear. But it puts the information from the non-linear side into a demonstration that you can see on the page.

You have probably heard about the difference between the right and left hemispheres of your brain. For right-hand-dominant people, the left side of the brain processes in analytical, sequencing, and linear ways, including use of language. The right side processes in a more holistic manner, typically taking into account a felt-sense of things such as imagination, intuition and rhythm. For most left-handed people, things are reversed and the differentiation is not necessarily as strong.

Psychedelics tend to throw differentiations out the window and let you experience sources of inspiration and understanding from both sides of the brain. Mind mapping holds the intention of letting you get this "both" intention or memory down into form so that you can keep working with it. The felt-sense, intuitive and imaginative appears in a way that can be understood and remembered by your analytical and sequential self. This can also feel like a liberation or relief for all parts of you in that you have it out of you and do not have to carry it all inside you.

How To Do It

Preparation in advance

1. Create a safe and sacred space that you have devoted to your psychedelic integration. This can be the same space you dedicate to meditating.
2. Build an altar that speaks to you, with both spiritual and physical interests of yours being represented.
3. Have your paper, markers, pens, and pencils laid out on your table.

Instructions for the exercise (Time: Twenty minutes to forty-five minutes)

- Sit for a moment and reflect on the general theme of your psychedelic experience. This could be for five minutes or a couple of days. (In many situations this could be one or up to a number of themes. My request is to attempt to integrate no more than three main themes). For example, Theme: Drink.
- Start by placing the main themes in circles in the center of your paper.
- Explore for a moment what thoughts relate to the main theme. These are your sub themes; think about them as your branches. For example, Sub theme: tea, coffee, and water.

- Continue writing; keep the branches short phrases or words that reflect your psychedelic experience.
- Incorporate symbols, names, and colors to your sub themes. Challenge yourself to expand even more from your sub themes. For example, detailed sub themes: white tea, cold press coffee, and sparkling flavored water.
- You are finished when you have exhausted your thoughts regarding the map.

You will find later in the book many exercises that work in a more artistic or metaphorical manner; for instance, beginning with a blank mind and sheet of paper and letting images or shapes come forward. In this exercise, I begin with conscious ideas, thoughts or images that you recall from your journey or want to bring into your journey.

There are several benefits of using this cognitive-based mind mapping integration exercise. To begin with, some people integrate more comfortably through beginning with words, concepts and thoughts. Others might more easily integrate beginning with pictures, symbols, colors or other non-linguistic forms. No matter which camp you are in, or if you are somewhere in between both extremes, I believe mapping in this cognitive fashion can develop your experience in ways that might be surprising, expanding, and grounding. Because psychedelic experiences are often hard to hold onto, grounding them with words, concepts, and other cognitive forms can help bring them into "reality" and make it more likely that you hold onto and grow from the experience.

This exercise can be used in many different ways. You could just use one main theme on a single piece of paper, or you could incorporate your whole psychedelic experience on one larger piece of paper. As I noted at the outset of this exercise, you could also map out your intentions, apprehensions, or hopes around an upcoming experience. In a way, this might plant seeds that will grow into branches, limbs and leaves in your actual experience.

Ultimately, the goal of mapping your experience will give you another lens to process and integrate your work. Many times I have had the chance to go back days later and add to a mind mapping diagram I thought was finished, only to uncover another "rabbit hole."

CHAPTER 6

CHANNELS OF INTEGRATION

In later chapters, I will talk about integration at different stages, with different psychedelics, for different types of people, and for people with different interests and goals. In this chapter, I want to share some ways of thinking about integration through different channels of your being. Staying aware of integration wanting to happen through different channels can be helpful in any form or stage of integration. Very importantly, inviting a "change of channels" can help move integration forward and work around blocks that may be arising in your life process.

I have borrowed the word "channels" from psychologist Arnold Mindell, whose ideas are discussed below. In essence, talking about "channels" recognizes that our path toward healing and wholeness emerges through different parts of us.

For most of us, some parts of ourselves are mostly unknown. They are there waiting for us to discover. Put another way, we have been trained by our culture to compartmentalize or even negate parts of ourselves. Aside from cultural influence, each of us has certain tendencies of personality that mean some parts of us are less developed as open channels of expression than other parts. Bearing in mind the possibility of different channels of integration can help you move forward and very often "break through" when you feel stuck.

Mind, Body and Emotion

Mind-Body-Emotion (or head-gut-heart) is a very common way of talking about what feel like different parts of us. As I mention throughout this book, I encourage you to bring all parts of yourself into one process or flow. But I know that many of us do not experience much access to our hearts or our bodies. To some extent, we may have been trained to separate out these parts because our culture has many divisions that contribute to feeling separations. Many people today live mostly "in their heads" and do not have much contact with their heart or body.

While most of us want to move toward wholeness of our entire being, there is importance to being able to feel different parts within us. Feeling into your body, mind, and heart is a great place to begin to notice that your attention can go to many different places, including most anywhere inside you. You may remember that in Integration Exercise 1, I encouraged you to notice all the places where your attention could go.

Many systems for spiritual growth recognize the value of feeling head, heart, and body as different sources of being. You may remember our discussion of the Enneagram and spiritual teacher Gurdjieff, who traveled around the world to investigate different spiritual teachings and developed a personality system based on whether people find their primary motivation in the workings of the head, heart, or gut. I will talk in more detail later in this chapter about the chakra system, which describes energy centers associated with head, heart, and body, though the chakra system has seven (not only three) different locations of body-energetic centers.

I am going to hit "pause" for a moment in our narrative and invite you to explore yourself at this moment. This is an exercise I use with clients or group members before starting many sessions:

> *I welcome you to get into a comfortable seated position. With your feet firmly on the ground, I invite you to bring full awareness to the sensations in your hands. This might be your first time today of being aware of your hands. Without judgment, simply pay attention to the physical body sensations....*
>
> *Having brought some attention to your body, now take a deep breath and allow yourself to simply be where you are....*
>
> *Now, transition your awareness to your mental mind. Immediately recognize all the thoughts that surface. I ask you, again without judgment, to put these thoughts on a shelf, knowing that you will always be able to come back to them. See if you can feel the difference between sensing your body and being with your thoughts and mind. Bringing your awareness to a calm, clear mind, take a few moments to be present to what comes up....*
>
> *Now having brought some attention to both your body and your mind, take another deep breath and allow yourself to simply be where you are....*
>
> *I now ask you to shift to the seat of emotion, that being your heart. Again without judgment, focus on what comes up. This could be a person, a spiritual higher power, or a feeling overcoming you. Bringing awareness to all of these sensations, find peace, a sense of calmness, and your own presence.*

Now I count down from 5 to 4, without judgment, exploring the sensations of your body... from 4 to 3, exploring the sensations in your mind... from 3 to 2, connecting the sensations in your emotional heart... and from 2 to 1, opening your eyes to see the room and yourself in a different way.

How are these channels helpful for integration?

- Notice if you favor your mind, heart, or body when assessing what is real and meaningful to you. Is it harder to "feel" your heart? Your body? Your mind?
- When you are working with integration of any experience, you might think about integrating from parts of yourself you do not usually favor.
- Try different exercises that integrate from each of these parts of yourself.
- With anything that is happening, check in with your mind, heart, and body to see what you might know or feel.

Verbal vs. Non-verbal

Most of us think about psychological work as involving talk therapy. In the last few decades, many therapists (like myself) have learned to encourage their clients to feel into their bodies and allow expression to come up that is non-verbal. The exercise I just shared gives you a taste of how that might work. Many other non-verbal ways of working with ourselves are now available: yoga, meditation, dance, and authentic movement. Several forms of therapy involve both talk and non-verbal expression. Some examples are psychodrama, Gestalt therapy, bodywork, or massage.

I find great potential in combining non-verbal and verbal forms of integration. This includes not only bringing non-verbal methods into the picture, but also using talk therapy to unpack and expand on the non-verbal realities of your being and life, including working with psychedelics. As I have shared, I wrote my master's thesis on the value of bringing talk therapy together with non-ordinary state experiences. I find this important for several reasons:

- The simple expression of talking about deep experience in a safe, non-judgmental environment can help affirm and "make real" the experience.
- There is value in having dialogue with a trained professional to process all the details and hidden components of the experience; after all, the original enthusiasm around LSD arose because the experience tended to open up the unconscious for more profound therapeutic work.

- Quite a few people, after experiencing psychedelics, have a part of themselves that is wondering, "Am I going crazy?" For many people, psychedelics tend to show them how their mind is operating, and they may start to feel a separation from the "operating system" and what they previously thought was "them." Talking with a therapist about this kind of experience can provide reassurance and grounding.
- Talk therapy can provide education about different ways to integrate psychedelic experiences such as I am sharing in this book.
- Perhaps most importantly, many people might end up feeling alone after a psychedelic experience; talking out an experience with a therapist, partner, or close friend can bring companionship and support into the experience.

Although verbal expression of your experiences is important, I do not feel that it is enough for most people. Psychedelics tend to encourage you to become one whole person (mind, body, emotions—and I can add spirit). To join all parts of yourself together through integration, you need to add non-verbal channels.

More on Right-Brain Left-Brain

When you think about integrating psychedelic experience, you might consider moving back and forth between methods that involve your different brain hemispheres. This involves combining verbal and non-verbal methods, but there is more to it.

In the Mind Mapping Exercise, I touched upon the well-known differentiations between the functions of right and left-brain hemispheres. For right-handed people, the analytical and language functions operate mostly through the left brain, while the creative, non-verbal, and holistic functions operate through the right brain. This is reversed for most left-handed people. In recent years, it has been shown that this polarity between brain hemisphere functions is not exact and may vary by individual. I find it fun to note that I am left-handed and many of the editors of this book are right-handed, so I think I have both hemispheres covered in putting together *The Psychedelics Integration Handbook*.

In general, drawing on your different brain hemispheres is a way to think about an oscillating (one-two, one-two, one-two) style of integration. You may focus your attention on a right-brain holistic understanding of where you are moving, finding what may be emerging from you in ways that feel creative and non-linear. Often this involves allowing symbolic representations to come forward. Remember that I drew upon Jung's understanding that the unconscious communicates through symbols, which never have just one meaning but that point toward relationships and wholeness.

Following symbols can take us deep into the unconscious, where everything is whole and connected. Then you might allow your left brain to find language and other linear, analytical representations for the most important parts of what you are discovering. I find this allows you to hold onto what is emerging from the right-brain land of symbols and wholeness. With these more analytical representations (words, a story, a list, a mind-map), you can communicate with an integration therapist about your work or have entry points for many exercises or techniques that take you once again back into the right-brain land. Again, one-two, one-two, one-two.

Just as important in considering right-brain/left-brain is the fact that the left side of your brain controls the muscles on the right side of your body, and vice versa. For instance, if you want to raise your left hand, the right side of your brain sends the messages down your neurons to your left arm and hand. This reversal is called decussation. There are some exceptions—for instance, smell (a very old function evolutionarily) is not reversed at all; visual processing is only partly reversed; and auditory processing involves both sides but has an important place on one side.

It can be profound to consider playing with the symmetry and non-symmetry in your body-mind when working with psychedelics and integration. Martin Ball, who works with 5-MeO-DMT, is adamant that parts of the body (for instance, the arms and hands) naturally move symmetrically when you are integrating non-duality during deep work with this medicine.

There is something about embodied symmetry that touches us at very deep levels. Similarly, breaking up symmetry can shake things loose. When feeling back into psychedelic experiences, you might experiment with symmetric movement or posturing in dance, authentic movement, or yoga. Then see how it feels when you break symmetry. See if any emotions or memories come up.

It can be very interesting to start doing things from the non-dominant side of your body. Try using your non-dominant hand in drawing or art projects. This helps pull out information, experience, and feelings from the non-analytical side of you. Around the house, see what it is like to spend a night or day or weekend using only your non-dominant arm. After a left hand injury and stiches, I had to keep my left arm in a sling for several weeks. I used my right arm, hand, and side almost exclusively during much of that time. Strangely, even while I was hindered, there was something that began to feel more whole and even peaceful for me in how I moved and just plain *was*.

Later, my team doctor confirmed that several people had reported this experience to him. He believes this emerging sense of wholeness relates to the hemisphere split and the value of including all of your body in your movements and sense of self. In his work, he often coaches people in the value of consciously moving from both sides of themselves.

In experiencing the forced reliance on my non-dominant side, I noticed many memories and emotions come to the surface, seemingly out of nowhere. Many came from my childhood and adolescence. Then, when I began using my dominant side again, even more memories and feelings came up. This was good grist for the integration mill.

The Jungian Functions

One of Carl Jung's contributions to psychology was to notice four ways of processing information: **thinking, feeling, intuition, and sensation.** The popular personality assessment called Meyers-Briggs (developed by a mother-daughter pair with those names) asks questions to find where we land on the range of these dimensions. Jung realized that each of us "leads" with one of these functions, which is called our dominant function. The "opposite" function then becomes our "inferior" function. It works like this:

Dominant function	Inferior function
Thinking	Feeling
Feeling	Thinking
Intuition	Sensation
Sensation	Intuition

I find these dimensions useful to consider with integration work. Suppose you're someone who leads with "thinking" and your "inferior" function is "feeling." When your head is racing with thoughts, you can teach yourself to examine, "How do I feel?" Feeling in the Jungian functions is not exactly about emotions (which Jungians might call affect) but is about how you value something. Feeling answers the question, "Does this feel good or not?"

On the other hand, if you lead with feelings, you might move toward wholeness by looking for "What do I think about this?" This gets back to the dimensions of head and heart. And you might remember that I described integration in our Entryway as "feeling your thoughts" and "thinking your feelings."

Thinking and feeling are both rational functions because they involve reflection. Intuition and sensation are described as irrational because they involve perception and reaching an understanding with less reflection. These functions may be a bit harder to feel (or think) into.

Those of us who lead with intuition (I do) will have an "intuitive" sense of "the whole" before we can notice particular parts or break things down. This is like receiving "data" from the unconscious. If you lead with intuition, you are comfortable with apprehending entire truths all at once based on what comes from the inside. Jung wrote:

> In intuition a content presents itself whole and complete, without our being able to explain or discover how this content came into existence. Intuition is

a kind of instinctive apprehension, no matter of what contents.... Intuitive knowledge possesses an intrinsic certainty and conviction.[97]

Sensation, on the other hand, involves taking in sense impressions from the external world. Impressions are based on what is received from the outside. The sensation function may also focus on bodily sensations in a concrete way, but this may feel as though the body is a source of information separate from you.

Working with psychedelics sometimes leaves us in places that feel mostly intuitive. This may be true even if you are usually very good with sensate functions. After working with psychedelics, it can become a spiritual practice to make sure you attend to practical details. Your life partners and family will appreciate your not making *them* deal with all the practical details while you are working on yourself.

More generally, if you tend to be an intuitive (even "spacey" person—and I describe myself that way sometimes), it can be very grounding during a life process of integration to make practical and sensate details part of your spirituality. I have some techniques I share with people when they seem stuck in a "spacey" space. Here are a few:

- Touch parts of your body a few times in an orderly and circular way: tap your knee, feel your knee; tap your shoulder, feel your shoulder; hold your heart, feel your heart beat. Cycle through this three to five times.
- Connect with the sensate details of the outside world: ask yourself things like, what is the temperature now? Is it raining or snowing or sunny? Do some simple math exercises that you make up spontaneously—for example, what is 3 + 7?
- Consider: what are the three main things I'm working on now in the practical part of my life? What are the five things I need to do today?
- Sometimes holding an ice cube in your hand (not to cause pain, but to feel temperature) can bring you into sensate reality. You can find other exercises like that for your own style.

I feel the exercise of "moving into sensate" can help shift people into new understandings and perspectives if they are accustomed to spending much of their time in their imaginations. In a way, this is the opposite of the "active imagination" exercise Jung developed to encourage letting go into the emergence of unconscious ideas. Bring yourself out of imagination into practical functionality of your daily life—and see what might shift. The focus is on *functionality* in this real world.

On the other side of the intuitive-sensate continuum, people who are very connected to the practical details of life are sometimes challenged to let go into the realm of the whole. Releasing into the whole may feel as though you are losing the order that you place upon the sensate world. If it is any consolation, sometimes you find that the realm of the whole contains order at an entirely different level than you expected. Remember my discussion in Chapter 5 of the implicate order described by physicist David Bohm.

Sometimes sensate people have trouble accepting the "reality" of working with consciousness, which often requires leaps of faith in our current culture. It may be hard to trust what comes from the unconscious as opposed to the external sensate world. In part, this is why I included a section on the "new physics" so that we can know that the "big picture" behind the ideas I am sharing can be grounded in hard science.

There is nothing wrong with needing to have step-by-step explanations or proof of things before we can accept something (sensation and thinking types). If this is you, then you might want to follow up on some of the reading and research leads I give you. Don't take my word for anything, but convince yourself piece by piece of whatever realities feel right to you.

In a big way, exploring psychedelics for many sensate and thinking people helps the letting go into what may feel like the chaos of the whole. Ultimately, though, it is not about taking things on faith, but about realizing that the most important realities come through your own consciousness and experience rather than what the mainstream materialist paradigm implies to you. In a sense, this is about trusting yourself.

Another dimension Jung noticed is more familiar to most people—introversion and extroversion. Being an extrovert or introvert is not just about whether you like to be the life of the party or talk to one person on the sofa. A good touchstone is whether you get energy from being inside yourself or from reaching out to the world (and other people). I talk about the value of integrating alone or with others in different places in this book. When you consider your preferences for how to integrate, you might notice your tendency towards introversion or extroversion and experiment with living "how the other half lives."

Considering how you relate to these dimensions can help your integration at any stage. If you would like to find out where you land on the Jungian functions, just put Meyers-Briggs into your search engine and you will find some free assessments to give you information.

The Chakra System

If you're reading this book, you are probably familiar with the chakra system to one degree or another. But let's take a look at how the chakras can work as channels for integration.

Since the 1960s, Eastern spiritual practices have made their way into the West, offering us many ways for self-exploration. Underlying many of these practices is awareness of seven major energy centers of our bodies. Actually, it is more accurate to understand **chakras** as the centers of the many layers of energy systems in our bodies, from the dense physical to very subtle.

In the Hindu tradition, balancing the chakras is part of spiritual and physical health. Opening the chakras is part of spiritual development. This means that energy at different layers becomes more free-flowing and connected to energies outside your own energy system.

The chakras are the energy components of the physical body system understood in Eastern medicine. This system includes energy meridians connecting all the parts of the body. Acupuncture, for instance, activates these meridians to encourage healing in the physical body. It is important to remember that chakras are energetic but also intrinsically connected to the physical body. In a way, these are the connections between our physical plane and more spiritual realms.

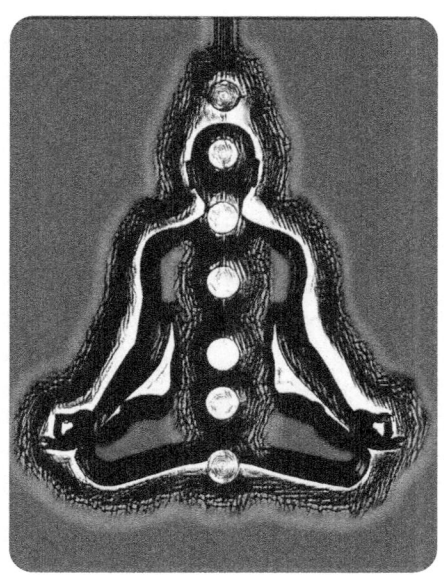

The Chakra System

When different chakras open, life experiences associated with those chakras tend to come your way. If you consciously integrate the meanings and impact of these experiences, you are moving along an ancient path of spiritual development. The more you integrate, the more the chakras may open; and the more the chakras open, the more experiences may come your way for processing.

I will encourage you to find your own learning about the chakras if you are interested. But I will note this basic guide:

Chakra	Qualities	Location
First	Root, physicality, sense of safety, life and death, connection to Earth.	Base of your torso or bottom of vertebrae

Second	Family, tribe, sexuality, close relationships.	A few inches below your navel (though may be experienced more in the groin or sexual organs)
Third	Power, warrior energy, will, individuality, agency, "gut truths," confidence, clarity.	Solar plexus, "gut"
Fourth	Heart, love, compassion, empathy, multiple perspectives, where the spiritual and physical meet, grief, longing.	Center of chest, heart
Fifth	The first of the truly spiritual centers; finding your voice; learning clear and clean communication; discernment; releasing codependence; speaking your truth without blame or judgment; knowing when to remain silent.	Throat
Sixth	Intuition, inner knowing, access to other realms, extra-sensory perception, non-attachment, acceptance of paradox.	Mid forehead (or various parts of head or eyes)
Seventh	Connection with the divine, awareness of the sacred, where grace may be received, "no limits," ecstasy, liberation.	Crown of head

In my experience, the chakras are not metaphorical. These are real centers of energy that often become activated in some way during non-ordinary states. From my work in Holotropic Breathwork, I know from personal experience (and witnessing the experiences of dozens of people) that activation of energy centers during non-ordinary states can involve a strong (and often difficult) need to release blockages.

Sometimes trauma seems to be correlated with (or perhaps stored in) the areas of the body associated with the relevant chakras. For instance, sexual trauma may feel "stored" in the second chakra; issues of abuse of power or finding one's own power can feel physically associated with the gut (third chakra). Really experiencing compassion for oneself and others, being able to grieve, and finding the capacity to give and receive love can involve what feels like a physical opening in the chest or corresponding area of the back (fourth chakra). Pressure for heart opening is very common in non-ordinary state work, particularly breathwork. Correlations to the other chakras (first and fifth through seventh) are also common, and you might imagine what that would be like (or you may have experienced them).

One of the most important understandings about spiritual awakening from the Hindu tradition involves **kundalini.** Often described as the serpent that awaits release at the base of the spine, some people experience a flow or rush of energy up through the body, the chakras, or the energy system. A sense of physical blockage near the base of the spine is also common during non-ordinary state work. You may ask your guide or facilitator to put their hand on that area or to offer you some pressure. Various yoga postures also seem to help. People often find themselves moving into postures that open up the base of the spine during non-ordinary journeys.

Sometimes, the sudden awakening of *kundalini* can be extremely destabilizing, even resulting in what the mainstream psychiatric system will label as a mental disorder (typically schizophrenia or bipolar disorder). I discussed the interplay between spiritual awakening and labels from the mainstream mental health system in Chapter 5.

As I noted, Christina Grof experienced and wrote about her own challenging *kundalini* awakening. This led Christina and her husband Stan to develop the idea of **spiritual emergency.** Often these experiences have strong physical correlations that can be tracked to some extent through the chakras.

Hillevi Ruumet wrote a precious short book called *Pathways of the Soul: Exploring the Human Journey.* Through decades of work as a Jungian therapist, Ruumet noticed that people working on their psychological development tend to cycle through issues that can be associated with the different chakras, which she calls Centers. Building on the chakra model, Ruumet describes the developmental journey many people take through the chakras in their unfolding life. There is integration "work" for us at each of the chakra levels.

Hillevi Ruumet

As Ruumet explains, we tend to complete one round of transformation involving one chakra, and then cycle back to other chakras, completing more work there, and continually move back and forth along a pattern of cyclical development. I return to Ruumet's understanding of developmental processing at the end of the next chapter.

When integrating psychedelic experiences—and even during psychedelic sessions —it can be very helpful to bring consciousness to what may be emerging in your chakra system. Knowing the chakras can also be helpful, in my view, for guides and facilitators of non-ordinary state work. This does not mean that either you or your guides bring pre-conceived judgments about what may be emerging energetically. Rather, it means that you might be able to understand as completely natural some of the things that emerge during non-ordinary state processing, which otherwise might seem strange or even worrisome.

Processwork (Arnold Mindell)

Arnold ("Arnie") Mindell is an American who trained as a Jungian analyst in Jung's native country, Switzerland. Since the late 1960s, he has been an innovative and influential therapist and teacher, first at the Jung Institute in Zurich and later worldwide, with a home base on Oregon. In his analytic practice, Mindell worked with the dreams of hundreds of people. This led him to realize that the body brings forward, as sensations and symptoms, the same information that dreams are trying to bring to consciousness.

Mindell developed processwork, or process-oriented psychology, assisted by his wife, Amy Mindell. In integration work, the understanding that "process" emerges through different channels is very useful. The four channels identified by Mindell are:

- Visual
- Auditory
- Movement (kinesthetic) and
- Body feeling (proprioceptive).

Arnold and Amy Mindell

Mindell teaches that most of us reach an "edge" in our process where we have trouble releasing something or taking the next step "off the cliff" in our development. One of the ways to step off the cliff is to notice something emerging in a "different channel."

From my experiences in Holotropic Breathwork, I find it very common that a shift happens when something is pushing through in a different channel. It is quite common for the "inner healer" in breathwork to offer images that are profound and have my complete attention. Then we may notice (or a facilitator may help us notice) that a sound, a movement, or a body feeling is on the verge of coming forward. Quite often, letting the "channel switch" is what allows the depth of healing (and adventuring) to come forward. Some of the most useful things I have heard from facilitators in breathwork have been:

- "If there's a sound, let it come."
- "Let your body do what it wants to do."
- "Okay, so you're feeling that [somewhere in your body]. Is it okay if I put my hand there? Can you breathe into that place?"

Many experiences in psychedelics are less body- or emotion-based than in breath-work, but allowing channels to switch in psychedelics can also be helpful. Moving among channels in integration of psychedelics experiences becomes very important. For instance, in working with psychedelics, you may have astounding visual or auditory information. To take the next steps to integrate that information, it may be helpful to "switch channels" into body feeling or movement. Again, this is the reason for many of my experiential offerings in this book.

Internal Family Systems (IFS)

In the world of integrating psychedelics, it is important to embrace many different options for working with your experience. One of the goals of psychedelic integration is to understand your **true self**. I think of finding your true self as letting go of defensive parts that no longer serve you. Psychedelics are particularly good at showing you these defensive parts if you are willing to look. Your relationship with these defensive parts becomes an important channel for your integration.

To discover and understand the role that your psychedelic experience is opening to you, I would like to offer a therapeutic theory called **Internal Family Systems (IFS)**. This method was created by Richard Schwartz as a way to recognize and integrate the many different parts that each of us carry within us.

IFS can be explained by understanding that people have a positive true self with positive characteristics (including the ability to heal ourselves). But we also have wounded parts, called *exiles* in the IFS system. Exiles are usually hidden from the outside world and even from ourselves. Unconsciously, we feel we are preventing damage or avoiding acting out by excluding our exiles. But without giving some life to the exiles, they remain inside us, sometimes sapping our energy and life force. Bringing the parts together is the essence of integration work.

To understand the basic components of the Internal Family Systems theory, it is valuable to learn some of the fundamental language that is associated with the method. Key concepts that help develop your true self include:

- **Managers:** Those parts of the self that protect the wounded parts of the self (exiles) from further damage and manage the negative outward effects of the exiles.
- **Exiles:** Those parts of the self that have been hurt or damaged; when triggered, they usually have a strong emotional and sometimes acting out component.
- **Firefighters:** Those parts of the self that get "called in" automatically when an exile is activated in order to both control and protect the exile from acting out in public. The work of the Firefighters is analogous to a *Post Traumatic Stress Disorder (PTSD)* reflex.
- **Self:** The self has many parts and qualities. The "true self" is believed to be always present and contains characteristics such as perspective, compassion, curiosity, confidence, and healing.

The goal of using this work is for the "true self" to begin leading with less and less need for the manager or firefighters. When damaged parts of the self are exposed, they may be healed and will no longer control or dominate your behaviors. The IFS model can help you work with addiction, obsessions, or any other psychological issues. As you develop conscious relationships between the healing parts and the damaged parts, you progress toward your true self and come to gradual terms with your discoveries about why the managers, firefighters, and exiles came into being.

I have a friend who works with her partner in facilitating psychedelic experience, usually with 5-MeO-DMT. She introduces IFS work at the beginning of a retreat to give participants tools to work with the psychological material that may come up during the session. This can play out in many ways, but she gives one particular common example. People often have amazing experiences with 5-MeO-DMT that open them up to unconditional love and how it feels to know you are absolutely okay. As you come back to your more customary mindset, you may feel overwhelmed by what seems like all kinds of things from inside yourself intruding on this basic knowledge that all is beautiful. For example, an exile based in shame might try to persuade you that the experience was not real. IFS wisdom can help put a name and face to the different parts that seem to be present when this or other processes emerge during psychedelics sessions.

It can be very important to *work with* the managers, firefighters, and other parts as they struggle to get to know each other. This type of tool can make a big difference in whether you integrate or dissociate from experiences you have just had.

The IFS tool is just as important for ongoing integration. As you re-enter your day-to-day living after a psychedelic experience, you may find yourself falling into *"sub-personalities"* or what I would call *"inner voices"* or *"parts."* For example, a part of *me* may attack the more authentic *me* for participating in this work, then another part feels lonely or hurt, and then still another part takes over and makes me ignore all the voices. Being able to bring consciousness (and language) to these normal reactions helps us understand that the parts are not just patterns or feeling states, but more like individual personalities with their own needs, fears, ways, and agendas.

This is why the system draws on the model of a family, because these different parts are, in a way, separate people who all live together and influence each other. We may feel all our parts think the same way; however, with processing, we can begin to feel the dissonance and struggles that actually exist within us, as well as all the strengths and resources that we have. Then we can start to feel *good* about the value of all the parts and accept everything that is part of us. We can start to *incrementally* incorporate each part or voice into our true self.

As I have shared a few times already, Stan Grof offers the concept of an *inner healing intelligence* as a way of understanding our internal guide to our true healing. Within the Internal Family Systems method, Schwartz recognizes the existence of a competent Self (capital S) that is analogous to the inner healer. As we work with our parts, the Self becomes increasingly strong and integrated with the other aspects of our being. Working with a therapist, including someone familiar with IFS, can greatly assist this process.

Using the Internal Family Systems model, the integrative therapist or psychedelics guide:

1. Helps an explorer find the parts that are dominating the experience. You can also do this verbally or non-verbally through integrative exercises.
2. Then asks the *managers* or *firefighters* to "step back" to give the experiencer some space. As managers and firefighters separate from the participant, she can be vulnerable and come to face *IT,* whatever IT may be. Asking managers and firefighters to step back can also allow the experiencer to stay with the intensity of the psychedelic experience longer in order to help it ground in the person.
3. Lastly, the participant, once done with the psychedelic journey, can benefit from the support, safety, and guidance of the guide to become immersed in internal healing with their "true Self."

The Internal Family Systems model is one valuable tool in your tool belt for bringing flexibility and strength to your work with psychedelics. You can read more in *Internal Family Systems Therapy* by Schwartz.[98] As a basic take-away, I encourage you to understand that:

- Psychedelics may show you defensive parts that are part of your psyche.
- There are strong parts of your psyche that want to heal you that psychedelics will reinforce.
- Forming a relationship with all these parts can be helpful. Let them get to know each other, and love them all.

Dan Siegel and Mindsight

In recent years, the ancient practice of being aware of one's sensory experience in the present moment ("being mindful") has taken a prominent place in discussions among clinicians, educators, and the public at large. For many people, putting these ancient practices into the language of contemporary neuroscience is helpful.

Dan Siegel is a psychiatrist and author of the internationally acclaimed book *Mindsight: The New Science of Personal Transformation*.[99] He is a leader in the field of neurobiology and founder of the Mindsight Institute, an educational center devoted to promoting insight, compassion, and empathy in individuals, families, organizations, and communities.[100]

Siegel describes **Interpersonal Neurobiology** as an inter-disciplinary approach that integrates independent fields of expertise for the purpose of painting a picture of the healing of the larger whole. Siegel brings together mathematics, varied social sciences, and other disciplines to solve for the greater concern. This is an excellent model for understanding the different disciplines that can be useful to you personally as you reach out into the theoretical and academic world to find the particular support you need to unpack, understand, and integrate what comes to you through psychedelics.

During medical school, Siegel made up the word **Mindsight** to describe the healing potential of looking into those parts of ourselves that are not integrated. These parts hold a **charge** that can act as a thread back into the part of ourselves that need healing. These are individual channels unique to you that may lead you toward a sense of healing and wholeness. In this way, Siegel puts into neurobiological language, and with the credibility he carries as a mainstream professional, the same threads that have been involved in psychospiritual work for generations. Some of the basic questions Siegel encourages us to ask with Mindsight are:

- Is there a memory that torments you or an irrational fear you can't shake?
- Do you sometimes become unreasonably angry or upset and find it hard to calm down?

- Do you ever wonder why you can't stop behaving the way you do, no matter how hard you try?
- Are you and your child (or parent, partner, or boss) locked in a seemingly inevitable pattern of conflict? [101]

The Wheel of Awareness is a concept invented by Siegel as a model for integration. What is being integrated, in his view, includes yourself and others, your right and left brains, and the internal dialogues always taking place between different parts of yourself. In the Wheel of Awareness, the hub represents the experience of awareness itself—knowing—while the rim contains all the points of anything you can come to know. One can send a spoke out to the rim to focus our attention on one point or another on the rim (for example, seeing a beautiful sunrise). In this way, the wheel of awareness becomes a visual metaphor for the integration of consciousness as we differentiate rim elements and hub awareness from each other and link them with our focus of attention. The hub is a form of knowing. In the sunrise example, the calmness we feel looking at a beautiful sunrise is brought back from the rim into the hub. We can then use that calmness when bringing attention to other things on the rim.

Let me put this into practice with an example of how you may feel after a psychedelic session. You might feel an overwhelming sense of *interconnectedness* with the universe; this is another way of perceiving a rim element. By using what Siegel calls a spoke, you then follow this down to a hub, which in the realm of a psychedelic experience brings you to any number of feelings that you associate with interconnectedness, potentially peace, joy, or contentment.

Another concept described by Siegel involves moving between rigidity and chaos in how we hold elements of awareness. Many experiences in psychedelics feel so fluid that we may not know if we can hold onto them or make sense of them. We may have an instinct to immediately label them with meaning of a rigid nature, which helps us feel we will not lose them. On the other hand, that kind of reduction might deflate the miracle of the gift, which has come from the realm of complete interconnection.

Siegel recommends that we work with our awareness in becoming comfortable at different stages of the continuum between rigid hold on a thought and chaotic release of any hold. Ultimately, finding a consistent flow down the river and avoiding either the bank of chaos or the opposite bank of rigidity can help us find attentiveness, responsiveness, and healthy processing towards wholeness.

What are some takeaways for integration work?

- Siegel's work can help you expand your understanding of integration into both grounded academic disciplines and practical tips for working on yourself and your relationships.

- Anything in your experience that holds a charge is a clue back into yourself worth exploring (and I return to this idea in Chapter 8, with the Awareness Positioning System (APS) of Tav Sparks).
- Learn to play with your awareness from hub to spoke; this is particularly useful in using positive experiences you have in psychedelics to help heal wounds or habits that hold challenging charge.
- Become comfortable with moving between holding onto something as part of your narrative and releasing it in order to make room for change.

Inter-psychic Channels

The channels of integration mentioned above involve **intra-psychic** integration. This is when you integrate by focusing on channels for integration within yourself. There are also powerful methods to help you discover **inter-psychic** channels of integration. By this I mean integration involving other people and groups. Since the human potential movement began after World War II, so many methods have developed for working on yourself with others. I will mention just a few to give you the idea of what is possible.

Psychodrama is a potent modality for exploring emotional issues through enactment in groups. With the assistance of a trained facilitator, individuals take turns in creating scenes that allow a working through of unresolved or emerging issues holding a great deal of charge. The person working on an issue invites others in the group to play the part of people in their lives with whom they have issues. The facilitator invites everyone involved in the scene to "drop into" what they are feeling in their bodies and emotions and to spontaneously "play out" (under structure from the facilitator) what arises through interaction with each other. This creates an inter-psychic experience where channels arise among all those involved that permit processing in a group setting.

Another modality, similar to psychodrama, is *family constellation* work. There are many styles and facilitation techniques around a common theme of bringing forward patterns and issues within family systems and family heritage. Often, unresolved and even unknown issues are draining energy and vitality from the individual and his or her family. In family constellation work, facilitators explore an issue with an individual who then invites, as in psychodrama, others in the group to stand in for family members. These can be known family members or even deceased ancestors who were not known to the person but may still be exerting influence in the present. Sometimes someone stands in for an entire lineage or nationality of people. Group members serving in the constellation (and those observing) often find within themselves what may have been missing from awareness, verbalization or resolution in the family system.

One of the leaders in developing family constellation work was the German psychotherapist Bert Hellinger. He taught that a **knowing field** comes into action that often allows shifts in ways that we relate to our ancestors, particularly our parents. Hellinger believed that many of us, even as adults, remain tied to our parents by the feeling they did not give us the right thing or *enough* of what we needed—and that they still owe us. His work showed that accepting what parents were able to give and creating one's own life allows a free-flowing energy.

> When the family has been brought into its natural order, the individual can leave it behind him while still feeling the strength of his family supporting him. Only when the connection to his family is acknowledged, and the person's responsibility seen clearly and then distributed, can the individual feel unburdened and go about his personal affairs without anything from the past weighing him down or holding him back.
>
> —Bert Hellinger

In psychedelic experiences, some of the most powerful openings relate to interpersonal relationships with family members. Very often it becomes possible to understand on an embodied experiential level the strands of psychological issues and story lines within families that have not previously come into awareness but may be holding an enormous charge and unresolved conflict. Often this involves trauma or things that could not be shared or spoken about. Such embodied psychedelic experiences provide an entry point into energies that may be integrated, and channeled forward, through family constellation work.

Family constellation work takes forward the compassion, forgiveness, and loving understanding that often comes as a gift within psychedelic experience. An excellent workbook for exploring your family lineage is *The Constellation Approach: Finding Peace Through Your Family Lineage* by Jamy and Peter Faust, who also lead family constellation workshops. [102] A family constellation worker who trained with the Fausts once told me there is nothing more powerful than working on your family's issues and beginning to feel the chain of your ancestors standing behind you and supporting you. I find this particularly useful for psychedelics work because it is possible to feel our ancestors in the field we enter through this work.

There are also many profound formats for inter-psychic integration that have no verbal or speaking elements. For example, **authentic movement** involves spontaneously allowing your body to express itself in the moment while being compassionately witnessed by others. Many people find the non-verbal aspect of such practices particularly powerful for developing healing connections between people and inside themselves. The non-judgmental witnessing component in this practice can be particularly healing—and resonates with my recommended practice of group integration work without interpretation or questioning (see Integration Exercise 8).

Energetic and Physical Body

Most of us are accustomed to experiencing our consciousness as separate from our bodies. When we are injured or experience illness or pain, we often think of our bodies as alien to us, causing us discomfort or threatening our viability. In the last few decades, much has been written about **embodiment** and the return to experiencing our bodies as ourselves. For many people, this is an important component of transpersonal psychology, as well as feminist psychology.

In my discussion about channels in this chapter, I began with the interplay of mind, body, and emotions. I want to leave this chapter with a suggestion that you might want to understand your energetic and physical body as the focal point in your psychedelic experience. This may be particularly true for some psychedelic medicines, such as Ayahuasca.

By this I mean that you may feel that your conscious mind takes a back seat to transformation that begins from inside your body. Your *awareness* remains present and may feel connected to your mind. But the field you enter may seem to have much more to do with your body. Your brain will feel as though it is part of your body, but not necessarily the source of what is you. In other words, your awareness may begin to understand your embodied physicality as a field connected to the larger field of universal consciousness. Your awareness witnesses the dance between them. You may come to feel that you and "the universe" are interchangeable focal points of awareness looking at what is in your body and in the universe.

This gets to the paradox that we are consciousness not tied to the material world, and yet we manifest and discover our particular life destinies through our bodies and the material world. I am touching upon the concept of surrender, which is important in psychedelics and all spiritual work. You surrender into your physicality (and ultimately into your eventual death), and from there you are released into all that is. This process of surrender may be the most important channel.

Sometimes "surrender" is the only effective channel when working with psychedelics medicines. Many people feel that psychedelics (again, particularly Ayahuasca) work to purge blocks or traumas that become lodged in the body (energetic or physical). You may feel as though the medicine (or the spirit behind the medicine) has entered your body in order to dissolve or remove a block. If you are working with an experienced facilitator or shaman, he or she might actually be assisting or causing this process.

When this happens, the channel for allowing this process may feel as though you are simply opening into what is happening, perhaps stepping out of the way of what is happening, and allowing these energies to enter into or through you. Because there is often some part of us that resists this process, the word "surrender" is a very useful term to describe the opening of this healing channel. When your process becomes one of surrender, you may feel as though no amount of preparation or intention was all that relevant to what happened. On the other hand, preparing to surrender into such experiences may be very useful. This may work as an invitation or acceptance of cleansing or purging energies. Bringing care to your body can be very helpful in preparing for these experiences, which is why most guides recommend attention to what you eat and drink in the days before a session.

If working with non-ordinary states is your path, eventually you will very likely understand all the channels I have mentioned as existing and working together simultaneously. Your attention during a non-ordinary state experience may move from one channel to the other depending on what is happening and where the medicine is bringing your energy and healing. For now, I want to end this chapter by mentioning the possibility that your body takes the lead during psychedelic experience, so that the main task of your conscious awareness may involve releasing the mental (or physical) blocks between experiencing the transformational and cleansing flow that can be part of this work. Paradoxically, the cleansing flow may seem as though it comes from within your body or energetic field—or it may feel as though it enters your body or energetic field from an external source. In the end, you might realize that there is less separation between internal and external than we are led to believe.

All this said, I know that many psychedelic experiences seem to involve consciousness completely leaving the body and exploring all kinds of amazing realms. This is part of the work, and yet when you come back, I encourage you to bring what you explored into the physical realm, starting with your body.

Now Your Turn

In this chapter, I touched upon several channels that may be involved in integration. I have found that shifting into channels that are new for you is one way to jumpstart integration and encourage breakthroughs—or simply growth in new directions. Before shifting into new channels, it helps to know where you are more comfortable. Looking back at the information in this chapter, I encourage you to ask yourself:

What have been your typical ways of relating to the world?
_____
_____
_____
_____
_____

How have you usually processed your experiences as they happen?

_____
_____
_____
_____
_____

Do you feel inclined to integrate with left-brain activities (for example, writing or verbally processing)? Or do you usually process with right-brain activities (for instance, dancing, art or collages)?

_____
_____
_____
_____
_____

Do you feel that you lead with your mind, your heart, or your physical self? Do you have a sense of where you might land on The Enneagram?

_____
_____
_____
_____
_____

Are you a thinking, feeling, intuitive, or sensate person? Which of these functions might be least developed? Can you move into new space with these functions?

_____
_____
_____
_____
_____

How do you express yourself, more verbally or non-verbally? Do you feel mostly introverted or extroverted?

_____
_____
_____

As you become conscious of your tendencies, are there places you might grow through new activities? You do not need to force change upon yourself—rather, you might just try some activities that draw out different parts of yourself.

And lastly—how do you feel about changing the channels?

Integration Exercise 6: Body Awareness

What You Need

- A comfortable place where you can lie down (e.g., your bed, sofa, mat)
- Tape recording of progressive muscle relaxation script (optional)
- Your journal.

General Background

Progressive muscle relaxation, or body scanning, is a great way to quietly turn inward, away from the stress and strain of external demands. This process soothes the central nervous system, eases physical tension, lowers heart rate and blood pressure, and slows down racing thoughts. You might want to do this exercise right before your first night's sleep after a psychedelic experience. This integrative exercise is one of deep relaxation. Progressive muscle relaxation can put you to sleep as you continue to advance through the experience.

There are different viewpoints about progressive muscle relaxation exercises. One school of thought is that you can manifest and learn to move energy around the more you work with your body. In this view you are moving through your physical body into your energetic system. The other view is that muscle relaxation exercises support you when you feel unable to connect to your physical body. When you feel scattered, you may benefit from coming back into your body. I feel it is a "both/ and" situation. I feel body awareness gives a sense of empowerment as well as control of your personal body.

Why this Exercise is Important for Psychedelics Integration

As I shared in the chapter you just finished, integrating from all channels of your body-mind-spirit is the ideal way to work your experiences. This exercise helps you feel the sources within you where insights, feelings, and information come from. In the Entryway, one of the ways I described integration was that you will be thinking your feelings and feeling your thoughts. This exercise helps you learn how to do this by bringing the different forms of awareness together.

Body scanning is especially important because most people in our culture have trouble accessing what is in their bodies. As you will discover if you stay on an integration path, the body often holds onto a great deal of information, from unexperienced trauma to insights to preferences to things you want to avoid. Learning how to better access this information can be helpful.

I take the liberty of noticing how this exercise provides a counter-point to the mind mapping exercise at the end of the last chapter. Rather than feeling into your mind, here you are feeling into (and thinking into) your body. Because emotions tend to be stored in the body and often dissociated from the mind, this exercise brings you in touch with your emotional as well as embodied self.

How To Do It

Preparation in advance

1. Step one is optional. The day of a psychedelic session it can be nice to have your bed made and your room organized. This is part of having the right mindset (set) and environment (setting).
2. Create or find a progressive muscle relaxation script that works for you. Some people don't like the sound of their own voice, and some people can be annoyed by other people's voices. (Script instructions for the exercise are below).
3. Have your journal by your bed if you want to write down what comes or if you want to be sure to record a dream when you wake up.

Instructions for the exercise (Time: 10 minutes to 15 minutes)

Get comfortable in your bed or mat. Stretch out on your back. Get any aches or tension out by shaking and moving.

Close your eyes and concentrate fully on your breath. Breathe air in through your nose and out through your mouth. It is important that you feel how the air enters, reaches into the lower parts of your lungs, and then leaves again through your mouth.

After breathing this way for several minutes, when your breath has become more regular, give yourself the following instructions:

- Wrinkle your forehead. Raise your eyebrows toward your hairline for ten seconds. Relax. Let go of thoughts.
- Close your eyes as tightly as you can for ten seconds. Relax.
- Draw the corners of your mouth back and grimace for ten seconds. Relax. Let go of judgment.
- Extend your arms in front of you and clench your fists tightly for five seconds. Relax. Let go of control.

- Extend your arms out against an invisible wall and push forward with your hands for five seconds. Relax. Let go…
- Bend your elbows. Tense your biceps for five seconds. Relax. Let go…
- Shrug your shoulders up to your ears for five seconds. Relax. Let go…
- Take notice of your lower back. Bring all your focus on your spine and back. Relax. Let go…
- Bring your attention to the front of your body. Tighten your stomach muscles for five seconds. Relax. Let go…
- Tighten your buttocks and feel your hips opening and dissolving into your bed. Relax. Let go…
- Tighten your thigh muscles by pressing legs together as tightly as you can and let go of the tension. Relax. Let go…
- Bend your ankles toward your body as far as you can for five seconds. Relax. Let go…
- Curl your toes under as tightly as you can for five seconds. Relax Let go…
- Give yourself gratitude and notice what comes. If you are doing this exercise before sleep, let yourself drift off into the night world.

The body scans alternates between a wide and narrow focus of attention—from focusing on your little toe all the way through the entire body. The body scan trains your mind to be able to move from detailed attention to a wider and more spacious awareness from one moment to the next. Any part of your body becomes someplace you know from the inside out.

CHAPTER 7

INTEGRATION AS PROCESS

In the last chapter, I talked about ways of holding the internal process of integration, as well as introduced inter-psychic integration. In this chapter, I explore how the internal and external blend together into a possible integrated flow of life, learning, and development. I call this chapter "integration as process." I could just as easily talk about process as integration. For kicks, let's look at a few dictionary definitions:

- **Integrate** is a verb meaning "to combine (one thing) with another so that they become a whole."
- Something is **integral** when it is "necessary to the completeness of the whole."
- **Integration** is "the action or **process** of integrating."
- A **process** is "a series of actions or steps taken in order to achieve a particular end."[103]

I think of *process* in the psychospiritual sense as moving along your life and bringing awareness to what happens internally and externally. Often this involves looking at the relationship between the internal and external. Something happens in life, and then you feel and think into how this impacts you inside. Conscious attention to what happens inside seems to bring more experiences that are relevant to your developing self. I talked about the same idea when I described Carl Jung's idea of synchronicity.

Integration, as I suggested in the Entryway of Chapter 1, involves bringing all that is happening into one flow. Other ways I described integration involve thinking your feelings and feeling your thoughts. Now that I have given you some maps of consciousness and some understanding about different channels of integration, I can say that integration is about using these sorts of tools to continue opening yourself into the person you are meant to be with the life you are meant to live. All that comes to you is brought through your process into your developing self.

Returning to the definition of **holotropic** coined by Stanislav Grof, I consider integration as the process of **moving towards wholeness**. But you get to decide what wholeness looks like to you. The fun thing is that you probably do not know for sure at any given moment what your idea of wholeness looks like. By definition, it is a process of unfolding evolution.

One way to think about psychedelics focuses on their ability to reveal where you may be out of sync with how you want to be—or feel you are meant to be. Just as likely, you may be shown where you are exactly on track and feel the connections you have to all that exists.

Often in psychedelics you may understand that everything is perfect "just as it is." But this can mean an understanding that given the way things are psychologically (internally), the external situation could be no other way. This can also mean that given the way things are internally for those involved, the way things are internally for others involved could be no other way. The perfection of things "just as they are" involves the understanding of wholeness and connection. This also involves an understanding of incremental development and the birth of a form of patience. Peace tends to arise because you understand all is unfolding as it can unfold.

But this does not negate the path of transformation. Change may seem even more important because you have a sense of relationship and consequence. External changes may become necessary, but you understand the inextricable link between internal and external.

With these understandings of wholeness, you can see how processing into "what is" can allow you to grow into yourself and the world as it is unfolding. Because psychedelics tend to show the relationships of all things in a wholeness, then you often have a chance of understanding how you (as a microcosm of the whole universe) fit into the scheme of things. You understand that following your own transformation can lead to the transformation of others and the world around you. This invites you to ask questions of yourself, which become part of your integration. Is the life you are living congruent with your deepest intentions and desires? Where are you congruent, and where are you growing?

One way that I talk about integration work is as **reconciliation.** One of the definitions of "to reconcile" is "make (one account) consistent with another, especially by allowing for transactions begun but not yet completed." [104] When psychedelics push us toward a new way of being, then we need to reconcile this new way of being with our actual lives both inside ourselves and externally out in the world. This is usually **hard** work.

We can stay safe in our heads and let our psychedelic experiences stay contained within us, or we can start to move these experiences into the places where they bump up against our internalized stories about ourselves. Even more challenging, we can start to let our psychedelic experiences challenge our behaviors and structures in our external lives. If we allow this to happen, we might feel as though we are becoming more authentic. Only through beginning to interact with the world from our new places does our psychedelic work actually start to integrate. The process is a series of actions or steps in your movement toward wholeness or authenticity, whatever that is for you. The functionality of your life becomes a flow from your sense of who you are. This almost always involves incremental changes, which are not always easy.

What gets complicated is that we tend to get feedback from the world about any differences we make in our ways of being. Maybe this is more appropriately called "pushback" in many situations. This is where we become challenged to live the transformation offered to us by non-ordinary state work. The challenge includes the need to keep pushing through the friction you may receive back from the world. Working in that space is the inception of integration. Dealing with the pushback, and where it takes you internally, is what integration is all about.

I also want to make a contrast between "reconciliation" and "acceptance." There is no doubt that acceptance is an important part of many psychospiritual journeys. As noted near the end of the last chapter, "surrender" is an essential aspect of spiritual work. But surrender does not always mean passivity. I find myself remembering the serenity prayer written by the American theologian Reinhold Niebuhr and often recited in Alcoholics Anonymous gatherings:

God, grant me the serenity to accept the things I cannot change,
Courage to change the things I can,
And wisdom to know the difference.

If there are external things that you cannot change, then integration involves processing through your honest feelings about the continuity you need to hold. For instance, almost all of us have times when we feel obligated to caretake for others, whether they are children, parents, loved ones, or friends in need. Often these others may be difficult people not able to bring much consciousness or health to their lives. If we decide we cannot change our path to stay present and helpful to them, then we can process and integrate all our feelings around what is happening. This too is experience that can be reconciled with who we are and who we are becoming.

With reconciliation, I mean to emphasize the **work** that can be done to take our experiences forward, to adjust them slowly, to let them meet the outer world, to feel back into where we go from the external feedback, and to move through all that arises cognitively, emotionally, and spiritually—through the many different possible channels I talked about in the last chapter.

"Process," Not an Event

This may be the most important thing I will say in this book. Using psychedelics in ways that will be integrated is not about having a single experience ("event") through a particular substance. Rather, it is about understanding your experience as one part of a transformational *process*.

This process has the potential of "reconciling" who you are at the moment of the experience with who you are becoming. This can bring into one flow all physical, emotional, mental, and spiritual aspects of your life. Using psychedelics is not just one moment in your life, but a catalyst along the track of ongoing, unfolding process.

Returning to a bit of physics, we can think about the way the "quantic entities" that make up the universe (e.g., electrons) are neither particles nor waves. This is the famous "wave-particle" duality. In the non-dual version, there is a particle (a snapshot) at the moment of observation, but the "real" event is an ongoing flow. You are not one static person, but you are a flow. Your consciousness is the main event in the flow, but your external actions and experiences are representations and participants in the flow.

This book is designed to help you figure out how your ongoing flow will work for you—not for anyone else. When throwing yourself into this process, psychedelics can be:

- An astounding catalyst to healing and growth in your life
- An open door to secrets of the mind and the universe
- A mundane kaleidoscope of hallucinogenic images without obvious significance
- A torrent of difficult memories or instinctual emotions or drives
- An invitation to a deep sleep or hypnogogic state that might heal body, mind, or spirit outside conscious awareness
- Any number of many other things.

Any of these experiences may be woven into a deeper process of understanding and development, i.e., may be "integrated." Approaching everything that emerges in your life—both from within yourself and from outside yourself—as part of a single flow that is *yours* is something that happens to many people involved in non-ordinary state work. But it is not something that is easily explained. Rather, it is something you have to "get" as it comes to you.

If you start experiencing everything as part of your process, then it becomes hard not to feel into everything that happens in your life as having some meaning in your unfolding journey. This is not to say that everything that happens—in psychedelic experience or in life—has a recognizable meaning that can be brought into any particular one place in a narrative. Sometimes things happen that feel "random" and will actually remain random. Feeling into the "randomness" of life can itself be integrated and become part of a journey.

Rather than considering happenings as "random," I can think about them as part of the mystery of life. Not to make things too organized, but I think about some happenings as falling into loose categories, which may shift and change:

- "I know what this is."
- "I don't know what this is right now, but it may reveal itself later."
- "I may never know what this is, and that's okay."

Integration of events can happen at any one of these levels. Just as likely, working on integration about something may shift from holding something at one level into another. I feel this is one of the ways that you make your integration process your own.

Now in closing this subsection, I want to say a word about something I call **colonization**. Like I defined "reconcile," I will draw on a definition of "to colonize" as "to take over (a place or domain) for one's own use."[105] Here we have to think about one part of us trying to take over a part of our unfolding process for another part of us. The colonizer part wants to keep itself safe and in control. From these basically legitimate motivations, however, the colonizer may take the transformational energy out of new experiences in order to keep the status quo in control. Given this natural tendency, it can be helpful to "watch out" for the colonizer when it comes into play. Thinking back to the Internal Family Systems method I introduced in the last chapter, the "colonizer" might be a manager or firefighter who thinks he is performing a good role, but may stop your unfolding process.

This can be seen very clearly in working with dreams. Sometimes we want to give a dream symbol a particular definitive (and finite) meaning that feels good to us. I remember working with someone who shared a dream in which a white horse was under water in a clear pool of water. The dreamer quickly interpreted the white horse as an animal ally that would carry her on her spiritual journey. She saw the dream as meaning she needed the courage to help the horse come out of the water and sail through the sky like Pegasus. Fair enough (and it was *her* dream).

But I was left wondering whether the part of her needing an uplifting story had colonized a dream that may have been more complicated. The dreamer did not want to consider whether the "dream image" of the horse was suffocating or drowning under water. She did not want to feel into what the horse might feel like not being able to breathe. She was not interested in whether the dream was showing her something that was not "breathing" in her mindset about her process.

This is an example of colonization. The part of this dreamer that needed to continue the one narrative that kept her safe prevented the new energy from unfolding or being unpacked. In my version of her dream, it's not that she wouldn't be able to ride Pegasus into the sky, but that her journey would be much richer if she were able to experience the feeling of drowning and see where that went.

In resisting the colonizer, usually we need to have the courage to go into the grief, anger or trauma that is often lodged between us and real transformation in our lives. Moving into these unknown places, and resisting colonization, is another way of defining integration. Giving yourself space to "know," "to not know," or "maybe to know later" can help guard against colonizing your process.

Observe, Open, Obtain

As a therapist, I spend a great deal of time helping people unpack experiences. I find it important to begin by teaching people to become sacred witnesses of their own story. In some psychological or spiritual systems, this is called developing an *observer* self. I talked about the observer or witness self near the beginning of the book. This is a developing part of you that becomes increasingly good at witnessing your emotions and reactions. Over time, this observing part starts to get familiar with your typical narratives or "scripts" for understanding your life. Then you can detach from getting "hooked" into your routine stories and projections—and you can stop the scripted parts from colonizing your growth points. Your observer self becomes able to "witness" not just you, but other people and even "spiritual" realities with increasing objectivity. I call this the three avenues of reflection:

- Intrapersonal (observing yourself)
- Interpersonal (observing yourself in relation to other people)
- Transpersonal (observing yourself in relation to the universe, particularly spiritual realities).

This brings me to the first part of my "Observe, Open, Obtain" model. When working on something that has a charge for you, the first step is finding a way to **observe** what is before you. Really observing what is there involves separating from your emotions and reactions, as well as from the story you may have already developed. These stories are often unconsciously formed as a defense in order to avoid a sense of shame or judgment from another part of yourself. It helps if you can learn to move past the defending part of yourself long enough to see the charged issue with some distance.

Sometimes when a "story" about something takes over, it helps to get really concrete and look back at what happened chronologically. The *observe* stage can get really tangible in terms of "this happened" or "I saw this" or "I felt this." This gives equal weight to mind, body, and gut. You begin to separate out the different pieces in order for them to come back together in a way that is more real and congruent with where you are transforming.

Once you have a handle on observing, you can work on being **open** to what may actually be present. Maybe it goes without saying that if you are using psychedelics, you are open to being open! However, I have found there is always more room to be open to cultivating what can come through or what has "shown up" in your experience.

Drawing once again on my guidance in therapy, there comes a stage where I encourage people to become open to different vantage points on the events or experiences giving them charge. Almost by definition, many of the experiences we have in psychedelics arise from the places of charge percolating inside ourselves. These charged places are probably the places where we have a tendency to shut down, project out, or "go into story." By this last phrase, I mean starting to explain or justify or even "give meaning" rather than just feeling and allowing something to be.

When approaching these charged places, it is very important to develop a practice of being **open** to consider what may lie beneath or around or above these experiences. Give them space. Be open to things having started at a place other than where you think they started, and consider the possibility of moving towards a place other than what you expect.

To put this simply, when we approach a charged experience during integration, we detach from it enough to **observe it** and then find enough space to be **open** to what it may be bringing forth that is different from what we already know or say about ourselves, our lives, or how the universe operates.

By *obtain* I mean gaining information or "take-aways" for working with—or *integrating*—the parts of your experiences that continue to have energy. Think of it this way: You have observed something that is part of you, you have opened to what else might be there, and now you hold onto what is emerging from this piece in order to let it develop.

Sometimes some piece will just disappear if it does not have the energy to keep going. Or sometimes there is continued "juice" that turns up a whole path that you will follow. Feeling into the difference between something that has run its course and something that opens a new life path is a valuable skill to continuously explore because it gives rise to understanding what is important in your integration. Again, I will say that it is useful to watch for *colonization* as some part of you wanting to spin back new experiences into old ways of being.

S-A-F-E-T-Y Revisited

I return to the word "safety" as a way to talk about some important elements within the process of integration. To allow yourself to unfold into new areas, as I am encouraging, you need to feel safe. Now for an expanded explanation of the elements of our acronym:

S stands for **security,** which is what you need before you reach into processing your psychedelic experience. It is imperative to remember that "S for security" comes first in my "safety" acronym. This is because you will not be able to integrate the challenging experiences that come to you through psychedelics *unless* you have security within yourself to move out of your comfort zones. For instance, you will need to feel comfortable with any groups or individuals (professionals or people in your life) who will play any role in your integration process.

Otherwise, you may find that you go into fight, flight, or freeze mode when your experiences come into contact with other people. Without security in a partner you share with, you might end up in an argument with that partner. Or you may find that you shut down, go into shame, or simply dissociate from your experiences as a "flight" process. Without security, your experiences might "freeze" within you. If you find yourself involved with fight, flight, or freeze, what could have been positive potential for growth and transformation can become not just a missed opportunity, but a source of trauma or suffering.

A stands for **accessible**. Once you feel secure, you have the chance to find the places inside you that are accessible to growth from the psychedelic experiences. This is a delicate process because it cannot be forced. In the next section, I emphasize the word "incremental" about integration, because you need to slowly find the ways that are available to you for processing based on your unique self and experiences.

Next is **F** for **fluidity**. I find that exploring psychedelics in general—no matter which medicine or means of experience you choose—opens up the possibility of fluid psychological and spiritual experience. As I sometimes say to clients, "It's always moving."

When you turn your attention to integration, it is important to allow the process to move and flow like a river. The flow of a river moves over and around obstacles, eventually wearing them down, but always renewing itself, changing direction sometimes, maybe forming a lake here and there, but taking a path back into the ocean.

E is for **empowering**. All psychedelic integration is ultimately for the goal of allowing yourself to become more fully who you are meant to be. The goal is also to move into alignment with all that is around you. This includes your relationships, your community, your work, your family, this crazy planet we call Earth, and the whole universe, including unseen realms.

Integration allows you to come into your own power through digesting the psychedelic experiences you receive and allowing them to assist you in walking in accordance with your authenticity. You need to find your mojo—your empowering juice—in order to do this.

This brings us to **T** for **transformational**. It is fairly common for people using psychedelics to realize, "I'm never going to see the world the same way again." With integration of this moment—whether it comes in your first or your fiftieth psychedelic journey—you open yourself to change from the depths of yourself and the universe.

Y is "yours." I can never say enough how much I believe integration is a personal process. This book contains thousands of suggestions and opinions and exercises. But in the end, *you* have responsibility to do whatever you want to do with your psychedelic work. These experiences are deeply personal and belong to you. So does integration.

Incremental Integration

I have already referenced incremental integration several times, but I feel the point deserves a whole section. In my experience, integration takes place step by step, one day at a time, one moment at a time. Sometimes integration slips forward, sometimes moves backwards, sometimes stays still. Even so, there is usually a slow progression forward, though this often feels more like a cycling through and around. I will talk in more detail about spiraling integration at the end of this chapter.

All the while, I do not want to minimize the possibility of enormous, sudden breakthroughs that immediately send us into a new place that feels like (and is) a permanent change. This is one of the hallmark possibilities of working with psychedelics. The trick can be finding ways to anchor those permanent changes. Incremental integration, for me, is a fluid back-and-forth process between where we go during non-ordinary states and where we engage with our lives inside ourselves and outside ourselves.

I remember a particular session with psilocybin when the practice of **explore and surrender** came to me. At one stage of the session, I felt as though I was being rained on by a torrent of DNA information of the universe. I felt nourished by the information I was receiving, but it was overwhelming to the point where I said, "This is too much. What am I going to do with this?" It was as though I was being given the chance to absorb or digest an enormous amount of insight, but there was so much to absorb that I needed to sit back in some way.

A friend, who had had sent to him the Thoth deck created by Aleister Crowley, had recently introduced me to Tarot cards. In my psilocybin session, with the torrential rain of information pouring down on me, when I said, "This is too much," the image of the Heirophant from the Crowley deck appeared to me. The Heirophant is often described as a priest or teacher who supports the search for hidden truth. His goal is often to assist knowledge and enlightenment as an experience separate from religious dogma and science, though he can embody religious structure at times. [106]

In a matter-of-fact manner, the Heirophant conveyed to me (telepathically, not in exact words), "Simply surrender." I translated this as advice to integrate what was coming to me through just surrendering before I tried actively to understand. The Heirophant conveyed that I should do this at my own pace, which is to say, incrementally.

Basking in the afterglow of the Heirophant's advice, still feeling the intensity of the DNA download, I felt within myself the dual urges of "actively open to take in more" and "back off and integrate it." From this, the words came to me that psychedelic work can be about **explore and surrender.** You feel into the intensity of what is coming to you, and then you back off and surrender into what is there without actively *trying* to work on it. At the right increments, you move back into a place of working with it—exploring it—and then you just surrender into what is there. This is one way of explaining what I mean by incremental processing.

Establishing Relationship with Universal Consciousness

Most of us working with psychedelics feel that we are receiving information or experience from a source of higher consciousness during the psychedelic journey. In Chapter 5, I described various maps of consciousness to help make sense of the transpersonal nature of consciousness. Revisiting this basic idea, most of us feel our sense of ourselves reaches back into parts of our psyche that feel unconscious and maybe ancient, where the archetypes (like the antelope) play. From there we sense connection to deeper and deeper realms beyond ourselves, eventually to a realm of what may be pure universal consciousness. This feels like Source to many of us.

You may be comfortable calling this source God; or you may experience different manifestations of source (for instance, angels or white light beings or aliens, etc.). Some facilitators believe there is only one unified field of consciousness that we are able to join through psychedelics (or other forms of spiritual experience). For instance, Martin Ball writes about experiencing *nonduality* through 5-MeO-DMT, an experience in which our consciousness releases into the one unified field and knows that we (along with all other forms of consciousness) are God and part of the unified field.

No matter how you experience or label this source, it can be very helpful during integration—and during your life journey more generally—to have a tool belt of what I will call divination tools. These are practices that help you connect with "the other side" and receive information or guidance. Often the guidance can affirm your thoughts or emotions as you tackle some particular aspect of change or decision-making. Just as often, some blockage or warning signs can be shown.

Sometimes this guidance can be hard to hear if it does not affirm what you want to believe or where you *hope* you are going. But very importantly, guidance from the other side can help you notice and halt any colonization of your experience by that part of yourself attached to a particular narrative that might not actually be your true calling for transformation.

Some of the most useful divination tools are:

- Tarot cards

- Astrology
- Rune stones
- I Ching.

You may also find yourself drawn to other practices or experiences that help you connect with universal consciousness. Almost all spiritual traditions have particular rituals or techniques for connection to higher source. As I touched upon in Chapter 2 and return to in Chapter 11, many ways of experiencing psychedelics incorporate these ritual practices into the journey and beginning of integration.

In other situations, you may create or join a ritual practice after a journey, often the following day. For instance, my Canadian friends sometimes follow up a Holotropic Breathwork daylong experience with a sweat lodge the next day. This additional experience helps ground the non-ordinary state session and begins integration in a beautiful way that goes beyond any words or possibilities for explanation. And of course, many people create their own rituals for connecting to Source.

Revisiting Astrology

In Chapter 5, I introduced astrology as a map of consciousness. Now I return to astrology as an aid in your unfolding process of integration. Contrary to what many people think about astrology, it is not a system for predicting your fate in a fortune-telling sense. Rather, it is a system for understanding the blend of archetypal influences that are most important for you as a unique person, and for understanding what influences may be most active at particular times. This can help orient you in your unfolding process.

As I noted in Chapter 5, your particular astrological map that carries through your entire life can be seen in your **birth chart.** With respect to your unfolding and evolving life process, I turn to the system of **transit astrology.** This is a means for looking at the motions of the planets as they influence your life experience over the course of time. "Life experience" includes both your internal process and what is happening in your external life.

In Chapter 5 I mentioned **archetypal astrology**, developed by Richard Tarnas and colleagues, as a serious branch of academic study. Grounded in the psychologies of Carl Jung and Stanislav Grof, archetypal astrology draws upon the understanding that planetary archetypes give insight into an interrelated set of themes and possibilities for unfolding of experience.

These themes and possibilities are **multivalent** in the sense that there are infinite possibilities for manifestation of the archetypal influence. While there are infinite possible manifestations, the particular archetypes push for manifestation in *some* form at particular times in a person's life. For example, if the planetary archetype of Uranus (liberation, freedom, breakthrough) is influencing you at a particular time, the manifestation might involve your leaving a job that no longer serves you and moving across country to take a new opportunity, suddenly understanding something you had never understood before, or taking steps to bring liberation to a group of people you had been trying to assist. How the manifestation happens is up to you —and to some extent, fate.

As I suggested earlier, receiving advice about your astrological transits on a particular day might give you a sense of what experiences you might have in any non-ordinary state work on that day. After you have the experiences, you may gain insight into the experiences and the influencing archetypes by looking back at the planetary archetypes impacting you that day.

For instance, a friend of mine had the most powerful psychedelic experience of his life on a particular day in October 2017. Looking at the astrology, the planet Jupiter was transiting that day over a grouping of planets in his natal chart. The natal planets involved Neptune (planet of non-ordinary states and immersion in the universal flow), the Sun (planet of identity and sense of self), the Moon (planet of emotions and hidden parts of the self), and Uranus (planet of sudden breakthrough). Jupiter tends to make experiences "big" and to offer blessing. In my friend's experience, it was very much like a visit from the gods—or an excursion to heaven. Understanding the transit astrology helped him integrate the meaning and significance of the experience—and also to understand that this was a special blessing that was brought on this particular day.

More generally over time, working with an archetypal astrologer will help you understand the themes that may be manifesting for your life journey in particular months or years. Psychedelic experiences tend to bring to the surface this archetypal content pressing for manifestation in your life.

Understanding the archetypes pressing for manifestation at any juncture can help you interpret and make use of the experiences that come to you in psychedelic work. At the same time, *feeling* the way in which universal archetypes are manifesting within you helps you understand yourself—and your individual consciousness—as part of one universal field of consciousness that is forever growing, evolving, and manifesting.

These concepts are explained in depth, with reference to particular archetypes, in Renn Butler's *Pathways to Wholeness: Archetypal Astrology and the Transpersonal Journey*.[107] Many people look to Butler's book before a non-ordinary journey to feel through the meaning of transits happening on the planned day. You would need to know the planets involved in your particular personal astrology, and then use the book for in-depth understanding about the archetypes.

Renn Butler

My friend mentioned above explored *Pathways to Wholeness after* his experience with Jupiter-Neptune-Sun-Moon-Uranus and felt confirmation with explanations such as: "Jupiter expands Neptune's impulses toward mystical union, softening people's boundaries and allowing them to access new and unseen layers of meaning" and "In these liberating alignments, Uranus brings a sense of unexpected new freedoms, dramatic awakening, and resolution of problems, while Jupiter one of divine benevolence, expansion, and success." [108]

His psychedelic experience was synchronistically aligned with this transit without his planning the day for the experience based on astrology. In other words, he did not know about the transits and then seek out the experience. Rather, various circumstances brought the experience on a particular day, and he later looked back and saw how it all made sense in transit astrology. This sort of alignment of "fate" often happens given the way synchronicity works. But you can also see how you might work with an archetypal astrologer to find optimum times for non-ordinary state work (or perhaps to be mindful about whether you want to avoid non-ordinary states during challenging astrological transits).

To put it simply, journeying with psychedelics offers you the possibility of experiencing the archetypes as they exist as real, actual manifestations in the universal field of consciousness. Astrology can assist you in bringing understanding of these elements into your consciousness awareness, helping you accept your role in the unfolding narrative of the universe as manifesting in your time and place.

Integration as a Developmental Process—Spiraling Through Stages

Developmental psychology studies how people change over their lifetimes. I don't want to get too complicated on you, but I think some of you might enjoy reading how transpersonal psychology talks about psychospiritual growth. This might help you put your own journey into some perspective. Originally focusing on infant and childhood development, the developmental branch of psychology expanded to include adult development. Transpersonal psychology added its own focus on stages where people begin to seek spiritual connection. Remember that *trans*personal means connecting with something *beyond* your individual sense of self.

Many people have heard of psychologist Abraham Maslow and his description of **peak experiences,** as well as his theory of a hierarchy of needs. Maslow (1908-1970) was in communication with some of the early transpersonal thinkers near the end of his life. His hierarchy of needs is often presented in a triangle, with the stage of **self-actualization** at the top. People on a path of self-actualization often find themselves moving from psychological growth to what I call psychospiritual growth.

Abraham Maslow

As Maslow explained, we need to have our basic needs met before we can try to meet "higher" needs. The progression is from survival needs (food, water, warmth, rest) to safety needs (free from danger) into psychological needs of belongingness and love. From there we can move into self-esteem needs (prestige and feelings of accomplishment) and then on to self-actualization, which involves trying to achieve our full potential.

Creativity and peak experiences tend to happen with self-actualization. Maslow described peak experiences as "rare, exciting, oceanic, deeply moving, exhilarating, elevating experiences that generate an advanced form of perceiving reality, and are even mystic and magical in their effect upon the experimenter." [109]

You have probably noticed how Maslow's description of peak experiences could be a description of many experiences people have with psychedelics. Without a doubt, many experiences in psychedelics have the capacity and power to fuel a path of self-actualization.

By encouraging integration, I hope to expand your focus from "experience" into what Maslow would understand as the self-actualization stage of development.

While Maslow laid some groundwork for understanding psychospiritual development, several transpersonal theorists writing after Maslow gave attention to the complexity of navigating a path that is both psychological and spiritual. There are several different transpersonal models of development. Here, I draw mostly on the model of transpersonal teacher and Jungian therapist Hillevi Ruumet.

In Chapter 5, I mentioned Ruumet's realization that people tend to spiral through experiences associated with the seven chakras when they are on a spiritual path. I encourage you to read Ruumet's short (and sweet) book in its entirety, *Pathways of the Soul: Exploring the Human Journey*. But here is a very condensed description of her seven developmental centers as they correlate to chakras:

One	Physical/Survival
Two	Emotional/Kinship
Three	Egoic Power
Four	Aloha Waltz (Heart/Love)
Five	Finding your Voice
Six	Embodying Spirit
Seven	Transpersonal Journey

As we journey along a psychospiritual path, Ruumet found, we tend to spiral between centers with these dyad relationships:

- Three (Egoic Power) and Four (Heart/Love)
- Five (Finding Your Voice) and Two (Emotional/Kinship)
- Six/Seven (Spirit and Transpersonal) and One (Physical Survival)

In the remainder of this subsection, I make some observations about integration and non-ordinary state work in these spirals. Borrowing from Ruumet's basic structure, I try to give you an abbreviated sense of how these spiraling dances between energetic centers might play themselves out in your psychedelics integration process. I also give attention to some specific experiences that tend to occur during non-ordinary states and how they might be understood as relating to the chakras or centers.

Ruumet's Aloha Waltz (Third and Fourth Chakras)

From being with people as they talked through their lives, Ruumet realized that many people in our culture who are working on themselves are doing what she calls the **Aloha Waltz**. This is a dance between the Third Center of Power and the Fourth Center of Heart and Love. The Aloha Waltz, Ruumet writes, seems to start with an "invitation of the heart." This is "a subtle, growing, insistent feeling… like homesickness for a place or something we do not know but have a deep, vague feeling will finally make us happy." [110]

Having spent many years living in Hawaii, Ruumet names this movement the "Aloha Waltz" because she understands *aloha* as recognition of the divine:

> The spirit of *Aloha*, as I learned it during my years in Hawaii, encompasses empathy with the pain *and* joy of others; the idea that we are all equal parts of the Creator and therefore to harm another is to harm oneself; extending open-hearted hospitality whether to friend or stranger; stewardship of the Earth and sky and sea, which sustain our life; and gratitude for all we receive, taking from nature only what we need and saying thank you. [111]

Ruumet calls movement toward the heart a **waltz** because you do not suddenly inhabit your heart place. You feel it, and then you return repeatedly to the egoic stages in order to work through your issues, which are also your family's issues and your culture's issues. Ruumet writes, "The road is not straight. Go back and deal with unfinished business at [the Egoic Center]. You must dance the Aloha Waltz until Love and Power work out a balance and your Egoic skills follow Love's lead." [112]

Working with non-ordinary states, I know this process is not just in the head, but involves our body and energetic levels. While the energetic bodies are complicated, you might loosely think of this spiraling as involving the opening (or cleansing) of your physical-energetic third and fourth chakras.

As I have already shared, it is common in breathwork experiences to feel a pressure or need for pressure on the center of the chest. This is the area of the energetic heart (as well as physical heart). People often feel an opening from this area that involves a great deal of emotion and compassion for self and others, as well as processing of grief and love-based memories or images from all the levels of the psyche. Weeping is very common with these experiences. The opening of the heart can feel like the birth of gratitude. You are less concerned with demanding or proving and more concerned with appreciating.

Similarly, it is common to feel stirrings in the area of the third chakra that seem associated with a movement into power or a physical-psychic struggle against abuse of power. Such physical-energetic experiences can be an entry point into release of power issues. It is important to remember that from a non-dual perspective, those who abuse power and those who are abused represent two sides of a human dilemma. It is not uncommon during non-ordinary states to experience the ways in which victim-abuser may be two sides of the same experience. This is by no means to excuse abuse, but rather to invite understanding and release.

During the spiral between the third and fourth centers (or chakras), many people gain a new appreciation for their bodies and the ways in which emotions and traumatic memories are stored in their bodies. Paying attention to what is within your body becomes important. You begin to realize your body holds your emotions, your history, even your karma.

With psychedelic medicines that involve purging, you may find physical-emotional-energetic-karmic release by literally and metaphorically throwing up energetic blocks associated with memories, insights or traumas. Breathwork can later help you really move into and release what starts to emerge from your body. As I quoted Ralph Metzer in Chapter 2, "these intensive breathing and body-methods use dynamic energy to break through conditioned inertia-resistances imprinted into the cellular and organ tissues of the body."[113]

How is it helpful to know about the Aloha Waltz?

- You can nurture in yourself the development of empathy, stewardship of nature, and gratitude for the experiences you are having.
- You can engage in embodied psychospiritual activities that physically assist heart opening—this is what many yoga postures were designed to help.
- You can witness your engagement in egoic and power issues, and have compassion for yourself and others as these issues are played out (welcome to Western civilization!).
- You can consciously intend for Love to lead Power.
- You can work with an integration therapist on these issues; any sensitive humanistic-oriented therapist, even without much knowledge of non-ordinary states, can probably help you skillfully with your particular version of the Aloha Waltz.

Finding Right Relationship (Fifth and Second Chakras)

Remember that process moves in many ways and through many channels. You do not necessarily "complete" the Three-Four Aloha Waltz before starting what Ruumet calls the **Descent Tango**. This involves spiraling between the Fifth and Second developmental centers. Here you work on issues of **Finding Your Unique Voice** and **Coming to Right Relationship with Kinship and Emotional Bonds**.

Ken Wilber was one of the first transpersonal developmental theorists, though he has preferred the label *integral* over transpersonal since the mid-1990s. In his early book *No Boundary*, Wilber talked about "the start of self-discovery" by developing the ability to become "the cause of your own feelings, and not the effect." [114] I associate self-discovery with the Descent Tango. Carl Jung's idea of individuation also resonates here.

Ken Wilber

We have all been conditioned by our kinship ties and by the clans we belong to in our culture. But the time comes when some of us want to decide for ourselves—from inside ourselves. Taking responsibility for our feelings becomes a road into discovering who we are uniquely as separate beings. From there we begin to find and use our unique voices. We come to know ourselves as separate from others, and then we become willing to say who we are.

Becoming honest with ourselves about ourselves involves accepting a lot of complexity and what feel like contradictions. Wilber wrote about a stage where people begin to:

- Understand that opposites can be true at the same time.
- Realize that viewpoints are skewed for unconscious reasons.
- Take back their projections, "to make room in yourself for an understanding and acceptance of all your various potentials, negative and positive, good and bad, lovable and despicable," rather than project the undesirable characteristics out on other people.
- "And thus to develop a relatively accurate image of everything your psychophysical organism is."

Wilber names a *Centaur* Level, where you begin to realize that you are your body, even if you are also consciousness that has existence separate from the material world. He writes about discovering blocks in your body that you can feel into and release—and learning that this has something to do with repressed emotions. Finding "buried feelings" usually involves "a release of tears, a good scream or two, ability for uninhibited orgasm, a good old-fashioned temper tantrum, or a temporary but enraged attack upon pillows...."[115]

At these stages, Wilber says you develop a "deep sense of responsibility" because you are no longer blaming or crediting external sources for how you feel and what happens in your life. Other people are no longer the source for your bad feelings or your sense of safety, though of course, relationships continue to be important and become more authentic.

These issues could be part of the Three-Four Waltz, but it can be helpful to feel into the deeply buried kinship ties that may be associated with the Second Chakra (physically as well as cognitively). You should be able to feel how easing out of unconscious kinship ties seamlessly leads to finding your own unique voice (Fifth Chakra). You find your unique voice by being able to speak your own truth to those you have previously been unconsciously merged with.

In Chapter 10, I write about addictions. Considering addictions very broadly, we have attachments not only to substances that may be harmful, but also to behaviors and relationships that hold us in patterns that do not allow us to find our true voice. Codependence has been a popular phrase the last few decades. I understand codependence as being tied (often energetically through the kinship center) with someone who is enacting addiction, poor mental health, over-dependency, irresponsibility, or immaturity.

This is not to judge anyone for where they are, but to note that staying tied without boundaries to others who are in such places prevents you from finding and living from your own true voice. Drawing boundaries may be painful and threaten you with loss of love and identity, but I encourage you to imagine finding yourself rather than abandoning someone or something else.

Very often through psychedelics we are given glimpses into codependent patterns that may have existed in our families for generations. Integrating these understandings into our lives becomes our chance to not only release ourselves, but to impact our energetic lines back through our lineage and into the future of the next generations.

In non-ordinary states, you may work with many feelings, issues, memories, and blocks that are associated with your groin area. Sometimes these involve sexual or family abuse issues. These can be considered second chakra issues. There are techniques in breathwork to help energetic releases that seem to involve such issues and body areas. Sometimes it feels as though you are birthing yourself through an energetically enacted birth or pushing out ties to others at deep emotional and kinship levels that are ready to be released.

Similarly, Fifth Center (and chakra) issues often work themselves out through the area of the neck and throat during non-ordinary states. There may be images of having your voice strangled. Maybe you remember a time in a past life where you fought against injustice and you were condemned and hanged. Purging in psychedelic sessions draws from many different parts of you, but the physical fact of something within you passing out through your throat can feel like a cleansing, which leaves you with a voice that is more yours.

How is it helpful to know about the Five-Two Spiral?

- Sometimes we do not want to face the reality that living our true voice usually means creating better boundaries with those people (usually our families and sexual partners) with whom we have deep and probably unconscious ties.
- Though we don't like to think about it, the areas of our throats and groins are the places we take in things from outside ourselves and release things from inside ourselves. This includes nourishment, release of body fluids and waste, and sexual activities. It can help to bring consciousness to these processes as relating to intertwined psychological, physical, and energetic issues. (Remember Freud and the oral, anal, and genital stages?)
- Finding more clarity and less toxicity in these areas prepares you for the surrender that is necessary if you keep going on the path.

Ruumet's Embodied Transcendence (Sixth/Seventh and First Chakras)

Ruumet describes the movement toward the higher chakras as embodied transcendence. This is a good phrase for the connection between the Sixth and Seventh Centers (spiritual opening and connection) and the First (grounding and physicality).

I talk more about surrender in our final chapter, but this is the place in the spiral where the challenge of surrender emerges with full force. This is paradoxical, because at this stage you increasingly learn to fully inhabit your body—and to inhabit the physical world around you—and yet through that *becoming* you are released from attachment to the physical. In other words, you move toward transcendence of physical attachment by becoming embodied and become embodied by moving toward transcendence of physical attachment.

This is not something anyone can tell you how to do. Rather, you need to figure out how to move out of your own way and let it happen. Ruumet writes that in this spiral:

> It is not really a task that we do. *It* does *us*. It is really not a doing at all, but a dissolution process in which we cooperate: a shedding and releasing of everything Ego has clung to, especially what we thought of as our identities. We do not practice, we are practic*ed*. We do not transform; we are transform*ed*. We do not integrate; we are integrat*ed*.[116]

In working with psychedelics, you may come to the point in an experience where you really feel you are dying. Dying, of course, is the ultimate release, the ultimate surrender. When you feel you are dying in a psychedelic experience, it may feel like real physical death about to happen, not a metaphor. Often this involves a sense that your heart is about to burst or stop or that you may have a stroke in your head. This is First Chakra material. Quite literally, you may decide to allow yourself to die, and then a great shift may happen, where possibly you become all that there is.

Working between the First and the Sixth/Seventh Chakras in non-ordinary states often brings people to re-experiencing issues of survival or trauma. Once again, this is a working through of the issues of the spiral between these centers. In Ruumet's model, Center One is the "physical/survival center" where most of us learn to live comfortably in a physical body. But sometimes:

> [T]his did not happen adequately because outer conditions such as poverty, ill health, parental neglect or criticism, a physical handicap, or even abuse, violence or war, instilled insecurity and fear rather than courage and confidence, [so that] we were left with growth tasks to take up in the future.[117]

In order to move into the deeper stages of transcendence, it may be necessary to heal such wounds, whether they are large or small. The specific issues involved in your personal lifetime may need to find experience and processing in safe circumstances. In addition, whether or not we personally have experienced survival or abuse issues, we need to deal with the existential fact, if we are honest with ourselves, that physicality and survival is a moment-to-moment risk. Accepting this finds connection with moving toward transcendence.

Many people working with psychic or extrasensory perception have learned that those of us who have suffered horrific abuse at some point in our lives (often early on) are often able to open our psychic abilities in astounding ways. This may result from learning to dissociate consciousness in our early years, but I suspect there is also involvement with the spiral connection between transcendent spirituality and issues of survival and abuse. Entering these realms with consciousness can be terrifying and should always have support from competent and trustworthy others.

In working with non-ordinary states, we need to be prepared for the embodied **regression** that is sometimes necessary to heal specific traumas. Our inner healing intelligence (to use Grofian language) may take us back to early infant or young-child stages for healing. We may need to revisit, re-experience, or heal traumas or unmet needs. Sometimes the embodied regression looks very much like the behaviors we have as infants. Very often it is hard to have linear or conceptual consciousness about what is happening. This could be because we had not yet developed mature cognitive processing abilities when the trauma or neglect happened.

It is also possible that we move back to early "survival" stages under the pressure of a psychedelics journey. The challenging nature of some information or experiences may lead us to seek the comfort of earlier states. Facilitators may notice a sense of fear or confusion or inability to process that seems regressed. This may be completely natural and exactly what needs to happen, though careful assistance (not too much, not too little) is very important.

Don Beck is another developmental theorist who understands the full range of human potential. He calls his system Spiral Dynamics because he too recognizes the movement back and forth between levels of experience as we learn to master more and more comprehensive ways of being.

One of Beck's students, Ian McDonald, described what might happen when we need to return to early stages of development due to challenging adult life circumstances. I find his description resonates with what sometimes happens when we revisit traumas or experience challenges during non-ordinary state work. McDonald writes:

> At times of great illness we may re-visit [a survival stage], or if we become totally overwhelmed by the outside world, we may retreat into it. The complexity of thinking is very elemental, and we are largely driven by the survival skills embedded in our reptilian brain. Emotions may well be very basic, principally fear-based and close to biological impulses, and there may be little sense of time beyond now. [118]

If you are the experiencer, it is important to be able to reach out for help and nurturance if you find yourself having feelings or memories that feel raw and *early* in ways that may resonate with this stage. If you are a guide, friend or facilitator, it becomes important to provide nurturance as requested—while being mindful of not projecting your *own* needs from this or other stages onto the experiencer. And, as always, watch those sexual boundaries. Remember that Freud wrote about the existence of strong sexuality at early nonverbal stages.

None of this is to say anyone will *try* to move into regressed stages during non-ordinary states or integration. But I can say that it is very common during non-ordinary state work for people to seek the kind of holding and comforting that soothes babies or young children. For an adult regressing to early stages, this can provide healing physical-emotional contact. This reaching out for contact often happens after a person has revisited trauma or felt deeply into important issues in non-ordinary states.

While regressed states can be challenging, they also may open us to the deepest forms of healing and connection. There can be a precious innocence and willingness to receive and give unconditional love. The possibilities of a pure sense of bonding are enormous.

Most development theorists describe the earliest stage of development as **symbiotic** because of the infant's experience of merger with caretakers. The infant does not cognitively sense any separation from the outside world. The outer world is either "good" because it takes care of your needs or "bad" because it does not. This is an early stage before ego has developed, but resembles in some ways the transpersonal experiences of merger.

Ken Wilber famously wrote about the **pre/trans fallacy**, meaning that we know the sense of oceanic connection with "no boundaries" as infants before our development of a sense of separation and then return to this sense of connection when we reach *trans*personal ways of being. Because many modern psychiatrists and psychologists (including Freud) thought mystical states were *only* regression to infancy, Wilber called this assumption a fallacy. In other words, those who think that trans-personal experiences are just regressing back to stages before we had an ego do not really understand transpersonal experiences. In actual transpersonal experiences, the ego remains available but has learned to release itself into something larger.

Enlightenment?

I have a friend who is quite concerned with enlightenment. He hopes it is possible to reach a state in this lifetime where he is peaceful and whole and resides in the energies of unconditional love. His search feels very innocent and pure to me. But I have to say (and I apologize for saying it) that some of the talk I hear about enlightenment from self-identified spiritual seekers feels very competitive and even narcissistic. I have seen people chatting with an air of animated and ostentatious sophistication about enlightenment while they ignored (did not even meet the eyes of) others sitting in the corner who were obviously lonely and uncomfortable. Suffice it to say that I suspect that anyone who actually might be "enlightened" is not going to talk about it but will likely unobtrusively move through the world with an attitude of compassion and service.

All that said, the possibility of enlightenment is built into religions practiced by millions of people. I do not rule out this possibility, but accept that most of us will continue to work on ourselves through our lifetime—and maybe through another few thousand lifetimes thereafter.

There are people I have seen (often from India) who seem so completely open spiritually that they transmit unconditional love and being-ness to anyone who comes physically near them. Sometimes if you come into contact with these people, you feel an energetic transmission of love that is physical, sometimes reducing you to tears. This blessing may be called *darshan* within Hinduism. While I believe these states exist, I recognize that most of us will not reach a permanent state of enlightenment, but grace may allow us to glimpse moments of these states, often in psychedelic experiences. The memory of these states may then guide us like a star along our continued journey.

Susanne Cook-Greuter is a developmental theorist who writes about an advanced stage of being she calls **unitive**. Here are some of the characteristics:

- You respect the essence of other people and do not need them to be different than they are; you realize no way of being is better than another, they are all just part of the evolution of what is.
- Humility comes naturally because you realize everything passes and there is no way to know what impact drops in the ocean may have.
- Without trying, unitive people may act as catalysts or inspiration to others because their nonjudgmental acceptance allows others to be; "because they see the dignity in all manifestations of life, others feel worthy and whole in their presence."
- "They are concerned with global justice, spontaneity, existence, and creativity but create no undue tension around goal achievement. Rather than being passive, the non-attached, impersonal stance allows for greater and more direct and powerful action where action is needed."
- Strong boundaries may be drawn, but "non-attachment to outcomes is an essential and liberating aspect of witnessing and acting out of non-defensive, spontaneous insight."
- Unitive individuals "feel interconnected with others as all sentient beings struggle to survive and make sense of their existence… [they] feel tolerance, compassion and an affiliation with all manifestations of life. The simplest flat-worm is in some way as close to the truth as the most sophisticated thinker."
- "Peak experiences no longer have an out-of-this-world quality, they have become a familiar way of being and experiencing." [119]

Susan Cook-Greuter

At these stages, there may be moments of overwhelming beauty in everything that exists and deep knowledge that everything is exactly as it needs to be. And yet from glimpsing these moments, the real work begins. Not just on yourself, but on the world, for as you move into these places, just by being yourself, challenging people and situations may come to you as you ever-more accept whatever roles are handed to you in the evolution of our planet.

How Much Structure to Bring to Your Process

In closing our chapter on process, I want to talk about the very basic issue of how much "structure" you want or need in your personal journey. For many people, the psychedelic experience is so *wonder-filled* and colorful they feel no need to *do* anything with the experience. Some great books have been written about amazing kaleidoscopic journeys through consciousness and the universe. Sometimes reading these books can suggest an emphasis on the event, without considering the long haul of process. The question then arises—do we really have to *do* anything with our experiences? Do we really have to integrate? Why should this feel like work?

Here is once again the paradox. Of course you do not need to *do* anything; and as Ruumet shared, you may start to feel that *you* are *being done* rather than actually doing anything. On the other hand, by writing this book, I am suggesting that you bring some intention and structure to your work with psychedelics.

One way to think about the question of structure is to put **ritual** at one end and **shapelessness** at the other. You can think of "the most structure" as holding a ritual intention (emphasis on form) and the other end of the continuum (holding no intention for bringing any structure to your process) as allowing shapelessness. This continuum applies from the preparation stage to the session itself to the post-session integration stages. But often the post-session phase is where I have the most difficult time with "how much structure." This is where many of us start to get lost. This is probably why I hear so many people confused about "how to integrate."

Here are some ideas for structure after sessions:

- You might commit to re-engaging with your session at a certain time every day (or every other day) and you might always do this in the same place (by your altar or on a walk on a particular path or sitting on the same bench in the park).
- Similar to what you might do before a session, after a session you might commit to following certain dietary guidelines.
- You might decide to start a completely new journal and commit to at least one entry every day after a session.
- Dreamwork can be important.

- As a commitment to working on integration from *this* experience you just had, you might consider committing not to experience another hallucinogen (even such as alcohol or cannabis) until you have worked on integration for a particular period of time.
- You could decide to carry with you for a period of time something that reminds you of your experience. In some circles, we are invited to bring an object for placement on the group altar during the journey. You might, for instance, decide to carry your object with you for a day or a week or a month after your experience.

At the other end of the continuum from ritual is what I call **shapelessness**. There is value at this end of the spectrum. Too much structure leaves no space for miracles or spontaneous shifts that you did not work to make happen. Sometimes going "shapeless" is like surrendering into your process.

On the other hand, if you leave things completely shapeless, you might find yourself in what some people sadly describe as a post-session void. The experience just seems to disappear, or you feel you have dissociated from what happened. You could be left with only an event—and an event that you can hardly even remember.

You might return to my suggestion to **observe, open, obtain.** This can involve "using some structure" and "seeing what you get," and then "releasing into shapelessness." Eventually you will find your own rituals and your own processing habits and rhythms.

While I offer suggestions, you need to decide what structure, if any, works for you. Even just a baseline intention for some structure within a multitude of possibilities can leave you with the freedom of expression to integrate in an individualized manner. Choosing how much structure you follow for integration, and what that structure may be, becomes part of your integration process.

Now Your Turn

If you were to commit to some post-session rituals, what are you feeling or thinking might work for you?

_____
_____
_____
_____
_____

What kinds of post-session ritual practices have not worked for you in the past?

_____
_____
_____
_____
_____

What practices are you drawn to in your ordinary life that you might work into conscious psychedelics integration? For example, fasting, artwork, creative writing, sexual experience, isolation, or other adventures?

_____
_____
_____
_____
_____

Integration Exercise 7: Exploring with Divination Tools

What You Need

- Tarot cards, medicine cards, or any other divination cards or tools: there are hundreds to choose from. Please select a deck that you are drawn to.
- Related guidebook that matches your tool
- Your journal.

General Background

Tarot reading is an intuitive, ancient system of knowledge that has been taught in many early mystery schools. The Tarot cards can be viewed as a map, with symbolism and signposts to understand yourself. As I have already suggested, divination tools of any kind can help connect you to source. Rather than viewing such tools as magic, I understand them as connected to source through synchronicity.

Correctly using the Tarot cards can be an integrative tool, drawing on the synchronicity that they offer. You can read about the meaning of the cards you draw or simply meditate on the images. I feel some of the older decks have ingrained themselves deeply into the archetypal realms. This suggests they carry a great deal of energy, or "mana."

Medicine Cards give you another tool for achieving personal growth and balanced living. By learning the meaning of animal signs, you can feel into how these signs are connected to psychedelic experiences. It is another opportunity to connect to a deeper source for finding potential lucidity around integrating your psychedelic sessions. Some facilitators I know place various divination tools on the altar for people to explore before and after a journey. Probably this is better for pre-journey or following a period of aftercare.

Different ways to use the cards include:

- Pull cards after a psychedelic session, which can bring reassurance, clarity and a deeper understanding of your psychedelic experiences.
- Pull cards in the morning as a ritual to start your day.
- Brainstorm multiple questions you may have surrounding psychedelic experience or any other part of your life.

Like many of *The Psychedelics Integration Handbook* exercises, this exercise is designed to introduce you to the work. If you start to feel really connected to a source of divination, there are many books, videos, and expert resources to help you learn more or even become a master at your tool of choice.

Why this Exercise is Important for Psychedelics Integration

I explained in prior chapters the way your awareness can reach back into your personal unconscious, and then back into the collective unconscious, including the archetypes, and then you are in the place where the Akashic records exist and from which all form emerges. Part of this reality is that synchronicities (coincidences, manifestation of fate) seem to come from this same deep source of manifestation. The cards you read in using divination tools are playing out this kind of synchronicity —sharing meaning with you for possible guidance.

Feeling into this place can be exciting and transformative and sometimes even a bit frightening with the tools' accuracy. Very often they seem to tell you things that you need to hear but not necessarily things you want to hear. I believe this is not only interesting and informative—but helps you establish connection with these archetypal places.

Having increased connection with the archetypal realm can serve you well not just in your personal growth and integration, but also in your psychedelics sessions. This realm communicates to you in your experiences. Particularly with some forms of medicine (for instance, 5-MeO-DMT), you may feel you have entered into the source of all being. Frequent reaching out to this source through divinatory work helps you become known in that realm.

I might mention that working with the symbolism of dreams is another way to become known in that realm. Jungian analyst Marion Woodman shares an image a friend has remembered for years about the *work* involved in remembering and exploring dreams. Woodman gives the image of hacking your way through thick underbrush in a forest to find your way to the river of dream wisdom. She believes that as you work hard to find your way through the brush to the river, the Dream Maker is matching your every move, hacking through the brush on the other side of the river to meet you at the waters. I suggest that work you do with divination and taking seriously the meanings you uncover—and working with them psychologically and spiritually—will help encourage "the other side" to meet you with recognition in your psychedelics journeys.

The exercise I suggest is directed to questions about your psychedelic experiences, but I encourage you to work with divination tools regarding any aspect of your integration work (which is essentially any aspect of your life).

How To Do It

Preparation in advance

1. Create a safe and sacred space that you have devoted to meditating.
2. Build an altar that speaks to you, with both spiritual and physical interests of yours being represented.
3. Lay out your preferred deck.
4. Have the particular guidebook and your journal.
5. Consider writing down questions you have regarding your psychedelic experience.

Instructions for the exercise (Time: five minutes)

- Sit for a moment and reflect on the general theme of your psychedelic experience. This could be for five minutes or a couple of days. When you're ready, start to mix the cards.
- Hold the cards in your hands and close your eyes for a while. Take a few deep breaths.
- For just a minute, let go of everything.
- Bring your attention to your psychedelic experience or a question you have created.
- Open your eyes and mix the cards again.
- Follow your intuition when and how you personally shuffle the deck, always having the psychedelic session or your question in your mind.
- Draw a card and observe it.
- Use your guidebook to learn more about what the card means and explore any synchronicities that come to your attention.

As you work through integrating your psychedelic experiences, sometimes you can be drawn to new ideas, religions, and schools of thought. The Tarot and Medicine cards can help you develop a vast array of connecting points with your psychedelic integration. The systems of decks are endless. I welcome you to explore different methods and decks of cards you are drawn to. There are many other divination systems using stones (runes) or sticks or coins (I Ching). Follow your intuition, but I happen to like the archetypal images on cards.

CHAPTER 8

INTEGRATION AND THE OUTER WORLD

In the last chapter, I began moving into the relationship of external events and your internal process. I want to continue that exploration in this chapter. I will focus more intentionally on models for incorporating the external parts of your journey into a process that unfolds with non-ordinary state work.

Tav Sparks and the "APS" System

Tav Sparks, transpersonal teacher in the Holotropic Breathwork movement, describes a way of working with ourselves when we have emotional charges reaching into our depths. You may remember that neuro-psychiatrist Dan Siegel writes about finding the parts of ourselves that hold an emotional charge and following the thread from those parts back into the central places within us that need healing. Sparks begins with the same basic idea.

Tav Sparks

In his book *The Power Within: Becoming, Being and the Holotropic Paradigm*, Sparks shares his experience from teaching Holotropic Breathwork facilitation for many years. This includes his **Awareness Positioning System (APS)** for **catching ourselves** when we are about to engage in some way with the external world when we could first work on whatever emotional charge or wound is moving us into action. These are the times when we start an argument or create drama or escalate conflicts or dramas started by others.

There is something inside ourselves that might be called "our stuff" that has a charge and fuels something we can call "acting out." We are "acting out our stuff" when we bring the charge of our internal unresolved or unprocessed emotional material into the external world and engage with others. I talk in the next section about the healthy necessity of speaking our truths, but for now we are shining some light on the process of "acting out."

Through his APS system, Sparks imagines a vertical axis that reaches down into our past narratives and experiences. This includes what has happened in our biological life, what may have happened during our birth process, and what we may bring into this lifetime from past lives. The upper half of the vertical line is that part of you seeking wholeness and spiritual connection—that part of you metaphorically reaching up towards a higher power.

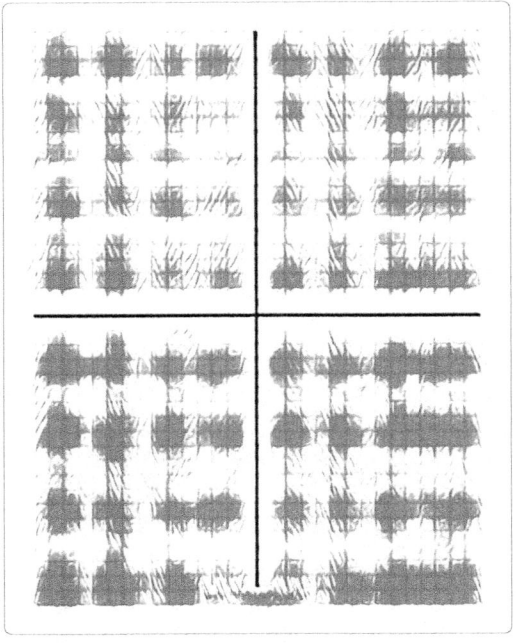

The Axis

The horizontal axis in the APS system goes outward to what is happening in your relationships with people and the circumstances playing themselves out in the external world. Sparks cautions that most of us have the inclination to unconsciously play out our inner wounds and "stuck" narratives through our relationships and external experiences. Sometimes people wonder whether the right and left sides of the horizontal axis have different orientations. The answer is, not really—you just find yourself reaching outwards, probably more in a 360-degree fashion, to play out your issues through your life.

For example, you may have a wound around betrayal. Someone close to you in the past may have turned against you abruptly and caused you to feel not only loss, but also the acute wound of having mistakenly trusted someone. Because of this wound, you may expect betrayal and experience it even when it is not really happening, or you may unconsciously act in ways that bring real betrayal back to you. For example, you may be so frantic about people taking things away from you that you hold onto things in a way that eventually results in a reaction to your charged emotion and actions.

This tends to happen with any consistent psychological theme in our lives. As I mentioned in Chapter 5, Stanislav Grof calls these phenomena a **COEX system** (a *system of condensed experience*). A COEX is a set of related experiences organized around a charged emotional center. This is similar to Carl Jung's idea of a *complex*. Many of the images and experiences that come to us in non-ordinary state work bring us back to our COEXs and offer a chance to heal and release tied up emotional energy.

In the Awareness Positioning System, when something has a great charge for us, Sparks encourages us to ***take it vertical***. We do this by digging down deeply into our past to find "what does this remind me of?" For instance, if we are charged because we feel someone is about to betray us, we have a choice. We can react emotionally from our wound and "act out" something with them on the horizontal plane. Or we can "take it vertical" and find the original experiences of wounding and process through those experiences. This almost always includes feeling tough emotions of grief or anger, often cycling through both. Sometimes the emotions are not clear and may feel like a frozen, stuck place. In the APS system, you will need to move into that place long enough to find the actual charges that have been frozen.

In working with therapy clients, I find that the stuck place is often associated with deeply imprinted beliefs that have helped defend against the painful emotions. Much of the work in therapy involves reaching an appreciation of the source of the beliefs in order to be able to sort through what really happened historically and what continues to happen as the narrative replays itself out in more recent life circumstances. As the hardened belief system softens, the emotions may come to the surface for feeling and release of the stored charge.

Non-ordinary state work tends to bring these charges (or COEXs) to the surface. Rarely is this a clear and linear process. As I have suggested in earlier chapters, the surfacing may be through images, thoughts, memories, sensations, body movements, or emotions. Often there is no clarity about the source, unless you move towards what is emerging and let it play itself out in whatever happens without stopping the process. As I have said, this is typically an *incremental* process that unfolds in non-linear stages and can be greatly assisted by the types of exercises and intentional process work I have been recommending.

In psychedelics work, it is useful to bear in mind the difference between processing something internally and engaging with external exploration. This becomes particularly important *after* the session, when incompletely processed things that have emerged may have a tendency to play themselves out externally.

For example, if you have glimpsed God in a psychedelics journey, that glimmer may have also brought to the surface wounding you have around organized religion. You may become annoyed (or even enraged) by all the people around you who seem to mindlessly follow organized religion and even play out their own "stuff" unconsciously through religion. You can work on these issues internally by feeling through your history and the associated emotions—or you can start a fight with your religious grandmother. Your choice.

This does not mean I devalue working on a horizontal level. In fact, most of the rest of this chapter turns to specifics of developing a relationship with the external that supports integration. This is hard to explain, but you will come to *feel* the difference between engaging horizontally in a way that is healthy processing versus projecting **charged** unconscious parts of yourself outwardly in a way that does not move you forward.

Given the complexities of life and the human psyche, these are not either-or experiences. But for the sake of understanding, I talk about them as two ends of a spectrum. I start in the next section by continuing with the language of Tav Sparks, now turning to horizontal communications.

Healthy Horizontal Communications

The idea of "taking it vertical" is easy enough to understand. But knowing how to "go vertical" is *way* more difficult than it sounds. Most of us are not accustomed to looking within for the source of our emotions and beliefs. To be honest, I find it rare that people have been raised to even consider whether emotional charges are something for which they can take responsibility.

Maybe we are taught to watch our anger or not be so clingy, but really taking responsibility for our emotional lives is not something our culture excels at teaching. For the most part, we are not trained to excavate for the sources of our emotional charges. Typically, the sources of our problems are considered outside us: something happened to us or someone did something to us. Blame is the name of the game. Things get complicated because often we believe we are not blaming someone else for our emotions, but blaming them for doing something that is *wrong*, for treating us unfairly or violating some rule we have internalized.

Typically, people do not realize the emotional sources of their hardened judgments or beliefs. The shift between thought-based judgments and the felt-sense of emotion is something that needs to be excavated along the way. This is why I talk about integration as feeling your thoughts and thinking your emotions.

Near the end of the last chapter, I talked about developmental models. I quoted Ken Wilber about his idea of a *Centaur* stage of development on the way to spiritual maturity, where we find a deep sense of responsibility for our own emotions. We stop blaming or crediting others for how we feel and shift into owning control of our emotions (and our beliefs as well).

Having encouraged the search for our charges, and their healing through internal processing and integration, I turn toward the importance of healthy horizontal communications. Importantly, we need to recognize that the instruction to *take it vertical* is not the complete answer to living your life. Engagement with the outside world is necessary for life and psycho-spiritual growth. For one thing, the instruction to *take it vertical* can function to suppress the development of our voice. I consider this a serious weakness in the way the APS system is sometimes understood and relied upon.

As I noted in Chapter 7, part of our spiritual growth is learning to separate from the unconscious (and codependent) ties that repress development of ourselves and may keep us from naming and moving away from relationships and situations that are not good for us. A necessary part of this development is learning to speak authentically. Sometimes our emotional charges are protective of our growing authenticity and separation. Sometimes the charges allow us to break through and name things (or people) that we need to leave behind. Sometimes the charges are useful (even necessary) in setting boundaries with other people or situations. Becoming our own unique person lies at the heart of Jungian **individuation** and is the goal of many psychological and spiritual paths.

If we *only* take all our charges vertical, we may leave ourselves under the domination of external people or static circumstances. Usually these people or situations are acting from a place of power rather than love, though people may be acting from a place of mixed love and codependent need. As many of us quickly learn in transpersonal communities, the admonition "take it vertical" or "this is your stuff" can sometimes be a helpful reminder to look into ourselves. But just as often it may be a consciously or unconsciously manipulative or defensive move from the other person to assist them in avoiding hearing or absorbing information that challenges them. Very often this is a move to preserve a power differential.

Many psychological and spiritual systems work with this very issue by encouraging us to notice our charges and work very hard to discern between whether our desire to act or speak horizontally is "acting out" or a genuine communication. Beginning in the 1960s, during a time of widespread emotionally charged social issues, Marshall Rosenberg began describing **nonviolent communication**.[120] This is a way to approach difficult conversations from a place of compassion. His basic teaching is that we reach points of conflict based on miscommunications about our competing human needs. The focus of nonviolent communication involves speaking from our needs while avoiding manipulative or coercing language that will cause shame, guilt, or fear in the other.

Transpersonal visionary Angeles Arrien was known for her teaching of the **four-fold way**, which presents a similar path. This involves four remembrances:

- Show up and be present (The Way of the Warrior/Leader).
- Pay attention to what has heart and meaning (The Way of the Healer).
- Tell the truth without blame or judgment (The Way of the Visionary).
- Be open to (but not attached to) outcome (The Way of the Teacher). [121]

I can say simply that the more you resolve charges inside yourself, the more likely you will be able to communicate from a place of compassion. That said, sometimes communications are necessary *with* charge in order to carry your point and find your authentic voice. Without a doubt, Gandhi and Martin Luther King were effective visionary leaders for their paths of nonviolence. But consider what would have happened if the world just *took it vertical* when faced with powerful and harmful leaders such as Hitler or others that may come to mind in more recent times.

Working with charges in the world is work. Do your best, and when you make mistakes, you have precious gems for integration. Gradually, you may learn when it works for you to engage and when it works to stay internal.

You may also find that you become increasingly "safe" for others to turn towards in their own journeys. The good news is that you might be able to help them; the bad news is they may unconsciously try to work out their own issues with you. Sometimes you become the object of projection. As you move toward understanding that everyone is simply doing what they are doing given who and where they are, you might learn when and how to engage with others and when to side-step and let the world turn on its own.

Metaphor of the Lemniscate

As an alternative to the geometric axis used by Sparks, I have drawn an infinity wheel to represent continuous engagement between the vertical and the horizontal in a cycling fashion. The *lemniscate* is a mathematical symbol used to represent the concept of infinity. I appreciate this symbol as a representation of the experience of integration. This is true for all aspects of integration and particularly true for integrating external and internal experiences.

The Horizontal

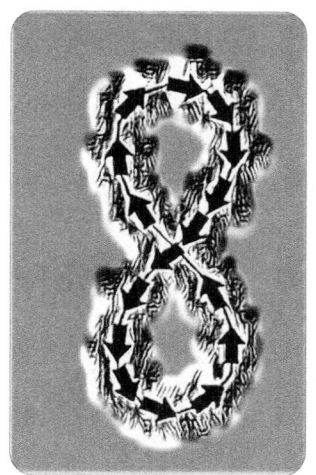

The Vertical

No matter where you begin on the lemniscate, you necessarily go around and up and down and then around and down and up and then find yourself back at the place you started. You can think about this when working with your charged issues. You do your best to find the sources and work through the charges, and then you take what you are discovering back out into the world.

What you learn about the source of your charges may give you insights about things you need to change in your external circumstances as well as yourself. Guaranteed, you will get feedback along the way from your loved ones, friends, and maybe even people you hardly know. Then you take that back around the circle and work with it. This is called integration.

It can be fun and revealing to work with the lemniscate as you consider any issues or challenges that you are facing. You can assign whatever qualities you want to the x-axis and the y-axis, or to the four quadrants created by the axes. You can also use the lemniscate to consider your personal process of integration. In reading the earlier chapters, you may have gotten some maps or tools to get to know yourself in how you process and integrate.

I invite you in the space below to consider qualities that may be involved in your current integration journey. For example, you may know that you begin with your thoughts and then journey around into your emotions, then loop back down into your past history, then come up around the bend into your current relationship situation, then skate back around into physical symptoms you may be having. Or you may be focused on your professional life and where that takes you, or you may be active in the political sphere and be fighting for justice, safety, or other values.

The value of the infinity symbol involves understanding that your integration journey is not linear, but rather cycles around and through and back and forth and up and down. An even better symbol would have a third or even fourth dimensional component, suggesting the ways that you move through past, present and future, and through all the corners and ups and downs of your life history and future possibilities.

I invite you to draw your own infinity symbol and label your drawing in any way you want to experience what you are now integrating in the present and where and how that integration weaves you into and through different areas of experience for your future.

Psychedelics Melt Together Internal and External

One of the classic experiences of psychedelics—in fact, a bit of a stereotype—involves what is known as *synesthesia*. This is where senses blend together and you "hear" something that is visual or "see" a sound or "feel" as a kinesthetic experience something that is external to you. As I talk through the impact of synesthesia, keep in mind these five traditional physiological senses:

Sight	Hearing	Taste	Smell	Touch

You might pause right now to "feel into" each of these senses. See if you can make each sense, one by one, the only sense in your awareness. Consider what it would be like *not* to have that particular sense. Consider that your physical form as a human evolved over millions of years for these senses to be your way of taking in the external world—then reacting to what you take in.

Most humans are predominantly visually focused. Sometimes it is interesting to imagine ourselves as another animal—for instance, a dog. Dogs are not so visually focused, but rather give great attention to smells and sounds. What would it be like to get such nuanced information about the most important things through smell? What would it be like to hear at ranges above and below typical human range? Feeling and "knowing" what it is like to be another animal on the sensory and experiential level are common to non-ordinary states.

The ability of psychedelics to expand senses into each other can be fun—it's a "trip," as they say. But we are talking about something more general and deeper with respect to melting together of internal and external. I use synesthesia as an example —a metaphor—for the ability of psychedelics to help us move around through different channels or lenses of experiences.

Can you "see" through what you "hear"? Songs often bring us back to visual or emotional experiences. Every time a friend hears the Seals and Crofts song "Summer Breeze" (not so much anymore, probably a good thing), he is fifteen years old and standing on his front lawn in New Orleans, smelling pine trees and waiting for his friend to pick him up for a party. Smells and images and feelings come through the auditory experience.

Non-ordinary state experiences tend to come in ways that blend many things together. For instance, in one non-ordinary state experience, this same friend felt himself at the edge of an indigenous village, watching the sun set over a jungle. An old native man wearing only a toga walked out of the jungle with a large stick as a cane. Within that image as it came to him was a simultaneous understanding of the aging process, the wisdom that comes with age, the way every day ends into a night, the imperceptible release of the day's heat, and how the emotions around all of these experiences blend together into a moment of life. Because the image was sensory as well as visual, he "got" a full moment where sensations and understandings were merged.

This way of learning from non-ordinary experiences can help us to

- understand in new ways
- experience more deeply
- exist more holistically.

Perhaps the most important back-and-forth movement is between the external and the internal. This movement is the largest part of integration work. In the big picture, this is how spirit manifests into our plane of material existence.

With psychedelics, what is inside us can shift what we sense outside us—and what we sense outside us shapes what we experience inside ourselves. This is why we pay so much attention to "mindset and setting" in working with psychedelics, which I discussed in chapter 3 and revisit in Chapter 11.

For now, consider two ends of a spectrum for possible experiences with psychedelics. At one end, we ingest a psychedelic substance, put on an eye mask, and have an experienced guide sitting with us. Our guide is likely playing some carefully selected music to help hold our experience. We turn our consciousness inside and work with what emerges. We may reach outside for emotional or physical support, perhaps a hand to hold, a drink of water, or assistance in reaching the bathroom. But the journey takes place internally.

At the other end of the spectrum are the journeys that might be described as recreational, though I do not want this word to suggest that significant learning or exploration are not available. Here are the classic psychedelic trips at a festival or concert, hikes in the mountains, sitting in the forest, dancing at a rave, walking through a city all night, or a sexual experience.

Many experiences are not at either end of this spectrum, but somewhere in the middle. For all experiences, I encourage you to consider how the internal and external come together. This can allow important releases, insights, or shifts, no matter the setting or intention.

Some psychedelic guides may look down on using psychedelics solely for a synesthesia trip. For instance, sometimes I hear, "Well, he just wants to eat some mushrooms and go for a hike and watch the trees all melt together, but that's not really what it's all about." In other words, "going external" while using psychedelics is thought by some people not to make full use of the possibilities of the experience.

From my viewpoint, integration can happen anywhere along this spectrum. Aside from always recommending safety, I am not interested in judging anyone's choices for exploring psychedelics. Sometimes watching the trees melt together is exactly what a person wants and needs.

I have a friend who finds that a hike in the woods during a psychedelic experience connects him to "what is" and recalibrates him for his ongoing participation in a mainstream job, where he feels few people "get him." When the trees melt together, he experiences a blending of nature with his senses in a way that grounds him in the natural world and renews his faith in life and himself. It is not just a show of colors and images, but also a flow of energy from the life force of trees into and through him and joined into his movement on the trail.

If my friend wanted, he could engage in additional focused integration, to explore some of these issues further. There might be hundreds of nuances, memories, and unfelt reactions to his life that could emerge from unpacking his "hike on acid." I respect his choice about how much and what kind of integration he wants, but I am writing this book to offer ideas for integration no matter where your psychedelic session falls on this spectrum.

Relationships

One of the main places external and internal blend for us involves our relationships, particularly the intimate ones. The important "others" in our lives are separate from us, and yet we internalize them as they internalize us. It is often their very "otherness" that brings us something that we need inside ourselves. This something may be what makes us feel whole or safe.

The Relationship Work

To state the obvious, our relationships are important places where we do our deepest psychospiritual work. They are also very important when exploring psychedelics. Our relationships on a psychedelics path can be our greatest support—or our greatest challenge. Sharing your psychedelics experiences can be tricky in close relationships. This can be true whether your significant others are drawn to psychedelics themselves or not. The difficulties increase if a close partner does not understand your path or decision to work with "medicines."

Not everyone is enthusiastic or even accepting of psychedelics. The very idea of psychedelics can be extremely triggering for many people. This is very natural, but if we are excited about exploring the depths of ourselves and of the universe with psychedelics, holding compassion for someone else's triggers can be very challenging. It is common in couple relationships for one partner to hold the adventuring energy of the relationship and the other partner to hold the responsibility and carefulness container. Throwing psychedelics into such a partnership without careful and honest discussions can lead to explosions and suffering.

Sometimes one person in a couple is drawn to psychedelics for reasons that involve issues in the relationship. For instance, one person may know deep down (perhaps not even consciously) that there is something not working in the relationship. Not knowing how to articulate the feeling, much less discuss it, the person may be drawn to psychedelics as a way to escape the issue, to find the answer to the issue, or to find support for dealing with the brewing need to face a painful relationship issue. Probably all of these things are true at the same time for some people.

Even if the relationship is mature and healthy, one person in a partnership might feel deeply threatened by the choices made by the other partner to explore psychedelics. They might be touching upon their own abandonment issues, their own fear of their unconscious, or spiritual-religious issues or wounds. You might remember the link between "high end" spiritual work and touching upon issues of death and bodily survival. Unconsciously, a partner might be picking up on these energies without being able to explain what is happening.

It gets even more complicated when one partner, who is not happy with the other partner's psychedelic exploration, has a perspective and observations that might carry a lot of truth. For example, sometimes the exploration of psychedelics *is* an attempt to avoid something rather than find something. In addition, sometimes our choices around ways to experience psychedelics, or people to trust in facilitating or sharing the experience, are questionable choices. I talk about some of these issues in the next two chapters: Chapter 9 (The Shadow Side) and Chapter 10 (Addiction).

In a perfect world, hearing criticism about your psychedelic exploration voiced by a partner could be helpful. But in our imperfect states of being, these perspectives from a partner can be difficult or even inflammatory. Knowing our human tendency to project out internal issues can help navigate through these situations.

Things can get *very* tricky when one partner talks the other partner into psychedelic exploration when there really is not free choice and consent on the part of the other partner. Psychedelic exploration is a deeply challenging—and yes, sometimes dangerous—path to choose. I believe the choice needs to be made independent from someone else's desires.

I met a couple who both participated in an Ayahuasca ceremony that was strongly desired by the husband. The wife only joined because it was something her husband wanted. Unfortunately (and probably not surprisingly), she had a very bad experience during the ceremony. Difficulties in their relationship emerged during the session. Now, these occurrences can be fruitful for integration work, both involving the "medicine" path and the relationship. But you can see the potential harm and trauma that can happen.

On the other hand, many couples—or close friends—explore psychedelics together. A deepening of the relationship can happen, and the relationship itself can become a lens for understanding oneself, the other, and all that exists. As I have discussed, sexual or deep kinship bonds are part of life and important for exploration in spiritual development. Integration of non-ordinary state experiences shared between two people can be very powerful, a true blessing. With some other couples, one person is interested in exploration and the other compassionately assists the exploration through giving time and a safe container, but has no personal need to join in the actual psychedelic journey. This can be quite beautiful as well.

Most facilitators have a great deal of experience in guiding couples through the preliminary self-exploration of issues surrounding relationships and psychedelics. If you anticipate the possibility of challenging couples issues, you might want to work with a facilitator who has a background in marriage and family issues.

Some facilitators actually refuse to work with one partner in a couple if the other partner has any misgivings about the work. One facilitator I know offers to dialogue with the "not sure" partner to answer any questions or concerns that may arise. His perspective comes from years of experience watching the suffering that may occur after one partner has an enormous opening, or experiences deep challenges, when the other partner did not fully support the decision to explore. Unless my facilitator friend is positive there is clean and clear acceptance by the non-instigating partner, he declines to become involved in the instigating partner's psychedelics exploration.

Other facilitators do not have this level of concern and are willing to work with couples dealing with relationship complexity. For instance, one facilitator I know invites a meeting with both partners to explore the various issues. This facilitator's meeting is primarily to make sure the "not sure" partner understands very clearly the nature of the medicine and the practical scenario that will unfold. This facilitator helps the partners make decisions about the level of involvement of the "not sure" partner in what is being planned. Of course, it probably helps that this facilitator has years of experience as a marriage and family counselor.

Even if your exploration is mostly on your own, and these partnership issues are not in your field, you will almost certainly have to make choices about which friends, extended family members, co-workers, and acquaintances are brought into your psychedelic work through your sharing. The issues I described above will play themselves out with everyone in your life, though not with quite the same charge as with a life partner.

All this said, many people find that psychedelic journeys give them extremely valuable information about their relationships. I know one journeyer who often has the experience in non-ordinary states that he can think about anyone important to him and come to understand what feels like their perspectives, wounds, hopes, and dreams—including with respect to him. He finds this information enormously helpful for his own understandings and healing for these very relationships. He knows it would not be fair to assume his "insights" are completely accurate, much less take the liberty of sharing such insights as "reality" with others. But nonetheless, the information is invaluable. This is where working with a professionally trained, and neutral, integrative therapist can become important. You can process all this information as "real" without seeming to make claims to people close to you about them.

If your exploration is mostly on your own, it will help to find a friend (or integrative therapist—see next section) who is interested in hearing about your journeys and your integration process. The key qualification of such a friend, in my experience, is the quality of non-judgmental listening. It can be helpful if the friend understands the terrain of non-ordinary state work. But this is not always necessary if your experiences are truly held with compassion and respect. No matter what, it is important for you to find ways to know you are not alone in your exploration.

Therapy

I will confess to having a strong affiliation for working with a trained therapist for ongoing integration of psychedelic experiences. This is because exploring psychedelics opens up so many possibilities for profound self-examination and personal growth. While you can do much on your own, it helps to have a companion in your exploration.

The ideal is a companion who knows the terrain. By this I mean a "psychedelics integration therapist"—which is a specialization that is developing though not yet completely recognized by the mainstream psychological community. In Chapter 3, I talked about the possibility of experiencing psychedelics supported by a facilitator who is also a trained therapist. Here, I am focusing on working with a therapist to integrate psychedelic experiences—which may be called integrative therapy.

At our current social juncture, the problem exists in finding an appropriate therapist. An Internet search can lead you to many people advertising themselves as practicing this work. But it is not easy to know their qualifications. There are few therapists with traditional training and licensure who have the experience and perspective necessary to work with someone following a path including psychedelics.

Because this is a unique skill among the broad range of therapist skills, the Multidisciplinary Association for Psychedelic Studies (MAPS) maintains a list of integrative therapists. These people have a clinical background in therapy in conjunction with expertise in integrating non-ordinary state work. I refer you to the list maintained by MAPS for seeking someone in your area with whom to work. If there is no one in your area, you can consider videoconferencing, which is more and more common in many forms of therapy.

Generally speaking, you will still need to pay attention to finding a therapist with whom you personally feel comfortable. I believe therapy is driven by the core value of a healthy relationship between the therapist and the client. Characteristics of a healthy therapist/client relationship include:

- Non-judgment
- Empathy
- Meeting you where you are
- Openness
- Feeling comfortable even if you can't explain why
- Warmth
- Authenticity
- The office feels congruent with the therapist
- The therapist lets you own your own life.

When talking about psychedelics in therapy, all of the above considerations apply, but you also want to consider whether the integrative therapist has:

- Accurate knowledge about psychedelics
- Experience with using psychedelics (including your choice of medicines)
- Exposure to cosmologies consistent with what tends to be experienced with psychedelics
- Experience with the difference between spiritual emergence and mental health issues that might need assistance through mainstream psychological support.

One of the concerns about psychedelics is that a "trip" might push someone into a mental breakdown ("a psychotic break") they would not otherwise have. I discuss this possibility in several places in this book. Coming back to it, let us all take a deep breath. This possibility may be one of the chief elephants in the room when we talk about psychedelics or begin to have psychedelics come out of the closet into the mainstream world.

I will return to the social shadow issues involved in this situation in the next chapter. For now, I want to stay with the question of whether to work with an integrative therapist. If you have any concern that an experience with psychedelics may be "making you crazy," I strongly encourage you to find a qualified integrative therapist. It is important that you find someone who will *not* assume immediately that psychedelics make people crazy and demonize your experience or shame you for where you are finding yourself. However, I find it equally important to suggest working with someone who is not so enamored with psychedelics that they will not speak clearly to you about assistance you may need from a mainstream mental health perspective in moving through your experience.

There is no doubt that experiencing non-ordinary states sometimes cracks open parts of us that carry a huge amount of energy. We might have a beautiful experience "on the mat," but then find that Pandora's box of anger or shame or trauma has come to the surface. This energy can be transformational in very positive ways, but can also be extremely hard to accommodate. Again, this is where integration with someone familiar with both psychotherapy and non-ordinary states can make all the difference in the world.

Integrating in Community or Alone

Being alone or in community is a complex question regarding psychedelic work. I have talked a great deal regarding the multitude of variables that are to be contemplated when getting ready to do a psychedelic session. Integrating psychedelic experience can raise the same spider web of questions. Are you drawn to integration alone or within a community? Do you thrive by processing externally or within yourself? The most important thing I can say would be: *this is your choice.*

In this section, I would like to explore the value of all the gradations between contemplation alone and in community. When you integrate alone, you can draw on the strengths of:

- Deep internal contemplation
- Understanding what is yours
- Safety to explore your boundaries and new insights without the sense of potential judgment
- Freedom to develop and practice your dialogue of expression without attending to other people.

Even if you explore psychedelics as part of a group, you still have the decision whether to stay mostly internal to yourself or whether to open yourself up. A good practice for integration group leaders is to allow people to make the choice in the moment of sharing or not, though often the leader will check in with you just enough to make sure you are doing okay. Even within group settings, I want to encourage you to take care of yourself. You can always fall back on: Do you want to give it more time?

Integrating in community has many potential values, including:

- Expression that reaches other people
- Exploring vulnerability
- Validating similarities
- Advancing your skills in empathic listening
- Sharing your authentic voice
- Experiencing support for your non-ordinary state work.

It's your choice, but I recommend that you experiment with both individual integration and sharing your integration work in groups. Stay within your comfort range, and test your ability to do things differently. Test your ability to trust—both your own instincts and the goodwill and safety of other people.

Group Sharing

Okay, so you have made the decision to explore psychedelics or psychedelics integration in a group. Let's say you're mostly an introvert, but you have opened up to the possibility of sharing in a group. You might be preparing for an experience that will happen later, maybe the next day, or maybe in just an hour or so. Or, you might be in a post-experience stage; a ceremony may have just concluded, or you might be gathering the morning or afternoon after a group session.

What do you need to bring to your awareness? Working in a group is different than working one-on-one. Here are some ways to think about the differences:

- Groups bring out behaviors in people that might not be apparent outside group situations. For instance, some people shut down in groups, while others flourish or open.
- Structures within groups may differ, so you may need to notice what is happening with the structure in order to keep yourself feeling safe and present.
- At the same time you are noticing what is happening within yourself, you are noticing what is happening in the group around you, so your attention is split.
- There might be a compounding potential for healing in that you might learn something from someone else's process simply by witnessing their process.

In a group, **empathetic listening** supports an environment for safety and maximum healing and integration. What do I mean by empathetic listening? I mean that you listen with your heart and suspend any tendency to judge, fix, or reach an opinion.

All of us have needs to discern and make sense of what we hear from others. So I do not ask you to lose your need to make your own sense of what you hear from others. But I recommend that within group sharing, everyone put those needs aside temporarily and open their hearts to each other. I recommend you try meeting others exactly where they are.

Similar to empathetic listening is the practice of **holding space.** You hear this phrase frequently now in working with relationships, any form of therapy, and with groups. I mentioned "holding space" in Chapter 3 when I talked about the different types of facilitation or guidance in psychedelics work. By holding space, I mean bringing your fully authentic self, and your full attention, to what is being offered to you by other people or by a group.

Empathetic listening is used in the sense of suspending judgment and meeting others where they are, but there is also a more active component of bringing a safe energy to the "space" that is created between and among people. This can be understood as a "presence" that may come forward. Often this is a mixture of sympathy, empathy, compassion, understanding, and love.

Group Therapy

Learning to find your inner empathetic listening, your ability to hold space, and your presence is one of the main values of integrating non-ordinary state experiences in groups.

Post-Session Life Choices

Another caution you will hear after working in non-ordinary states is "don't run out and make any big decisions." You want to be cautious when you return to the outer world after being in non-ordinary space. Here is what I often share with people after a Holotropic Breathwork session: "If changing jobs or getting divorced or moving to a new country is a good idea now, it will still be a good idea three months from now."

Even with healthy and incremental integration of a psychedelic session, there is still an afterglow that may leave you thinking:

- Everything is perfect.
- There is no danger in the world.
- I will be protected no matter what.

When you have the glow, enjoy it and bring that joy into your being in ways that last. And yet, this is a time when you really should use caution to remember safety and **prudence**. I love that word "prudence" and actually use it frequently as I "process the shit out of everything." I will even give you a definition of being prudent: "acting with or showing care and thought for the future." Synonyms are "wise, well judged, sensible, politic, judicious, sagacious, sage, shrewd, advisable, well advised."

I talked about Tarot cards earlier. In my favorite deck (the Crowley Thoth Tarot Deck created by occultist Aleister Crowley and Lady Frieda Harris), the Eight of Disks is known as the Prudence card. My favorite book about this deck, *The Crowley Tarot: Handbook to the Cards*, by Akron and Hajo Banzhof, has this to say about the energy of prudence:

> Energetically this card symbolizes self-discipline, weighing of details, conscientiousness, and spiritual knowledge of the lawfulness behind the course of all events in nature as well as behind all human actions. The high standard of bringing oneself back into balance with creative nature not only requires a pure motivation and selfless striving for wisdom, but also the spiritual sensibility that chaos and order, destruction and development, creative intelligence and emotional motivation do not contradict, but rather reciprocally give rise to each other. [122]

Prudence involves giving time for things to fall into a new order. Let the big picture issues described by Akron and Banzhof incrementally work their way through you. Basically, I recommend integrating concrete reality *and* the depths of your experience **slowly and kindly.**

In the meantime, there are some tried and true practices for beginning your engagement with the outer world after psychedelics. Some of the most commonly recommended ways for grounding after non-ordinary state work include:

- Walks in nature
- Hot baths
- Heavy food—or light food?
- Refraining from alcohol, cannabis or other recreational compounds
- Drawing or painting
- Moving or dancing
- Sitting quietly
- And, most importantly, just giving yourself space to be with what happened.

Making it Your Own

Even though I am giving advice in this book about integration, it is significantly important for you to remember that integration is your personal trip. At the end of this chapter on process, I want to give your process back to you. To one degree or another, I recommend you guard your integration process as your own throughout your life journey. This chapter is about what happens as you begin to work with your experiences in relationship to the outer world.

As you engage incrementally through who you are becoming, you may find that feedback comes to you from many sources. As I have seen, these can include:

- Your life partner
- Your parents
- Your children
- People you work with
- Your friends
- Your therapist
- The city you live in
- The media as it seeps into your life
- Anything and everything else.

What gets even more complicated is to consider that you have an internalized image of all of these "others" that has a life of its own inside you. For example, you may assume that people you work with have certain judgments about you or what you are doing or who you are becoming. There may be some basis in reality for your assumptions, but you probably need to sort through your assumptions and what actually is coming from them that makes any real difference to you.

In psychology and throughout this book, I use the term "projection" to describe the common practice of making assumptions about someone else and their motivations and meanings. "Introjection" is an inverse term. This describes the practice of bringing these imagined versions of other people inside ourselves. As you guard your process as your own, it is important to work through your projections and introjections to find that unique space inside yourself that is safe and truly owned only by you.

For now, it is crucially important to hold onto what comes from psychedelic work as rightfully yours. No one can—and no one should—take this away from you. No one should judge you for your search and your desire to learn and grow. Full acceptance; it's yours.

Ultimately, by taking on ownership of your experiences, you gain freedom, but you also find responsibility. It becomes your responsibility to engage in psycho-education to learn about risks and benefits. It becomes your choice to find the psychedelics and the experiences that best fit who you are and your intentions. It becomes your responsibility to find the appropriate people and settings for your non-ordinary state work.

Although people rarely talk about what I am about to say, many people do not *really* want freedom or responsibility. If we take full responsibility for making integration our own, we might come right up against the existential reality that we are alone. If we become the authorities on our meanings and choices around psychedelics—not our family, spouse, friends, or coworkers—then we might not have the sense of these people supporting us. We might realize fully for the first time that we were born alone and that we will die alone.

BUT: if you take full ownership of your experiences, this is where empowerment comes from. You might find yourself feeling intimately connected with who you are becoming and the realities beyond yourself that you discover in psychedelics. Very likely, you will come across new people who are on similar paths as you are choosing. Or, you may find that people who have always been in your life want to take the journey along with you and open themselves in ways that surprise you.

Now Your Turn

I invite you to consider some questions that you may hold throughout your integration process:

How do you process?

_____
_____
_____
_____
_____

What style of processing do you feel comfortable with? For example, do you gravitate towards verbal or nonverbal, movement or silence?

_____
_____
_____
_____
_____

What are things that are of primary significance to you? What are your pillars that you stand for?

_____
_____
_____
_____
_____

Describe your support system. Who are the people that are safe for you to discuss this work with?

_____

How do you walk your walk?

This work is an ongoing teacher. What are some of the questions you would like to ask? What do you long to learn from this work?

Can you define where, how, and from what you find comfort?

Integration Exercise 8: Sacred Circle: Group Sharing, Empathic Listening

What You Need

- Yourself and other people (that is, a group setting)
- Open room (sacred space)
- Chairs, "back-jacks," or meditation cushions
- Sacred objects for "collective altar"
- Timer
- You might consider having a "shaker," a device that asks for mindfulness on the part of the person sharing (and someone to keep a general sense of time)
- Your journal.

General Background

Many people experience psychedelics in a group setting and have the benefit of group sharing before and after the experience. If you have never had this experience, I encourage you in this exercise to find a group of some kind to stretch yourself with your empathic listening skills. You can find psychedelic integration circles now in many communities. I focus on psychedelic integration circles in this exercise, but you can experience this form of sharing in many different groups.

Psychedelic exploration is not only about sharing what you have gained yourself. We can learn so much by listening to what others have to share, and we can also develop our compassionate, non-judgmental listening skills. Many sharing circles in the realm of psychedelic integration follow a **talking circle** model, drawing on practices in indigenous communities. A talking circle recognizes the equal right of everyone to their own experiences and the obligation of all to respect and honor each other.

Empathic listening is a technique that can help you manage and avoid disruptive and projected behaviors. This empathic listening technique can be used in one-on-one experiences (such as a client with a therapist) or collective groups where everyone participated in the psychedelic event. A key component involves agreement not to engage in cross talk—that is, not to question or challenge what anyone else says, but simply to listen and take it in. This is a practice that is common in addiction communities and creates a great sense of safety.

Talking, sharing and healing circles are useful when the topic under consideration has no right or wrong answer, or when people need to share feelings. Moral or ethical issues can often be dealt with in this way without offending anyone. The purpose of talking circles with psychedelics integration is to create a safe environment for people to share their points of view and experiences with others. This process helps people gain a sense of trust in each other. They come to believe that what they say will be listened to and accepted without criticism. They also gain an appreciation for points of view other than their own.

Why this Exercise is Important for Psychedelics

Exploring psychedelics can be such an intense experience of focusing on yourself that it can be very important from the beginning to remember to focus on other people and their experiences and their life journeys. Including others begins the integration process as you move back into your "ordinary" everyday life. It is a return to the "outer world." Like it or not, that outer world is where much of your integration will be shaped.

Somehow, sharing with others and *listening to others* helps you to remember your own experience in a deep way. This also helps you learn to trust a community. For many people, the communities they find around working with non-ordinary states become the first community they *really* trust.

How To Do It

Preparation in advance

1. Create a circle with chairs, blankets, or "back-jacks."
2. Create an organic "collective altar" with flowers, candles, and sacred objects to focus on.
3. Have enough space for group members to be comfortable.
4. Have a timer and "shaker" to monitor time (optional).

Instructions for the exercise (Time: Forty-five minutes to ninety minutes)

- Everyone that participated in the psychedelic experience enters the circle.
- An intentional silent meditation opens the circle.
- Sacred sharing is done in "popcorn" style or may go around the circle.
- Not everyone needs to verbally participate. But usually if people do not share, a facilitator might check in with them to be sure they are okay.
- A predetermined "rough" time frame is discussed for group sharing prior to the sharing session.

Empathic Listening Skills

- Provide the speaker with your undivided attention. This is one time when "multi-tasking" or "rapid refocus" is not recommended.
- Be non-judgmental.
- Read the speaker. Observe the emotions behind the words. Be quiet.
- Assure your understanding through "holding space" and "sacred attention."
- After each participant shares, reflect in silence until the next person wants to share.

Sacred Sharing

- Share from a heartfelt space. It is not a "play by play" of your experience, but more of a selection of moments from the heart that represent the aspects of your psychedelic experience that you want to share.
- Participants share when they are drawn to share, often in a "popcorn" manner so that people speak only when they are ready to speak.
- The facilitator of the group may want to control the time and open space to share. Continue to organically explore sacred sharing and empathic listening until it feels a natural completion has been reached.
- The circle is traditionally closed by the leader of the group with a ceremonial completion that is traditionally agreed upon by all members of the group.

I have observed repeatedly that experiencing psychedelics in a collective setting (a group workshop, healing ceremony, festival, or home exploring session) can be a profound opportunity to learn about not only yourself, but our woven connection to others too. The emphasis of a sacred sharing group is to allow each person to speak about whatever they wish as it relates to their experience of the psychedelic work in a safe and non-confronting atmosphere.

This sacred sharing circle will be developed with trust, offering a safe, confidential haven for us to speak and be heard. Everything said by group members is held in the utmost confidence. This part of the integration work is designed so that each individual is heard and all develop their listening skills as well as a deeper sense of empathy.

CHAPTER 9

THE SHADOW SIDE

In the last chapter, we saw how the internal and external are intertwined with each other. I now turn to the murky subject of shadow. This is another way of understanding how our psychologies—both individual and collective—intertwine with and create the external world. The concept of the shadow—which I talked about briefly in Chapter 8—comes from the psychology of Carl Jung. The shadow is a potent part of the psyche that is beneath awareness, but close enough to the surface to act out in ways that can be noticed if you are willing to look.

The Shadow

The shadow contains the rejected, abandoned, undeveloped or demonized parts of yourself. These may be characteristics, emotions, or unlived possibilities of life. The shadow holds things you do not want to see about yourself or your culture. Jack E. Othon writes:

> Rather than confront something that we don't like, our mind pretends it does not exist. Aggressive impulses, taboo mental images, shameful experiences, immoral urges, fears, irrational wishes, unacceptable sexual desires—these are a few examples of shadow aspects, things people contain but do not admit to themselves that they contain.[123]

If you hear someone (including yourself) talking about owning their shadow, you might be suspicious whether this is really shadow. By definition, what is in shadow does not want to be seen or talked about. When shadow starts to become conscious, there is usually shame, guilt, fear, or anger. It is difficult to share actual shadow without embarrassment.

Making shadow conscious involves admitting to yourself that you are not all that you like to believe yourself to be. It may also involve admitting that the culture you hold as yours is not what it wants to believe. Making shadow conscious takes work and pain around your conception of yourself or your affiliation with parts of culture that you consider part of yourself.

The shadow is a *complex* in the sense of holding emotional charge. The charge is often very strong, even violent. Most of us have been so trained to repress these charges that we become unconscious of their existence. Because many of them first arise during adolescence and puberty, they may be repressed before we even get to know them. But they leak out.

Shadow tends to project itself out onto other individuals, groups, ideas or behaviors. Jung wrote that "Projections change the world into the replica of one's own unknown face."[124] What you do not face within yourself, you imagine in others outside you. As Jung said, typically there is some "hook" in these others on which you hang your projection. But the charge you bring involves your own repression and inability to face all that exists within you.

Many characters in fiction and film embody our semiconscious awareness of shadow and how shadow operates. Like these characters, our shadow complexes have the capacity to deflect, defend, or twist reality to avoid being detected and experienced. These characters are sometimes very attractive on the surface but may turn out to be dangerous. For the psyche, what is dangerous is often something that is painful to admit because it contradicts ideas or images we like to hold about ourselves or those with whom we are identified.

There are two primary **defense mechanisms** operating with shadow. The first, as we have seen, involves **projecting something out** so that we do not have to integrate it within ourselves. The second is simply **defending** against taking in the understanding by putting up barriers and rationalizations.

A good example of both defenses can be seen with a sense of inferiority. None of us really wants to feel lesser than others. But almost all of us feel insecure in one way or another, sometimes deeply insecure. To project out a sense of inferiority is to consider another group of people less worthy than ourselves—flawed or stupid or immoral or wanting to take something from us. To defend against a feeling of inferiority is to put up a hostile front to anyone or anything that might call attention to your insecurity. The defense can also include refusing to believe anything that contradicts your projections.

Shadow wants a way to get out, but our psyche resists. Unconsciously, we do not want to experience the emotions or sense of deflation that arises if we make shameful things about ourselves conscious. It is very difficult for many people to hold onto the idea that life is complicated and not easily divided into categories that always hold true. In the process of working with shadow, you have to give up distinctions of good/bad. Accepting shadow usually involves owning things like fear, anger, resentment, violence, and desires to dominate and abuse. If that is you (or at least a potential within you), can you live with yourself?

Making shadow conscious involves **integrating** these impulses into your mind-body feeling state. You become honest with yourself about the impulses and understand this is part of life. You find ways to "take back" what you project onto other people and feel it all inside yourself. You do not feel bad about yourself, but understand all these instincts are part of our humanity. You know that none of us is all one thing or another. With light comes darkness and with darkness comes light. The "dark-ness" can feel like heritage and provide a kind of strength that helps you feel solid.

Why do I talk about Shadow with Psychedelics?

The concept of shadow is very useful in working with psychedelics. Psychedelics want to show you what is in your unconscious mind. Shadow is the mechanism by which your psyche does not want to see what it does not want to see. Learning about shadow can help you understand and make sense of what is being revealed to you in working with psychedelics.

In his first session with Ayahuasca, my friend Jay Dufrechou, author of the book *Moving through Grief: Reconnecting with Nature*, was shown how his mind projects out from what is painful and defends against taking in experiences that could be painful. He could start to recognize this mechanism and feel into it. Understanding this, it became easier to stay with things that were coming into awareness but were hard to accept. For instance, he could take in the realities of how he had hurt particular other people through actions that he had rationalized or blamed others for causing.

Staying with such things sets the stage for processing and integration after the psychedelic experiences. Within an Ayahuasca session, the way it works for Jay is that he starts to feel sick, and then consciousness about something he has not wanted to see begins to form. He knows he does not want to accept what is being shown to him, so he resists for a time. Then he feels worse and worse. Finally, he knows that the only way to feel better and move through what is present is to take in what is being shown, even with the associated feelings, often guilt, shame, or fear. Then Grandmother Ayahuasca brings a purging (literal and energetic) that feels as though something is released while integrated.

During his first Ayahuasca experience, Jay also understood the way that acting from projections and defenses creates the fabric of our lives. By avoiding something, you do something else. The projections and defenses then bring back experience after experience that teach us. Whether you consider this fate or simply the mechanics of interacting with other people, it seems to be true that when you project and defend, things come back to you that may wake you up.

Jay had a teacher at the Institute of Transpersonal Psychology, David Goff, who shared a wise saying: "What I do to defend myself is offensive to others." This is one way of understanding what comes back to us. All things considered, it may be easier to let the medicine wake you up than bring life experiences to you that knock you around.

There is another fundamental reason the concept of shadow is helpful in working with psychedelics. Shadow is a mechanism of dividing things off and creating dualities. Good/bad or us/them are very basic splits into which many other splits could be categorized. Psychedelics show us the unity of all things. This is not an idea, but a reality. As I have seen, some guides working with psychedelics focus on the experience of nonduality. This experience is available with psychedelics, possibly more with some medicines than others. Shadow from the perspective of nonduality becomes a way of understanding the unseen connection between things and events.

From a nondual perspective, you might understand that something has been repressed from consciousness, but you might also see that this causes an impact somewhere else. Perhaps something repressed from your conscious mind causes acting out of your emotions, a symptom in your body, or a problem in your relationships. If something is projected out, there will be a response of some kind from those carrying the projection. Everything weaves together if you become open to understanding and if you can carry the painful awareness that may open up to you.

From a perspective of nonduality, shadow can be seen as the interaction or connecting waves between different manifestations of interrelated parts. This necessarily involves awareness that consciousness is transpersonal and participates in collective consciousness and unconsciousness. This brings us to collective shadow—our focus in the next subsection.

But before approaching collective shadow, let us revisit the idea that everything in our culture finds some way inside us. In other words, we have our own personal shadow, but our shadow includes many repressions we have inherited from our culture. Erich Neumann, a psychologist, philosopher and student of Jung, described the way collective aspects of shadow inhabit our individual unconscious:

> All those qualities, capacities and tendencies which do not harmonize with the collective values—everything that shuns the light of public opinion, in fact — now come together to form the shadow, that dark region of the personality which is unknown and unrecognized by the ego. The endless series of shadow and doppelganger figures in mythology… again and again such figures have appeared and made their bow before human consciousness, but the psychological meaning of this archetype of the adversary has not yet dawned upon mankind. [125]

It is one thing to have this "adversary" existing within our individual unconscious. But something else entirely happens when shadow takes hold in the collective unconscious. Then we get a powerful and sometimes terrifying intermingling of collective shadow arising at a moment of historical time with the powerful energies of ancient archetypes that might seem to be gods or demons.

Collective Shadow

Jung wrote:

> It is a frightening thought that man also has a shadow side to him, consisting not just of little weaknesses and foibles, but of a positively demonic dynamism. The individual seldom knows anything of this; to him, as an individual, it is incredible that he should ever in any circumstances go beyond himself. But let these harmless creatures form a mass, and there emerges a raging monster; and each individual is only one tiny cell in the monster's body, so that for better or worse he must accompany it on its bloody rampages and even assist it to the utmost. Having a dark suspicion of these grim possibilities, man turns a blind eye to the shadow-side of human nature. [126]

Living through the twentieth century world wars in Europe, Jung was aware of the way societies become hypnotized into acting out collective shadow. This usually happens through creation of adversaries that carry projections of our own aggressions, feelings of inferiority, and instinctual fears. Real social and political issues are often involved. But the tone becomes vehement and seems to reach back into unconscious realms with more energy than the issues justify. Reality takes a back seat to the need to deflect and blame. Self-righteousness and victimhood often hide aggression and anger that are being denied and projected.

Enactment of the collective shadow draws from the deep energies of the collective unconscious. In this realm are archetypal complexes sufficiently split from wholeness that they act as objectively evil. Psychologist Stephen Diamond writes:

> Jung differentiated between the personal shadow and the impersonal or archetypal shadow, which acknowledges transpersonal, pure or radical evil (symbolized by the Devil and demons) and collective evil, exemplified by the horror of the Nazi holocaust. Literary and historical figures like Adolf Hitler, Charles Manson, and Darth Vader personify the shadow embodied in its most negative archetypal human form. [127]

Jung is said to have once seen Hitler passing by in a parade. As the story goes, he turned to his companion and said, "That man is possessed." This was possession by a collective shadow for which Hitler had become the living vehicle. The need of a leader for constant energy from crowds ready to direct anger and judgment against others suggests possession by archetypal shadow. Willingness to demonize others and ignore reality takes on an otherworldly quality that is hypnotizing for some and terrifying for others.

If you are not pulled into the collective shadow, history passing before you in times of collective shadow may seem like a bad dream. Deep splits are created as those resisting the collective shadow react to the sense of danger from falling into a lack of consciousness. When the collective is involved, the projected shadow is more likely to take on archetypal characteristics and energies. Mythological themes become constellated. Issues of policy with the possibility of rational debate turn into imagined epic battles between good and evil where there is no ability to consider alternatives. Religious images are invoked. Those who disagree do not just have different opinions, but become bad and wrong and dangerous. Slogans arise and crowds cheer and jeer.

In non-ordinary states, you may reach places where you can feel very deeply the power that constellates around collective shadow. There is an instinctual and raw element that can feel invigorating, primal, even with sexual overtones. What might ordinarily seem coarse or immature starts to feel like blood running through the veins of those in the collective energy: it can feel like a pack ready to descend on a kill or a dominant about to mount a submissive in a sexual encounter.

Both sides of these energies can be experienced. You may feel how these energies can lead to destruction and chaos: the enactment of cruelty and consuming of other. These energies can be truly terrifying. It takes great centering to allow them into yourself. Psychedelics may provide the strength and centering necessary to experience the dark possibilities of the collective shadow.

When a culture enacts archetypal shadow, it is possible to understand the occurrence as part of a healing process. Such divisions might happen when movement toward wholeness has pushed towards a point of crucible. Jungian theory is not alone in recognizing that movement in one direction tends to create an opposite reaction. Because the individual and collective psyches are living systems with compensatory mechanisms, when a new element of light is added to the system, some elements tend to adjust in response by arising in negativity, in darkness. Jung had this to say:

> The enlargement of the light side of consciousness has the necessary consequence that the part of the psyche which is less light and less capable of consciousness is thrown into darkness to such an extent that sooner or later a rift occurs in the psychic system. At first, this is not recognized as such and is therefore projected—i.e. it appears as a religious projection, in the form of a split between the powers of Light and Darkness.[128]

Whether or not healing occurs from these archetypal rifts is perhaps a matter of fate. What can individuals do? Probably the best work is staying conscious and witnessing what is happening—and, if necessary, protecting yourself and your loved ones from harmful effects.

The History of Psychedelics and Shadow

What does all this mean for exploration of psychedelics? What does this mean for integration of psychedelics? Shadow is very important to consider when facing the history of psychedelics in the Western world. There are two aspects of shadow I want to discuss. On the surface these may look like two completely separate issues, but once you look deeply, you can see them as mirror images of each other.

- The first is the cultural shadow that has been projected onto psychedelics by mainstream culture. This is essentially the story of the demonization of psychedelics in the 1960s, 1970s, and into the present. If you are interested in psychedelics, it is important to understand this history and to separate out what is shadow and what might have some reality.
- The second issue involves the shadow that exists in the psychedelics community (or some psychedelics communities). Here are the things that we do not want to acknowledge or that we dismiss too easily if we support exploration of psychedelics. This may include our tendency to write off those "others" who have concerns about psychedelics being widely used. If we repress taking seriously the concerns about psychedelics, then others will end

up carrying them. If we reject these others, then we are enacting shadow projection and continuing duality.

In this section I will talk about the cultural shadow projected onto psychedelics. I will return in a later section to the shadow within psychedelics work. I wanted to mention the two together at the outset, however, because it is important to understand the relationship between them.

I follow talking about integration in relationship with the outer world with talking about shadow because all of the craziness that exists in the outer world about psychedelics will necessarily become part of your integration if you are willing to explore a deep process. This includes the projections of insanity and criminality and irresponsibility that are placed upon psychedelics by some in the culture. I reserve the subject of addiction for our next chapter because addiction is an enormous topic on its own. But you can see how the issue of addiction can be both a projection of shadow from mainstream culture and a shadow element that psychedelics culture may at times avoid.

Let us return to the historical narrative of LSD. In earlier chapters, I shared the story of Albert Hofmann's discovery of LSD in the Basel, Switzerland, Sandoz laboratory in 1943. I pick up now with Hofmann's realization of the shadowy turn taken by LSD's explosion into popular culture. As Hofmann wrote in *LSD: My Problem Child: Reflections on Sacred Drugs, Mysticism and Science,* his initial joy at having fathered a drug "with such fantastic effects on mental perception" was tarnished beyond anything he could have foreseen. This happened "when LSD was swept up in the huge wave of an inebriant mania that began to spread over the Western world, above all the United States, at the end of the 1950s." [129]

In this mania, we might see the collective split between projections of light and projections of darkness recognized by Jung. There was so much enthusiasm for psychedelics, much of it ungrounded, that compensatory shadow emerged. As Hofmann put it:

> The publicity about LSD attained its high point in the years 1964 to 1966, not only with regard to enthusiastic claims about the wondrous effects of LSD by drug fanatics and hippies, but also to reports of accidents, mental breakdowns, criminal acts, murders, and suicide under the influence of LSD. A veritable LSD hysteria reigned. [130]

Hofmann hit upon some of the high points of the darker perceptions about psychedelics during the 1960s and 1970s. I will reframe these in my own words:

- Using psychedelics will make you go crazy (induce psychosis or paranoia).
- You will have flashbacks forever and will never get back to normal.

- Only criminals delve into psychedelics.
- Psychedelics will make you do dangerous things, like jump out of a window or off the top of a building.
- LSD and mushrooms are addictive, just like heroin, and will lead to your death in a ramshackle abandoned building in a bad part of town.
- Even if psychedelics do not make you go "crazy," they will scramble your mind so that you will no longer think clearly, as with the famous television commercial of the frying egg: "This is your brain on drugs."
- Using psychedelics makes you have sex with anyone and everyone (including orgies).
- Psychedelics are the work of the devil.

Even those of us who find positive benefit in working with psychedelics may have residue of such cultural projections living within us. This residue may mix with our own prudent fears and concerns and, at the very least, cause the need for conscious work about the lines between projected falsities and reality.

Even if we have minimal introjection of cultural shadow around psychedelics, it is very possible that those around us (loved ones, acquaintances, people who seem to come out of nowhere) may in some ways embody aspects of the cultural shadow projected onto psychedelics. If you become a psychedelics warrior, some of this energy will likely come towards you. This becomes a place for integration work.

I'm going to take a break from this narrative to let you feel into your own orientation around this heavy topic.

Now Your Turn

Do any of these projections into psychedelics carry a charge for you?

_____
_____
_____
_____

If so, can you close your eyes and center yourself and trace back that charge to its source? What do you learn?

_____
_____
_____

Do you know any people who think or feel these things about psychedelics? If so, can you imagine having a mature and calm dialogue with them?

Cultural Shadow and the Psychedelics Renaissance

Getting back to the cultural projections into psychedelics, I continue the story of the turbulent 1960s and 1970s, and then turn to present times. Many books have been written about the history of psychedelics coming into Western culture and the splits that arose within our culture. I look back at this time as a fascinating period well before I was born. For some older people, the most turbulent struggles were happening when they were children or in their early teens, but they may remember the sense of great opening and great reaction.

Psychedelics—and war—became two of the primary fault lines for the cultural divide of the 1960s. I do not think these two fault lines are unrelated. While the cultural factors were many, thousands of people were having experiences of love and unity through psychedelics that contributed to a desire to end what seemed like an insensible war. While all wars are horrible, what was happening in the jungles of Southeast Asia seemed based only on the power needs of people who were unable to take in the sanctity and sacredness of life.

Collective Shadow

The "generation gap" of this time period was notorious. Berkeley Free Speech Movement activist Jack Weinberg was the source of the famous saying, "Don't trust anyone over thirty." In later years, Weinberg explained that he was not trying to make a huge statement, but was attempting to get a reporter to back off from suggesting the Free Speech Movement was a Communist plot. As the statement went viral in the press, it was used to exacerbate an emerging generational divide full of projections from one side to the other.

As we have seen, one of the consequences of this history was the prohibition of psychedelics, which halted all research into the healing and creative properties of many substances. While this represented one closed door, the impact of the openings of this time period continued—and brought long-term reactions.

Interestingly enough, a strong cultural divide is finding an echo in our current times. There are ways to see this divide as resulting from the openings that occurred in the 1960s and beyond. Some of the openings included civil rights for minorities, new roles for women, sexual freedom, acceptance of ranges of sexuality, decline of many traditional social organizations, a faster pace of life, increased mobility and travel—and in the last few decades, globalization through communications and international immigration and economics.

After the cultural explosion of the 1960s, many people ceased identifying with organized religion and became interested in "spirituality, not religion." It is easy to see the growth of religious fundamentalism and suspicion of immigrants (movements that are worldwide) as a response to some of these openings.

As we move into the third decade of the twenty-first century, the fault line in the United States is along geographical and cultural lines rather than generational. But the sense of a split with strong energies (archetypal?) is cause for concern. Numerous commentators have observed that the United States has not been this divided since the Civil War of the 1860s.

For us, there is a strong sense of shadow emerging worldwide—and certainly in the United States—from what feels like demonization of some peoples or groups. This seems to involve projected issues of power, dominance, fear, loss, aggression, and anger. As many observers have lamented, facts and truth seem to be taking a back seat to the desire to blame and demonize. The appeal of grandiosity, sloganeering, and crowd mentality seems fueled by archetypal energies. Social media has made this easier.

Psychedelics have not (yet?) been caught up in the contemporary "culture wars" being experienced in the United States and other Western countries. The researchers and therapists currently bringing psychedelics back into mainstream culture have been extraordinarily careful to comply with mainstream rules and regulations. The mainstream media has for the most part been respectful of these efforts.

As I have said elsewhere, it helps that some of the impetus for opening MDMA therapy involves assisting the thousands of military veterans suffering from post-traumatic stress disorder. Veterans are traditionally held in high honor by the conservative groups who might otherwise demonize psychedelics. This fact, I hope, will continue to protect the new research and MDMA projects.

Nevertheless, I notice the reports of overdoses by famous people that sometimes include reference to psychedelics. I personally suspect the drug actually leading to death in these sad stories was one of the opiates or amphetamines (or alcohol). But I note that a psychedelic is sometimes mentioned, which I find a bit worrisome.

Given the split that currently exists among many people, I want to encourage consciousness about the possible reemergence of shadow projections into psychedelics. I also stress that the shadow projection, in my view, involves not just psychedelics but any work with non-ordinary states of consciousness. Many people find such work unhealthy or even demonic.

"Belief" or "faith" is enormously popular among some people in our time. But finding one's own way to spirituality can be suspect. The fundamentalist religious base fueling politics in the last few decades seems very fond of a split between good and evil. Some people find it "good" to "believe" in the authoritarian interpretations of religion and "bad" to question external authority. Adherence to the "external" beliefs of a crowd can be labeled "good," and seeking one's own way through the internal realms can be labeled "bad."

Looking back at the 1960s and 1970s, it is not an overstatement to say that the fight between good and evil (or light and darkness) was projected into the story of psychedelics. Western culture (particularly the United States) loves to replay this epic struggle. I do not want to minimize the actual dangers and irresponsible actions that existed among some psychedelics users during that period. But I believe the projection of "evil" into psychedelics had much more to do with shadow projection than with reality. I want to be mindful that this projection can happen again.

When cultures grapple with collective or archetypal shadow, the response to these strong shadows has to involve individual work, person by person, and willingness to have compassion for all, with appropriate boundaries. Working directly with collective and archetypal images necessarily takes place through our individual life stories.

Sometimes it can help to align yourself with positive ancestral energies when working with non-ordinary states. When collective shadow emerges in a particular historical time, it can help to take a long view of history. I believe that in all times there have been souls who were able to ride out shadowy eras with wisdom and compassion. Can you imagine an ancient teacher or guide who might come to you to provide assistance if you feel challenged by projection of shadow into psychedelics in our times? What would this ancient teacher look like? How would she or he act? Can you feel this guidance inside you?

What Underlies the Negative Cultural Projections into Psychedelics?

Each of us will have our own understanding of what underlies the mainstream cultural shadow projections into psychedelics. But I offer two suggestions that ring true to me.

As you will remember, shadow begins with the repression of something. There is something that is not accepted or defended against. Then projection of "evil" tends to happen onto something that carries a hook or represents the threat. Sometimes shadow begins with the repression of a fear. I call our first suggestion about mainstream cultural projection as the fear of **Opening Pandora's Box.**

Ultimately, I wonder if the central projection about psychedelics involves the fear that using psychedelics will break down the culture and bring chaos. Unconsciously, people may understand that exploring psychedelics throws open everything in the psyche, and this could lead to desires for drastic changes and restructuring in the external world. The fear involves loss of existing social and political structures. Within this fear is the concern about chaos during transformational times.

Oddly enough, there is some truth in this possibility. Psychedelics may open enough people to the harmful ways of current culture that changes happen to our culture. As I noted above, it is easy to recognize the role played by psychedelics in the many openings and changes that happened during the tumultuous decades of the 1960s and 1970s. Should we be afraid of such changes?

I return to the reality that psychedelics do not *do* something to your consciousness, but rather, open doors of perception. Psychedelics are catalysts and provide ignition. In this way, some of what comes into individual awareness, and then cultural awareness, involves the things that may be missing or unhealthy in current culture. In this scenario, deep down there is knowledge that many things are not working. Rather than face this possibility, there can be a strong hold onto the status quo. Something that might open up the minds of people to the need for change can be demonized in order to uphold the repression.

For example, many people during non-ordinary state journeys reach a place of deep anger or grief about environmental degradation. This may manifest as anger directed towards corporate greed or the political agendas of certain groups. Simultaneous understanding may emerge about the ways that organized religions do not honor the Earth. With this, identification may emerge with past spirituality based in nature. Many ways of experiencing psychedelics, of course, honor connection with nature.

When these understandings are brought back into modern culture, they may in fact be dangerous to the existing political, corporate and religious systems. Indeed, the backlash of "the man" against psychedelics and counter-cultural movements was part of what happened in the 1960s and early 1970s. As we move through what many people are calling the "psychedelics renaissance," we might continually watch for ways that dominant culture or powerful interests might begin to push back at new openings through psychedelics. The way forward is not to make any emerging splits worse, but to understand and respond with compassion and rationality.

The second energy behind negative projections into psychedelics may involve what I will call **a fear of the power of the sacred.** Through psychedelics or other forms of spiritual awakening, you may reach a place of understanding that mainstream culture has virtually no sense of the sacred. You might find that what passes for religion and spirituality causes immense suffering for millions of people. There are dark, horrible things in our culture that hide under the canopy of good and righteous.

I feel there are two forces in the contemporary West that make it difficult for many people to feel a sense of the sacred. The first involves the outer shell of many organized religions. In our times, it is impossible not to notice the attraction to strong-arm authority, the need for good/bad mentality, and the tendency toward "us/them" divisions that exist among many people who portray themselves as religious. I feel this leaves many people without a home base in religious heritage where they have touched a sense of the sacred.

The second force is what Stanislav Grof calls "monistic materialism." Grof has written:

> The leading philosophy of Western science has been monistic materialism. Various scientific disciplines have described the history of the universe as the history of developing matter and accept as real only what can be measured and weighed. Life, consciousness, and intelligence are seen as more or less accidental side-products of material processes. Physicists, biologists, and chemists recognize the existence of dimensions of reality that are not accessible to our senses, but only those that are physical in nature and can be revealed and explored with the use of various extensions of our senses, such as microscopes or telescopes, specially designed recording devices, and laboratory experiments.
>
> In a universe understood this way, there is no place for spirituality of any kind. The existence of God, the idea that there are invisible dimensions of reality inhabited by nonmaterial beings, the possibility of survival of consciousness after death, and the concept of reincarnation and karma have been relegated to fairy tales and handbooks of psychiatry. From a psychiatric perspective, to take such things seriously means to be ignorant, unfamiliar with the discoveries of science, superstitious, and subject to primitive magical thinking. If the belief in God or Goddess occurs in intelligent persons, it is seen as an indication that they have not come to terms with the infantile images of their parents as omnipotent beings that they had created in their infancy and childhood. And

direct experiences of spiritual realities are considered manifestations of serious mental diseases—psychoses.[131]

Given this paradigm, many educated people feel they would be succumbing to naiveté, ignorance or mental illness if they *really* believed in the existence of God or held a sense of the sacred as anything other than a passing sentimentalism. Because psychedelics receive attention as opening to God and the sacred, negative attributions can be projected into psychedelics and those who work with psychedelics in order to avoid what lies underneath the hard layer of monistic materialism. What lies underneath is an enormous well of grief and anger that we live in a civilization without God.

None of us really knows what is going to happen next in our own lives, much less in the unfolding history of our country or the world. All I am saying is that I feel there are cultural forces at play in our times that might easily project into and once again demonize psychedelics. Holding onto a sense of the sacred may be the one anchor that works.

What else can you do? Possibly you can open to whatever shadowy projections come to your attention and develop compassion for all involved. What happens when we really feel these negative projections? Well, many of us cry and wail and weep and are held during non-ordinary state work as we allow ourselves to feel through these things. Others react with anger at the cultural forces that have held them in the dark. But eventually, you may reach a place where you accept that everything is unfolding in the only ways that it can.

The Other Side of Shadow

For those of us knowing the benefits of psychedelics, it is easy to talk about the projections of mainstream culture as misguided or even ridiculous. But it can be more difficult to own the shadowy parts of psychedelics use and advocacy. Even more difficult may be examining shadow within psychedelics communities. Once again, the issue is that real shadow is unconscious, and working with shadow involves making conscious parts of ourselves (or our communities) that we *really* do not want to see.

Not long ago, Jay Dufrechou attended a talk on shadow in the psychedelics community at a large conference on transpersonal topics. The young woman giving the talk expressed concern about sexism, racism, and lack of diversity in the psychedelics community. Looking around him, Jay found it interesting that no one in the audience seemed bothered or even surprised by the discussion. Of course, there were relatively few people of color, but there were many women, perhaps the majority in the room. If this was community shadow, you might expect some tension or pushback.

Maybe this was shadowy complacency, but the lack of tension in the crowd made Jay wonder whether these were actually unconscious shadow issues in the community. Perhaps there was such complete denial that no emotions were roused, or perhaps these concerns—while real—were not quite reaching shadow. While Jay would never discount these issues, which are quite serious in our world, he had been hearing similar concerns in transpersonal communities (mostly in California) for nearly three decades. There was not much edge in the topic within the community in his experience.

On the one hand, the concerns of the speaker signaled that these issues still existed and still needed attention—which of course is true. Jay wondered whether she had identified *problems* more than shadow. Looking for emotional undercurrent, Jay wondered whether the lurking shadow might not actually involve anger, perhaps even rage. Perhaps one of the shadows in the psychedelics community—which values love and unity—is anger.

The young woman actually struck Jay as very much on the edge of anger. Of course, then Jay had to wonder to what extent he was projecting his own anger into his observation of the woman. After all, he is a white guy. As you can see, this moves us into terrain that is personal as well as collective. In my experience, the personal edge is an entry point into shadow.

In this gathering, a well-known member of the audience raised his hand and observed his surprise that "sexuality" issues were not mentioned as part of shadow. Jay thought some slight edge rose to the surface in the speaker (and some members of the group) but then dissipated as the conversation moved on. Without reaching any conclusions about this particular example, our point is that the really difficult manifestations of shadow are likely to be hard to see and hard to discuss.

That said, we have to start somewhere. Elsewhere in this book, I have touched upon some of the possible shadow issues among those of us who find the positive within psychedelics. Using a very broad-brush stroke, I repeat some of the main possible issues:

- Psychedelics can in fact catalyze the emergence of serious mental health issues in some people; in particular, the greatest risk might involve people in the age group 18-26 with a predisposition to schizophrenia (or other serious mental health issues). Some of these people might move toward a "psychotic episode" (or other manifestations of difficulty) through opening doors with psychedelics use.
- Although most psychedelics do not carry serious physical risks in dosages anyone would use, some substances falling into the psychedelic tent are dangerous. As I have seen, these probably include ketamine and ibogaine, possibly also Salvia divinorum.
- Addiction (see next chapter).
- Avoiding facing responsibilities and real-world life challenges.

When I described basic understandings of shadow projection, I noted that projections often find a "hook" that is real in order to attach. You will note how some of the issues I consider with respect to the shadow of psychedelics are the same issues I think culture inappropriately projects onto psychedelics. In other words, some of the overblown, unfair projections by mainstream culture into psychedelics find a hook in some shadowy realities within psychedelics culture.

Because we react to the demonization of psychedelics, many of us do not like to acknowledge even to ourselves the possibilities of shadow in use of psychedelics. I am personally clear that culture projects many things into psychedelics that involve repressed elements of culture and are not necessarily true about psychedelics. But I am also clear that it is not wise to reject out of hand all negative beliefs about psychedelics. To put it very simply: the rock needs to be turned over.

Earlier in this chapter, I invited you in a "Now Your Turn" to examine how you feel about some of the projections made into psychedelics. Now I invite you to consider any blind spots you might have around psychedelics. I start with some of our ideas about issues that may exist in the broad psychedelics community.

Some Issues of Shadow in Facilitation and Setting

Facilitator Shadow

I talked about the importance of being mindful about your choice of facilitator in our discussion of setting and along the way in other chapters. Without repeating those discussions, I want to bring the discussion of facilitator shadow into the place in your head where you think about shadow—both your own and that of the culture. Sexual abuse or, in milder form, enactment of sexual arousal and attraction might be an issue of shadow among some facilitators and in some communities. I discuss this issue at length in Chapter 3.

In general, I believe that any aspect of shadow in the facilitator will likely play itself out in your experience of your work with her or him. Sometimes this can lead to abuse or trauma. In other instances, this can be a place for you to learn. By this I mean that your facilitator's faults or foibles might become places for you to make conscious and find your own voice and power around. But I do not want you to get hurt. So be careful.

Where the work gets hard is that you may have a tendency to project out your own shadow issues onto the facilitator—and blame her or him for various things. If this happens, you will need to work **very hard** to separate out what might be real issues that come from the facilitator (their shadow) from what is your own projection. Depending on the contract you have with the facilitator, you may have the chance to work through these issues with your facilitator, or you may need to take them into your solo integration or your work with your therapist or integration guide.

Psychedelic Tourism

Today a simple search of the Internet will allow anyone to find an Ayahuasca ceremony in Peru, a psilocybin mushroom experience in Jamaica, ibogaine treatment in British Columbia, or a purification journey with Bufo alvarius in many places around the world. While thousands of people have positive experiences in psychedelic tourism, some people are hurt.

Without seeming to discredit any particular services, I suggest a prudent look into the shadow side of these psychedelic "tourist" experiences. You may want to spend time with research, understanding, and awareness when it comes to integrating these experiences. Here are some thoughts on:

Safety. When exploring and learning about these destination "retreats," don't just dive in with blind faith because they have a nice website or a friend of a friend told you about it. Make sure you do the research you need to do before making the choice to travel and do the work. In recent years there has been an influx of causalities both mentally and physically when it comes to the tourism of psychedelics, and this is due in a large part to safety.

Education. Not just for your safety, but also to have the best experience, investigate the reputation of any groups you may visit. What compounds are they using? How long have they been doing this work? Now is not the time to simply "trust the universe." Dig into what you need to know about the experience: read books, talk to people, and do your due diligence.

Legality. It is one thing to risk illegal conduct in your home country. It is another in a foreign place. Many forms of psychedelics are legal in many other countries. But understand where you are going and whether others have had rough experiences with the law.

Expertise. There are scary stories about abuse by pseudo healers. This may be our biggest concern. Especially when someone is working outside their scope of understanding, damage might be done on many different levels. I am not just joking when I say things could happen that might take lifetimes to undo! When you are there, remember you always have the right to leave or to say no to anything you're not comfortable doing.

Cultural appropriation. I mentioned this issue when I described Ayahuasca ceremonies in our times. The issue of cultural *mis*appropriation can also be considered an issue of shadow in psychedelics work. Over the last fifty to sixty years, Western culture has imported many eclectic traditions of other amazing cultures with remarkable results. However, when there are issues of imperialism and financial or cultural exploitation, we need to consider shadow.

Relating to psychedelic tourism, this issue goes back to R. Gordon Wasson when he met Mazatec curandera Maria Sabina. As I noted in Chapter 2, Sabina ended her days regretting the woes she brought to herself and her culture through allowing exploitation by the mainstream West.

Integration. A significant concern relating to psychedelic tourism is that people usually leave a remote area after their experience without any integrative support. Often they travel before they are ready. As an integrative therapist, I have supported a handful of clients who have come back from their experiences only to feel abandoned and isolated. They did not know where to start with integration or even what integration might mean. Fortunately, they did their research to find support in their home country.

As I have continuously stated in this book, integration is a process that is ever expanding and a continuation of the experience. So when you do this work in other countries, consider whether you will be able to have a continued relationship at some level with the staff and people with whom you had the experience. Consider the support you will have when you get back home. Building a strong foundation of safety, education, and awareness is very important.

Working with Shadow During Psychedelic Sessions

I suggested how you might think about what is revealed to you in psychedelics through the concept of shadow. Much of what you learn about your own psyche might involve things that you were holding back from yourself. You might also come to really feel how the repression, projection, and defense mechanisms work in your mind.

In Chapter 4, I talked about the experience of a "bad trip." Sometimes people think about bad trips as involving shadow. Experiences of fear, anxiety, terror, dread, or sickness could be considered "shadow" emerging from your psyche or from the cispersonal or transpersonal realms at the depths of your psyche. But I do not necessarily think about "bad trips" as always involving shadow. It may not be that things relating to your experience have been repressed or ignored by you. It may simply be that your "inner healer" has offered you the experience, or you have channeled something around you or within you that was ready to surface.

But what if something appears to you *as* a manifestation of shadow? In other words, what about shadowy figures or monsters or archetypal images that might appear to you and embody shadow in some way?

I share a story from my teens. Experimenting with psychedelics with a group of friends, I was riding as a passenger in a car. I suddenly felt that a threatening wolf was running along the side of the vehicle. The wolf seemed objectively real as an animal running along the car. I felt it was either trying to get me or get my attention. I had the ability to ask the driver (who was sober) whether there was actually a wolf running alongside the car. When the driver said no, I put my attention onto objects and people that I knew were real in order to have an anchor in reality for when I went back to experiencing the wolf.

In retrospect, I remember feeling the wolf had dark, threatening energy. I found a way to allow the wolf to run alongside the car, but that was the extent I worked with the wolf at that time. Mostly this was what I call damage control. Given the recreational setting and the fact that most of my friends were under the influence, I knew intuitively that I did not have a good way to really face the wolf. Of course, at the time I was "riding" between believing the wolf was real and having enough anchor in the "real" world to know it was part of the psychedelic experience. This is one way to handle shadowy manifestations that appear in an experience.

In later life, having more of a history of working with psychological theories, maps of consciousness, and ranges of experiences in non-ordinary states, I tend to work more actively with shadowy or fearful images that may come during non-ordinary states. In a Holotropic Breathwork experience, I relived an experience from my youth that had been abusive. Someone who had harmed me returned energetically to me, and I was reliving the abusive experience.

In the safe set and setting of breathwork, I was able to interact more consciously (and in a more empowered fashion) with the image of the abuser as the experience worked through me. Quite literally, I fought back. In the setting, I was able to safely enact what I would like to have done at the time.

When I had this adult experience in breathwork, Jay Dufrechou happened to be working with me. Jay observed me embody a form of rage that I directed quite clearly to the image of the abuser in the shape of pillows and through physical and emotional catharsis. I ripped apart my own t-shirt that I was wearing in a form of defiance to the abuse. (This later became a souvenir for me.) I later shared with Jay that I sensed a breakthrough with respect to how I held those early experiences.

Over the following years, I was able to recognize the ways in which I had acted out experiences that might be considered abusive of others. The relationship of my own potentially abusive actions to what I had experienced sunk into me and could live through me. These insights only came by sticking with the experience (I had the t-shirt, after all) and letting it unfold and work its way through me.

Sometimes shadowy images actually hold some of the shadow that exists around psychedelics. I return to my early experience of the wolf running alongside my friend's car. From my perspective all these years later, I recall that the wolf seemed to hold many voices of the negative perceptions of psychedelics that were all around me. When the wolf felt threatening to me, the threats included many of the bullet points I noted about society's judgments about psychedelics. While I as a teenager rejected (or ignored) these judgments, they seemed to have appeared in the form of a wolf.

When I saw the wolf, I thought I might be going crazy. I wondered whether I was harming myself or if I was going down a road from which there was no return. Even then, I had enough understanding of the big picture to know that I needed to let the wolf run along the car, but ground myself in external reality.

From the perspective of integration, throughout my life I intuitively developed ways to journal, draw, bring music into my life, and find other ways to unpack these experiences. For me personally, finding love as the central glue to my psychedelics experiences helped me work through the pieces that felt threatening or negative.

Encountering Manifestations of Archetypal Shadow

Shadowy experiences during psychedelics may be complicated by the possibility that what appears to us has some objective reality that is separate from our individual psyche. Challenging energies that exist in archetypal realms may actually manifest in some images or experiences that come to us. While this is a tough subject to talk about, I need to mention the possibility that archetypal entities might manifest during experiences with psychedelics. I encourage you not to assume this will happen, because it is very rare.

One of my favorite books written by Stan Grof is *When the Impossible Happens: Adventures in Non-ordinary Realities*.[132] Grof explains that after a fire in his home burned his library, he decided to write a book about his own experiences, which was possible without his usual references. In a story titled "Interview with the Devil: The story of Flora," Grof explains that:

> Experiences of encounters with various wrathful deities and demonic forces are very common in individuals who have taken psychedelics, participate in sessions of Holotropic Breathwork, or are undergoing spiritual emergency. Careful examination shows that evil entities manifesting in these states are closely connected with extremely difficult and painful traumatic experiences in the present or past life of the individual, such as anoxia at birth or prenatal distress, near drowning, life-threatening events, or physical or sexual abuse. On the collective level, evil archetypal beings and motifs seem to be the moving forces behind wars, bloody revolutions, genocide, and other forms of tragedies and atrocities.[133]

From the days when administering LSD in psychiatric treatment was lawful, Grof recalled working with a woman in a psychiatric hospital. The woman was suffering a great deal of emotional trauma. During one of the woman's psychiatric treatments with LSD, Grof encountered what seemed to be possession of the woman by an evil entity. You can read the fascinating details in Grof's book. This included the entity, speaking through the patient, knowing confidential and potentially damaging information about the hospital program that she would have no way of knowing. Threatening to reveal this information, the entity tried to blackmail Grof and other physicians into abandoning the patient to him.

Grof's instinctive response, in a situation he found out of films such as *The Exorcist* or *Rosemary's Baby*, was "to put myself in a meditative mood and visualize a capsule of white light enveloping both of us."[134] Grof held his patient's hand for over two hours in this meditative state. Amazingly, Flora, the patient, made a surprising recovery from the depths of her psychiatric condition. Grof remarked on the irony of his psychiatric training seeming to pale in the reality of what was essentially shamanic work with an archetypal entity.

Contact with collective shadow is something that can occur with experience with psychedelics. In my own experience, the white light available in the archetypal realms is a manifestation of unconditional love. In dealing with manifestations of archetypal shadow, finding centering in ritual space and responding with white light of unconditional love might be the best path to consider. There is no way I can say more because I would be entering mystical or shamanic realms where I lack qualifications. But I know these realms can be touched with care through non-ordinary state work.

Leaving Shadow

I hope I have suggested in this chapter that **integration** is the solution for shadow. This is because integration brings together what is missing and allows what has been rejected to rejoin the whole that is becoming consciousness. At the most basic level, shadow involves splitting, whether in the personal or collective unconscious. One of the benefits of psychedelics is offering you a path toward wholeness and nonduality. On this path you will find that the remedy for splitting and projection is integration.

Throughout this chapter I have tried to suggest that you take into yourself all the criticisms of psychedelics that may involve cultural projection and work through them on your own terms. Similarly, I have suggested you make the effort to see what you might not be admitting to yourself about the shadowy sides of psychedelics. This is something that happens little by little, day by day.

I leave you with the idea that working with shadow does not leave you always in the light. But incorporating shadow might help you become more real, more solid, and more able to embody all that exists.

Now Your Turn

After reading about the shadow, what does shadow mean to you?

_____
_____
_____
_____
_____

How have you experienced the shadow in your life?

_____
_____
_____
_____
_____

Explain in your own words what is challenging about working with psychedelics.

_____
_____
_____
_____
_____

Describe any beliefs you have that you identify as being dark.

_____
_____
_____
_____
_____

Integration Exercise 9: Exploring Your Fears Surrounding Psychedelic Experiences: Digesting Your Strengths

What You Need

- Your warm beverage of choice. This is a non-alcoholic beverage such as tea, coffee, or lemon water.
- A tea or coffee cup that has meaning for you
- Your prepared altar
- A candle
- Your journal.

General Background

> "I am an old man and have known a great many troubles, but most of them have never happened."
>
> —Mark Twain

I think Mark Twain's quote offers a beautiful perspective of how I look at fear. When taking on, experiencing, or participating in any psychedelic work, you may have a unique amount of trepidation or fear. This can come up in many different ways. Within this exercise I am going to offer a practice that may limit the fear associated with working with psychedelics; at the same time, I am offering a way to maximize the positive intention you will have going into your psychedelic experience.

This exercise works through exploring your fears and then cultivating innate "ingredients" that you put in your cup. You will face those fears and identify your strengths for both preparing before a session and integrating after a session. Then you will digest your source of internal strength.

Why this Exercise is Important for Psychedelics

In the chapter on shadow, I talked about how easy it is to repress things we do not want to feel or even see. There are many reasons for why we may not want to feel or see things, but sometimes the reason is fear. When working with psychedelics—like when sailing on rough seas or climbing a rock face or riding a spunky horse—a certain amount of fear is sensible.

While we do not want to repress all our fears, we also do not want to get paralyzed or forget our strengths. Feeling our fears, we want to find and energize our strengths. This is integration and moving toward wholeness. I think an intention to feel what fear exists and find our strengths makes for more mature and powerful work with psychedelic medicines.

How To Do It

Preparation in advance

1. Create a safe and sacred space that you have devoted to your psychedelic integration. This can be the same space you dedicate to meditating.
2. Build an altar that speaks to you, with both spiritual and physical interests of yours being represented.
3. Have your warm beverage and cup you will use for the experience.

Instructions for the exercise (Time: Thirty minutes to forty-five minutes)

- Start boiling the water for your tea, coffee, or lemon water.
- While the water is boiling, sit in silence in front of your altar.
- In silence, bring focus onto the fears surrounding your psychedelic work (three minutes to five minutes).
- Write down three bullet points surrounding your fears that came up. Explore the nature of where they came from. Are they real? What can you possibly do about them? Ask your self-reflective questions.
- Turn your attention to your strengths. In this exercise I am calling your strengths your "ingredients." These can be psychological, emotional or physical (for example, I have a loving family… I am safe in my relationship… I love my job… I am secure in my body.)
- Write down five "ingredients" you wish to place in your soothing beverage; these strengths would be your antidote to your fear.
- Grab your cup.
- Now prepare your warm beverage of choice. As the hot air rises from the cup and the aroma starts to engulf you, start to speak the positive strengths ("ingredients") into your cup. This can be done out loud or in silence. However, it is important to place focus on the cup and the warm air coming up from the cup.
- Place your hands on the cup. Focus your gaze on the air rising; smell the aroma.
- Sit for a moment and reflect on all the ingredients you just placed in the cup.
- Slowly drink your beverage, imagining all the "ingredients" with each sip.
- With each sip, mindfully bring attention to your strengths ("ingredients") by reminding yourself of your list of "ingredients."

- Finish the exercise by paying gratitude for your experience.
- Write in your journal about the experience.

This exercise can be done both as an intention when you feel fear arising before a psychedelic experience and after a psychedelic experience. This exercise can be an antidote for a "bad trip."

When you face your fears by labeling them, you can change your focus to your strengths, and you will find a new paradigm. This exercise is an experiential way to explore your fears and come to terms with how they affect you. It is a terrific chance to grow all the positive intentions you wish to integrate into your psychedelics work and your life. By approaching your fears and trepidations about psychedelics by directly working with them, you will have a greater chance to understand what are the potential blocks in your life.

Exploring the positive and adding "ingredients" into your body, you will start to build a confident vaccination for any troubles that may arise in your work. Ultimately, this exercise is to reclaim, remind and restore the true authentic person you wish to be through building strength and integrating all of your experiences, be they good or difficult.

CHAPTER 10

ADDICTION

I'm going to start this chapter with a few stories.

Story 1: You're sitting around a circle in a weekend "medicine" workshop in a gorgeous house in rural Colorado. From the moment everyone arrived earlier that day, the gathering has been held with a light seriousness that feels sacred and also fun. The group is honoring the deep psychospiritual work that will be done, and yet you are friends coming together for a good time—including people you are just meeting but who already feel like old buddies.

In the lineage of rituals held around the world from the beginning of human time, sacred space is built through trust, attention and kindness. The time with these friends feels ancient and yet totally right now. Before any "medicine" is ingested, the facilitators invite everyone to open into their intention for the work and to share as they feel comfortable sharing.

When it comes time for the medicine to be ingested around the circle, one of the facilitators slowly walks around the group, person to person, offering one by one the first dose of a psychedelic. As you sit waiting for your turn to pull in the substance through a pipe, you feel rising within yourself the same grasping, overpowering, bottomless sensation of **wanting** the substance, **needing** the substance, almost being willing to push aside all the people before you in the circle, and you think to yourself, *This is no different than when I'm pushing up to the bar in a crowded pub, looking for a drink.* And yet, giving yourself a break, as you have learned to do, you wonder, *What is it really that I am wanting—is it peace, is it dissociation, is it a wild ride, is it God?*

"Without integration, you're just taking drugs."
—Experienced Guide

Story 2: Sixteen-year-old Brad has been dropping acid since he was twelve. Not every weekend, but often enough. This one night, Brad is hanging out with his buddy Travis before going to the high school party of the weekend. They drip liquid LSD into Sour Patch Kids candies and eat the first one on the way to the party. Before they walk in, they eat another one because they didn't think the first one was strong enough.

At the party, Brad sees his now-and-then girlfriend, Sara, with Justin. Why is that jerk hanging around her so much? If Brad were sober, and if he were able to feel his adolescent feelings, there would be some hurt and some anger. But now he is tripping enough that he thinks he doesn't care. He goes outside by himself and finds an old swing set. He sits on the swing and slowly rocks himself. He eats one more Sour Patch kid and lets himself fall back onto the grass. Now he is looking at the constellations and he is swinging around the universe, seeing the planets go by, and watching the birth and death of stars. Everything is fine; he knows everything is fine; it is better than fine.

If he had been honest with himself, he might have known he was dropping acid in part because he didn't want to have some of the adolescent feelings he was having.

Years later, Brad would also understand the relationship between his draw to LSD and what was happening in his family at home. His parents drank their faces off every weekend and most nights during the week. When he was much younger, they partied at the houses of friends most weekends and had the teenage girl across the street babysit. She would rock him in the rocker and touch his penis in a way that felt good and bad at the same time. Eventually, when she was older, she had her own boyfriend over when she babysat, and Brad would get out of bed and see them rubbing against each other on the sofa. He felt sick and angry, feelings he would later know as jealousy.

For the rest of high school, all of college, and all of his twenties, Brad moves back and forth between alcohol and pot, now and then some acid, mushrooms, or ecstasy, narrowly avoiding arrest many times in the years he sold weed, and eventually learning about himself by going back to school for a master's in counseling psychology. He then becomes a therapist at a large counseling center, but his weekends go back to booze and herb as he cycles through relationship after relationship that all end badly.

In his thirties, Brad starts working with an Ayahuasca group. Over many weekends through three years, he purges himself of many traumas and memories. He starts to understand the origins of abuse, trauma, and jealousy. As he is getting better, Grandmother Ayahuasca starts to tell him clearly, *If you really want the life you say you want, you need to let go of alcohol and pot.*

Story 3: Joan is a talented singer and guitarist. She has struggled with alcoholism since her teens. When she was on the tavern circuit around the country, she was always sipping whiskey from a coffee cup sitting on the speaker next to her. Some of her best songs were written when she was soaked in alcohol.

For years, Joan was pretty good about only having a few before she performed. She could ride the buzz through the gig. But as the years wore on, and the contract with a big label never materialized, she was drunker and drunker during performances, until eventually a few blackouts got her blackballed from performing.

Having reached the proverbial rock bottom, Joan agrees to enter a rehab program her parents found and funded. She takes it seriously while she is there, but then enters into the spiral of abstinence, sobriety, and relapse. Her friends start smirking about her latest failed "spin dry" as they hand her a bottle.

A chance encounter with a woman at a coffee shop finally gets her into Alcoholics Anonymous. She becomes obsessive about attending meetings and following the Twelve Steps. Though she was initially sarcastic about surrendering to a Higher Power, she actually starts to get it. She starts doing yoga and meditation regularly. She learns to play the sitar and starts a sober round of writing and playing music. But it is not the same; she is background music, not the center of attention.

Now that her old friends have fallen away, she has some new relationships, but it all feels pretty controlled; the new people feel tight just beneath the surface of spiritual. When she meditates, she can reach a deep sense of sadness. She gets back to AA. But she starts wondering what is the point of living day to day when every day is a sad day. She remembers that thrill of being alive and creative that she used to know when she was drinking. She considers suicide.

More and more depressed, Joan finds a therapist who prescribes anti-depressants, but she falls deeper and deeper into depression. She reads an article about treating depression with ketamine. She never tried "special K" in the clubs, but she saw a good many people fall into a "k-hole." Still, she is becoming desperate. She travels across country to work with a psychiatrist lawfully using ketamine to treat depression.

The first couple of times seem helpful, but the depression returns. Even the whole experience is kind of depressing. She shows up at the clinic, the psychiatrist barely remembers who she is, asks a few questions. Then she is on a medical bed and feels herself outside herself, then comes back as though her head has been vacuumed. There is no counseling at the clinic, just the ketamine and the bill.

Her curiosity piqued by the ketamine, but once again feeling she is going down the wrong road, Joan starts reading online about the possibility of using psychedelics for healing of substance abuse problems. She reads about the interest Alcoholics Anonymous founder Bill Wilson had in using LSD as a bridge toward profound connection with a higher power. Through chance, Joan comes across an underground therapist who offers individual private psilocybin sessions with an ongoing integration program, mixing one-on-one talk therapy sessions with group integration meetings. The feel of the group meetings is similar to AA meetings, but with a depth she has not personally found in any other setting.

Over the course of several psilocybin sessions, Joan comes to know deeply within herself the relationship of every experience of her life, and all life before her, to each moment she is living. She feels held by a Higher Power that is not just an idea, not just a substitute for being drunk, but a lived reality within her body. Little by little, Joan starts to feel as though her days are clear and clean without struggle, without deprivation, and with a sense of knowing she is alive.

Story 4: Jerome is sitting in a substance abuse group at First Step, an addiction treatment center in the inner city. He has to participate in the group as a condition of his parole from a prison sentence for robbery. Like most of the other men in the group, Jerome grew up in a culture where heroin and crack cocaine were a routine part of life, just like criminality. Toward the end of his five years in prison, Jerome started exploring spirituality through African American Muslim culture. He found community with other Muslims while he was on the inside, but when he got out, the First Step program dominated his life.

First Step follows a medication-assisted treatment (MAT) model. This model combines behavioral therapy, counseling, and use of an opiate-antagonist, such as methadone or suboxone. Even though Jerome was clean in prison, when he got out, the federal funding for the treatment program required him to be placed on methadone because of his history of substance abuse and criminal behavior. He goes every morning to a room in the Program Center to get "dosed." Then he sits through the mandated groups, physically present but mentally dissociated. He is consistently reminded by the group facilitators to "wake up."

In the First Step group, despite the sluggishness from the methadone, Jerome is trying to listen to what is being shared. He thinks most of what he hears is bullshit. He knows that nearly 80% of the men in the program will end up using again and will be back in prison. He thinks about speaking his mind now and then, but it just doesn't come to the surface.

Jerome doesn't like the physical feeling of the methadone, and this starts to make him feel hopeless. In the back of his mind is the question of what is going to happen when he is finished with this program. He is now staying in a halfway house associated with the program. Heroin and crack are easily available there, and he knows what it will be like if he goes back to the part of town where he is from.

When the group is over one day, Jerome walks around the block to the halfway house. In the living room, one of his housemates, an Asian guy named Ty, is watching a YouTube video about something called ibogaine. Ty is also struggling with the effects of the methadone. Jerome sits down and watches the video. He starts to feel a deep connection to what is being said. Men and women who look like him and the people he knows are talking about how they finally got away from methadone addiction (which follows a lot of people into their private life) through a session with this substance. He likes that ibogaine comes from the bark of the roots of an African plant. This feels right to him. He is connecting to the place he knew with the Muslim group.

The problem is, ibogaine is illegal in the United States. He is on parole and does not have the money it would take to find a treatment program in some other country. Nor would he get permission to travel. He knows in a heartbeat how to find heroin or crack, but has no idea how to find help with ibogaine in his situation.

What is Addiction?

One of the fastest-growing epidemics in the world is addiction. This ranges from alcoholism to street drugs to the opioid crisis. In our culture, people also suffer from *non-drug*-based addictions involving behaviors such as gambling, shopping, video games, or sex. According to the American Psychiatric Association, "addiction is a complex condition, a brain disease that is manifested by compulsive substance use despite harmful consequence. People with addiction have an intense focus on using certain substance(s), such as alcohol or drugs, to the point where it takes over their life."

The American Society of Addiction Medicine has the following "short" definition of addiction:

> Addiction is a primary, chronic disease of brain reward, motivation, memory and related circuitry. Dysfunction in these circuits leads to characteristic biological, psychological, social and spiritual manifestations. This is reflected in an individual pathologically pursuing reward and/or relief by substance use and other behaviors.
>
> Addiction is characterized by inability to consistently abstain, impairment in behavioral control, craving, diminished recognition of significant problems with one's behaviors and interpersonal relationships, and a dysfunctional emotional response. Like other chronic diseases, addiction often involves cycles of relapse and remission. Without treatment or engagement in recovery activities, addiction is progressive and can result in disability or premature death.[135]

Now let's get back to real life. It is hard to imagine anyone with any relationship with addiction finding much use in those definitions. "Duh!" comes to mind. But where is anything helpful?

Like many (if not most) people, we have our own addictive tendencies. From inside the experience of addiction, these definitions from mainstream psychology do not feel relevant, no disrespect intended. It feels like professionals talking to each other without including anyone they are trying to help.

Plus, these descriptions do not really get to the heart of the experience of addiction. It's like explaining a sunrise as a gaseous body appearing on the horizon and the visual image hitting the rods and cones of the eye and transmitting the image to the brain. True enough, but nothing to do with seeing a sunrise.

Over the last few decades, the "disease model" of addiction—concerning alcoholism in particular—has become popular. Supporters of the disease model point out the following:

- There seems to be a genetic disposition towards addiction, suggesting it should be treated like other inherited diseases based in biology.
- The disease model helps us move away from the past moral stigma and shaming surrounding addiction, which has never been helpful in recovery.
- Understanding addiction as a disease helps us understand that it will not go away but is a constant condition that can only be managed.
- Given the compulsion that seems to drive addiction, assuming individuals have control over addictive behaviors is not realistic.
- A disease model encourages treatment rather than punishment.
- Treating addiction as a disease encourages insurance coverage, which helps not only individuals but also their families and society.

The three primary criticisms of the disease model are that:

- Viewing addiction as a chronic, incurable disease may encourage some people to reject considering themselves an "alcoholic" or "addict," thus enabling their continuation of behaviors they might otherwise consider changing.
- The disease model—particularly when framed as a neurological brain disorder—may distract people from examining the deep psychological roots of their addictions.
- Being encouraged to consider oneself as having a disease can be depressing and demotivating, leading one commentator to observe, "Thinking of myself as a diseased alcoholic is enough to drive me to drink."

In typical American fashion, the disease model of addiction has contributed to growth of an enormous industry of addiction treatment centers. If you open any issue of the popular magazine *Psychology Today,* you will find advertisement after advertisement for addiction treatment centers, many with their own particular brand or spin.

My head spins at all the money spent on marketing and all the talk-talk going on in corporate board meetings of such for-profit programs. Not that I don't think some people are helped, but like most everyone else, I know many people who have been in and out of such programs. I also know many people who cannot afford them and do not have insurance coverage to help.

I do not want to argue with the American Psychological Association or discourage the healthy dialogues around addiction. From my perspective, all of the things noted in the mainstream definitions are true—to some extent and for some people. I have deep respect for Alcoholics Anonymous and Narcotics Anonymous programs. Many lives are saved and communities formed. For God's sake, if you are in trouble with alcohol or drugs, give AA or NA a try as well as treatment programs, if you can afford them or live in a state that will help you.

AND—returning to our consistent theme of individual empowerment and choice —I encourage you to consider some different ways of framing the draw to substance as you read this chapter. Mostly, as an integration guy, I encourage you to think/feel into your own possible relationship to addiction. I would encourage a "soft grasp" on the various opinions around addiction. Notice if you are attached to—or resist strongly —any one point of view about addiction. If so, ask yourself why that may be.

Transpersonal Models of Addiction

From my perspective, the most important model of addiction comes from a transpersonal perspective. This model understands addiction as a spiritual desire for the experience of what I will call God. In *The Thirst for Wholeness: Attachment, Addiction, and the Spiritual Path*, Christina Grof describes the yearning for the divine that she believes underlies all addictions. In trying to convey "the craving behind addiction," she writes:

> As far back into my childhood as I can remember, I was searching for something I could not name. Whatever I was looking for would help me to feel all right, at home, as though I belonged. If I could find it, I would no longer be lonely. I would know what it is like to be loved and accepted, and I would be able to love in return. I would be happy, fulfilled, and at peace with myself, my life, and the world. I would feel free, unfettered, expansive, and joyful. [136]

As Christina unpacks throughout her book, this may be the yearning that underlies all addictions—and this is essentially a spiritual longing. She continues:

This deep yearning goes beyond the very real physiological craving of those of us who become hooked into the cycle of chemical addiction, and it is different from our desire to escape pain through addictive behavior. Our innate longing to rediscover our spiritual nature is an often-unconscious driving force that many of us feel throughout our lives.

Until we acknowledge its presence, until we give way to its vital potency, we will experience a disquieting undercurrent of dissatisfaction with our existence. [137]

Carl Jung had this same insight many years previously. Christina Grof quotes the classic passage in Jung's famous letter to Bill Wilson (aka Bill W.), the founder of Alcoholics Anonymous. Writing about one of his patients, Jung wrote: "His craving for alcohol was the equivalent on a low level of the spiritual thirst of our being for wholeness, expressed in medieval language: the union with God." [138]

I have absolutely no doubt in the truth of the spiritual understanding of addiction. Of course, things get complicated, as Grof suggests, when the desire to avoid pain and stressful life circumstances become part of the picture. Use of substances to escape pain and stress then leads—more for some people than others—to neurochemical and brain reliance on substance. Then down and down the rabbit hole we go.

But at base, aren't we looking for the experience of love and being "all right" that Christina describes? Isn't this why we keep coming back to addictive behaviors?

Many addictive chemicals or behaviors might give some version of this "all right" experience on a temporary basis—usually with a high price. But it is interesting to note that many people find the deep knowledge of being "all right" through serious work with psychedelics. We may find unconditional love, forgiveness, and understanding that start to feel more and more permanent. All the pieces may start falling into place. Whatever word you are comfortable using, "God" may be present. You may come to know there is order to the universe. Everything is "all right," and you *know* this.

Importantly, serious psychedelics work has the potential of providing not only such experience, but also the means to unravel all the things that have become lodged within us that make it difficult to feel "all right." But to unpack all this in a way that lasts, integration work is necessary.

There is a corollary understanding of addiction that involves the loss of nature in contemporary technological-industrial life. Like a growing number of people, I believe that humans have a desire (often unconscious) to live in sync with nature and the Earth. The craving involves being able to experience the natural world around us as sacred. Addiction is understood as a way to fill the void that is left when we feel alienated from the natural world—and the pain that exists (perhaps unconsciously) when we know humans are destroying nature.

Pioneering ecopsychologist Chellis Glendinning unpacked this idea in a remarkable book called *My Name is Chellis and I'm in Recovery from Western Civilization*. [139] Playing off the introductory statements people make in AA and NA meetings, Glendinning suggests that Western culture itself pushes us into an addictive process. She understands the source of this process as our loss of connection with nature.

Glendinning writes: "You and I are not people who live in communion with the Earth, and yet we are people who evolved over the course of millions of years—through savannah, jungle and woodland—to live in communion with it." [140] Rather than living within nature, she continues, we find ourselves "dislocated from our roots by the psychological, philosophical, and technological constructions of our civilization, and this alienation leads us to our suffering: massive suffering for each and every one of us, and mass suffering throughout our society." [141]

One of the primary addictions noticed by Glendinning is our addiction to treating the Earth and all its nonhuman inhabitants as fodder for our consumption. Our (relatively) recent addiction to technology, now expanding exponentially, is part of this trajectory.

In his book *Moving through Grief, Reconnecting with Nature*, Jay Dufrechou describes the grief many people feel—often very deeply during non-ordinary states—when coming to really sense their disconnection from the Earth. [142] As he describes, ultimately this is a disconnection from sacred source—from the same kinds of feelings described by Christina Grof.

Many of us working with psychedelics come to experience a draw to nature as sacred. If you follow this draw, you may return to feeling oneness with nature that feels like a return to source. Many of us find nature very healing when working with addictions and the issues underlying addiction.

Narratives about Psychedelics and Addiction

If you work with psychedelics, I believe it is helpful to make conscious—and to work through—the various narratives that exist in our culture about psychedelics and addiction. There are both negative and positive narratives. Unfortunately, because research with psychedelics has been stymied for several decades, the light of reality through research has not had much chance, until recently, to start to create narratives based in reality. But we are getting there.

Even with more research, I do not believe there can be any one narrative about psychedelics and addiction. But we can each become willing to make conscious what is out there in the collective field. Before suggesting our own narrative, I want to clear away some of the strong narratives I find in the collective field about psychedelics and addiction.

Narrative #1: Psychedelics make you feel good, which means you are avoiding reality, which means psychedelics are addicting. The American Psychiatric Association, when writing about addiction, includes psychedelics in the category of substances that may become addicting *because* people may "feel good" or "feel pleasure" or "feel better" or "do better."

Without going into a dissertation on American culture, I might note the tendency in our social history to believe suffering equals being righteous or good—meaning feeling good means you are not good. An argument could be made that those cultures with less attachment to the righteousness of suffering find an easier time being realistic about whether psychedelics are actually harmful and need to be illegal. When integrating psychedelic experiences, it can be useful to unpack our internalization of the narrative that feeling good = addiction.

Narrative #2: In the backlash against the freedoms emerging in the 1960s and 1970s, a narrative was created in which psychedelics, particularly LSD, were portrayed as addictive and dangerous. I can remember Richard Nixon calling Timothy Leary "the most dangerous man in America." In the midst of the Nixonian "War on Drugs," the public consciousness was encouraged to lump together a variety of drugs —including heroin, marijuana, and psychedelics—as dangerous substances. This happened with absolutely no backing in research to suggest that particular psychedelics were addictive. Nevertheless, in the minds of many (if not most) people, psychedelics are just as addictive as other substances that in fact have enormously strong physically addictive properties, such as heroin. This is another narrative you can work through in your integration.

Narrative #3: Using any psychedelic leads to use of other drugs that are undeniably addictive. For instance, if you use LSD, then the next thing you will be using is heroin. Terms thrown around in this narrative include "cross addiction" and "gateway drug." When integrating psychedelic experiences, you might want to examine whether you have any fears or concerns that working with non-ordinary states through psychedelics might lead you into using drugs that are undeniably dangerous, even deadly. Try to separate out this line of thought from the very real need to consider the actual possible dangers of any particular psychedelic you are considering taking.

NOW, from the other side...

Narrative #4: There is no proof that psychedelics are addictive. Among many in the psychedelic community, there is a strong belief that psychedelics do not have the addictive properties of other substances, being less addictive even than coffee, certainly less addictive than alcohol. At the extreme, this narrative denies the potential of any addictive elements in the use of psychedelics. *I believe it is crucial in working with integration of psychedelics to examine any denial we are* *experiencing about the possibility of any addictive elements in our exploration of psychedelics. I think this denial is a shadow element of psychedelic exploration.*

Narrative #5: Rather than being addictive, psychedelics help cure addictions to other substances, such as alcohol or opiates. There is a growing body of research indicating the benefits of using psychedelics in recovery from addiction. This narrative has a strong basis in reality. However, I believe very strongly that taking a psychedelic is not a once-and-for-all answer to addiction, but rather an extremely useful tool in moving through addictions, particularly if coupled with dedicated integration work.

I have seen many people strongly disappointed after they have one session with a psychedelic and do not feel an immediate cure for their addiction. I feel this is a carry-over from the way we treat ourselves as machines that can be fixed by some pharmaceutical or surgery. In this fantasy, you just need the right chemical "fix" and you are corrected without any effort from you. Sometimes a "fix" can happen with some medicines and some conditions (antibiotics do work for infections!). But there is no quick fix without effort when it comes to addiction recovery.

And yet, treatment with ibogaine, with appropriate change in lifestyle, might come close to a one-time change of life around addiction *if* there is careful support and follow-through. But remember, ibogaine is dangerous for some people, even deadly.

And now, our narrative:

Because there are so many different psychedelic substances, it may not make much sense to have a blanket statement about addiction and psychedelics. It is possible that some substances within the psychedelics panoply have some physically addicting properties, but it is undoubtedly true that hysteria and politics have confused the mainstream public vantage point when considering psychedelics and addiction.

I believe this much is true:

- There is nothing wrong with feeling good, but feeling good can become a preoccupation.
- The Nixonian "War on Drugs" included psychedelics for political and social reasons having almost no relationship to whether or not psychedelics were addicting or harmful. None of the psychedelics are as physically addictive as substances such as heroin, cocaine, or methamphetamine; nor are psychedelics as addictive as cigarettes, alcohol or coffee.
- There is no hard evidence that using psychedelics is a "gateway" into other drugs based on biochemical processes, but we should consider the possibility of social, personal, or even spiritual links between using psychedelics and using other undeniably harmful substances.

- While it is important not to be fooled by the unproven assertion that psychedelics are addictive, there is value *on the personal level* to considering our relationship to addiction when considering our motivation and practices when engaging with psychedelics.
- There may be no greater tool in recovering from addiction than working with psychedelics. Let us say this again: *there may be no greater tool in recovering from addiction than working with psychedelics.* Ibogaine and psychedelics with DMT may be particularly useful. Some people report that working with psychedelics moves them very quickly toward the experience of "I do not want alcohol" and away from the experience "I want alcohol but can resist drinking day by day." When this happens, it can feel like a miracle.

Integration Moves Past Narratives

Thinking and feeling into the various narratives around addiction can be a useful part of integration. But from my perspective, integrating your personal relationship to addiction moves you past attachment to any particular narrative(s).

Another story will illustrate what I mean: Mario has a conservative Catholic mother (Teresa) whose nephews have had problems with methamphetamine. Mario has struggled with alcohol since his early teens. His late father was an alcoholic but had been out of the family home for years before he died.

Mario did not have much ambition in school or in his first jobs. Having drifted for many years, Mario went back to school, got a degree in health care administration, and finally has a very good (but demanding) job. He has a close circle of friends, mostly from work. He remains close to his mother.

Through one of the doctors at work, Mario found an Ayahuasca group led by a wonderfully grounded man who trained with indigenous shamans. Mario attends ceremony about once a month in a yoga studio out in the suburbs. He is finding monthly work with Ayahuasca very healing. This includes the sense he no longer even "wants a drink" after a stressful day at work. He has started to meditate and even does yoga. He is losing weight and eating much better. The group also meets for integration discussion and for barbecues and hikes in the woods. These people feel like family, and Mario has witnessed the healing of many people in the circle.

Mario is so proud of this accomplishment that he tells his mother about his journeys with Ayahuasca. This was the first she knew his overnight ritual experiences involved "drugs." Teresa became very upset and launched into a lecture about how risky it was for Mario to experiment with this drug given the family history. She was worried he would go down the same path as his father and his cousins. "This is how it starts," she said.

Mario reacted by arguing that she was sucked into propaganda about drugs and she didn't know what she was talking about. He refused to acknowledge that his growing attachment to the Ayahuasca rituals might have anything to do with addictive tendencies. Deep inside, not only were his feelings hurt, but he also began to doubt his own experience. All his life, Mario has assumed his mother knows more than he does, even if he sometimes fights back.

Rather than struggle with who is right and who is wrong in this storyline, I would encourage Mario to feel into his thoughts and emotions around the conversation with his mother—and around addiction as it has impacted his family and his life.

From the perspective of healing through non-ordinary state work, no one narrative is absolutely true over another, but all narratives become entry points into what lies tangled within people like Mario and his family (and they are like all of us). Through psychedelics combined with various forms of integrative work, Mario might release not only blocks within him, but also strands that have challenged his family lineage for quite some time.

Once he feels he has worked through some of these issues, Mario might invite his mother into an integration circle that includes family. If he is honest with himself about his family lineage and addiction, he will probably find that Grandmother Ayahuasca has a great deal of support and information for him. He will probably come to understand so very much about his ancestors and cousins that his heart may expand more than he can hold. He may find forgiveness he did not even know he was lacking.

Integration work might take advantage of entry points into Mario's feelings around his dialogue with his mother and his memories of all those involved, including his father and his cousins. Conscious attention to these issues would likely loosen up some important places in his energetic/body system, assisting Grandmother Ayahuasca in her next sessions of work with him.

Now Your Turn

Are there any addictive qualities that you feel you have?
_____
_____
_____
_____
_____

What are the addiction tendencies that you have in your family?
_____
_____
_____
_____

Describe what it would be like to be free of any addictions in yourself or your family lineage.

_____
_____
_____
_____
_____

Do mainstream addiction treatment models have a role in working with psychedelics?

I have the benefit of having worked as a therapist in addiction treatment for many years. I know the mainstream addiction treatment models grow out of conceptualizations of addiction not completely in sync with transpersonal views. Nevertheless, I find it helpful to know something about the mainstream models and their possible application working with psychedelics. Here are some reasons why:

- If the new research studies provide support for working with psychedelics to help with addictions, psychedelics may eventually enter the picture in some mainstream addiction treatment centers. When that happens, a blending of mainstream addiction models and understandings from the psychedelics community may arise. In this scenario, people in the psychedelics world should know some of the language and ideas from the mainstream addiction treatment settings.
- People finding their way to underground psychedelic sessions for addiction treatment will probably have been working with some of the mainstream models in other settings. As I have said repeatedly, psychedelics are not a one-time cure for addictions. So treatment models from the mainstream world will continue to be important as the follow-up to psychedelic sessions.
- Even if you are not concerned about addiction tendencies, there are ways to understand living in our culture—and even the challenge of being human—as facing challenges with addiction. The issue of "surrendering attachment" that becomes part of many spiritual paths is related to releasing addiction. Generally speaking, I believe addiction models can help if they are loosely held and if the models themselves become entry points for processing around your path.
- If you are working with psychedelics in a group setting, knowing something about mainstream addiction treatment models can be helpful in understanding the experience of others in your community.

More on Models

Fortunately, mainstream addiction treatment is well past the old idea that addicts are morally deficient. Once upon a time, the edict was that you just had to be strong and resist the urge. If you couldn't, you were basically labeled as weak and shamed.

I talked about addiction narratives with a broad-brush stroke earlier in the chapter. Now I would like to introduce five ways to look at addiction in the mainstream addiction treatment world.

1. **Neuro-scientific model—Brain Disease Model.** In the model of the addicted brain, desire leads the process and learning continues the experience. Addiction exerts a long and powerful influence on the brain that manifests in three distinct ways: craving for the object of addiction, loss of control over its use, and continuing involvement with it despite adverse consequences. While overcoming addiction is possible, the process is often long, slow, and complicated. The idea is that you are working with a hard-wired brain, and the wiring is against you.

2. **Biological Model—Nature vs. Nurture.** In this theory, we begin with the realization that no one starts out intending to develop an addiction, but many people get caught in its snare. Understanding that substance abuse is based on neurobiological structures can make it easier to understand addiction and spot problematic substance abuse. But you have to consider both biology and social life. **Nature:** Delta Fos B is a protein in our bodies, and it's the main character in the nature side of understanding addiction. In the "reward system," dopamine is the chemical that makes things feel good. Most addictive drugs stimulate dopamine, which gives us incentive to do more of them. Despite the explanation of how the short-term reward of substance abuse affects the user and how they become addicted, there are various external factors that contribute to whether an addict chooses to engage in substance abuse. **Nurture:** Obviously, our environment has a role as well. Studies with twins show that the environment and surroundings play a significant role in the "inherited" addiction. For example, moving away from family and being introduced to some "new" lifestyle separate from addictive culture can make all the difference. Often what we need to move away from involves association with traumatic events.

3. **Psychological Model:** This model may lead to classical therapies, and these techniques are broad and vast. The main idea is that people tend to use alcohol and drugs or participate in addictive behaviors as a way of coping with traumatic experiences or negative relationships, many of which originated earlier in their lifetime. The term self-medication comes to mind, and the addiction comes from experiences that people

repress through their addiction. Psychotherapy is then implemented to help support recovery from these addictions. (I note that if you add perinatal and transpersonal experiences through the Grofian model, you might have traumas associated with birth or with past life experiences as having a relationship with present-life addictions).

4. **Rational Choice Model:** With this model, the assumption is made that people make a lifestyle choice and then must be helped to change the choices they are making. People get addicted to many things such as alcohol, tobacco, cocaine, and other substances; however, people also are highly addicted to consuming behaviors, such as work, food, sex, and other activities. The rational choice model assumes that, when deciding whether to consume something or not, the individual may evaluate the behavior in order to see the lack of value or value in doing it. From this point of view, there are risk and time preferences to consider. The Rational Choice Model is usually explored after some level of treatment has been established. You may also think of this model as it relates to exploring psychedelics. There is always a choice.

5. **Bio-Psycho-Social-Spiritual (BPSS) Model:** This model is considered an integrative approach to dealing with addiction. It is a holistic approach that works with a diverse range of understandings of causation and cure. The general framework identifies addictive behaviors on a vast continuum of severity, specific conduct, and/or chemicals. In this model, I believe that complex interactions of biological, psychological, and sociocultural factors, similar to those which contribute to the appearance of addictive behaviors and experiences, also contribute to other less persistent or less severe forms of addiction. By exploring the vast spectrum of your biology, psychology, sociology, and spirituality, you will gain perspective on your whole self. This is ultimately integration.

Addiction Cycle

The stages of the cycle of addiction can be matched up with stages of behavior change and their relationship to recovery. Considering cycles and stages can help you recognize some of what you might be doing in your approach to psychedelics regardless of whether you feel there is any "addictive" element involved. You can also consider these stages with respect to whether you are ready to seriously work on integration. Remember the quote earlier in this chapter: "Without integration, you're just doing drugs." So you can think about any resistance you have to really working on integration through ideas about addiction.

1. **Precontemplation** – The person facing addiction has not yet considered stopping the behavior or use of substances.
2. **Contemplation** – The individual is starting to consider making a change in behavior.

3. **Preparation** – The person is mentally and, possibly, physically preparing to make a change.
4. **Action** – The individual has taken an action, such as seeking treatment, self-help groups, or counseling. Treatment has been provided, and the addict has stopped using.
5. **Maintenance** – The person in recovery is maintaining his or her new lifestyle and behavior, following serious work on all the issues involved with addiction.

Post-Psychedelic Session Integration Work in Addiction Treatment

Many of the people who come to psychedelic medicines for addiction treatment will probably have tried other mainstream treatment methods. They may have tried and failed. Perhaps they have tried and failed many times. These folks will probably have significant motivation to change and possibly some shame around past failures. The psychedelic medicines may begin to show them their strengths as motivation and support. The medicines may also show them some of the reasons they have not previously been successful.

Assuming the psychedelics give them a boost toward success, they will need to change the world around them to keep on track for leaving their addictions behind. There is an amazing little book by Peter Frank and Eric Taub called *Ibogaine Explained: Everything You Need to Know about the World's Most Powerful Psychedelic*.[143] These authors describe using ibogaine as ***addiction interruption***:

> Ibogaine does not cure addiction—people have developed the term "addiction interrupter" to describe its abilities. Ibogaine completely eliminates withdrawal symptoms from opiates. It also gets rid of cravings for opiates, cocaine, meth-amphetamine, and alcohol. Cravings are sometime eliminated permanently, but it is more common for cravings to return after weeks or months, albeit in a weaker form. This means that ibogaine alone is usually not enough to kick a habit; people also need therapy and a change of lifestyle. In some cases, they must move to a new city and be in a whole new environment.[144]

Frank and Taub are writing about ibogaine in particular. But their description of phases provides a model for post-psychedelic work directed at healing addictions with any medicine. With ibogaine, the experience itself (Phase One) is extremely tumultuous. Frank and Taub give a description of how it usually goes. After a twelve-hour session, with the first six hours the most intense, you can move around and eat, and then you tend to sleep. For days after the session, you feel energized, but exhausted. You need to take care of yourself. Frank and Taub write that many people feel they have "resolved an issue that was causing them a lot of pain" even if that was not the reason they sought the session.

But then the real work begins. Frank and Taub say this involves spiritual healing, emotional healing, and even physical healing. In the first phase after an ibogaine session, you might find release from many of your psychological issues. You might get to that place of "being all right" that Christina Grof wrote about.

Phase Two moves back toward normal, but you feel like "a dishtowel that has been wrung out, over and over." You may cry a lot and experience ranges of emotion such as fear or sadness. It helps to have someone with you who can hold your process and reassure you. You are probably still close enough to the revelations about your life and psychology that you can consciously process many of these issues, particularly if you have help from an integration therapist.

In Phase Three, your cravings are gone, you are thinking clearly, and you have stable emotions. You may never have felt this good. But Frank and Taub are clear that this is a temporary state, and you need to use it to build a new life. They strongly recommend working with a therapist. They also give some unique and particular perspectives and recommendations:

- You do not necessarily need an addiction therapist, but you need someone you respect, not someone you can manipulate or intimidate.
- Frank and Taub believe your therapist should be the same gender as you because "many providers have found that addiction stems from unresolved emotional issues with the same-sex parent."
- Join a therapy group for ex-addicts. Because you need to distance yourself from people who supported you in taking drugs, you need a new group for "support, encouragement, and companionship when hard times inevitably arise."
- "Do not return to your old scene, even if you are not experiencing cravings. People who do this invariably end up using again, because the social pressures are overwhelming. If you want to help your friends who are still addicted, tell them about ibogaine once and then leave them alone to make their own decisions. Spend a few years getting clean yourself, and perhaps you will then be in a position to help others."
- In some cases, particularly if you were using cocaine or meth, you should move to a new city. You need to be in a place where you do not know how to reach a dealer.
- Find enjoyable ways to spend your time; consider spiritual practices like yoga, tai chi, or martial arts. Enjoy your creativity and start to write or paint.

I also want to stress that therapeutic work with addiction has implications for many groups of people other than the people facing addiction themselves. These include families, researchers, practitioners, policy makers, treatment programs, investors in treatment programs, and people who make their living as addiction counselors. I recommend being gentle with all these people. If psychedelics help you and you come to feel others have failed you, please try to see that everyone has probably tried to do the best that they could given their understandings, training, and perspectives.

It is very possible that lawful use of some psychedelics in treating addiction will become part of the mainstream, regulated medical system in Western countries. This concerns me just a bit, because I am mindful about the impact of profit motive on medical care in the United States and other countries. However, I have great trust in those people conducting the research and guiding the training programs that may usher in addiction treatment through psychedelics.

I hope these new programs (and any individual therapists working with addiction and psychedelics) will hold a soft and broad approach. Any framework for the conceptualization of addiction must allow for the bottom-up development and integration of working with the *whole* bio-psycho-social model. I hope all of the players will be flexible, accountable, reflexive, and integrative in identifying what works and what does not work for each individual.

A "drug" to get rid of a "drug"

I need to touch upon the firm aversion some people in the addiction recovery communities have to the idea that psychedelics can help cure addiction. Some folks just cannot accept the idea of "using a drug to get rid of a drug." When you talk with these folks, you may feel they cannot understand the basic idea that psychedelics open the psyche to healing possibilities rather than simply providing a chemical high. Many people in the addiction recovery communities are very attached (and you cannot blame them) to the idea that they need to keep false substances out of their bodies and their process.

Please remember that these folks are absolutely right about their own paths. You do not need to surrender your own reality to theirs, but you also do not need to argue with them. Even people not within the recovery community may have trouble with the idea of "using a drug to get off a drug." Granted, substances like Suboxone and Methadone (synthetic opiates) are widely used and sometimes mandated in programs receiving government funds. But these substances seem to have the approval of the mainstream medical system. If you find healing from addiction with psychedelics, you will probably need to work through all the various projections into psychedelics that I have discussed throughout this book. You might also stay open to listening to any concerns or questions that feel well intentioned and prudent.

If you need to defend yourself about "using a drug to get rid of a drug," remember the openness of AA founder Bill Wilson to the possible healing from addiction with psychedelics. Although Bill W.'s words on psychedelics remain controversial for some, he was an intimate friend of Aldous Huxley. You will remember Huxley as one of the first proponents of the spiritual value of psychedelics. Bill W. is said to have himself experienced LSD and then written:

> It is a generally acknowledged fact in spiritual development that ego reduction makes the influx of God's grace possible. If, therefore, under LSD we can have a temporary reduction, so that we can better see what we are and where we are going—well, that might be of some help. The goal might become clearer. So I consider LSD to be of some value to some people, and practically no damage to anyone. [145]

Bill Wilson

Astrology, Addiction, and Psychedelics

I mentioned early in this book that astrology can help you understand not only yourself, but also your experiences in psychedelics. While I cannot do justice to a full explanation in this book, it bears noting that the archetype of the planet Neptune reaches into the experiences of both addiction and psychedelics. Since this idea is an echo of the transpersonal understandings of addiction, it feels right for ending this chapter.

Liz Greene is a Jungian analyst and prolific author of books exploring the psychological depths of astrology. My friend Jay Dufrechou has found that reading Liz Greene has been some of the best reading he has ever done in psychology, though her subject was more specifically astrology. Greene wrote a long book called *The Astrological Neptune and the Quest for Redemption.* At the risk of reducing a complicated archetype to one sentence, I note Greene describes the Neptune archetype as involving "deception, illusion, disappointment, and addiction, as well as creative urges and mystical insight, primary narcissism, hysteria, projection, karmic obligation, renunciation." [146]

Greene suggests Neptunian influence is like immersion in water or a return to pre-existence. She writes:

> Such a return occurs at death, and in the throes of the mystical experience, and in the twilight world of the drug-induced trance. It can also happen whenever primal emotions rise up and flood consciousness, so that the "I" disappears. [147]

Archetypal astrologer Richard Tarnas describes Neptune as governing "all non-ordinary states of consciousness." In *Cosmos and Psyche: Intimations of a New World View*, Tarnas lists Neptunian qualities similar to those noted by Greene:

> It is associated with the impulse to surrender separate existence and egoic control, to dissolve boundaries and structures in favor of underlying unities and undifferentiated wholes… melted ecstasy, mystical union… with tendencies towards illusion and delusion, deception and self-deception, escapism, intoxication…. [148]

Astrologer Steven Forrest, in his introductory text *The Inner Sky*, breaks down positive and negative poles of Neptune:

> Function: The decentralization of ego in self-imagery. The creation of a point of self-observation external to ego. The weakening of the barrier separating conscious from unconscious, ego from soul. The development of an awareness of what I may call God.
> Dysfunction: Confusion, laziness, daydreaming, spaciness, escapism, drifting, drug and alcohol dependence, poor reality testing, glamorous delusions. [149]

Neptune

What this means is that—astrologically speaking—many of the experiences we have in psychedelic exploration, including the very experience of a non-ordinary state of consciousness, are part of an archetypal wholeness including addiction and many of the more problematic components of addiction, such as escapism, self-delusion, and delusion of others. The basic urge to release oneself into some larger whole plays a part in our yearning for psychedelic experience and in the addictive thirst of alcoholism and drug addiction.

As with all planetary archetypes, we each have our own particular "placement" of Neptune in our natal astrological charts, as well as our own timing of transits when Neptunian influence is particularly strong. I have a placement of Neptune in the astrological "First House," meaning an astrologer would talk about my need to enact Neptunian themes in my presentation and embodied experience in the world. You might consult an astrologer to learn about your own placement of Neptune and the times in your life when Neptune may be most influential.

For integration, this means that exploration of psychedelic experience and addictive themes are part of a whole. Rather than separate out these experiences, I encourage you to explore the lived experience of Neptunian themes in their interconnected wholeness, following the particular strands into your depths and noticing where they may merge into each other. By bringing consciousness to all the pieces, and not rejecting any, you will find a natural movement toward the healthier manifestations of the unified archetype containing both psychedelics and addiction.

Now Your Turn

How can an addictions perspective help you on your psychedelics integration path?
_____
_____
_____
_____
_____

What are other ways to view psychedelic therapy other than the "magic pill" as it relates to healing addiction?
_____
_____
_____
_____
_____

How do you think the psychedelics and addiction communities could better support each other?
_____
_____
_____
_____
_____

Integration Exercise 10: Creating an Integration Altar

What You Need

- Space designated for integration altar
- End table, shelf or any form of board for altar
- Candles, figures of deities, pictures, tapestries, and heartfelt objects
- Your journal.

General Background

The care you give your *altar* is a sign and symbol of the mind of your intention. An *integration altar* can serve as a central point for meditation or become the focus of a sanctuary where you can go when you want that peace, serenity, and connection with your source of inspiration. As it relates to integrating psychedelics, the impact an altar can have is significant. Sometimes altars of this nature are called "sacred altars," but I want to honor the specific integration work you are doing and also give space to those of you who may not resonate with the word "sacred."

An integration altar is one of the pillars of creating a safe setting to integrate your psychedelics work and your spiritual practice. By dedicating space in your home to integrating, you prepare your mind—and your loved ones—to consider that peace, quietude, and connection with your personal growth is an ever-increasing priority.

Why this Exercise is Important for Psychedelics

Integrating your psychedelics experiences is about moving into ongoing awareness and into your external life what you are bringing forward in your non-ordinary state work. I know this happens incrementally and not in any linear fashion. Sometimes the most important things do not begin as thoughts or even images, but as general senses or feelings that can be drawn intuitively or instinctively to symbolic manifestation long before they form into understandings or cognitive thoughts.

If you are drawn to something to put on your altar, you might find that you have brought forward something you did not really understand, but that needs to sit with you and work on you as you face your altar and let it sink into you. As I have said with other exercises, it can really help to bring these things outside of yourself and into the world for them to reflect back to you.

You might also find a great deal of support by placing comforting figures or images on your altar. These might bring to mind deities to whom you are drawn or family members or friends who have helped you or who give you peace. Some people place photographs or memorabilia associated with ancestors on their altars. Sometimes it feels as though this is an invitation for these ancestors to bring their presence and their love to you as you work with your experiences. In some cases, the ancestors may know that you are healing them along with your entire family lineage.

There is also something to be said about the space on your altar. The sense of space in your internal sense of self can become more solid as you manifest comfort with an external space with boundaries on your altar. Your altar is a concrete space that is yours and into which you invite only what you want and need. By being with this space, you can start to feel how you can do the same thing with what is inside yourself and from which you connect to others and all that is. Because an altar is finite and concrete, it can help you establish an intuitive sense of boundaries inside yourself. You can move items close to each other or you can move them apart. You can add something or you can take something away. *It is all yours.*

How To Do It

Preparation in advance

1. Clear the space; the importance of this cannot be overstated. You have to create the space for the altar to exist. Clear and consecrate a dedicated area of your home such as a room, a corner, a table, or the shelf of a bookcase that will be solely used for this integrative and spiritual purpose. This is important because you are committing to allocating a percentage of space for integration. It helps you to create the time within your life for Spirit as well, because you are committing to the idea behind it.
2. Place the integration altar where it is most comfortable to you; this may change.
3. Start to collect heartfelt objects that resonate with your integration work; for example, deities, stones, crystals, pictures, and mantras. The altar is not to be a stagnant space, rather a fluid expression of your psychedelic integration work.

Instructions for the exercise (Time: Ten minutes to many hours)

- Gather all your sacred objects and place them on your integration altar.
- Arrange your altar.
- Maintain your altar.
- Use your altar.

Creating an integration altar is another vital component to laying the foundation of psychedelic integration exploration. Your altar doesn't have to please anyone but you, so make sure that you are choosing how to set up your altar based on what YOU like. Place everything with intention. Intend for each item to represent the integration and spiritual realm for the altar itself to be a powerful, sacred place for you.

It's important to keep your altar clean. Don't allow it to become a catchall. Depending on your integration process, you may want to save drawings or rotate deities. Often your altar will represent not only your psychedelic work, but also the season of the year.

Your altar is not there to hold cups or your keys or spare pieces of paper. Don't allow dust to cover it. Keep your items clean. Dedicating that space solely to integration is a powerful tool to keep YOU reminded to keep your spirit clean too. If you are neglecting your altar, ask yourself if you are neglecting your spiritual life.

Once you've created your own personal altar, use it! You might meditate in front of it, bring flowers to brighten it up, or just look at it on your way out the door for an extra lift, smile and prayer before you start your workday. This is a great way to integrate into life all the valuable lessons you are learning about yourself throughout your psychedelic work.

The care you give the external environment is a sign and symbol to the mind of your intention. The outer reflects the inner.

CHAPTER 11

INTEGRATION STAGES: POSSIBILITIES AND PITFALLS

In the last two chapters, I went through two important issues relevant to working with psychedelics: navigating shadow and considering addiction. Having gone through two chapters involving potential darkness, I want to bring back the larger spectrum, including the astounding glimpses into the transcendent that are possible through psychedelics.

In this chapter, I invite you to feel through integration in the various time periods following a psychedelic session. I start off with "Pre-Session" just to get us rolling. Then I take you through six possible stages after a journey.

There is no way to isolate one post-session time period from another in any definitive way, but I think it helps to consider a template of the possibilities and pitfalls in different stages after a session. Here is how I roughly break down the time periods after a psychedelic session:

Stage 0	Pre-Session	Countdown
Stage I	Immediate	1 to 6 hours after
Stage II	Grow Slow	6 to 24 hours after
Stage III	Next Steps	1 to 3 days later
Stage IV	Moving Through	4 days to 2 weeks
Stage V	Embodying IT	2 weeks to 6 months
Stage VI	Ready again?	3 to 6 months?

Some thoughts for each stage….

Stage 0: Before your Session

In Chapter 3, I talked about Mindset (Set) and Setting for psychedelics work. Here I revisit the preparation phase of your session, but with some more practical orientation. The benefits of a proper integration start when one creates the intention to work with what comes up during a session, not simply to take psychedelics. This intention forms when you approach a session and moves with you through the session and into the phases afterwards.

One of the countless ideas of integration is finding wholeness; this happens as you combine the goals you had before the session with what happens during and after the session. Before the session starts, you have your intentions and hopes, but you do not know what will really happen in the session. Even from this wise place of "not knowing," it can help to have an intention to integrate whatever happens with the intentionality you are bringing to the session. You might hold your specific intentions for what you would like to learn loosely. But consider having a serious intention that you will honor what emerges through a commitment to integrate.

You also want to prepare practically for your comfort and sustenance after your session. If you are working with a group or facilitator, some of these issues may be taken care of for you, but you always want to remember to take responsibility for yourself. You can never prepare for all you may want or need. For instance, after a session, you might have a spontaneous desire for an exotic fruit or to talk with a specific person who might not be available. However, you can have a list of things that traditionally bring you immediate comfort and connections to self, while also staying open to spontaneous integration with who and what appears.

For those who have been exploring psychedelics for a long time, you might already have developed an intentional integration *ritual* or *handbag*. Maybe you know that you really need some slow-cooked onion soup or that special blanket when you come out of a session. Developing an integration ritual and handbag can be an important part of intentional integration. You enter the experience knowing you have the things that will help you stay with your experience and start to digest it.

Before a session I encourage you to formulate a plan; it can be as specific or as general as you desire it to be. The importance lies in creating a rough idea of what you are expecting before, during and after the session.

Working with the same facilitator and group can really help you to know the basic structure of what will likely happen. This may let you feel into your own space in a way that is safe and gives you leeway for the experience to go where it goes. In other words, you may not have unconscious concerns or worries about what things are going to look like when the psychedelic experiences tapers down.

With some settings, being spontaneous is just part of the experience. For instance, having an experience at a festival or on a walk in nature, you have to be prepared for what may unfold. I hope some of what you have learned in this book can help you in any setting. This is because having your integration intention within you can help you integrate no matter the setting. The bigger question is opening up to your intuition.

At the end of Chapter 7, I talked about how much structure to bring to your process. I come back to the idea that some structure helps you hold onto an experience and make the most of your possible transformation and healing. But there is also a place for spontaneity. Spontaneous integration is really being open to what you need. You have a plan, but you stay present to yourself to follow what emerges. That is why I encourage the idea of practicality. Ultimately, it will be like going on a vacation where you planned a handful of things to do, but then, depending on the weather, your energy, and your schedule, you follow what is there.

Stage I: Immediately afterwards – One to Six hours post-experience (Aftercare)

Stage I highlights:

- Affirmation of safety
- Emotional—physical reassurance
- Basic essentials—water, food, warmth, security
- Balancing the desire to extend and the need for grounding
- Working with what is still happening and towards going through it
- Identifying emotions and connecting.

Here I return to the idea of **aftercare** as something slightly different from integration. In the period just after a psychedelic session, aftercare is extremely important. Here is where it is necessary to have compassionate support for your physical, emotional, and mental self from someone or a group you trust. This is particularly true if you have had a challenging experience.

Let us set the stage for the period right after a session. It goes without saying that any experience of non-ordinary consciousness does not end at a definite moment. On the other hand, these experiences do taper off and we find ourselves returning, usually gradually, to what feels like our more ordinary consciousness.

Safety in your setting as you are coming back is paramount—and I talked about this in our chapter on Mindset and Setting. Now I want to focus more directly on you and how you navigate as you come back. This is a dance between caring for all parts of yourself and beginning to integrate what happened. This is a dance because you need to be safe and well cared for in order to start integrating what happened; and if you stay with what happened in a way that involves integration, you may need to keep paying attention to caring for your body, mind, and spirit and reaching out for the assistance and safety you need.

Let's get back into the moment when you are coming out of an experience. The type of medicine you chose, your particular experience, and your setting create some variations, but in the end, you are coming back into yourself after having been in another realm of consciousness. Most people come back gradually, feeling one part of themselves still immersed in another world and another part of themselves awakening back into the surroundings. At the same time that you are reconnecting with your surroundings, you are coming back into your customary sense of yourself and how you inhabit your mind, body, and spirit.

You may want to lie quietly so that you can slowly feel into your body and see what might be there. By way of analogy, some people who work with their dreams have learned to wake up slowly after a dream and even stay in the same position in which they awoke for a while. This gives the body (and mind-spirit) time to slowly let the contents of the dream (which seems to come from some other place) to find a place in the body. This slow coming back may help you retain what you have experienced deeply within your body and have it stay (more or less) accessible to the conscious waking mind.

One of the true gifts sometimes received in non-ordinary state work involves a body-sense of how it would feel to be in the world (or to deal with a particular problem, trauma, relationship, or issue) from a different felt-bodily sense than one usually occupies. Sometimes this felt-sense involves how it would feel to be in the world having moved past a certain belief about yourself, the world, the universe, etc., and into another form of being. Often a felt-sense of knowledge and trust is present.

It can be particularly important to lie (or sit) quietly while this felt-sense really finds a way to **be remembered** in your body. You might want to associate the felt-sense with an image that you received or a particular insight or message—this can help you bring back the felt-sense when you invoke the image or message. Sometimes some slight motion (rocking or slightly shifting in position) can help lock this felt-sense into you.

It could be that you have come to know deeply within yourself that there is love and consciousness in the universe and that you are part of this love and consciousness. That can be a felt-sense deep within your body-mind-spirit *before* it is an accepted belief. For this reason, it can be important to stay with this felt-sense while it takes hold within your physical (as well as mental, emotional, and spiritual) form. If your mind later starts to tell you that what happened was only a passing experience, that it was not actually real, then the felt-sense memory in your body may bring you back to your new reality.

For some people, as they come back from some experiences, there is a deep processing (even catharsis) of strong emotions. Staying with these emotions can be important. Just as in the psychedelic session itself, you might follow these emotions with your awareness and attention into where they lead in terms of your biographical history, your psychological work, or what you have been shown or taught about yourself or the universe. You will want to remember insights that are coming (maybe take a few notes), but not move too quickly into an analytical mode that might disconnect you from your continuing openness to the experience.

Strong emotions, if they were present, may begin to release into states of relaxation or processing of what is present. You may want to let these emotions take the lead on their own time. In the Holotropic Breathwork community, this is a stage where trained facilitators ask "breathers" who are returning from their experience how they are doing in their bodies, minds, and emotional selves. Most guides in psychedelic sessions will have a similar "check in" with experiencers.

Very often, as you are coming back, you may find there is something in your body or emotional self that wants to process in a physical and emotional way. This may be obvious or it may be subtle. Something may not feel finished. It may feel heavy or empty or full or just like an entry point. It may feel like sadness or confusion or hurt; or it may feel very positive, like joy or memory or a place God has touched you. Sometimes these feelings are located in a specific place in the body, and sometimes they feel more like a general mood.

One way to work with these possibilities is to breathe into what feels present and perhaps "make it bigger." If something is emerging, then let the physical or emotional process play itself out. Support from a guide or facilitator can help, but it is very important that you own the process. Do not let others impose their own assumptions or models on you. Training in facilitation of a Breathwork modality can provide solid experience in giving this form of support to experiencers in any non-ordinary state work. The mantra is to let the experiencer lead in whatever is emerging and not impose any system or agenda of the facilitator.

Eventually, as you come back, you may begin to sip some water or tea or even have an interest in some appropriate food. Here is where you start to develop a fuller sense of what happened. It is important not to make this only a mental compartmentalization or absolute final framing of what happened. Instead, let it find its own way of rooting itself and having footing within you.

Here is where I can talk about an integration pitfall. Rushing through this stage of simply *being* with the experience might in some way make it difficult for the process to find its own resolution within all parts of you. Another pitfall is to allow a story or stories (a belief or beliefs) begin to colonize or control whatever happened. Sometimes it is better to leave an experience as a felt-sense (even if it feels vague) than to turn it into a narrative or affirmation of a belief too quickly.

Recording the experience or some parts of the experience is a natural instinct shared by many of us. This represents another dance. In the Holotropic Breathwork community, the culture at this stage is to invite creating a mandala with art supplies or cutouts from magazines. The idea is to find images that allow the experience to root itself within you and have some lasting visual reminder, but not to define or limit the experience in an analytical manner. At this stage, symbolic representations work well because symbols point into wholeness rather than specificity.

On the other hand, some psychedelic medicines, with some people, tend to offer messages or insights in verbal form that you may feel are important to record as closely as possible to what came. You might write down what you saw or heard and then let things unfold a bit more in writing. Sometimes these "messages" do not yet make sense, but just need to be recorded. Similarly, you may receive very specific geometric or other images that you feel you need to record exactly as they came to you rather than symbolically. Often these visual or verbal messages are symbolic in their own way and do point towards wholeness.

Whether and how you want to communicate with others is also an important dance. There are many different ways to navigate through this stage, depending on your guide or whether you are working alone or with another experiencer. You may want to verbally share your experience, usually in a quiet way that is not rushed and completely without feedback or judgment. Many people like to journal about their experience so that they are pouring out what happened, but only to themselves. The imprint is still deeply within you, so getting it out in any way that lets you feel as though you will retain the experience can be valuable.

If you write in the early post-session phases, I recommend an approach of recording what happened rather than making conclusions or a narrative based on beliefs or definitive assumptions of meanings. On the other hand, very often we have insights that do seem to convey explanations of the meaning of something—often we want to write those out.

If you have journaled or created a drawing or mandala, you may want to come back in the coming weeks or months to what you have recorded as a place to start in some intentional integration work. If you are working with an integration therapist, you may want to share what you have recorded and allow these records to be touchstones as you find ways to work together. Any part of your record can help you expand and embody what has come to you—and to gradually, incrementally allow belief systems, relationships, and ways of being in the world shift along the trajectory of transformation coming to you.

If you are ready, and feel you have recorded enough of the experience so that it will stay with you, you might want to go outside. Taking a walk, particularly in nature, or sitting quietly where you can look at the natural world can be very grounding and moving. Being quietly around other people can help, or sometimes being alone feels right.

If you have experienced psychedelics with a facilitator in a day-only session, at this point, someone close to you might enter into the picture in order to take you home and care for you in the coming hours. This is an important transition stage. I talked earlier in the book about the importance of communicating with those close to you about your and their feelings around your psychedelics work. I also talked about the care that is important in sharing with others. The ideal situation here would be a gentle handing off from your facilitator to the person who is taking you home. Honest communication about *your* needs will be important.

It is important to remember precautionary measures for coming back into society and returning to your relationships with the people who have not had your experience. Some of the tried-and-true recommendations I often hear are:

- Operating heavy machinery (cars!) should be approached with care.
- Starting charged discussions with people not in tune with the work might not be a good idea.
- Being gentle with yourself (and your loved ones) involving your vulnerable state is very important.

A standard problem I have seen after a session is difficulty knowing when a session is over and when integration begins. Sometimes there can be confusion and lack of definition that can feel unsafe. Psychedelics tend to remove boundaries, so there can be a lack of boundary for leaving the non-ordinary world and coming back to your setting. Sometimes it can be important for a guide or facilitator to gently (but perhaps firmly) remind you that it is time to start *being here*.

If your facilitator gives you the advice "it is time to come back," please try to work with it gently but seriously. To be honest, sometimes I have felt facilitators have rushed things. In that case, it is fair to say, "I need a little more time." But way more often, the reminder to "come back" is an appropriate and necessary boundary for your own process as well as those who may be in community with you.

Each person does make his or her own covert or overt request for starting to integrate his or her work. Guides, facilitators, or friends can offer the opportunity to begin integrating through different possibilities, but ultimately this is your decision. My recommendation is to gently stay present to what is happening for you while also allowing the non-ordinary experience to close.

I hesitate ever to say any one thing is wrong in the psychedelics realm. But I find it helpful to make conscious some potential pitfalls in the various stages after a session. At least you can think about whether any of these apply to you and your experiences.

Pitfalls in Stage I:

1. Coming back too soon—rushing re-entry
2. Not coming back at all

3. Acting out when you are not yet grounded
4. Leaving energetic blocks unprocessed
5. Resisting guidance to stay safe and in yourself
6. Paying attention to someone else more than yourself.

And, yes, I get the contradictions between some of these potential pitfalls. Again, I am back to encouraging you to find your own "Goldilocks" place in the immediate post-session stage.

Stage II: Six to Twenty-four hours afterwards – (Reentry)(Grow-Slow)

Stage II highlights:

- You're still in it or close to it, so don't be afraid of continuing the process with questions inside yourself: asking how, what, where, when, and why?
- Stay with your emotions and let them flow, but please find help if you feel yourself overwhelmed.
- As you are reentering, you may want to keep track of your emotions (for example, on a scale of 1 to 10)—checking in with how "back" you are mentally, emotionally, and physically.
- Pay attention to your extended sense of safety and security; you may think you are back, but you are probably still very vulnerable.
- Try to either have someone with you who has an eye to your safety or create a separate sense of yourself watching for your safety.
- Continue to explore direct aftercare needs—this involves your individual desires around food, hydration, rest, support, and mental health.
- Consider using stabilizing and grounding techniques (see below) to help you reenter your ordinary world.
- Stay mindful that you are probably not ready to jump full force back into the world, particularly with any new decisions or activities.
- Begin to understand your pace of integration.
- Nurturing—cultivating—patience.
- Be gentle.

In the reentry stage, the most important task is to continue grounding yourself without losing what happened. Rather than jumping into life, stay with your internal sense of yourself and with what is coming up. The information is probably still coming even though you are not in the depths of the experience.

Continuing to pay attention to safety is very important. This need continues after you "go home" if you had your experience somewhere other than your home. If you are able to have a trusted someone stay with you for this first twenty-four hours, that can be helpful, but this person should know to treat you gently and not to force any one thing on you.

Facilitators realize that sometimes people in this first twenty-four hours have ideas that do not seem dangerous to them but might not be safe. For instance, I know a facilitator who was taking a walk with an experiencer about eight hours after his journey. The experiencer said he felt an urge to jump off the top of a bridge they were crossing. He knew not to do this, but it helped to have the facilitator present while he felt the urge and let it go. (I realize this story feeds into one of the shadowy urban legends used to fear-monger about psychedelics, but this is a true story.)

In the first six hours, when you start to drink and eat, you are still in a strong aftercare mode. As time goes on, you have more space to slowly feel into what you might want to taste, touch, or bring to yourself. This feels more like finding what feels good or right or secure. Soothe and nurture yourself. This helps you ground back into reality while allowing the process to take deep root within you.

What grounds you is unique to you, but I find the most grounding things involve the senses and not the mind. Some examples:

- A cup of tea
- A warm or hot bath
- Walks in nature
- Massage
- Touch from a loved one
- Gentle music.

If you are heading well into twenty-four hours and find that you have just not really come back, you might consider more intentional grounding techniques. My strong recommendation is to reach out to your facilitator or someone with experience in integrating non-ordinary state work. They can talk you through what you are experiencing and make sure you are staying safe.

If you are on your own, reaching out to a family member or friend can be very important. From the perspective of safety, it is extremely important to be comfortable sharing with family, friends, or a professional any concerns or non-traditional patterns that start to arise in your daily life. Things to watch out for:

- Are you isolating?

- Are you considering dangerous behaviors? (Call your local emergency department if you are having thoughts of harming yourself or others.)
- Any "uncommon thoughts" that are not your usual way of thinking can be a sign to reach out to someone, particularly any paranoid or delusional thoughts that persist after a session or arise in the following days.
- Manic behavior, depression, or an intense sense of meaninglessness should be treated gently and with help.
- Is your sleep being affected since your psychedelic experience?

If you do not feel finished and have the assistance of someone with experience, deep breathing might take you to a part of your experience that did not finish. You might be able to complete that part of your process and have a firmer sense of coming back. If you are on your own, you probably want to stay only with gentle breathing just to see if this helps bring you back, but not to restart an entire process.

In the six-to-twenty-four-hour period, pitfalls might be:

- Getting back to your ordinary routine too quickly.
- Acting out emotions rather than processing them.
- Sharing (or over sharing) with people not able to honor your experience.
- Neglecting basic needs (e.g., letting yourself become dehydrated, weak from lack of food, or manic from lack of sleep).
- Getting thrown off by a **crash.** I talk about this in depth in the "general pitfalls" section of this chapter. For now, by crash I mean a variety of experiences that feel negative, such as physical, mental, or emotional symptoms, or even just a simple exhaustion or disappointment of expectations not being met.

As you move out of Stage II, you will start to explore your dance between structure and freedom of choice. Anchors or tethers can help as you continue to integrate. I mean certainties about your experience that remind you that what happened was real and give you concrete basics that you trust and on which you can build. With these foundations you can begin to build your house of integration. There are so many activities that you can enjoy. This could take the form of individual or group exercises that will support you in a direction you may feel you need. Try working on your own and also working with others.

By having structure, you are not prohibited from genuine enjoyment and a fulfilling integrative experience. It is similar to a chef and their kitchen staff who get a handful of ingredients together from the farmers' market without a fixed meal plan. The chef needs to see what is fresh, in season, and available. Moreover, they might have a general vision, but the outcome is not clear. Other staff might have an inspiration or direction. They might even just want to improvise and not have any outcome, only to stumble upon an amazing dish. Try to gently find the balance between structure and spontaneity during this period.

Consider that different parts of you are the chef and kitchen staff and even the ingredients. Ultimately, sticking with some kind of shared agenda or direction, a chef and their kitchen staff all the while agree to stay within a chosen framework, or create within a pre-selected direction, and allow something to emerge within the structure of what is there. This is our hope for being open to a loose structure with integrating psychedelics. I am not dictating "hard and fast" mandates; rather, I am offering a guideline for successful integration within stages.

Artistic Expression throughout the Stages

So many of us have resistance to artistic expression of any kind because I "can't draw" or "don't paint" or are "not creative." If this is any part of you, I encourage you to let this go for the sake of making the most of your non-ordinary state experiences. Sometimes I call this *creative expression* rather than artistic expression. Creative expression is not about drawing or painting well, but about expressing your experience in ways that hold onto and continue the actual experience—without an analytical or narrative-based colonization of your experience.

If you *are* an artist, then more power to you! You may find it easier to tap into those parts of yourself that can bring something into manifestation that embodies your experience. On the other hand, sometimes artists have to work their way out of their usual mindset when doing their art. Sometimes this is the same thing as working your way out of your usual sense of yourself. The goal is to allow whatever comes from the experience, which may seem nothing like your other work, and which the disciplined artist part of yourself might even try to judge before it emerges.

Psychologist/healer Ross Heaven writes about the healing effect of art on consciousness, particularly in staying connected to psychedelic experience. He quotes from Grant Eckert's essay *Art and How it Benefits the Brain*:

> Art is very important in helping the brain reach its full potential.... It introduces the brain to diverse cognitive skills that help us unravel intricate problems. Art activates the creative part of our brain—the part that works without words and can only express itself non-verbally.

Heaven finds that making art after a psychedelic session helps you become a *walker between two worlds*. This is because the creativity of art and the creativity of psychedelics are very similar:

> [Both are] non-rational and nonverbal, the insights coming at an almost cellular level through a remodeling of the self. Trying to capture this experience in words is too limiting for those who have undergone it. By splashing paint on paper, however, they put themselves back in connection with the experience and reengage with the creative process that took place then. Because they are no longer completely "in" the experience, however, they can also glean more information from it as they record their sensations in art. They become, in a sense, walkers between worlds as well, not quite of this world and not fully in the psychedelic one that they have explored and re-emerged from. [150]

Heaven makes an important point about *integration* in this paragraph. He mentions three main components of integration:

1. Finding ways to hold onto and continue the experience (often nonverbal ways).
2. Using your witness self to *glean more information* from your experience without shutting down your experiencing self.
3. Becoming a walker between two worlds as your psychedelic experiences stay with you, but you begin to transform yourself and your interaction with the world through an incremental integration process.

When is a good time for artistic expression after a psychedelic experience? *Any time*! That said, the most beneficial times probably depend on the particular psychedelic and dose, as well as your setting and your particular experience. For example, in the Holotropic Breathwork community, breathers are invited to create a mandala just after they "come back" from their experience. But many psychedelic experiences require more extended aftercare and a slower returning process. With many psychedelic sessions, aftercare and s-l-o-w return from the experience may last the first twenty-four hours or longer, so finding your way to artistic expression may come more slowly.

Tools and Guideposts in Stages III through IV

Throughout all the next stages of integration, your tools and guideposts for integration work will mostly stay the same, but you will shift as you gain perspective and integrate. Your basic tools will be:

- Your mandalas, artwork, notes, and any other expressions you have made or continue to make from your experience.
- Your work with your guide or integrative therapist.
- Integrative exercises.

Your guideposts will remain:

- Remembering to include your emotions and your physical body.
- Noticing (with compassion but some objectivity) the narratives you are developing.
- Catching yourself when old patterns or beliefs start to come back and possibly negate your experience or transformation.
- Remembering to make it your own.
- Controlling how much interaction you want with others (and the outside world in general) about your experience.

Stage III: Next Steps – One to three days post-experience

I envision Stage III as the period of one to three days after the experience. Usually this is a time when an afterglow from the experience is still with you. How long this lasts depends on the medicine, the nature of your experience, and your setting. Sometimes, you may still be in a workshop setting or in the place to which you traveled for a session. Things may still be different from your ordinary life, and I encourage you to make the most of any differences for really investing time in your integration.

While there may be afterglow during this period, there may also be some crashes or sudden intrusions from something that happened or didn't happen in your experience. Sometimes this results in part from biochemical aftereffects in your body (and this varies from medicine to medicine). The period of one to three days is not exact for these possibilities, but is a rough estimate.

During Stage III, I encourage **reassurance** from yourself to yourself or from others to you. This can include:

- That you are back, you are here, and you are okay.
- That you will continue to have support for your experience (continuation of what helped you feel safe).
- That whatever you experienced is okay and can be unpacked over time—you don't need to figure it out all at once, and you don't need to judge it.

One way to think about days one through three is that usually your ordinary habits of mind and frames of reference start to come back. You can think of your **ego** coming back online. For this reason, it is important to find ways to hold onto your experience (your artwork, your notes, your relationship with your guide if it is continuing) while also being gentle with your normal ways of being. You will have time to transform and do not need to start a fight with yourself—or start a fight with other people you may assign as holding a judging or challenging role of your ego.

Days one through three are still a time of **collecting** and not a time of judging or evaluating. The meanings and memories from your experience will have time to incubate and settle in on their own.

Pitfalls in Stage III:

1. Getting back to your regular life as though nothing happened. This is the time when we might tell ourselves, "Wow, that was fun…" and just leave it at that—as though we went to a party and got loaded and just let it start to fade away.
2. Not listening to your body about what you may need—you may still need more sleep than usual, different kinds of foods, a slower pace.
3. The "New Year's Resolution" syndrome—we have an intention to integrate and begin a process, but when it comes down to commitment, we keep putting it off and putting it off and then it all fades away. If you intend to create integration structure, it is important to have taken some steps during days one to three.
4. Letting ourselves be derailed by people in our lives who don't want us to change. This can be subtle, but if people who do not want you to change intuit that you have had a profound and possibly transformative experience, now is the time they may take conscious or unconscious efforts to keep you where you have always been. This may be a comment from them here or there—or a withholding of affection or connection. If this is happening, you will probably need to deal with the issue eventually if the person is important in your life—but you are still too close to the process to allow yourself to be pulled into something challenging. So if this happens, please just notice it, be compassionate for yourself for the reactions you are keeping inside yourself, and be

compassionate for them around how they may be feeling. Or, if this happens, it may not signal any long-lasting problem, so you may simply want to reassure them and it will be okay.

Stage IV: Day Four to Two Weeks

This stage is when you **consolidate** what happened. You are pulling together what happened and starting to look at it. This can be like stepping away from a dream and beginning to understand how you will work with it.

From around day four to two weeks is when you will decide whether you want to devote real time to integrating your experience and what that might look like. You might have a strong intention to integrate consciously and with structure, but you may not end up choosing to really do that work. If you let integration go, do not beat yourself up or feel guilty. You may come back to it later, or you may engage in more integration structure the next time you have an experience.

But if your path is integrating *this* recent psychedelic experience, during this phase:

- Explore what integration means to you.
- Consider how much engagement you want with the outside world.
- Find your integration pace.
- Identify the most important take-aways from your experience.
- Now that you have more distance from your experience, take another look at your mandala, artwork, expression, or any other notes or information from your session.
- Explore themes with a guide or integrative therapist who understands this work.
- Find the integration and grounding exercises that work best for you and fit into your life.
- Remember to gently avoid destructive thoughts or negative judgment.
- Extend your creativity and exploration of experience through activities you may not yet have included—dance if you have done art, do art if you have danced.
- Consider practices that are not strictly focused on integration but give you general space for your spiritual, psychological, or physical unfolding, such as meditation, physical exercise, or other types of reflection.
- Revisit any themes or goals that were intentions.

Pitfalls in Stage IV:

1. Shutting it all down. To be honest, this is the time when most people return to their ordinary life and their psychedelic experience fades away. Maybe there are some

lingering memories and maybe even some lasting healing or shifts. But ordinary life takes over, and there is no space for conscious continuation of the experience.
2. Going back to your usual pre-session narratives. This would most likely happen unconsciously or semi-consciously. For example, if you live your life with a background of shame, and had an experience of "being completely okay" in your session, now is the stage when the usual narrative "I'm not okay" may slip back into your life. Therapy can help!
3. Delaying reaching out to a therapist or integrative guide specializing in the work. If you don't do it now, you may never do it.

Stage V: Embodying IT – Two Weeks to Three months? Six months? Next time?

Because I anticipate that many of you are on an extended journey with psychedelics, I assume that you may have another session at some point. Stage V is that period when you are settled into your integration work and doing the work, but you have not yet decided to have another session, assuming you will have one. If you do not anticipate other psychedelic experiences, then this is the extended period when your experience merges into your life and you find whatever transformation has come from the experience.

In Stage V, you have moved into your intentional methods for integration. Here is where all of the perspectives and exercises offered in this book might support you in working with all the issues that come up with psychedelic work. Only you will know what you are called upon to embody within you internally and what you will begin to include or transform in your external life as part of your integration. Some examples of where many people find themselves focusing through integration work:

- Working through unresolved traumas.
- Healing or separating from family of origin problems.
- Releasing addictions or addictive behaviors.
- Facing and working through relationship issues, particularly those that might be labeled codependent.
- Forgiving yourself and/or others for past occurrences.
- Letting go of dependencies or habits that no longer serve you.
- Placing importance on improving your physical health (e.g., adding exercise or eating habits more beneficial to you).
- Gravitating towards a spiritual community, or releasing attachment to a spiritual or religious community that no longer serves.

- Shifting toward employment (or volunteer work) in sync with who you are becoming.

You might want to look back through earlier chapters of this book and see if you are drawn to perspectives after your experience that may not have seemed compelling to you before. If there are exercises I have offered or that you find elsewhere, I encourage you to really work through them so that you **embody** what was given to you during your session and then consolidated into you in the first weeks afterwards.

Notice the difference between having an experience and **embodying** the experience into your body and life. As I said in earlier chapters, this is an incremental process—little by little, often not conscious, but involves an intention to hold onto what is happening and let it keep happening to you and through you as your own.

Also, notice the difference between forcing yourself to do something or work on something and following transformational energies that arose in your psychedelic work. This can feel like the difference between responding to a stick ("I know I should work on my relationship with my mother…") and following a carrot ("I felt that sense of love and compassion for my mother for the first time in years, and I want to see if I can follow that…").

This might seem strange, but as you move through this stage, you might end up with one or more symbols that are impossible to explain, but connect you with your integration. Just as an example, you might keep thinking about some part of your experience or an image or an archetype that was part of your session. Such symbols tend to feel sacred or numinous. As the session itself becomes part of your body, this one (or two or three) images might settle into you as a portal that moves you forward into next phases.

In addition to working on personal issues, you might find yourself interested in learning about something or researching some area of knowledge. Often this involves an interest in psychedelics themselves as a subject of inquiry or as an unfolding phenomenon socially and politically in our times. But any area of inquiry may come to you. My teacher, colleague, and friend Rosemarie Anderson developed a research method called Intuitive Inquiry to guide scholars (or students or anyone) in feeling into the questions or concerns that feel compelling to them.[151] This is a way of learning that makes a partnership between intuition and discernment. Through an Intuitive Inquiry, the researcher works on and through herself at the same time she seeks to gain and contribute knowledge about something.

I have found that in this stage, we often develop interests we did not necessarily have before. We find ourselves reading books, watching films, listening to types of music, or visiting museums that feel like they are filling in or expanding our experience. I recommend you follow any of these leads— whatever they may be!

Synchronicities often come to help move you along. You may find new people, activities and things coming into your life—and perhaps some aspects of your prior life falling away. I suggest you do not force any of this; just embody what is happening, incrementally.

Pitfalls in Stage V:

1. Starting to believe what happened was an event (with a story, or a meaning that you will create) and not the beginning of a process that you **need to follow.**
2. Not staying open enough to surprises or synchronicities.
3. Fear that if you really change, you will lose more than you gain (and I firmly believe you will gain more than you lose—but that is your decision and your choice). For instance, I know a woman who stopped doing experiential work because she had recently married and she realized if she kept doing the work, she would lose her marriage. This was not because her husband disapproved, but because she realized the work was starting to make her change and that she would probably leave the marriage behind. She didn't want to do that. Her decision, her choice.
4. Being unrealistic about the reality that you may need to face some loss (or leave some things or people behind) if you really follow your process. In other words, denying the fear I mentioned just above but probably acting it out in some way.
5. Falling back into the Western habit of analysis or thinking *about* something (and giving it an explanation) rather than staying in a place of not knowing and following your process. Another way of saying this: thinking you can control your process rather than feel into it and follow it. Remember: explore—surrender. Let it continue to work you.

Stage VI: Ready yet? Three to six months? Next experience?

There are different opinions about how long we "should" wait until we dive once again into a psychedelic experience. I put "should" in quotation marks because I do not want to impose any requirements or judgments. But I do want to encourage you to be mindful about your process of deciding when next to take the dive.

Some experts strongly recommend waiting at least six months. In *The Psychedelic Explorer's Guide,* Jim Fadiman cautions against taking another psychedelic voyage too soon:

> The rule of thumb is *the more profound the experience, the longer you should wait before doing it again.* The Guild of Guides suggests a minimum of six months between entheogenic journeys because it takes at least that long for the learning and insights to be absorbed and integrated into your life.[152]

According to research cited by Fadiman, it takes at least a year "for deep-seated personality change to stabilize."[153] This means you may want to keep integrating profound experiences for up to a year to give them a chance to really settle into your life. Fadiman also notes that some people who have truly profound experiences have no desire to do more psychedelics work for several years—and sometimes never again. If this is you, then honor your intuition.

Fadiman makes two other valid points that are worth noting. The first is that "chasing the high almost never works." The numinosity may lessen if you climb the mountain again too soon. Second, if we feel we "absolutely *must* take a psychedelic again as soon as possible," there may be something that we're avoiding. You know what I'm going to say next: you might be avoiding doing the hard work of integration.

Jay Dufrechou had a personal exchange with Fadiman where he jokingly inquired, "That recommendation about waiting six months, that doesn't apply to me, does it?" With his characteristic sense of humor, Fadiman replied, "Of course not, waiting six months is only for those who take working with psychedelics seriously, so it doesn't apply to you." Jay took his point.

On the other side of the spectrum is the perspective of Martin Ball, who writes about "energetic therapy" through psychedelics, particularly 5-MeO-DMT. Ball writes: "Giving yourself time and space to do this once a month can be very fruitful. If you feel more urgency, then once every two weeks, or once a week, can also be productive."[154] To appreciate Ball's perspective, you need to remember he is focusing on clearing energy blocks that have manifested in our physical-energetic embodiment. Ball believes we are the physical manifestation of energy and that removing tangible energy blocks is necessary to free us to be who we are able to be. Why not work as quickly as possible to remove the blocks?

The purpose of working with psychedelics, according to Ball, "is to enhance your experience of energy, expand into yourself, encounter your blocks, projections and attachments, and then work through them energetically, so that you can have a release of stuck energy and process through what needs to be processed through."[155] This is not just an idea that came to Ball, but represents his experience with his own journey and from working with many people. Because this is a physical process, Ball believes, the process can be effectively continued with monthly or weekly frequency.

Thinking about Ball's perspective, I am reminded of physical therapy after an injury or surgery, when you need to teach your muscles to work together again—usually in a better way than they have ever worked together before. Your physical therapist might recommend coming into therapy once a week or twice a week or maybe every other week. While the muscles are learning how to reinvent themselves, you would not want to wait several weeks or months between sessions. Then your muscular system might go back to its old habits and the work you have already done might be wasted. On the other hand, you might need at least *some* time between sessions for the excitation of what happened to settle down.

While he endorses relatively frequent sessions, even Ball provides similar cautions to Fadiman. More than a few times a month, he writes, "is unlikely to be helpful, and is probably an indication that you're attached to the experience and most likely not making real progress." Ball believes you are probably ready for a session if you feel you are, "but check in with yourself and your heart. Always remember that psychedelics can easily be used by the ego as a form of distraction, attachment, and escape from everyday reality and responsibilities."[156]

Another valid reason for more frequent psychedelics work involves participating in an ongoing community. For instance, some facilitators of Ayahuasca work offer sessions every few weeks, sometimes following various moon cycles. Often working with Ayahuasca with a *curandero* is similar to what Ball is talking about — you are working on energetic blocks in your body-mind-spiritual system, so continued work makes sense.

In addition, if you are in such a community, you may be benefitting from comradery and ritual in the community and may want to attend regular sessions. Being part of such communities can have great meaning to support you in your integration and transformation. That said, you could still fall into the problems with avoidance through attending a session every month—going to ritual instead of doing your hard work.

My rule of thumb is waiting three months, though with a strong caveat of *it depends*. I have found that twelve weeks generally gives us time to settle into what we have experienced and a chance to identify and work with the issues and potentials that have arisen. I also like the idea of quarterly sessions, one in each season. This means up to four times a year. The number four is solid and has much juice from various spiritual systems, such as Native American honoring of the four directions.

What factors are involved in *it depends*?

1. Know your own relationship with **addiction**. (See the addictions chapter). This does not mean you should not follow your instinct for another session, but that you might be honest with yourself about the role of addiction or simply "wanting to get high" that is playing itself out in your process.
2. Consider your **intention**. Are you doing energetic work and staying on top of your process? Are you participating in a community? Or are you hoping to heal deeply rooted traumas that you might need to face on your own time? Might it be wise to sample more slowly and carefully?
3. The **particular medicine** is an important factor. Factors here are the intensity of the medicine, the duration of the experience, and how easily you come back to your life.

4. Consider **exactly** what you are working on. For instance, I once cancelled my participation in a medicine workshop because I realized I was working on being able to stay present during difficult communications. I realized that the embodied insight from three months before had not fully settled into my body—and knew even more that another dive could have helped avoid the difficult feelings that were being worked through.
5. Do not be afraid to give yourself more time.

Don't forget to consider other modalities for inviting non-ordinary states of consciousness—and processing—between psychedelic sessions. For instance, Holo-tropic Breathwork works very effectively in helping *integrate* what has already come into your body-mind-emotional system through psychedelics. Breathwork usually involves more possibility for embodied (and emotional) integration. This is due to the level at which breathwork impacts most people (in the body and emotions) and also because breathwork allows you to better control the rushing in of new material.

Other modalities to help integrate, but let you feel you are touching into the realms you reach in psychedelics, would involve meditation, shamanic work, ecstatic dancing, and many of the modalities I have mentioned throughout this book.

Pitfalls in Stage VI:

1. Taking the "waiting period" too literally—if you are still in month two and a friend wants you to eat some mushrooms and walk in nature or go to a concert, give yourself a break and maybe do it (but do check in with yourself and make sure you're following a positive invitation and not returning to addictive behavior you want to leave behind).
2. Waiting too long—depriving yourself as some kind of masochistic act or "control thing."
3. Forgetting that you can keep your process going with non-psychedelic modalities (or less potent psychedelics).
4. Turning the decision of "when to go again" into more of a head-trip than it needs to be.

As I finish talking about stages, I want to emphasize the importance of making the stages your own. There are no definite lines between stages of integration, but I do think it is helpful if you bring some mindfulness to the unfolding of your integration over time after a session. What is most important is that you find your own emerging balance between what is comfortable for you and what challenges you in moving forward in your process.

General Pitfalls

Pitfall Number 1: LOOPING

One of the topics of discussion among facilitators is how to handle what is often called "looping." This is when people keep having the same experience when they do non-ordinary state work.

It is hard for me to talk about looping because I do not want to seem judgmental or veer off from my general belief that your inner healer (or the universe—or however you want to think about the source of your experiences) offers you the exact right experience for any session. That said, I would be dishonest if I did not acknowledge that many facilitators worry that some people seem to keep having the same experience and do not seem to change much in their outer lives.

One of the lead teachers of Holotropic Breathwork facilitation is adamant that facilitators should not question the experiences of any participant. Hearing facilitators talk about a participant "looping" actually makes him somewhat angry. He considers this disrespectful to the person and to the person's inner healer.

That is one legitimate perspective to have. His view is that the inner healer will keep offering the exact right experience to the participant—even if this looks like the same experience from the outside or is reported similarly by the experiencer—until something inside the participant is ready to shift.

This is hard to question, but I do encourage examination of whether there is attachment (from either the facilitator or the experiencer) to continuing a certain aspect of what is happening in a way that could be considered codependent. Cynically, I might also note that if people really do change, they might not keep coming back to the circle (and paying the facilitator if there is a money exchange).

> "If you're doing it right, your sessions will be progressive and cumulative, even if you are working with a variety of medicines with very different effects and presentations."
>
> —Martin Ball

I also note that some people might never become ready to release whatever is generating experiences that look like "looping." But these people may be gaining tremendous support from being in non-ordinary state sessions and being in the communities doing this work. It may be that repeatedly having a certain type of session is exactly what is allowing this person to cope with their lives and their histories.

However, I do feel that you—as an experiencer—might benefit from considering whether you might bring some shifts to your integration work if you find yourself having—or reporting—the same experiences through many of your sessions. What might you do?

- Work with an integration therapist, who might be able to help you look outside the experience or begin to understand it or process it in ways that you have not yet been able to do.
- Bring an intention to do something different.
- Consider stepping away from the experience to look at the experience as if it were happening to someone else and see what you notice from a distance.
- Explore another modality of non-ordinary state work—for instance, try Holotropic Breathwork or a different medicine; or shift from group work to individual work with an integration-focused guide (or vice versa).

When talking about "looping," it is important to remember that we can "loop" with positive experiences as well as negative experiences. Some people spend many repeated sessions immersed in difficult experiences of trauma, and some people spend most of their sessions in bliss. There is nothing wrong with returning to the same places in non-ordinary states—it may be exactly what you need—but it may also be worth considering whether there is something that is ready to move if you invite something different.

Pitfall Number 2: Silos

What do I mean by silos in medicine work? If you have driven around farmland, you have seen huge isolated silos where grain is stored. That is one meaning of silo, but there are two other meanings. I think all three meanings are interrelated if you apply them to one of the pitfalls people encounter with integration. Here are the three definitions of *silo*:

1. A tower or pit on a farm used to store grain.
2. An underground chamber in which a guided missile is kept ready for firing.
3. As a verb, to isolate (one system, process, department, etc.) from others. [157]

In non-ordinary state work, I use "silo" to mean letting your experience (or part of it) become isolated and encased in a defensive structure. If you isolate something from your experience, then you are not integrating it. If you are not integrating it, you are not allowing it to move you forward in your transformation and life.

Having a silo in your psyche is similar to concepts developed by other theorists. This would include complexes described by Carl Jung, COEXs described by Stan Grof, and Internal Family Systems described by Richard Schwartz. Our psyches have a tendency to encapsulate and create separate structures for parts that carry something painful or fearful.

I have developed my own term—silos—because I like to emphasize the physical structure of a farm silo as well as the underground missile bunker structure. During psychedelics work, we sometimes have an internal physical sense that somewhere in our psyche is an area that is contained within itself and difficult to access. This **spatial** sensation can be important, because within a psychedelic space you might begin to work with the space around a silo or call for help in working with the silo.

Thinking of complexes, COEXs, or family systems can be helpful conceptually, but on a feeling level you may have a sense that you are just barely able to *feel* that some part of you is blocked off from other parts of you. In psychedelics work, if you feel or sense a part that is blocked off, you may have an instinct to stay away from it. But if you leave it as a silo, you may be missing an opportunity to heal—and to explore.

What is dangerous about "siloing" in non-ordinary work is that the experience, like a missile in a silo, can be triggered by mistake and cause some damage to you or others out in the world. Remember our chapter on Shadow.

How might we know if we are creating a silo? If we think we have figured out the final meaning, concept, or judgment about an experience, we might be moving toward a silo. Longstanding narratives, beliefs, or locked-away emotions might be linked with a silo. This is confusing territory, because meaning, concepts, and judgments can help us hold onto experiences and help them move us forward into new narratives and behaviors. This is the dance we must dance—using our language and analytical abilities to move us forward, but not holding too tightly, always being ready to let go.

How do you work with silos? Try coming back to the basics of integration work: check in with your **emotions, thoughts, and physicality.**

1. Ask yourself to identify emotion, describe your thoughts, scan your body.
2. Don't react.
3. Accept, rather than resist.
4. Be yourself.
5. Check in with a guide or integrative support system.
6. Let it go.

Pitfall Number 3: Fear of Integration

Fear of integrating your psychedelic experience might be conscious or (more commonly) unconscious. What do we fear? Well, with integration, we might have to re-experience trauma and allow our bodies, minds and emotions to process through experiences that really hurt. With integration, we might move through very intense emotions, including grief, anger, fear, shame, guilt, meaninglessness, etc. Or, with integration, you might have to experience ecstasy, bliss, complete acceptance, and ultimate meaning when part of your life narrative (and unconscious sense of safety) involves holding yourself away from those experiences.

It was Franklin Roosevelt who said: "The only thing we have to fear is fear itself." How to cope with fear?

1. Ease into it.
2. Remember the basics of integration.
3. Ask for help.
4. Go **through it** rather than around it.
5. Symbols, tangible objects, images, and internal safe places can help you with courage.

Pitfall Number 4: Getting Harmed by the Crash

With all medicines—and with some more than others—there can be a crash as you come back from your experience. I mentioned this briefly when talking about integration in the six to twenty-four hours after your journey. A crash might be a physiological symptom involving your biochemistry. For instance, you might be physically exhausted and need to rest or sleep to make sure you do not return to a fast life too quickly. Or you might experience headache, muscle ache, or nausea and need to again remind yourself to go slow.

A crash can also be mostly emotional, psychological, or mental. Sometimes the euphoria of a psychedelic session has a counterpoint in depression or dissolution. This can be a very fragile time when you could start second-guessing, blaming, or shaming yourself or others. It can be very important to hold onto your anchors and tethers and reach out to trusted people or professionals before a crash really goes too far.

I think it is important before a journey and after a journey to be consciously prepared for what may feel like a crash. There are steps you can take to help physiologically, such as magnesium for MDMA and some other supplements for various medicines. Keeping yourself hydrated is helpful. I do not endeavor to provide chemical advice in this book, but you can find helpful hints about supplements through the Internet.

With a crash, the harder work may be dealing with the psychological component. I like to use the analogy of making sure you have a parachute that will help you land slowly and carefully, but you still need to be prepared to hit the ground and roll if you have to. For some people, the crash can feel as though it entirely negates the benefits of the experience you had. I recommend that you prepare yourself for the possibility that you may feel terrible at some point and just be ready to tell yourself, *Okay, here it is, I am feeling the negation side, but it will pass.*

In addition to being a pitfall, I think turning a crash into a concrete judgment about psychedelics is a pity. But it is easy, when under the influence of a crash, to embrace a narrative that keeps you in a place of negation about your experience or about the possibility of your own healing and transformation. When you are in a crash period, those parts of yourself (you can think of them as silos if that helps) that want to hold you back from changing will take the opportunity to pull you away from yourself.

Once again, here is where it is **so important** to remember that using psychedelics is not a "one pill wonder." You would not expect to go to the gym once and then have a completely different body in terms of health or strength. The same goes for a path with psychedelics. So when you are in a crash period, be careful if you find yourself thinking, "This didn't work." Once again, you would not go to the gym for only one day and then two days later look in the mirror and say, "This didn't work, I'm not going back to the gym, gyms are a big fraud, I don't know what I was thinking."

Here again is where you might remember that working with psychedelics requires your active participation, not your passive standing by. If you experience a crash, that crash is just one more piece of your journey for you to work with and integrate.

Pitfall Number 5: Expecting Unicorns and Rainbows

This can be a pitfall for first-time experiencers but also for people who have used psychedelics many times. The issue is expecting marvelous and beautiful experiences as the only thing that will happen with psychedelics. You probably will have these kinds of experiences, but you may not—and I would be surprised if *all* that you have is unicorns and rainbows. The expectation (conscious or unconscious) is what creates the pitfall.

In a way, this pitfall is the same pitfall about fear of integration. If you are afraid of having experiences that are hard work, you might miss the most amazing possibilities for evolution of yourself. I am not discouraging anyone from being positive about working with psychedelics. But I am suggesting that some of us may unconsciously be looking for the positive, whereas there is no way to prejudge what is positive and negative.

Rumi's poem "The Question" says this beautifully. The great Persian poet explains the deceptive possibilities if you are seeking God. Yearning for healing water might actually burn like fire. Trying for unicorns and rainbows could end up keeping you in an unconscious prison without being able to see the walls or the chains. About the trickery of healing water and burning fire, Rumi concludes the poem: "Somehow each gives the appearance of the other. To these eyes you have now, what looks like water, burns. What looks like fire is a great relief to be inside."

Pitfall Number 6: Forgetting to Surrender

Those of us with a strong intention to work hard on integration also need to remember that in the end, you just need to let go. Remember my recommendation in an earlier chapter and throughout the book: explore, surrender. This is also similar to: sit with it, sit with it some more, frame an understanding, find some meaning, and then let it go; see what comes next.

Pitfall Number 7: Pretending You Can Put It Back

Psychedelics, by their very nature, can turn your understanding of reality on its head. I have noted throughout this book that sometimes people take a psychedelic journey and then forget it ever happened. That happens. On the other hand, I caution anyone who thinks they can open the box of their psyche—and their place in the universe—and then just close it back down. Maybe, possibly, you can do this. But I feel you should be prepared for psychedelics to change everything in a moment. This may happen in your first session, or it may happen in your fiftieth session.

If you decide to explore psychedelics—and I include deciding to "do it again" or "try a new medicine"—then please do not pretend you will be able to put it back after you open it up.

This is not to say you will have to keep going in directions you decide not to follow. Of course not. Nor is this to say that you need to stay at any particular level of intensity. Even those of us working seriously with psychedelics need to take a break from the intensity and just enjoy some "normal" life.

On the other hand, I recommend just noticing what is going on if you find yourself in a space where you think the toothpaste can go back in the tube. What to do if you feel overwhelmed by falling into the rabbit hole? Maybe consider the following:

1. Be gentle with yourself rather than needing an answer.
2. Explore all possible ways of doing something differently.
3. Have faith that if doors close, windows open.
4. Find people who are on the same path.
5. Trust yourself.

Integrating Pitfalls

I wanted to cover possible problems with integration. And yet I want to leave you with a positive understanding that any pitfall can become a beautiful entry point of discovery during integration. What is important is to reach out for help when you need it. The key is to find the link between any pitfall and you and psychedelic process. There is a *reason* you may have touched upon a pitfall. When you find that reason, it may be a gem that helps you change your life.

Now Your Turn

Here I return to some questions that may feel similar to questions I invited you to consider in earlier chapters. Now having read this chapter on stages of integration, you may ask yourself if anything has changed or shifted.

Do you gravitate to a certain kind of integration? Spontaneous and leave it open, or do you prefer more structure?

_____
_____
_____
_____
_____

Are there certain styles of integration you gravitate towards? Verbal, non-verbal, active or passive exercises? Do you enjoy more cognitive reasoning or artistic expression?

_____
_____
_____
_____
_____

Are there specific situations (settings) or experiences that you consider more interesting to you? Therapeutic or recreational? Group or individual?

_____
_____
_____
_____
_____

How do you see the course of "time" influencing your personal integration?

Integration Exercise 11: Food

What You Need

- Food you are interested in prepping
- Kitchen
- Cooking equipment
- Recipes
- Writing utensil
- Your journal.

General Background

Gathering food and cooking with presence is an opportunity to explore intense connections to the full spectrum of all your primitive senses. Mindfulness in the assembly, preparation, and finishing of a meal in the kitchen means staying fully engaged in the process, instead of rushing through it. Just like when creating, preparing, focusing intention, having a session, and integrating psychedelic experiences, just existing or *mindlessly* preparing your meal can be dissociative and not benefit the ultimate search for integrative wholeness. It means being expressive, open, non-judgmental, and improvisational with food, just like psychedelic experiences. Releasing control, surrendering to the *full body* experience.

The "six senses" full body experience of working with food gathering, preparation, and eating is a magnificent way to integrate your psychedelic experience and authentic self. I encourage you to use all five traditional senses—touch, sight, smell, sound, and taste. Along with the five senses, I have added my own version of a sixth sense—your intuition. In the following exercise you will explore being fully present in your gathering, preparation, and discovery of cooking. And just as with your psychedelic experiences, you may learn to use your full body and all your senses.

Some skills that will be heightened:

- Full presence
- Understanding improvisation
- Creating something new.

Why this Exercise is Important for Psychedelics

I hold absolutely no judgment about how people eat. To be honest, in the world of spiritual seeking, you run across a fair number of people who are fairly snobbish and often very demanding about their eating habits. That is their trip, but I might wonder whether they are keeping their body pure at the risk of sending out some judgmental and attachment vibes to those around them.

And yet, there is no doubt that what we eat influences how our minds, bodies and, yes, spirits interact with the world and with our development. Changing eating habits could solve most of the health problems in developed countries. That said, I know that so many of us have so many challenges that certain types of food can be comforting—and I also know the economic issues involved with food.

You may find that your work with psychedelics influences how you eat. Whether or not certain eating habits can be considered an addiction is controversial. But many of the issues involved with addiction can be considered with respect to food consumption.

Just as working with psychedelics tends to increase our orientation toward nature and all life forms, this work might influence how fresh and how "clean" we desire to have our food. Additives and even the way food is raised may start to become important. Having raised chickens for several years for eggs and simply for the experience, my friend Jay Dufrechou can now only buy grocery store eggs that come from free-range chickens.

Even if you only do it once or twice, preparing and eating a meal mindfully and with consciousness about each step can feel like a sacred ritual. After all, this is how our bodies, minds, and spirits take in some parts of the natural world and process those gifts for our continued life. Having come this far in this book, you can see how I make an analogy to processing (integrating) the experiences that come to us in psychedelics. Be mindful and *feel* them every step of the way.

Just as with a psychedelic session and with integration, I also recommend a combination of loosely following intuition and allowing change and following intentional structure. Have a plan for a meal, buy the ingredients you are called to buy, have a recipe, and then allow something sacred to emerge. After you engage in this exercise, consider how your actions reflect your approach to life and how you might be changing with your psychedelics experiences.

Preparation in advance

1. Take time and do the meditation exercise from this book.
2. Focus on the foods that you are naturally drawn to.
3. Make a list, knowing that you might deviate from the list.
4. Remember main meal ingredients and ideas.

5. Stick to the season and time of year for freshness.
6. Remember to gather slowly, not quickly; be present.
7. Clean your kitchen in a mindful, meditative way.
8. Organize and take out all the tools and utensils you think you need.
9. Create a musical playlist if this interests you.

Instructions for the exercise (Time: Two hours to six hours)

Gathering the Food

- When you enter the store, be aware of all your senses.
- Using your basic list, start to collect the items on it.
- Build upon your list; explore different items you are drawn to.
- Create a mindful pause between each item you pick.
- Buy a few items that you are spontaneously craving.
- Spend time with local and seasonally fresh items.
- Place food in the cart/basket with care.
- When shopping and checking out, be engaged in the mindful practice of respecting others in the store.
- When you leave the store again, be aware of all your senses.

Preparing the Food

- Organize all your food items on the counter in front of you.
- Collect and put in place all your utensils, recipes, and tools to prepare this particular meal. (The French call this *mise en place*—put in place.)
- Clean as you go, through each preparation and move you make. Clean behind yourself.
- Incrementally ground yourself during the preparation; take time to breathe and connect with your body.
- As you make your meal, consider a minimalist approach in your choice of how to cook or not cook certain items. Remember to consider texture, temperature, and flavor.
- Take time to look at the food as you prepare it.
- Now, close your eyes and explore the food with your senses. You might improvise and change courses or direction in what you want to do with the food.
- As you finish preparing the food, pause and notice your creation.

Mindful Eating

- With the meal in front of you, pay your respect and gratitude in the way that you are drawn to prior to experiencing eating the meal.
- Pause and savor. Take a moment before eating to notice three of your five senses—touch, sight, smell. Observing the aroma is a great start. Go slowly.
- Now be mindful and observe the slow nature of lifting your utensil or food, and once the bite is placed into your mouth, be completely present in the act of chewing the food. Your two other senses, taste and sound, come into perspective.
- When thoughts, feelings, or other sensations arise within your "field of mindfulness," simply acknowledge them gently without judgment. And like clouds in the sky, let them drift by and go back to your breathing and eating.
- Throughout the meal, occasionally breathe in and breathe out, sit, and again pause and reflect on the gathering, preparation, and full experience you are having with your food.
- At the completion of your meal, don't get up too fast. Take a moment to mindfully again pay gratitude in the manner that you are drawn to.

A psychedelic experience and full-body food experience have many similar opportunities to integrate one's life and purpose. Mindfully preparing and participating in a bountiful meal (no matter if it's an elaborate smorgasbord of bite-size flavors or a simply crafted soup), you will find a deeper integrated connection to your psychedelic work and life. Mindful gathering and the integrative full-body food experience use all six senses. This experience of eating is a fantastic way to integrate your psychedelic work; every day we are able to stop and be present to slowing down and finding gratitude for the bounty of what is at our fingertips.

There is no real recipe for learning what you need or what works for you. Test some of the recommendations and feel into what is right for you. And at the end of the day, you might just need to be confident that being spontaneous is always an option.

CHAPTER 12

LETTING GO, DEATH, AND THE ULTIMATE MYSTERY

All through history, our ancestors lived in sacred relationship with Earth, cosmos, life and death. We may call their knowledge mythology, but they understood the unity of all things. Death was part of the fabric of life. I could never say they did not fear death. But I suspect they did not dissociate from death in the way that many of us do in our culture.

Life and death are not separable and not exclusive. I believe this paradox lies at the heart of awakening. Death of the body allows transition of the soul, but nothing is lost, only transformed. Birth leads to death, and death leads to birth, and the circle continues.

This is not to make light of our fears and our grief. There is nothing more painful than losing a loved one, nothing more terrifying for most of us than approaching the release of our consciousness into our own passing. But dissociation from the reality of death only leaves us separated from who we are and our place in the cosmos. Being continually aware of death is one of the bridges to maturity, agency, and accountability as an Earthling. I am not talking about a morose or depressing obsession with death, but a respectful awareness that all life on Earth is finite and, no matter how you look at it, brief.

It is hard to explain, but holding death in awareness seems to link us both to the Earth and to what is beyond the Earth, rather than separate us. Usually it is easier to understand this while listening to beating drums or whirling in a dance or crying in response to a sunrise than from a place of the rational mind. Working with psychedelics tends to offer an opening to this understanding.

Everybody who enters the physical body will face the inevitable experience of dying from the body. One of the pillars of integrating psychedelics is exploring the relationship we have with death. This is a matter of integrating the reality of death —death in general and *your death* in particular—into your experience of living.

As I touch upon later in the chapter, research has long demonstrated the value of psychedelics in helping people cope with the anxiety and depression surrounding a terminal illness. Typically this is not just an easing of fear, but a shift in understanding about the nature of reality.

In this final chapter of the book, I leave you with the big questions none of us can really answer. One of the shifts in working with psychedelics is often a movement toward curiosity rather than needing certainty. This is a place of opening to what is—which is also a place of acceptance of death. There is a place where you accept that *you* as you know yourself are finite. But you also know you are part of something that endures outside of time and space. From this place, most of us will become people who have more questions than answers. I call them seekers.

Let us turn to some questions.

Death and Enlightenment

Stan Grof made the following essential statement:

> There is no fundamental difference between the preparation for death and the practice of dying and spiritual practice leading to enlightenment.

How can we understand this statement? Well, maybe exploring psychedelics gives us a chance to understand our souls, figure out the meaning of life, connect more deeply with this planet and the universe, and the list goes on…. (You fill in the blank). I can envision this exploration as a preparation for death and a spiritual practice leading toward enlightenment.

To get more specific, I believe humanity's intention in the universe is to embody the experience of understanding, compassion, kindness, peace with the unknown, and ultimately, unconditional love, and going forth to share it. When we release into death, perhaps we meet our creator in this place of unconditional love.

Enlightenment is what happens when there is nothing left to grasp, nothing left to fear, nothing but love. There may still be questions, but there is no grasping for answers. There is awareness. If you open the cracks in awareness, there is love.

But what is the practice? How do we find an integration practice involving death? This brings us to what is known in spiritual circles as "ego death."

Ego Death

What do I mean by ego death? Some of us who hang around transpersonal gatherings may have the experience that talking about "ego death" can sound like one of the most ego-oriented things you can do. I say this in jest, at least in part. What I mean is that a strong desire for "ego death" is an attachment to an idea about an experience, sometimes with an unconscious desire to be able to consider ourselves better than other people who have not had an "ego death."

On the other hand, you might feel a pull towards an emptying out of yourself, and a letting go that is very complete and feels like what I imagine actual death might be. It's not about becoming *someone* without an ego, but about emptying or letting go. So in a way, it may be about becoming no one and everyone. This is a psychological process because what you release are your opinions, beliefs, needs, desires, hopes, dreams, experiences, understandings, projections, and defenses—all the things that feel as though they make you who you are.

Many of you will know this is terrain covered well by Buddhism. As I said when introducing myself, I had some identification and training in Buddhism in my early years, and transpersonal psychology draws in part from Buddhist understandings as well as from many other world traditions. I encourage you to explore the wisdom of these traditions surrounding death and release of attachment. But here, I will talk more directly about psychological experience—and experience during psychedelics work. I am less interested in belief systems and more interested in experiences you may have working with psychedelic medicines.

Some of this chapter will give you a chance to think about the many forms of emptying out that happen with psychedelics experiences. (And yes, I know purging is an emptying out! But I'm talking about something even more important.) In the very beginning of the book, I talked about the definition of psychedelic—*to make visible what is in your mind*. On the road to death—of the ego and then eventually the body-mind—you see more and more deeply all that is part of your conscious and unconscious mind, and then you let go.

When talking about emptying out, we start with gaining consciousness of those parts of ourselves we have not really seen or acknowledged. This is (of course) where psychedelic journeys help. Here I am talking about coming to see what can be called *shadow*, our projections and defenses, our hidden needs and desires and fears, our assumptions about right and wrong, our beliefs and judgments, and feeling them so clearly that they seem to disappear—and what is left is both you and not you. What is left is you, but it is also the universe, God, or whatever other words you like to use for all that is. As you experiment with letting go of all the things that (unconsciously) seem to be you, you will probably find yourself back to the place of thinking about actual death.

Questions about Death

When questioning about death and psychedelic integration, there is much to wonder. You will wonder how much is real and how much is imagined, just like me. A fundamental discipline that I will offer throughout this chapter involves questioning and contemplation about death.

- Is life after death real?
- Is there a greater reality beyond our five senses?
- Can we personally know, for sure, whether our loved one's consciousness continues after physical death?
- Can we grow into an emerging knowledge or awareness of the wisdom this experience gives us?

These are a few questions to consider as we integrate death and dying within our psychedelic experiences. These are also some of the questions that many people bring to their work with psychedelics. I have had death experiences in psychedelic journeys and have taken these as a glimpse as to what may come in the future; however, I have not died yet and can only ponder what the experience will be like. This is why I feel exploring death and dying through questions is an integral piece in integrating psychedelic experiences.

Working within the realm of psychedelics offers an amazing perspective not only to concrete sequential issues in your life on this planet. There is also the benefit of exploring psychedelics to catapult you into a readiness for the death experience, the afterlife, and contemplation around consciousness, spirituality, and our ascension into the beyond. Consider this as exploring your road map of death and dying. One of the ways to think about working with psychedelics is that you are practicing dying. Eventually, you may come to know the places that feel they are reaching towards death just as much as you know the physical world.

Building the Bridge Between the Worlds: One Foot In

Exploring psychedelics with healthy integration starts building a bridge between the two worlds—*Here and Now* and *Then and There*. By keeping one foot in the exploration of life and one foot in the preparation for death, certain ideas become unveiled to you. I cannot say what those ideas will be, but I believe they will come to you.

I cannot underscore enough the relationship between integrating death and your own integrity. Integrating the reality of your eventual death is practice for being able to face anything in life—and being able to integrate anything that you may remember as happening to you or that you may worry will happen to you or someone you love in the future. Just because death and certain topics are unsettling, if not threatening, to our egos or beliefs does not justify our ignoring or denying their potential importance.

These days, most people deny death, whether consciously or unconsciously. One of the themes of this book has been encouraging you to go towards, not away from, what arises within you. This is true whether you are exploring meditation, dreams, psychedelics, or any of your emotional or physical experiences. One of the paradoxes of life is that avoiding truths or dismissing them without process or integration—even when those truths are terrifying—can ultimately cause more insecurity, fear, or confusion.

Building your awareness is a tool that strengthens the soul. How do we manage to live in an open manner surrounding death and dying, when even *really* allowing ourselves to accept that we will die may cause us to dissociate? Well, you will have to figure that out for yourself day to day. But possibly strong attention, engaging in the exercises that psychedelics bring forth, and practicing love, compassion, and humility might help. Those are the basics of keeping one foot into the integration of your life through conscious exploration of death.

Clinical research confirms the value of carefully undertaken psychedelic journeys in relieving death anxiety. This seems to be true for those of us facing death sooner rather than later and for those family members and loved ones coping with knowledge that someone they love is nearing their transition. Offering psychedelics for coping with death anxiety is one of the first important therapeutic uses of psychedelics backed by a great deal of solid research. In *The Ultimate Journey: Consciousness and the Mystery of Death*, Stan Grof reviews the early studies in working with death anxiety through LSD, including sharing case histories.[158] He participated in developing the Spring Grove Program for working with cancer patients facing death. His summary evaluation of the important work was as follows:

> The changes I observed in cancer patients following psychedelic therapy were extremely varied, complex and multidimensional. Some of them, such as alleviation of depression, tension, anxiety, sleep disturbance, and psychological withdrawal, were of a familiar nature; they could often be achieved by traditional forms of therapy. However, many others involved phenomenon new to Western psychiatry and psychology and specific for psychedelic therapy, such as attenuation or even elimination of fear of death and radical changes in basic life philosophy and strategy, in spiritual orientation, and in the hierarchy of values. In addition to their influence on the emotional, philosophical, and spiritual aspects of the patients' existence, both LSD and DPT [Dipropyltryptamine, a psychedelic tryptamine] also often deeply influenced the experience of physical pain, even pain which had not responded to narcotic drugs.[159]

More recently, Charles Grob has replicated many of the early studies, primarily using psilocybin. Several other psychiatrists, neuroscientists, and cancer specialists have been following similar paths in the meticulous documentation of this most beneficial work with psilocybin. For instance, several researchers associated with the Johns Hopkins University School of Medicine and Medical Center conducted a study documenting, with statistical significance, the effectiveness "of a high dose of psilocybin administered under supportive conditions to decrease symptoms of depressed mood and anxiety, and to increase quality of life in patients with a life-threatening cancer diagnosis."[160] The authors summarized:

> Participants attributed to the high-dose experience positive changes in attitudes about life, self, mood, relationships and spirituality, with over 80% endorsing moderately or higher increased well-being or life satisfaction. These positive effects were reflected in significant corresponding changes in ratings by community observers (friends, family, work colleagues) of participant attitudes and behavior.

Not surprisingly (to me at least), there was a "strong association" between patients having a "mystical-type experience" in their first high-dose psilocybin session and lasting decrease in death-anxiety as well as substantial improvement in the quality of life. This new work points toward the eventual use of psychedelics for assisting death anxiety in "above ground" settings. I envision the ability of physicians to prescribe psychedelic medicines in controlled settings for people facing death as one of the first widespread lawful uses of psychedelics. Once legal, these journeys may become common and commonly accepted. I note that the mainstream culture may accept this use of psychedelics as not threatening any status quo given the circumstances and the recipients. An important link between medicine and spirituality —already growing in other contexts—may be further established. I am grateful to those scientists clearing this important path.

When You Die into It: Death Anxiety and Grieving Life

I say again, it is easier to talk about death when you are not facing your own death or grieving the death (or coming death) of someone you love. I bow humbly to all those closer to the death experience at this moment than ourselves.

I believe most of us need to work hard to allow ourselves to really face the experience. Let's be honest: the mystery of death is anxiety-provoking, and if you are not denying death, or dissociating from death, you will probably need to process through some intense fear and a whole lot of grief.

Fear can be paralyzing. Fear involves the head and the gut—and the whole body when you get that quick jolt of terror or that slow-cooking, numbing dread. With the head, maybe it is anxiety in a generalized sense; or maybe it is the racing of panic as one frightful thought leads to another. With the gut and the body, it usually feels more diffuse. This can be the realm of trauma.

These are normal experiences, and you can work with them. But it ain't easy. Facing the fear and grief of death can be your mission, if you choose to accept it. As I have said, I do not feel this is something that can be accomplished once and for all, but is a matter of incremental integration day to day. You are integrating death into life. How does that feel?

There are many techniques for working with fear and grief; full exploration is beyond the scope of this book. With fear, you can consider slow and gradual acceptance. Fear is a normal emotion, designed to protect us through evolution. So the goal is not to reject it, but rather to understand it and explore it. This probably involves acceptance and then release of the compounding thoughts of fear. Maybe you ease into your bodily fear responses and then feel your way out of the numbing anxiety. Human touch from those you love can be important. But ultimately, facing the fear of our own death is a personal matter.

Grief is more a matter of the heart. Grieving is very sad, very painful, and usually hard to understand. As I shared in Chapter 10, Jay Dufrechou wrote a book called *Moving through Grief: Reconnecting with Nature*. The book is more about the experience of grief (often including weeping) that comes up for some people when they open themselves up to nature than about grieving the loss of loved ones. But one of the observations in the book is that the experience of grief is multi-faceted and multi-layered.

In a sense, all experiences of grief are intertwined with each other such that moving into the reality of death tends to bring up the reality of all the losses that have existed in your life, those known and those not yet conscious. What are your losses? Can you feel them? Are you still holding onto them? Can you feel the grief and let it open your heart rather than close you down? You may need to weep your way through it.

Another observation in Jay's book is that grief and anger often layer over each other. If you open up to grief and feel it, quite often you then reach a place of anger. If you open into and express the anger, then usually you reach a place of weeping and heart opening, which is laced with grief. What are we ultimately angry about? Not having something we want? Loss of power? Inability to control? Being hurt? Not having the ability to express ourselves? Not counting? These experiences start to hover around the experience of death.

Imagining your Death

Here again I would like to open up the conversation. Design your death. Imagine into it.

Yes, there are tragic events that take people's lives. There are also peaceful deaths that come as an easing into the next phase. Someone once told me there are two ways to die: unexpectedly (as in an accident), or when you know you are approaching death and have time to move into and through the emotions and pains (often intense physical as well as emotional pain) leading up to death. Can you let yourself imagine which will be yours? How would it feel to have only a few seconds or minutes to know you are leaving the Earth? How would it feel to move through the fear and grief in a longer process—lasting, say, three years, a year, six months, a month, a week, a few days, maybe tomorrow?

In her famous book *On Death and Dying*, Elizabeth Kübler-Ross wrote about the stages of grief surrounding the approach to death: denial, anger, bargaining, depression, and acceptance. More recently, empirical research concluded most people experience some level of acceptance from the beginning, without as much disbelief or denial as suggested by Kübler-Ross. These authors identified *yearning*, an emotion not mentioned by Kübler-Ross, as the dominant emotion in grief around the coming loss of life.[161] Can you allow yourself to feel into these possible experiences? What path might your emotions take? This yearning, what would this feel like? What are we yearning for when we know we are approaching death?

Jay Dufrechou had an experience in his first breathwork that is with him every day of his life. He felt he was remembering successive deaths, many of them violent, followed by going back to God, then being sent (also violently) back into a body for another life. After these successive experiences, there was a final experience where he remembered lying on a bed nearing death and being surrounded by many people who loved him. Having this experience in his mid-thirties, he knew he could build his current life as though it was leading up to that moment.

Suppose you are asked, "What is it that you believe will happen when you die?" How do you envision your death? Do you have anxiety? Can you be with this fear long enough to imagine what is on the other side? I mean on the other side of life and on the other side of fear.

There is only one reality, and different ways of relating to it. As I talked about in Chapter 5 (Maps of Consciousness), we have a multitude of ways to look at this subject. Humans have evolved an elaborate set of assumptions about dying and what happens after our last breath. What is your imagined version? So what's stopping you from *dying* into it? I think working with psychedelics is a new zenith to a healthy way of coming into contact with death anxiety and opening up a vortex of possibilities for what's lying ahead of us all.

Experiencing "the Others" (Aliens? Angels?)

I would like to share two stories about working with death in psychedelic journeys. The first is a personal experience that changed the way I view my life here on Earth. The second is the narrative of a client living with inoperable brain cancer who had been told he was in the last few months of his life. He came to me for work on integrating an experience he had with psychedelics. Synchronistically, both stories suggest the potential of what the afterlife has to offer.

Working with a high dose of psilocybin, I had an experience that resonates with Jay's breathwork "memory." I came face to face with my death. I was lying on a bed in a room with all my family and relatives who were living at that present moment. In the experience, I feel the energy to follow for a move into death and am instructed to die into it. I continue to hear the invitation of the word play "dive into it" replaced with "die into it." And so I do just that by taking one last breath and proceeding to die.

Then all of a sudden, I find myself face to face with a group of beings I simply call "the others." They do not scare me; most people who have any engagement with them may call them aliens or extraterrestrials. I cannot confirm that I would call them aliens, though I have felt them most of my life, especially in the years of frequently engaging in psychedelic work. In many psychedelic experiences, I find an intimate and ongoing relationship with the others immediately.

During the experience, I was on the line between "is it okay to die?" and "letting go" into what was happening. I said to myself, there is an "inward healing" and "external awareness." This gave me safety and permission to let go into whatever happened. The others were guiding me, and I allowed myself to trust them. I asked myself what I meant by this, and said back to myself, "They live within this reality. I am a part of it." I went on to understand other people's notion that spirits don't exist at all, which I laugh about given my experiences. I remember these things daily through experiential integration and know deep inside myself what is my truth. While the experience arose through mushrooms, I *know* the experience as real, not a lie or a hoax of my mind.

Now to my second story. A client I will call Garrett came into my office to work on integrating psychedelic sessions. Garrett verbalized his history with meditation, yoga, and many other spiritual practices, and still he was nervous as he approached the end of his life. He shared that he had voluntarily stopped all medical treatment and had just done his first self-guided LSD experience.

Garrett was left confused after the journey. Being raised Irish Catholic, he had been told as part of his religious faith that you must repent all sins and put faith in God. However, what was introduced to him through psychedelics was not anything that he had learned in his church classes on Sunday mornings. He was introduced to a large group of what Garrett called aliens and "souls" that met him. He told the story of his naked self being lifted up by a tribe of spirits. During the integration session, he said the souls of the spirits were intertwined with his soul, strengthening him and helping him create a new bond between those of us in the physical life and those moving on.

Through the course of two more integrative sessions, Garrett came to peace with his awareness that he would trust what he learned during his psychedelic session and let go of the teachings of his youth. He was dying into his own death. Had it not been for the "others," Garrett would never have accepted his ability to sense control and power in his journey toward the other side. I feel the others taught both me and Garrett that life and death are not as separate as we sometimes feel. All is happening right now.

Approaching Death with Full Consciousness: Psychedelic Practice

I introduced Aldous Huxley, the famous author of *Brave New World*, briefly in Chapter 2. In his later years, Huxley became fascinated with psychedelics. He wrote the classic book *The Doors of Perception*, as well as the lesser-known *Heaven and Hell*, about psychedelic experiences and how they manifest and can be understood. [162]

In the annals of psychedelics lineage, Huxley's death holds a special and moving place. In her book *This Timeless Moment: A Personal View of Aldous Huxley*, Laura Huxley describes her husband's request for an intramuscular dose of LSD as he was approaching death. In the culture that has arisen around psychedelics in the last half century, Huxley's exploration of consciousness, including working with psychedelics, culminates in his journey toward death with the sacrament of LSD.

Laura was Huxley's second wife. His first wife, Maria, had died in 1955 (eight years before Huxley) from cancer after a long, painful illness. In working towards her description of Huxley's death, Laura draws on Aldous's own writing about the last days of Maria's illness. (I call Laura, Aldous and Maria by their first names given the intimate nature of this story.)

Maria had been hospitalized but was then brought home to her own room, where she could be near her family and friends and receive care from people she knew. Aldous wrote that Maria could still hear but had reached the point where she had increasing difficulty in speaking. He spent many hours sitting with her, "sometimes saying nothing, sometimes speaking." [163]

In the past, as Aldous wrote, Maria had "a number of genuinely mystical experiences, and had lived with an abiding sense of divine immanence, of Reality totally present, moment by moment in every object, person and event." Aldous described all of Maria's mystical experiences as associated with light, which she had come to associate with the desert. Her sense of light infused her love for the desert.

As she lay in her final days, Aldous would remind her of the desert and encourage her to open into waning desert light. "And I would ask her to look at these lights of her beloved desert and to realize that they were not merely symbols, but actual expression of the divine nature… of the peace that passeth all understanding… of the love that is at the heart of all things, at the core… of every human mind." [164]

Having reminded Maria of these truths—"truths which we all know in the unconscious depths of our being"—Aldous urged Maria "to advance into those lights, to open herself to joy, peace, love and being, to permit herself to be irradiated by them and to become one with them." Still more days passed, with Aldous periodically reminding Maria that "she must go forward into love, must permit herself to be carried into love, deeper and deeper into it, so that at last she would be capable of loving as God loves—of loving everything, infinitely, without judging, without condemning, without either craving or abhorring." [165]

Aldous encouraged Maria to leave her old memories behind. "Regrets, nostalgias, remorses, apprehensions—all these were barriers between her and the light." For the last hour of Maria's life, Aldous sat or stood with one hand on her head and the other on her solar plexus. Her breathing became more and more quiet, and he sensed her moving toward a release. Aldous went on with his suggestions, repeating close to Maria's ear:

> "Let go, let go. Forget the body, leave it lying here; it is of no importance now. Go forward into the light. Let yourself be carried into the light. No memories, no regrets, no looking backwards, no apprehensive thoughts about your own or anyone else's future. Only light. Only this pure being." [166]

Maria died in that way.

Eight years later, with Laura by his side, Aldous lay moving toward his own transition, from illness beginning with cancer. On the day he would die, Aldous wrote a note to Laura: "Try LSD 100 micrograms intramuscular." As she went to obtain the drug from elsewhere in the house, Laura noticed with irritation that friends and family were circled around the television. To her surprise and dismay, she discovered they were watching news of President Kennedy's assassination.

Laura administered the dose Aldous requested. After another hour, according to his wishes, she gave him another 100 micrograms and began to talk to him, echoing his words to Maria:

> "Light and free you let go, darling; forward and up. You are going forward and up; you are going toward the light. Willingly and consciously you are going, willingly and consciously, and you are doing this beautifully—you are going toward the light—you are going toward a greater love—you are going forward and up. You are going towards Maria's love with my love. You are going toward a greater love than you have ever known. You are going toward the best, the greatest love, and it is easy, it is so easy, and you are doing it so beautifully." [167]

Laura repeated similar words for several more hours, as Aldous became more and more still. His breathing grew slower and slower, then stopped. In Laura's words, "this ceasing of life was not a drama at all, but like a piece of music just finished so gently in a *sempre piu piano, dolcement....*" 168

Aldous Huxley

Can we imagine into the experience Aldous Huxley was having? Did he ask Laura for LSD to help him let go? Was he interested in a boost for his movement toward the other side? Could there have been an intuitive understanding of the benefit of reaching deeply into his own psyche—the mind of the man he had been and would release being—one last day before his consciousness moved back into the whole of Pure Being?

Considering Your Death Story

Not all of us will have the soul-cleansing "death privilege" that Aldous Huxley was given, where one lies in one's bed with loved ones, and just at the right moment is administered a large dose of The Food of The Gods. The story of the Huxleys provides a classic image of movement toward death, but we will each have our own stories —and our own needs as we move towards completion of our unique life journeys.

For many people, the archetypes, narratives, and rituals of various organized religions are a great comfort and template for considering death and moving towards transition. For instance, I believe that if you are connected to Jesus and have felt his love during life, then Jesus may well come to you as the bridge toward what is beyond this life. From my perspective, all of the spiritual systems carry their own truth and reality, although I am also clear that all of the religions carry their own potential for holding people in trauma, fear, grief, or codependence. But I am encouraging you to open into whatever is your path as you consider death.

I believe that with psychedelics there becomes less guesswork. With the coming of psychedelics into the Western world in the last few decades, several books have been written that give guidance in the practical realities of death and dying. Classic among them is *The Psychedelic Experience: A Manual Based on the Tibetan Book of the Dead*, a collaboration of Tim Leary, Richard Alpert (Ram Dass), and Ralph Metzner.[169] Throughout the book they introduce the Bardos, which are the in-between stages of death and rebirth in the Tibetan Buddhist culture. The authors compare the Bardos to different psychedelic experiences and parts of the psychedelic journey.

Other books draw on the understandings of other cultures. The **Ars moriendi** ("The Art of Dying"), **Egyptian Pyramid Texts**, and the **Tibetan Book of the Dead** are a few manuscripts sharing observations and detailed experiences of journeys into the afterworld. These writings account for the experiences of specific cultures and time periods and unique spiritual contexts. Their mythologies could be understood deeply by people in those time periods in which they were written. But we can even now feel into these systems for understanding and find our own resonance.

While insights from other cultures can be helpful, we each need to find our own relationship with death that makes sense in our own lives. One possibility is to participate in a psychedelic journey (perhaps most safely, a guided journey) in which you open to questions about death, including your own eventual passing. Jay Dufrechou was part of a beautiful several-hour session during which a gifted guide led experiencers through a series of questions inviting consideration of the moment of death. Using the structure of Egyptian mythology, the guide offered images helping the journeyers consider their life journey from the perspective of completion. The culmination was imagining the moment of actual death. When? Where? How? Who is present? How does it feel?

Another possibility is to let yourself imagine death as you are falling asleep in your own safe bed. What might death feel like? What comes up for you? Approaching sleep is a letting go. What if death is an analogous letting go, but with leaving the body? What if the transition state as we enter sleep and dreams has some similarity to the stages of consciousness after death? After all, in *The Tempest*, William Shakespeare wrote, "We are such stuff as dreams are made on, and our little life is rounded with a sleep."

Another possibility is an exercise I call Unlocking Conscious Awareness about death:

1. Examine your thoughts. What are the thoughts you have about death and dying? Let your mind be at ease with exploring the afterlife.
2. Feel your emotions. Are there certain emotions that are manifesting as you consider death? What if you start to think of loved ones or others? Challenge yourself to feel the emotions and the nuances that come up.
3. Explore your physical body—scan your body and pay attention to any sensations that start to become noticeable.

The more you develop this Unlock approach, you will be amazed at the preparation for exploring full consciousness. There is often an unconscious "block" against the very idea of death standing between us and really experiencing life. See if you can ease that block and move into whatever happens.

Now Your Turn

We all know we can't predict our death; however, what do you need to consider doing in preparation prior to the ultimate experience?

_____
_____
_____
_____
_____

How do you want people to handle your ceremony (if you chose to have one) after you pass on?

_____
_____
_____
_____
_____

Are there any rituals or services that you are drawn to that you would like to add into your life at this point to help understand the purpose of this work with psychedelics?

_____
_____
_____
_____
_____

After it's all said and done… What do you think is going to happen after you die?

_____
_____
_____
_____
_____

The Other Side During Psychedelics

Many of us who have experienced psychedelics feel as though we have had a taste of "the other side." There is no way to be sure this is where our consciousness goes after death. But it sure kinda feels like that. Actually, the experience may feel more like your consciousness has not "gone" anywhere, but has just become able to experience what is already here all around us all the time.

This possibility during psychedelic experience may be more likely with some substances than others, perhaps particularly with 5-MeO-DMT. In *When the Impossible Happens*, Stanislav Grof writes about his first experience with this medicine. The particular story is called "Gateway to the Absolute: The Secret of the Toad of Light." In sessions with other psychedelics, Grof wrote, he had always maintained a basic orientation of who and where he was. But with 5-MeO-DMT:

> [N]one of these dimensions even seemed to exist, let alone manifest. My only reality was a mass of radiant swirling energy of immense proportions that seemed to contain all existence in a condensed and entirely abstract form. I became Consciousness facing the Absolute.
>
> It had the brightness of myriad suns, yet it was not on the same continuum with any light I knew from everyday life. It seemed to be pure consciousness, intelligence, and creative energy transcending all polarities…
>
> I could not maintain a sense of separate existence in the face of such a force. My ordinary identity was shattered and dissolved; I became one with the Source. In retrospect, I believe I must have experienced the Dharmakaya, the Primary Clear Light, which according to the *Tibetan Book of the Dead*, the *Bardo Thodol*, appears at the moment of our death.[170]

I call participation in the "radiant swirling energy" being *in the field*. But I think there are probably many variations on "being in the field," and I do not pretend to understand them all. Some people have the sense that within the field there are answers to any questions, though they may also feel that answers are not relevant. There may be a sense of unconditional love as the same thing as light. But there may be a sense of something even beyond love, something more like absolutely everything together at once. This may be what some call **nonduality**.

With respect to our life stories—or past life stories—or ancestral stories—or stories of life on planet Earth—it may feel as though everything that has occurred is right there present in one moment. As Columbia says in "The Time Warp" (*Rocky Horror Picture Show*): *Time had no meaning, never would again.*

It may seem as though all relationships can be understood and are inevitable in some sense. What may be called karma seems to be the relationships that exist between one action or manifestation and another. The consequences of choices may seem as apparent as that a rock will roll down a gulley if you push it downhill on Earth.

In his description of his 5-MeO-DMT experience, Grof wrote that as he started to come down from the experience, he believed he was experiencing "the bardo, the intermediate state between my present life and my birth in the next incarnation, as it is described in the Tibetan texts." [171]

At first, he thought he actually was dead or dying. When he realized his life was not really ending, the experience of dying lingered. "I found myself in many dramatic situations happening in different parts of the world throughout centuries, all of them dangerous and painful." While he was shaking and hurting in various ways, "as my karmic history was being played out in my body, I was in a state of profound bliss, completely detached from these dramas." [172] In the field, death exists in the knowledge that "this is how life on Earth is set up." But the presence of all that has come before seems tangibly right there with you.

The sense of ancestors—and all of us being related—may come with experience in the field. A friend has described the experience of your ancestors all standing behind you, knowing you, loving you, wishing you the best in your choices and fate. How your ancestors linked together to form who you are, and the possibilities present in your life, may seem right there for you to experience. While you see they had choices, you also sense the ways all of their wounds and desires, past karma and future fate, fit together. People who are important in your life may seem to dance all around you (along with some spirits), and those whom you let go may seem to move into their own separate paths, even though all remains connected. After such experiences, you still live your life and have your preferences, values, and dislikes —but you know fundamentally you are part of a continuous whole of all that is and all that will be, like a fluid, continuous dance, infused with love.

Dying through Psychedelics Work

Fairly often during a psychedelic experience, people come to believe they are literally going to die, right then and there. Stan Grof shared his experience of believing he was dying in *Gateway to the Absolute*. Here we are not talking about a memory of a death that was somehow "us," as in a "past life memory." Rather, we are talking about lying there during a psychedelic experience and thinking, "I'm lying here in a psychedelic experience, and I am going to die from something that is happening in my body."

Jay Dufrechou and I have both had versions of this experience. For both of us, we had the sense there were literally physical symptoms that felt as though they were leading toward death.

We each felt as though we had the choice to resist these symptoms (and therefore resist death), or just let go into them and see what happened. Each of us thought, *God, this feels like I'm going to die; what a trip to die right here like this.* But there was also part of us thinking, *In terms of probabilities, this is probably just part of this experience.* When I went with it, I was then crying and felt there was no separation between myself and my therapy clients or all of the people in the world and all of their suffering.

For Jay, going with the experience of death led to a shift in awareness in which Jay disappeared into what felt like God, and Jay was looking out at all there is from the perspective of God, knowing he was God. This is not an experience of hubris or power, because you know that it is not just you that is God, but everyone and everything. This felt something like the part of Jay's first breathwork experience when it seemed he died and then died again and again and each time went briefly back to God before being sent back into a body. Interestingly enough, that experience was very much like the experience of "karmic history" described by Grof. Jay had not read Grof's essay at the time he had his analogous experience.

While I am personally convinced of the reality of these experiences, who knows? From a mainstream perspective, these could all just be drug-induced experiences. But if you have the experiences, you may feel (even know) they are more real than the material world around you. And yet again, I say the importance of death experiences in psychedelics involves not only reassurance about how the universe works, but being shown a template for serious psychospiritual work.

This brings us back to the experience of *ego-death*. As I have shared, I consider ego-death to involve a letting go that is best considered as a model for working on yourself. Even if you have moments (or hours) of merger with universal consciousness during psychedelic experiences, eventually you come back to yourself, and you still have an ego. I believe the letting go is mostly about letting go of illusions.

In psychological terms, it is about feeling and processing through your projections and defenses, as well as feeling and accepting your biologically based needs, desires, and instincts, while realizing they are tied to your physical incarnation—they are you, and yet you are also something else. You are part of the evolution of the Earth (a violent and needy place), and yet you are part of a universe grounded in the reality of love.

Here is one way to address the desire for ego-death. If you are thinking, "I want ego-death; I am going to go for ego-death," then consider whether you are attaching to something that involves a view of yourself or an ideology. Ask yourself what need you are fulfilling by that desire. On the other hand, if you are feeling into yourself, facing all the hard, painful, and even shameful realities about yourself with honesty (and then with honesty and compassion), and letting them fade away, then keep doing that and surround yourself with those who will help.

Martin Ball lists a series of beliefs we sometimes develop about our work with psychedelics, which he believes suggest egoic attachment. I may not agree with him completely, but if you find yourself (as many of us do) developing a strong attachment to these sorts of beliefs, you may try to bring yourself back to your own personal letting go. Ball says:

- [T]his is not about having profound mental breakthroughs or deep revelations. If you keep chasing after such, and keep returning to psychedelics because you think you're unlocking the secrets of the universe with all your mental activity, you're probably performing an act of mental/egoic masturbation.
- If you think you are developing psychic and magical spiritual powers, you are deluding yourself.
- If you think you are changing the world, processing for the collective, or healing others in your sessions, you are deluding yourself.
- If you think you are preparing yourself to ascend to a higher realm, you are deluding yourself.
- If you think you are receiving "downloads" of esoteric information, you're probably caught in an ego projection game.[173]

Again, I might not put things exactly as does Ball. But I admire his tenacity in advising the release of all illusions. I also find useful Ball's basic experience of the work as clearing out energetic blocks in our system. Specifically writing about 5-MeO-DMT, he explains:

> The goal of doing this work is to enhance your experience of energy, expand into yourself, encounter your blocks, projections and attachments, and then work through them energetically, so that you can have a release of stuck energy and process through what needs to be processed through.[174]

Ball describes the process as "unraveling the enigma of nonduality." In his experience, the "only relevant revelation is that you are God, and this isn't something that can be understood, though it can be experienced." He believes "the experience itself has infinite value as it helps you to learn how to relax into your genuine nature and be yourself without attachment and illusion."[175]

Letting go of illusions is not easy, particularly because we are usually not aware that our illusions are illusions. Perhaps more importantly, they feel as though they *are* us—unconsciously we believe that our habits of mind (projections, defenses, attachments) are the tangible essences that not only make us who we are, but that are necessary for us to exist. Allowing ourselves to see and then release these things, if you really do it, absolutely does **feel like death**. But I firmly believe you gain more than you lose.

When you work on your process, through integration, when you see and feel and then let go, and then see and feel some more and then let go some more, you gradually become someone grounded in unconditional love. How does this happen? It happens because what seeps through the cracks when you let yourself crack open is unconditional love.

Does this mean you become Mother Teresa, helping the needy, or that you go around expressing love to everyone you encounter? Absolutely not. Does it mean you allow yourself to be drained by all those in the world—or even those in your family —who are in need? Of course not. But it does mean you see reality more clearly and hold compassion for all in your heart. You are still you, but you have also expanded into connection with everyone and everything else.

Remember explore-surrender? If you just keep doing this—without struggling for your ego to die or attaching to an idea of ego-death—you just might find that those things you thought made you a person are still here, but are just holding up a form that is infused with a white light of unconditional love. This is "dying into it."

Ascension: The Continued Journey

The body dies, but the soul endures.

The new relationship I am offering through integrating both psychedelics and death is about the enrichment of our souls on both sides of these worlds. For that is what life is about: never-ending exploring and surrendering to what is. It is about the soul and the universe—all of it can be met with fear, love, grief, sorrow, elation, and above all, love. How will you moment-by-moment meet what is here for you?

I close this chapter (and the book) with the idea of ascension. The word *ascension* can be controversial. For some people, there is the image of Jesus or Mary ascending into heaven, which can be comforting or disturbing, depending on your relationship to Christianity. There is an image from some science fiction stories of becoming pure energy. The idea is that you have worked through all your earthly issues and transformed into the substance of angels or energetic beings.

I want to offer the word *ascension* as whatever you believe is the next step for you. How do you transcend yourself? How do you ascend into your next phase of being? I do not mind the image of moving *up* into something new and better, because honestly, that is the goal of many of us in psychological and spiritual work. But I do not exclude the moving *down into* yourself and all that exists in the earthly realm as part of ascension. You move down into what is there in order to process it all through yourself.

Ascension comes in the form of taking all your events, integrating them, and creating whatever meaning you choose to place on them. You may feel as though you want to surrender all of this to your designed creator or narrative. Nothing vital must be left undone as you consider your own ascension into the continued journey into death and beyond. As you ponder your ascension, questions may continue to arise. At some point, rather than driving further into the abyss, I encourage the idea of ascension through acceptance.

One of the hardest things about moving toward the later stages of an integration process is being in contact with death and dying, believing it is going to happen. This is particularly hard when we are young. Around the mid-thirties, some people have a moment when they realize—usually spontaneously—that they are really going to die. But this understanding can come at any time for any of us. This can signal transition into a new phase of life.

To experience the reality of death with psychedelics is to experience the present. This is how we as psychedelic journeyers explore the cartography and come to understand ourselves. Surrendering and ascending bring surprises. These revelations are crucial, or we would not journey further for the truth.

I want to close by acknowledging the reality that none of us really knows what is around the bend. I have offered many things in this book, some borrowed from others, some coming from my own heart and experience. In the end, what do I know?

What I *have experienced* is that you can find everything you need by going into yourself. Psychedelics are a gift from the gods that can open the doors into yourself —and beyond yourself into all that is. If you are choosing to walk through those doors, I send you Godspeed. I hope you will take some of my love and my hope for you through those doors with you.

Like moms and dads sending their off kids to nursery school or college, I hope you remember to integrate. Just like you, every time I take a journey, every time I open my eyes, every time I go inside to work on an issue, every moment, I try to remember to think and feel into what is there. If we keep bringing consciousness to what arises, we have the chance to discover ourselves and feel the entirety of creation happening now in our bodies.

In the end, patience might be the main ingredient to an easy relationship with both life and death. Ultimately, I will be granted access when the time has come. Maybe patience and integration are one and the same. Giving yourself the time to think and feel and be.

Take it easy, good friends. Be gentle.

Integration Exercise 12: Exploring Your Relationship with Death

What You Need

- Paper
- Pen or pencil
- Your journal.

General Background

"Obituary" is from the Latin word *obit*, meaning death. Since the early eighteenth century, the word *obituary* has been used to refer to a published death notice. However, written accounts of the life of a person at their death go back throughout human history. An obituary can be:

- A short story
- A long tale
- A straight-to-the-point death announcement
- An epic account of a person's life
- Poetry
- A chronological detail of one's life.

In working with psychedelics, we often encounter not only the reality and experience of death, but also the history of our lives. Often you may see for the first time the themes beneath the surface—what you were *really* learning and working on. Your life's purpose, meaning, and history can come up. Sometimes this is in relation to others in your life or your family lineage.

In this exercise I am asking you to write your obituary—what you would want written about you when you have passed away. Write whatever comes to mind, even if it feels like stream-of-consciousness. Use sentences if they come to you, or just jot down words and phrases. You don't need to over-think this exercise. Do not edit, censor, analyze, or critique your thoughts.

Take twenty to thirty minutes to complete this exercise. You can re-visit this exercise again in the future; so do not try to perfect your story now.

Questions you could consider asking yourself as you do this exercise:

- What and/or who did you impact or change? Why?
- Do you want to write about a psychedelic death-rebirth experience?
- How do you want to showcase yourself—via story, poem, etc.?

- What character traits and values did you consistently demonstrate over your life? At your core, who were you?
- Whom did you care for? How did you impact or change this person/these people?
- What were major accomplishments in your life? Think about certain ages of your life: for example, 40, 50, 60, 70?
- What did you show interest in? What were you passionate or enthusiastic about?
- What was your legacy?

Why this Exercise is Important for Psychedelics

Writing your obituary invites you to think and feel into the essence of your life. This integration exercise hits close to home about our impermanence on this planet while at the same time putting into perspective what our lives are really all about. The activity may be uncomfortable, but you will almost certainly find yourself considering the reality of your death and reconsidering your life.

You may notice avenues you have not yet pursued in life and might decide to make some changes. You may also find yourself celebrating what was important to you and thinking back with fondness on the adventures you have had. Writing your obituary at the end of our integration exercises helps you take stock of where you are and where you have been. I hope this brings you to the surface of yourself, so that you are ready for the most productive next steps in your psychedelics work and integration journey.

How To Do It

Preparation in advance

1. Create a safe and sacred space that you have devoted to meditating and your integration work.
2. Build an altar that speaks to you, with both spiritual and physical interests of yours being represented.
3. Have your chair and pillow set up in a comfortable position.
4. Organize your writing material.

Instructions for the exercise (Time: Twenty to thirty minutes)

- Dim the lights, or you may enjoy the natural daylight.

- Engage in a form of relaxation focusing on your life and death—for as long as you need (five minutes to ten minutes).
- Start to write in a non-judgmental manner.
- Don't edit or change anything.
- Be open to drawing or engaging in other "free flowing" ways to create your obituary; follow whatever desires are stirred up within you.
- After you are finished with your draft, revisit meditating for a minute or two.
- Read your obituary.

I hope you are able to honor yourself and your life through this exercise. None of us really controls how our lives unfold, much less how we leave our bodies with death. But exploring how you view your life and death at this moment is just one way to integrate yourself with yourself and practice being fully present right now. Perhaps the integration of both your psychedelics journeys and your life will remind you of who you are and inspire the rest of the time you are here.

Exitway

What are you leaving with?

_____
_____
_____
_____
_____

APPENDIX A

It's All Integration

This book has been created to support you in developing your authentic way of integrating your psychedelic experiences. I hope you engage in psychedelic experiences with information that reduces the risk, elevates the process, and enhances the clarity of your integration.

To understand integration is to know that it is all integration. The healing benefit of a psychedelic experience comes with the fluid process of contemplating all the aspects that go into the journey before, during, and after the experience. This means working with integration as an incremental approach. In addition, by associating with safe people who are familiar with the territory, you will solidify the chance to find healing and wholeness through psychedelics.

As you embark on your journey, here is a brief checklist to consider:

The Beginning: Educate and Develop Intention

- Explain your intention for the experience.
- Make sure that your mindset and intention are aligned with the offered setting, and that circumstances for safety and emotional support are fitting and within your consent.
- Listen to your intuition: some anxiety prior to an experience is normal, but do not force yourself into experiences you are uncertain about.
- Allow and honor any needs to cancel, reschedule, or change your mind.

Possible questions to consider:

1. Are you comfortable with individual work or curious about group work?
2. What training and/or experience does the guide/sitter/ partner have?
3. What is the purpose of your work? Recreational? Spiritual? Self-discovery? Healing trauma or addiction?
4. Are you conscious of the preparation and integration guidelines for this endeavor?
5. What is your comfort level with this work?

Assess possible outcomes and risks

- Know the psychedelic you will be working with.
- Understand the environment and people you may be with.
- Ensure that the quality and source of your medicine are reliable.
- Research, research, research to understand the appropriate range of dosage, duration of experience, common effects, and adverse reactions. Clear out any concerns *before* the experience.
- Recognize potential biological, psychological, and social ramifications.
- Find out what legal threats there are.
- Discuss concerns with your guide, and review any health conditions/medications/supplements with a healthcare provider.

Prepare for your experience

- Are you fasting or requested to fast?
- Get the best rest you can get.
- Stay well hydrated. Have a variety of refreshments.
- Have an assortment of nourishing snacks for energy.
- Organize transportation to and from journey location as needed.
- Refrain from energetic emotional/physical/social activity, and plan to be in low-pressure environments. For example, consider being in nature, having a safe place, being around safe people, and making space for one to two days before and after.
- Create a list of open friends, family, or supporters, and/or an integrative therapist with whom you can discuss the experience after.
- Focus on preparation for and integration of the upcoming experience through practices such as journaling, creative expression, meditation, exercise, bodywork, time in nature, or other suggestions that this book offers.

Ways to engage with the experience

- Exploring the intention through a ritual prior to the session or experience.
- Engaging with rather than judging, evaluating, or trying to predict.
- Connecting with your breath if frightened or overwhelmed.
- If it becomes too much, take it internal and go inside.
- Make it bigger! Work with rather than shut down.
- Never hesitate to reach out to your sitter or guide for support.

Starting the aftercare and integration process

- Go slowly. Grow slowly! There is no rush to do anything.
- Take time to scan your body, going from your feet up to your head.
- Allow time and space for contemplation of your experience so that it continues to unfold and cultivate.
- Hydrate and snack lightly if you desire.
- Start to consider the difference between nonverbal and verbal ways to express your experience. Over-sharing your experience too fast, or trying to make sense of it too early, may obstruct its full healing potential.
- Wait a few weeks before making any major life changes or decisions.
- Continue your integration process.

Other things to consider with integration

The first hours and cascading into the following days after the experience are a fundamental stage to start incorporating new perceptions into your daily life by engaging in regular integration practices. During this time you are most physically, psychologically, emotionally, and spiritually open to bring new understandings into life. It is also a cautionary tale to check in with your mind, body, and spirit along with friends, family, and professionals that work within this arena.

- Review your experience with regards to your original intention and goals. Start to explore and categorize patterns, themes, and internal emotional states you have.
- Be okay with letting go of some of the information; you can always come back to it. That's the value of jotting down everything you can.
- Avoid the *Moon Shot*. Short-term and long-term plans both take time. The Moon Shot is a goal that is too big and too easy to fail at.
- Make sure your chosen practice(s) are practical and you're able to incrementally incorporate them in a sustainable manner.
- A consistent spiritual or religious practice frequently provides a larger place for your integration work.
- Refine, refine, and refine your integration practices: As time progresses, micro and macro adjust your practices to incorporate new insights, and acknowledge any physical or emotional states that may have arisen during them. This book is designed to use over and over again.

- An elder, family member, friend, or trained integration therapist are all beneficial resources in cultivating and sustaining integration practices.

Things to look out for

Throughout this book I continuously talk about mental health and spiritual emergence. It is extremely important to be comfortable sharing with family, friends, or a professional any concerns or non-traditional patterns that start to arise in your daily life.

- Are you isolating and/or starting to give in to uncommon thoughts?
- Paranoid or delusional thoughts occurring beyond the normal duration of an experience should lead you to ask for help.
- Is your sleep being affected since your psychedelic experience?
- Are you having thoughts of harming yourself or others? (Call for some help, including a trusted family member or friend or even your local emergency department.)
- Manic behavior, depression, or intense meaninglessness are also warning signs.

Other Exercises to Consider

Art

- Collage
- Mandala drawing
- "Childlike" coloring
- Play-dough or clay work
- Nature collage (use items you found on a nature walk)
- Painting
- Photography
- Mask making
- Digital graphic art design
- Vision board making.

Writing

- Free association
- Storytelling of experience
- Mind mapping

- Journaling
- Research writing
- Poetry.

Physical Activities

- Nature walk
- Walking meditation
- Yoga
- Swimming
- Bodywork
- Drumming
- Playing music
- Bicycling
- Playing at a park
- Visiting an art museum
- Working out
- Sex
- Reading
- Researching your session
- Bathing/showering
- Float tank.

Religious or Spiritual Activities

- Prayer
- Participating in designed ritual
- Mudras
- Going to your place of worship
- Isolating with self
- Fasting
- Going into nature
- Dreamwork.

(This appendix may be copied and distributed as long as you give credit to author Ryan Westrum and provide the title of my book, The Psychedelics Integration Handbook.)

APPENDIX B

Questions to consider along the way

(Note that these questions can be seen from two vantage points—prior to any experience with psychedelics or as you integrate your psychedelic experience.)

How do you intend to use this work in your life?

What do you need to have through integration to verify your work? Describe what myths you have heard around working with psychedelics. How do you think psychedelics will support you?

What are the positive qualities of psychedelics, and what are some challenging aspects of psychedelics in your mind?

What would be an example of an intention you want to work on?

What will you need to continue to engage in this journey and feel safe?

What are some alternatives if you do not feel you are ready for psychedelic work?

Explain why you believe working with psychedelics will be beneficial for you and share what is your hope for the work with psychedelics.

Are there certain psychedelic experiences you want to have? For example, a therapeutic LSD session performed in a traditional manner?

What are the questions that you still need clarification on regarding the subject of psychedelics and the integration process?

How would you know that you are ready to dive in again to a psychedelic experience?

How does psychedelic integration tie into what you have already learned about this work?

How is psychedelic integration going to apply to everyday life?

Who are some people that you are comfortable enough to have conversations with about psychedelic experiences?

What are some of the questions that have come up as you integrate your psychedelic experiences? For example, consider cosmological, spiritual, family of origin, or mental health issues.

What is sympathetic to your psychedelic work in your life that will support your psychedelic integration for you? For example, practices such as fasting, artwork, creative writing, sexual experiences, isolation, or other adventures.

How has psychedelic integration helped support your understanding of your life's journey?

What do you consider as a certain tool for your psychedelic integration process, and what do you consider something you would like to try as it relates to integrating your work that may be a stretch for you?

When did you last come across something that changed the way you saw yourself?

How would you begin to integrate your psychedelic experience? In what ways will you know you are ready to experience psychedelics again? What needs are important to you regarding integrating psychedelics?

What are other ways to work on your self-exploration? How do psychedelics play a part in your life?

Where do you find safety in your life?

What would be an example of integrating psychedelics that is unhealthy?

What are some characteristics that give you reassurance that your psychedelic work is benefiting you?

What are some personal ways to integrate your psychedelic work that help you?

How do you foster self-care?

What is the basic limitation or concern you have with psychedelics?

What are the benefits you have received in your life when you have integrated psychedelics?

What do you want to do next as it relates to the topic of psychedelics?

What encourages you about the latest research around psychedelic studies? What concerns you?

(This appendix may be copied and distributed as long as you give credit to author Ryan Westrum and provide the title of my book, The Psychedelics Integration Handbook.)

BIBLIOGRAPHY

Akron & Banzhaf, Hajo. (1995/2014). *The Crowley tarot: The handbook to the cards.* Stamford, CT: US Games Systems, Inc.

Alpert, Ralph, Leary, Tim, & Metzner, Ralph. (1964/1992/2000). *The Psychedelic experience: A manual based on the Tibetan book of the dead.* New York, NY: Kensington Publishing Corp.

Anderson, Edward F. (1996) *Peyote: The divine cactus.* Tucson, AZ: The University of Arizona Press.

Arrien, Angeles. (1993). *The four-fold way: Walking the paths of the warrior, teacher, healer, and visionary.* New York, NY: HarperCollins.

Assagioli, Roberto. (1973). *The Act of Will.* New York, NY: Penguin Books.

Ball, Martin. (2017). *Entheogenic liberation: Unraveling the enigma of nonduality with 5-MEO-DMT energetic therapy.* Ashland, OR: Kyandara Publishing.

Bohm, David. (1980). *Wholeness and the implicate order.* London, UK: Routledge.

Butler, Renn. (2014). *Pathways to wholeness: Archetypal astrology and the transpersonal journey.* London, UK: Muswell Hill Press.

Campbell, Joseph. (1949). *Hero with a thousand faces.* New York, NY: Pantheon House.

Capra, Fritjof. (1975). *The Tao of Physics.* Berkeley, CA: Shambhala.

Capra, Fritjof. (1982). *The Turning Point.* New York, NY: Bantam Books.

Darenvogt, Willers T. (2013). *Rehab doesn't work: Ibogaine does.* W.T. Darenvogt and Iboga Books.

Dass, Ram. (1971). *Be here now.* San Cristobal, NM: Lama Foundation.

Davis, Stephen. (2004). *Jim Morrison: Life, death, legend.* New York, NY: Gotham Books.

Davis, Steven L. & Minutaglio, Bill. (2018). *The most dangerous man in America: Timothy Leary, Richard Nixon and the hunt for the fugitive king of LSD.* New York, NY: Twelve Hachette Book Group.

Dufrechou, Jay. (2015). *Moving through grief: Reconnecting with nature.* London, UK: Muswell Hill Press.

Edinger, Edward F. (1972). *Ego and archetype: Individuation and the religious function of the psyche.* Boston, MA: Shambhala.

Eliade, Mircea. (1951). *Shamanism: Archaic techniques of ecstasy*. Princeton, NJ: Princeton University Press.

Fadiman, James. (2011). *The Psychedelic Explorer's Guide: Safe, therapeutic and sacred journeys*. Rochester, VT: Park Street Press.

Faust, Jamy, & Faust, Peter. (2015). *The constellation approach: Finding peace through your family lineage*. Berkeley, CA: Regent Press.

Forrest, Steven. (1984/2012). *The inner sky*. Borrega Springs, CA: Seven Paws Press.

Frank, Peter & Taub, Eric. (2014). *Ibogaine Explained: Everything you need to know about the world's most powerful psychedelic*. Peter Frank.

Freud, Sigmund. (1913). *The interpretation of dreams*. New York, NY: Macmillan.

Glendinning, Chellis. (1994). *My name is Chellis and I'm in recovery from Western civilization*. Boston, MA: Shambhala.

Greene, Liz. (1996). *The astrological Neptune and the quest for redemption*. York Beach, ME: Samuel Weiser.

Grof, Cristina. (1993). *The thirst for wholeness: Attachment, addiction, and the spiritual path*. New York, NY: HarperCollins.

Grof, Stanislav & Grof, Christina. (1989). *Spiritual emergency: When personal transformation becomes a crisis*. Los Angeles, CA: Jeremy Tarcher.

Grof, Stanislav & Grof, Christina. (2010). *Holotropic Breathwork: A new approach to self-exploration and therapy*. Albany, NY: SUNY.

Grof, Stanislav. (1975/2009). *LSD, doorway to the numinous: The groundbreaking psychedelic research into realms of the human unconscious*. Rochester, VT: Park Street Press.

Grof, Stanislav. (1980/2006). *LSD psychotherapy: The healing potential of psychedelic medicine*. Santa Cruz, CA: The Multidisciplinary Association for Psychedelic Studies (MAPS).

Grof, Stanislav. (2006). *The ultimate journey: Consciousness and the mystery of death*. Santa Cruz, CA: The Multidisciplinary Association for Psychedelic Studies (MAPS).

Grof, Stanislav. (2006). *When the impossible happens: Adventures in non-ordinary realities*. Boulder, CO: Sounds True.

Grof, Stanislav & Grof, Christina. (1990). *The stormy search for the self: A guide to personal growth through transformational crisis*. New York, NY: G. P. Putnam's Sons.

Harcourt-Smith, Joanna. (2013). *Tripping the Bardo with Timothy Leary: My Psychedelic Love Story*. North Charleston, SC: Create Space Independent Publishing.

Harner, Michael. (1980/1990). *The way of the shaman*. San Francisco, CA: Harper San Francisco.

Hartelius, Glen & Wolfson, Phil. (2016). *The ketamine papers: Science, therapy and transformation*. Santa Cruz, CA: The Multidisciplinary Association for Psychedelic Studies (MAPS).

Heaven, Ross. (2013). *Shamanic quest for the spirit of salvia: The divinatory, visionary, and healing powers of the sage of the seers.* Rochester, VT: Park Street Press.

Heaven, Ross. (2016). *San Pedro: The gateway to wisdom.* Hants, UK: Moon Books.

Hinojosa, Octavio R. (2016). *The toad of dawn: 5-MeO-DMT and the rise of cosmic consciousness.* Studio City, CA: Divine Arts.

Hofmann, Albert. (1979/2005). *LSD, my problem child: Reflections on sacred drugs, mysticism and science.* Santa Cruz, CA: The Multidisciplinary Association for Psychedelic Studies (MAPS).

Huxley, Aldous. (1932/2006). *Brave new world.* London, UK: Chatto & Windus.

Huxley, Aldous. (1954/2006). *The doors of perception: Includes heaven and hell.* New York, NY: Harper Collins.

Huxley, Laura. (2006). Excerpts from Laura Huxley's This timeless moment: A personal view of Aldous Huxley. In Stanislav Grof (Ed). *The ultimate journey: Consciousness and the mystery of death* (pp. 319-326). Santa Cruz, CA: The Multidisciplinary Association for Psychedelic Studies (MAPS).

Jung, Carl G. (1912). On the Psychology of the Unconscious. *Collected Works 7: Two Essays on Analytical Psychology.*

Jung, Carl G. (1991). Aion—Researches into the Phenomenology of the Self. *Collected Works of C. G. Jung.* London: Routledge.

Jung, Carl G. (2009). Ed. Shamdasani, S. *The Red Book.* New York, NY: W.W. Norton & Company.

Kesey, Ken. (1962). *One flew over the cuckoo's nest.* New York, NY: Penguin Random House.

Kübler-Ross, Elizabeth. (1969). *On death and dying.* New York, NY: Routledge.

Lazslo, Ervin. (2009). *The Akashic Experience: Science and the cosmic memory field.* Rochester, VT: Inner Tradition.

Le Grice, Keiron. (2010). *The Archetypal Cosmos: Rediscovering the Gods in myth, science and astrology.* Edinburgh, UK: Floris Books.

Le Grice, Keiron. (2013). *The rebirth of the hero: Mythology as a guide to spiritual transformation.* London, UK: Muswell Hill Press.

Maitri, Sandra. (2000). *The Spiritual dimension of the enneagram.* New York, NY: Jeremy Tarcher, Putnam.

Maslow, Abraham H. (1964). *Religions, values, and peak experiences.* London: Penguin Books Limited.

Masters, Robert Augustus. (2010). *Spiritual bypassing, when spirituality disconnects us from what really matters: Learning to recognize and transform the obstacles that keep us from living life fully.* Berkeley, CA: North Atlantic Books.

McNamara, Patrick. (2006). *Where God and science meet: How brain and evolutionary studies alter our understanding of religion.* Westport, CT: Greenwood Press.

Metzner, Ralph. (2013). *The Toad and the Jaguar.* Berkeley, CA: Green Earth Foundation & Regent Press.

Naranjo, Claudio. (1994). *Character and neurosis: An integrative view.* Nevada City, NV: Gateways/IDHHB.

Neumann, Erich. (1963/1990). *Depth psychology and the new ethic.* Boston, MA: Shambhala.

Palmer, Helen. (1988). *The Enneagram: The Definitive guide to the ancient system for understanding yourself and the others in your life.* San Francisco, CA: Harper & Row.

Pinchbeck, Daniel. (2007). Introduction. *The psychedelic experience: A manual based on the Tibetan book of the dead* (pp. ix-xix). New York: Citadel Press Books.

Pollan, Michael. (2018). *How to change your mind: What the new science of psychedelics teaches us about consciousness, dying, addiction, depression, and transcendence.* New York, NY: Penguin Random House.

Read, Tim. (2014). *Walking shadows: Archetype and psyche in crisis and growth.* London, UK: Muswell Hill Press.

Riso, Don R. (1993). *Enneagram transformations: Releases and affirmations for healing your personality type.* Boston, MA: Houghton Mifflin.

Riso, Don R. & Hudson, Russ. (1996). *Personality types: Using the enneagram for self-discovery.* New York, NY: Houghton Mifflin Harcourt.

Rosenberg, Marshall. (2012). *Living nonviolent communication: Practical tools to connect and communicate skillfully in every situation.* Boulder, CO: Sounds True.

Ruumet, Hillevi. (2006). *Pathways of the soul: Exploring the human journey.* Victoria, BC: Trafford.

Schwartz, Richard C. (1995). *Internal family systems therapy.* New York, NY: The Guilford Press.

Shroder, Tom. (2014). *Acid Test: LSD, ecstasy, and the power to heal.* New York, NY: Penguin Group.

Siegel, Daniel J. (2011). *Mindsight: The new science of personal transformation.* New York, NY: Bantam Books.

Sparks, Tav. (2016). *The power within: Becoming, being, and the holotropic paradigm.* London, UK: Muswell Hill Press.

Strassman, Rick. (2001). *DMT: Spirit molecule.* Rochester, VT: Park Street Press.

Tarnas, Richard. (2006). *Cosmos and psyche: Intimations of a new world view.* New York, NY: Plume.

Wade, Jenny. (2004). *Transcendent sex: When lovemaking opens the veil.* New York, NY: Simon & Schuster.

Wilber, Ken. (1979). *No Boundary: Eastern and Western approaches to personal growth*. Boston, MA: Shambhala.

Wolfe, Tom. (1968). *The electric kool-aid acid test*. New York, NY: Macmillan.

ABOUT THE AUTHOR

Ryan Westrum, Ph.D., M.A. works as a psychedelic integration psychologist and end-of-life doula in the Twin Cities of Minnesota and through video conference nationally. His primary focus is working with individuals integrating expanded state experiences for healing and personal transformation. Ryan frequently works with people at end of life, terminally ill, living with death anxiety, depression, mental illness, stress, trauma, and grief.

Ryan is available for speaking engagements on a myriad of topics and leads experiential groups, like death and dying groups, dream work therapy, and psychedelic integration groups; and develops death and dying plans as well as psychedelic integration plans with people though therapy and coaching.

Ryan graduated from the University of Minnesota with a degree in psychology, followed by a master's degree in marriage and family therapy from Adler Graduate School. He then went on to receive his doctoral degree in transpersonal psychology from Sofia University.

Ryan is a certified end of life doula with the International End of Life Doula Association. He is also a registered integration therapist for Multidisciplinary Association for Psychedelic Studies (MAPS). He is a practicing psychologist in Minneapolis, Minnesota, where he lives with his wife and four children.

Ryan's website can be found at www.healingsoulsllc.com.

Are you interested in knowing more?

Tune in to The Psychedelic Psychologist found on your favorite streaming services.

INDEX

A

Active imagination, 163
Addiction
    definitions of, 316
    transpersonal model, 318
Aftercare, 340
    compared to integration, 18
Agosin, Roberto Tomas, 192
Akashic field, 174
Alpert, Richard. See Dass, Ram
Ancestors (and psychedelics), 3
Anderson, Edward F. 58
Anderson, Rosemarie, 354
Anger, 140
Archetypes, 162
Arrien, Angeles, 266
Astrology, 175, 241, 331
    Archetypal, 13, 176
Awareness, 35
Ayahuasca, 53, 91
ayahuascero vs. Curandero, 111
    effects, 55
    purging, 78
    tourism, 53, 148
    working outside awareness, 125

B

Bad trip, 145, 304
Ball, Martin, 72, 103, 113, 197, 356, 359, 385
Barefoot Walking Meditation, 136
Bipolar Disorder, 196
Blake, William, 40
Body awareness, 228
Body scanning, 228
Bohm, David, 172
Brain hemispheres, 203, 208
Bufo Alvarius, 69
Butler, Renn, 13, 242-243

C

Campbell, Joseph, 183, 191, 195
Capra, Fritjof, 173
Chakra system, 212
Cispersonal, 169
    definition of, 8
Cognitive Behavior Therapy (CBT), 35
Collective unconscious, 161
Colonization, 235
Complex, 162
Cook-Greuter, Susanne, 254
Cultural appropriation, 54, 303

D

Dass, Ram, 43, 383
Death, 371
Defense mechanisms, 287
Developmental psychology, 243
Diagnostic and Statistical Manual of Mental
    Disorders, 185
Diamond, Stephen, 291
Divination tools, 240, 258
DMT (N,N-dimethyltryptamine), 67
Doblin, Rick, 51, 53
Dose
    psycho-integrative vs. Dissociative, 124

E

Einstein, Albert, 171
    on God. 172
Eliade, Mircea, 116
Empathic listening, 283
Empathogen, 10
Enlightenment, 253, 372
Enneagram, 35, 180

F

Facilitators
    categories of, 113
    practitioner vs. Provider, 113
Factors shaping psychedelic experience, 11
Fadiman, James, 89, 101-102, 122, 355
    microdosing, 127
    pre-session exploration, 90
Faust, Jamy and Peter, 223
Fear, 146
Flashbacks, 187
Forrest, Steven, 177, 332
Frank, Peter, 328
Freud, Sigmund, 158
    model of the psyche, 159
    relevance to psychedelics work, 161

G

Glendinning, Chellis, 320
Greene, Liz, 331
Grob, Charles, 52, 376
Grof, Christina, 190, 318
    spiritual emergence/emergency, 24
Grof, Stanislav, 41, 61, 120, 165, 299, 385
    archetypal astrology, 14
    Basic Perinatal Matrices, 166
    cartography of the psyche, 165
    COEX (system of condensed experience), 8, 168, 263
    relevance to psychedelics work, 170
    spiritual emergence/emergency, 24
Group sharing, 275, 283
Guides
    underground (finding), 102
Gurdjieff, George Ivanovich, 180

H

Hallucinogen Persisting Perception Disorder, 187
Harm reduction, 130
Harmon, Willis, 122
Harner, Michael, 116
Haug, Diane, 79
Heffter Research Institute, 51
Heffter, Arthur, 51
Hofmann, Albert, 39, 41, 59, 293
    bicycle ride, 60
Huxley, Aldous, 40, 56, 331, 380
Huxley, Laura, 380

I

I Ching, 241, 260
Ibogaine, 73, 315, 328
Ichazo, Oscar, 181
Inner healer, 9, 168
Inner self, 82
Integration
    as process, 231
    channels, 205
    non-verbal channels, 207
Integration altar, 335
Internal Family Systems, 217
Intuitive Inquiry, 354

J

Jaguar, 68
Jung, Carl Gustav, 154, 161
    Individuation, 164
    map of consciousness, 157
    psychological functions, 215
    relevance to psychedelics work, 165
    shadow, 286, 289

K

Kesey, Ken, 44
Ketamine, 73, 125, 151
Kollisch, Anton, 49
Kübler-Ross, Elizabeth, 378
Kundalini, 190, 215

L

Laing, Ronald D., 193
Laszlo, Ervin, 173
Akashic field, 174
Le Grice, Keiron, 177-178, 183
Leary, Timothy, 42, 383
Lemniscate, metaphor of, 266
Listening, empathetic, 277
Looping, 359
Lysergic acid diethylamide (LSD-25), 59

M

Mandala Spirit Collage, 154
Manske, Richard, 67
Masters, Robert Augustus, 149
McKenna, Terence, 49
MDMA, 47, 65, 118, 151
    as empathogen, 10
Medicine cards, 258

Meditation, 34
5-MeO-DMT, 68, 385, 388
Mescaline, 56
Metzner, Ralph, 10, 68, 71, 77, 118, 146, 383
Microdosing, 126
Mind Mapping, 202
Mindell, Arnold, 205
Mindell, Arnold and Amy, 216
    Channels, 216
Mindset
    Defined, 85
    interaction with setting, 91
    pre-session, 88
Mindsight, 220
Mithoefer, Annie, 66, 118
Mithoefer, Michael, 66, 118
Morrison, Jim, 45, 160, 199
Multidisciplinary Association for Psychedelic Studies (MAPS), 51
Mysticism v. Psychosis, 191, 193

N

Naranjo, Claudio, 181
Neumann, Erich, 289
Nichols, David, 10
Nonviolent communication, 265

O

Obituary, 391
Observer consciousness, 35
Osmond, Humphrey, 6, 40

P

Palmer, Helen, 35, 181
Perry, John W., 192
Peyote, 56-59
Pinchbeck, Daniel, 141
Post traumatic stress disorder (PTSD), 118, 151
Progressive muscle relaxation, 228
Psilocybin, 44, 62, 376
Psychedelic Tourism, 303
Psychedelics
    alternate words for, 9
    commonly used, 9
    definition of, 6
Psychodrama, 222
Psychosis v. Mysticism, 191, 193

R

Read, Tim, 7, 169
    archetypal penetrance, 195
    cispersonal, 8, 169
Relationship issues, 149, 353
Religion (and psychedelics), 4
Rettig, Octavio
Riso, Don
Rosenberg, Marshall
Ruumet, Hillevi, 69, 78

S

Sabina, Maria, 40
Sacred circle, 283
Sacred sharing, 285
Sacred space, 82
Safety, 237
S-A-F-E-T-Y acronym, 20, 237
Salvia divinorum, 73
San Pedro, 56
Sandison, Ronald, 41, 120
Schizophrenia, 188
Schwartz, Richard, 217
Sexuality, 107
Shadow
    and psychedelics, 288
    collective, 289
    explained, 286
Shulgin, Alexander "Sasha", 49, 65, 181
Siegel, Dan, 220
Silos, 360
Sparks, Tav, 12, 261
    Awareness Positioning System (APS), 262
Spiritual bypassing, 149
Spiritual emergence/emergency, 24, 189
Stages of integration, 350
Strassman, Rick, 6, 51, 67
Symbol, 162
Synchronicity, 163
Synesthesia, 268

T

Talking circle, 283
Tarnas, Richard, 14, 176, 332
Tarot cards, 258
Taub, Eric, 328
Terror, 146
Therapy for integration, 150
Toad medicine. See 5-MeO-DMT
Transpersonal

definition of, 7
modei, 318
Twain, Mark, 309

W

Wasson, Gordon, 40, 304
Wasson, Valentina, 40
Whiteout, 123
Wilber, Ken, 248, 253
Wilson, Bill, 314, 319, 330
Witness consciousness, 35

Y

Yogic sleep, 124

Z

Zendo Project, 132

ENDNOTES

1. Strassman, Rick. (2001). *DMT: Spirit Molecule.* Rochester, VT: Park Street Press, p. 31.
2. Grof, Stanislav. (1975/2009). *LSD, Doorway to the numinous: The groundbreaking psychedelic research into realms of the human unconscious.* Rochester, VT: Park Street Press, p. 157.
3. Sparks, Tav. (2016). *The power within: Becoming, being, and the holotropic paradigm.* London, UK: Muswell Hill Press, p. 37.
4. *Id*, p. 37.
5. Hernandez-Avila, Inez. (1997/2000). Meditations of the spirit: Native American religious traditions and the ethics of representation. In Lee Irwin (Ed.) Native American spirituality: A critical reader (pp. 11-36). Lincoln, NE: University of Nebraska Press, p. 21.
6. http://www.medicaldaily.com/psychedelic-drug-use-united-states-common-now-1960s-generation-245218.
7. Huxley, Aldous. (1954/2009). *The Doors of Perception.* New York, NY: HarperCollins, p. 26.
8. Anderson, Edward F. (1996). *Peyote: The divine cactus.* Tucson, AZ: The University of Arizona Press, p. 49.
9. Id, quoting Slotkin, J.S. (1956). *The Peyote Religion.* Glencoe, IL: Free Press, p. 77.
10. Hofmann, Albert. (1979/2005). *LSD, my problem child: Reflections on sacred drugs, mysticism and science*, p. 47.
11. *Id.*, p. 49.
12. *Id.*, p. 50-51.
13. *Id.*, p. 51.
14. Grof, Stanislav. (2006). *When the impossible happens: Adventures in non-ordinary realities.* Boulder, CO: Sounds True, xxxiii.
15. Strassman, p. 31.
16. *Id.*, p. 266.
17. *Id.*, p. 276.
18. *Id.*, p. 277.
19. Metzner, Ralph. (2013). *The toad and the jaguar.* Berkeley, CA: Green Earth Foundation & Regent Press, p. 43.
20. Rettig Hinojosa, Octavio. (2016). *The toad of dawn: 5-MeO-DMT and the rise of cosmic consciousness.* Studio City, CA: Divine Arts, p. 38.
21. *Id.*, p. 89-90.
22. *Id.*, p. 90.
23. *Id.*, p. 164.
24. *Id.*, p. 51.
25.
26. Ball, Martin W. (2017). *Entheogenic liberation: Unraveling the enigma of nonduality with 5-Meo-DMT energetic therapy.* Ashland, OR: Kyandara Publishing, p. 55.

27 Frank, Peter & Taub, Eric. (2012). *Ibogaine explained: Everything you need to know about the world's most powerful psychedelic.* Columbia, SC: Peter Frank & Eric Taub; Darenvogt, Willers T. (2013). *Rehab doesn't work, ibogaine does: Everything you need to know about the overnight drug and alcohol abuse treatment that stops cravings and ends addiction without withdrawal.* Columbia, SC: Iboga Books.
28 Metzner, p. 80.
29 Rettig, p. 54.
30 Ball, p. 84.
31 *Id.*, p. 85.
32 Metzner, p. 81.
33 Fadiman, James. (2011). *The psychedelic explorer's guide: Safe, therapeutic and sacred journeys.* Rochester, VT: Park Street Press, p. 19.
34 Grof, Stanislav & Grof, Christina. (2010). Holotropic Breathwork: A new approach to self-exploration and therapy. Albany, NY: SUNY, p. 99-100.
35 *Id.*, p. 15.
36 *Id.*, p. 17.
37 *Id.*, p. 17.
38 Ball, p. 61-62.
39 *Id.*, p. 62.
40 Wade, Jenny. (2004). *Transcendent sex: When lovemaking opens the veil.* New York, NY: Simon & Schuster.
41 http://www.caminodoamor.org/progress/ayahuascero-vs-curandero-a-western-misunderstanding-of-shamanism/
42 Ball, p. 61.
43 *Id.*, p. 61.
44 Strassman, p. 306.
45 Pinchbeck, Daniel. (2007). Introduction. *The psychedelic experience: A manual based on the Tibetan book of the dead* (pp. ix-xix). New York: Citadel Press Books, p. xiii.
46 *Id.*
47 Metzner, p. 49.
48 *Id.*, p. 55.
49 *Id.*, p. 55.
50 http://journals.sagepub.com/doi/abs/10.1177/0269881116662634.
51 Metzner, p. 70.
52 http://www.jeremytaylor.com/dream_work/dream_work_toolkit/index.html.
53 Metzner, pp. 60-65.
54 Masters, Robert Augustus. (2010). *Spiritual bypassing, when spirituality disconnects us from what really matters: Learning to recognize and transform the obstacles that keep us from living life fully.* Berkeley, CA: North Atlantic Books, p. 1.
55 *Id.*, pp. 1-2.
56 https://www.military.com/daily-news/2018/06/21/va-reveals-its-veteran-suicide-statistic-included-active-duty-troops.html
57 https://www.usatoday.com/story/nation/2014/10/31/suicide-deaths-us-military-war-study/18261185/
58 See, e.g., Ryan, Isley C., Marta, Cole J., & Koek, Ralph J. (2016). Ketamine, depression and current research: A review of the literature. In Phil Wolfson & Glenn Hartelius (Eds.), *The Ketamine papers: Science, therapy, and transformation* (pp. 199-274), Santa Cruz, CA: MAPS, p. 214.
59 Jung, C.G. *Collected Works 8*, "The Structure of the Psyche," par. 342.
60 *Id.*, par. 325.
61 See http://jungcurrents.com/twelve-quotations-on-individuation.

62 Read, Tim. (2014). *Walking shadows: Archetype and psyche in crisis and growth*. London, UK: Muswell Hill Press, p. 261.
63 https://www.washingtonpost.com/history/2018/10/03/einsteins-letter-belittling-god-religion-will-be-auctioned-million-or-more/?noredirect=on&utm_term=.8d56ffbc8d4e
64 https://www.washingtonpost.com/archive/opinions/1985/12/22/einsteins-intoxication-with-the-god-of-the-cosmos/4b979fa2-7367-4814-b70c-109fb7642b1b/?utm_term=.480a4d257edc.
65 *Id.*
66 *Id.*
67 Bohm, David. (1980). *Wholeness and the implicate order*. London, UK: Routledge, p. 172.
68 Capra, Fritjof. (1982). *The turning point*. New York, NY: Bantam Books, p. 91-92.
69 *Id.*, p. 92.
70 *Id.*, p. 92.
71 Capra, Fritjof. (1975). *The tao of physics*. Berkeley, CA: Shambhala, p. 12.
72 Laszlo, Ervin. (2009). *The Akashic experience: Science and the cosmic memory field*. Rochester, VT: Inner Tradition, p. 3.
73 Le Grice, Keiron. (2010). *The archetypal cosmos: Rediscovering the gods in myth, science and astrology*. Edinburgh, UK: Floris Books, p. 179.
74 *Id.*, p. 179.
75 *Id.*, p. 207.
76 *Id.*, p. 209.
77 *Id.*, p. 209.
78 Palmer, Helen. (1988). *The Enneagram: The definitive guide to the ancient system for understanding yourself and the others in your life*. San Francisco, CA: Harper & Row; Maitri, Sandra. (2000). *The spiritual dimension of the Enneagram*. New York, NY: Jeremy Tarcher Putnam; Naranjo, Claudio. (1994). *Character and neurosis: An integrative view*. Nevada City, NV: Gateways/IDHHB; Riso, Don Richard & Hudson, Russ. (1996) *Personality types: Using the Enneagram for self-discovery*. New York, NY: Houghton Mifflin Harcourt.
79 Riso, Don Richard. (1993). *Enneagram transformations: Releases and affirmations for healing your personality type*. Boston, MA: Houghton Mifflin.
80 Le Grice, Keiron. (2013). *The rebirth of the hero: Mythology as a guide to spiritual transformation*. London, UK: Muswell Hill Press.
81 https://thedrugclassroom.com/video/hallucinogen-persisting-perception-disorder-hppd/
82 Halpern, J.H., Pope, H.G. (2003). "Hallucinogen persisting perception disorder: what do I know after 50 years?" *Drug Alcohol Depend*. 69(2) 109–19.
83 https://thedrugclassroom.com/video/hallucinogen-persisting-perception-disorder-hppd/
84 Grof, Stanislav & Grof, Christina. (1989). *Spiritual emergency: When personal transformation becomes a crisis*. Los Angeles, CA: Jeremy Tarcher.
85 Grof, Stanislav & Grof, Christina. (1989). Spiritual emergency: Understanding evolutionary crisis. In Grof, Stanislav & Grof, Christina (Eds.), *Spiritual emergency: When personal transformation becomes a crisis*. Los Angeles, CA: Jeremy Tarcher.
86 Grof, Stanislav & Grof, Christina. (1990). *The stormy search for the self: A guide to personal growth through transformational crisis*. New York, NY: G. P. Putnam's Sons; see also http://www.christinagrof.com/page-4/.
87 *Id.*, p. 11.
88 http://www.seedsofunfolding.org/issues/11_08/feature_english.htm.
89 http://www.seedsofunfolding.org/issues/11_08/feature_english.htm.
90 Read, p. 48.
91 Ball, p. 115.
92 *Id.*, p. 116.

93 Edinger, Edward F. (1972). *Ego and archetype: Individuation and the religious function of the psyche.* Boston, MA: Shambhala, p. 7.
94 Quoted in many places, including Davis, Stephen. *Jim Morrison: Life, Death, Legend.* New York: Gotham Books. 2004, p. 182-183.
95 Ruumet, Hillevi (2006). *Pathways of the soul: Exploring the human journey.* Victoria, BC: Trafford, p. 140.
96 *Id.*, p. 140.
97 Jung, "Definitions," CW 6, par. 770.
98 Schwartz, Richard C. (1995). *Internal family systems therapy.* New York: The Guilford Press.
99 Siegel, Daniel J. (2011). *Mindsight: The new science of personal transformation.* New York, NY: Bantam Books.
100 https://www.mindsightinstitute.com/
101 http://www.drdansiegel.com/books/mindsight/
102 Faust, Jamy & Faust, Peter. (2015). *The constellation approach: Finding peace through your family lineage.* Berkeley, CA: Regent Press.
103 See dictionary.com.
104 https://www.google.com/search?q=reconcile&oq=reconcile&aqs=chrome..69i5 7.1416j0j8&sourceid=chrome&ie=UTF-8.
105 www.google.com/search?q=colonize&oq=colonize&gs_l=psy-ab.3..0i20k1l2j0l2.4328013.4329973.0.4331140.10.9.1.0.0.0.141.702.5j2.7. 0....0...1.1.64.psy-ab..2.8.705...0i67k1j35i39k1.j_pr0MWYLsE
106 Akron & Banzhaf, Hajo. (1995/2014). *The Crowley tarot: The handbook to the cards.* Stamford, CT: US Games Systems, Inc., p. 44.
107 Butler, Renn. (2014). *Pathways to wholeness: Archetypal astrology and the transpersonal journey.* London, UK: Muswell Hill Press.
108 *Id.*, pp. 96, 175.
109 Maslow, Abraham H. (1964). *Religions, values, and peak experiences.* London: Penguin Books Limited.
110 Ruumet, p. 65.
111 *Id.*, p. 66.
112 *Id.*, p. 77.
113 Metzner, p. 80.
114 Wilber, Ken. (1979). *No Boundary: Eastern and Western approaches to personal growth.* Boston, MA: Shambhala, p. 101.
115 *Id.*, p. 115.
116 Ruumet, p. 117.
117 Ruumet, 33.
118 http://spiraldynamicsintegral.nl/wp-content/uploads/2013/09/McDonald-Ian-Introduction-to-Spiral-Dynamics-1007.pdf.
119 Cook-Greuter, Susanne R. (2013). Nine levels of increasing embrace in ego development: A full-spectrum theory of vertical growth and meaning making. http://www.cook-greuter.com/Cook-Greuter%209%20levels%20paper%20new%201.1'14%2097p%5B1%5D.pdf.
120 Rosenberg, Marshall. (2012). *Living nonviolent communication: Practical tools to connect and communicate skillfully in every situation.* Boulder, CO: Sounds True; or any of the many books written by Rosenberg or others on nonviolent communications.
121 Arrien, Angeles. (1993). *The four-fold way: Walking the paths of the warrior, teacher, healer, and visionary.* New York, NY: HarperCollins.
122 Akron and Banzhaf, p. 185.
123 https://highexistence.com/carl-jung-shadow-guide-unconscious/.
124 Jung, Carl G. (1955). *Aion,* Collected Works 14, p. 17.
125 Neumann, Erich. (1963/1990). *Depth psychology and the new ethic.* Boston, MA: Shambhala, pp. 39-40.

126 Jung, Carl G. (1912). "On the Psychology of the Unconscious" in *Collected Works 7: Two Essays on Analytical Psychology*, p. 35.
127 https://www.psychologytoday.com/us/blog/evil-deeds/201204/essential-secrets-psychotherapy-what-is-the-shadow
128 Jung, Carl G., as quoted on https://academyofideas.com/2017/10/carl-jung-shadow-profound-quotes/.
129 Hofmann, p. 79.
130 *Id.*, p. 84.
131 https://www.huffingtonpost.com/stanislav-grof-md-phd/science-and-spirituality-_b_680470.html.
132 Grof, Stanislav. (2006). *When the impossible happens: Adventures in non-ordinary realities*. Boulder, CO: Sounds True.
133 *Id.*, p. 288.
134 *Id.*, p. 292.
135 https://www.asam.org/resources/definition-of-addiction
136 Grof, Christina. (1993). *The thirst for wholeness: Attachment, addiction, and the spiritual path*. New York, NY: HarperCollins, p. 9.
137 *Id.*, p. 18.
138 *Id.*, p. 1.
139 Glendinning, Chellis. (1994). *My name is Chellis and I'm in recovery from Western civilization*. Boston, MA: Shambhala.
140 *Id.*, p. ix-x.
141 *Id.*, p. xi-x.
142 Dufrechou, Jay. (2015). *Moving through grief: Reconnecting with nature*. London, UK: Muswell Hill Press.
143 Frank, Peter & Taub, Eric. (2012). *Ibogaine explained: Everything you need to know about the world's most powerful psychedelic*. Columbia, SC: Peter Frank & Eric Taub.
144 *Id.*, p. 22.
145 McNamara, Patrick (2006). *Where God and science meet: How brain and evolutionary studies alter our understanding of religion*. Istport, CT: Greenwood Press, p. 253.
146 Greene, Liz (1996) *The astrological Neptune and the quest for redemption*. York Beach, ME: Samuel Weiser.
147 *Id.*, p. 5.
148 Tarnas, Richard. (2006). *Cosmos and psyche: Intimations of a new world view*. New York, NY: Plume, p. 96.
149 Forrest, Steven. (1984/2012). *The inner sky*. Borrega Springs, CA: Seven Paws Press, p. 154.
150 Heaven, Ross. (2016). *San Pedro: The gateway to wisdom*. Hants, UK: Moon Books, p. 98-99.
151 Anderson, Rosemarie. (2004). Intuitive Inquiry: An epistemology of the heart for scientific inquiry. *The Humanistic Psychologist, 32*(4).
152 Fadiman, p. 37.
153 *Id.*, p. 37.
154 Ball, p. 204.
155 Ball, p. 202.
156 Ball, p. 204.
157 https://www.google.com/search?q=definition+of+silo&oq=definition+of+silo&aqs=chrome..69i57.4192j0j8&sourceid=chrome&ie=UTF-8
158 Grof, Stanislav. (2006). *The ultimate journey: Consciousness and the mystery of death*. Ben Lomand, CA: MAPS.
159 *Id*, p. 232.
160 Griffiths, Roland R., Johnson, Matthew W., Carducci, Michael A., Umbricht, Annie, Richards, William A., Richards, Brian D., Cosimano, Mary P., & Klinedinst, Margaret A. (2016). *Journal of Psychophar-*

macology 30(12), 1181–1197; doi: [10.1177/0269881116675513]; https://www.ncbi.nlm.nih.gov/pmc/articles/PMC5367557/

161 Maciejewski, Paul K., Zhang, Baohui Zhang, Block, Susan D. & Prigerson, Holly G. (2007). An empirical examination of the stage theory of grief, *Journal of the American Medical Association, 297*(7) 716-723.

162 Huxley, Aldous. (1954/2009). *The doors of perception and heaven and hell.* New York, NY: HarperCollins.

163 Huxley, Laura. (2006). *Excerpts from Laura Huxley's this timeless moment: A personal view of Aldous Huxley.* In Stanislav Grof (Ed). *The ultimate journey: Consciousness and the mystery of death* (pp. 319-326). Ben Lomand, CA: MAPS, p. 320.

164 *Id.*, p. 321.

165 *Id.*, p. 322.

166 *Id.*, p. 323.

167 *Id.*, p. 325.

168 *Id.*, p. 326.

169 Leary, Timothy, Metzner, Ralph, & Alpert, Richard. (1964/1992). *The psychedelic experience: A manual based on the Tibetan book of the dead.* New York, NY: Kensington Publishing.

170 Grof, Stanislav, *When the impossible happens*, p. 255.

171 *Id.*, p. 255.

172 *Id.*, p. 256.

173 Ball, p. 204.

174 Ball, p. 202.

175 *Id.*, p. 148.

Printed in Great Britain
by Amazon